Cults and Nonconventional Religious Groups

A Collection of Outstanding Dissertations and Monographs

Edited by
J. GORDON MELTON
Institute for the Study of American Religion

WITHDRAWN

A GARLAND SERIES

Horatio W. Dresser
Lent by his daughter, Dorothea Reeves

HEALING HYPOTHESES
*Horatio W. Dresser and
the Philosophy of New Thought*

C. ALAN ANDERSON

GARLAND PUBLISHING, INC.
New York & London
1993

© 1993 C. Alan Anderson
All Rights Reserved

Library of Congress Cataloging-in-Publication Data

Anderson, C. Alan, 1930–
    Healing hypotheses : Horatio W. Dresser and the philosophy of New Thought / C. Alan Anderson.
        p.   cm. — (Cults and nonconventional religious groups)
    Originally presented as author's thesis (doctoral—Boston University, 1962) under title : Horatio W. Dresser and the philosophy of New Thought.
    Includes bibliographical references.
    ISBN 0-8153-0778-0 (alk. paper)
    1. New Thought—History. 2. Dresser, Horatio W. (Horatio Willis), b. 1866. 3. Philosophy, American. I. Title. II. Series.
BF639.A6776 1993
191—dc20   92-34575
                                                                CIP

Printed on acid-free, 250-year-life paper

MANUFACTURED IN THE UNITED STATES OF AMERICA

PREFACE
1992

It has been about thirty years since I wrote most of this work, as a doctoral dissertation in Philosophy in the Boston University Graduate School (available from University Microfilms as 64-389). Its current subtitle is its original title. It seems appropriate to call the book *Healing Hypotheses*, since it presents hypotheses that at once may be (1) about the nature of healing, (2) intended to promote healing, and (3) undergoing healing, in the sense of improvement of the hypotheses.

The title *Healing Hypotheses* avoids the possible implication of narrowness of focus. Although my central focus is Dresser's life and thought in relation to New Thought, I give considerable attention to others, including Dods, Quimby, and Evans; and in appendices I even present some of my own views. In addition, the tentativeness suggested by *hypothesis* is appropriate to the empirical approach emphasized by Dresser and by most of New Thought. That philosophical-religious movement scorns creeds and, at its best, looks for ever fuller understanding while practically applying the insights already at hand.

Over the years the dissertation was copied many times and it gained some recognition as it stood. When Gordon Melton recently recommended that it be published and Garland Publishing, Inc. concurred, I agreed to it, although I did not have much opportunity to amplify the work as I had assumed that I should do if I were to seek its publication. But the prime purpose is to make the work more readily available in essentially its original form; hence, there is no point in modifying it so much that a serious student of its areas of concern might be obliged to turn to both the original and the published versions. So, for better or worse, it appears largely as it has been for three decades, except for some slight improvements in wording, omission of the autobiography and author's photograph, a few additions (generally in brackets) in the main text, supplementary bibliographical information, appendices following Appendix H, and this preface. I have not shifted the viewpoint ahead thirty years, so, for example, the publication of Braden's 1963 book on New Thought remains in the future, as far as the main text is concerned. In the course of writing the dissertation, I eliminated much material on Quimby and Evans from the main body of the text, but preserved some of it in appendices. This was the first presentation of significant excerpts from Quimby's lecture notes, and in conjunction therewith public recognition of the early influence of Scottish Common Sense Realism on Quimby and his overall philosophical awareness. The lecture notes now are to be found in *Phineas Parkhurst Quimby[:] The Complete Writings* of Quimby, edited by Ervin Seale and published by DeVorss in 1988.

In Appendix I, I have added some fascinating material about Quimby and his most famous patient, excluded from *The Complete Writings* because, I believe, of its not being written by or to Quimby, and of its possibly controversial nature. By including that writing, I continue one of the work's purposes, to make more readily available previously-unpublished or long out-of-print writings of people who were involved with the immediate Quimby circle.

In rereading some of the writing by others included in this book, I have been struck again by how extremely valuable it is (regardless of whether one may judge it correct or incorrect), and how privileged I have been to bring it together. I feel as if the book were only in a small degree my own. Mostly it belongs to people whom I did not know in person (I missed Dresser by about a year, since I discovered his writing in 1955, very shortly after

Healing Hypotheses vii

I learned of New Thought). So, without any great pride of authorship, I am happy to help to send this compilation and distillation on its way in a new package.

I have relegated to new appendices the essence of much of what I might have included in an expansion of the study, may develop at greater length in another volume, and already have dealt with briefly in some of my other writings. Most of the present book is devoted to the past, but my appended writings deal largely with what I believe that the future metaphysics of New Thought should be.

Some of the new appendices give--without always meaning to imply direct influence--outlines of some ancient and modern roots of New Thought. In doing this it distinguishes (1) conventional New Thought, which takes for granted a traditional substance orientation, from (2) Process New Thought, which incorporates a newer understanding of the creative process, centering on the process-relational thought of Alfred North Whitehead and his followers, augmented by the spirit, if not all the details, of the personalistic vision that made Boston University famous. Portions of the writings of Quimby, Evans, and Dresser point toward such a Process New Thought. It is mainly with the uniting of New Thought practice and personalistic process-relational thought that I have been concerned in my research and writing in recent years.

In addition to the gratitude expressed in the original Acknowledgements section, I now add thanks to Gordon Melton for his appreciation of my work and for his proposing publication; to Garland Publishing Inc., especially to my editor, Claudia Hirsch; to Director Howard Gotlieb and his associates at the Special Collections of Boston University's Mugar Memorial Library; to Deb Whitehouse for much invaluable advice and word processing aid; to Curry College for its assistance in my scholarly endeavors for the past 25 years--especially now to Maryann Gallant for indispensable help in the mysterious process of electronically transmogrifying the work from typed pages to disk to laser-printed pages.

I am indebted in my thinking and otherwise to so many people, in and out of the academic and New Thought worlds, and to members of my family, including my son, Eric Anderson, and my parents, the late Carl and Helen Anderson, that I shall not attempt a full listing of them. However, it may be appropriate to add that working with the Quimby, Evans, and Dresser materials, and families, has been an extremely inspiring experience, from multiple standpoints of the worth of the writings, the warmth of descendants of these men, and the outstanding quality of the people who have shared in Quimby work over the years, especially Herman Aaftink, Igor Sikorsky, Jr., the late Dimas Avila, and the late Ervin Seale, as well as the late Erroll Collie, with whom I had less contact. Ervin Seale, whom I first contacted in, I believe, 1957, enabled me to find the Quimby material then still in Maine and much later to participate in the project that resulted in the publication of *The Complete Writings*. Among those whose work within the academic side of New Thought has been encouraging are Dell deChant, Larry Morris, and Robert Winterhalter. Through contact with them and others who are helping New Thought to grow ever newer I have been enriched far beyond any expression of it that I could put onto paper. To all whose lives have touched mine (and in a process perspective that includes everyone), I say a simple and sincere thank you.

ACKNOWLEDGMENTS
1963

    In emerging from the rather impersonal writing of the following pages, it seems appropriate to offer some contrasting words. They rightly come first, for they express what is most important. They say a simple thank you to all who have helped to make this work possible.

    Perhaps it would be best to leave it at that, for no verbiage can exercise sufficiently the privilege of offering thanks. But the opportunity is so welcome that it is difficult to refrain from attempting a somewhat fuller expression, although it must be largely a confession of inability to convey very much.

    Even a little reflection on anyone's indebtedness reveals such a complex network of causes for gratitude that the naming of everyone meriting thanks is impossible. In addition, the mere listing of names is inadequate, and the full indication of feeling--especially in relation to the invaluable contributions of human loved ones and the Source of all--is too personal for inclusion. So references here will be limited largely to more or less formal groupings of people.

    An outstanding aspect of the study reflected in this writing has been the occurrence of many occasions for discovering some of the most helpful, generous people imaginable, as well as for continuing to enjoy the support of others who also fall within that description. Despite the differing views of New Thoughters, New Churchmen, Christian Scientists, and others, they have been united in their hospitality and good wishes.

    The names of many to whom thanks are due will be found below, including footnotes and appendices. Two of the most important are written above [in the original dissertation: doctoral dissertation First Reader Peter A. Bertocci (1910-1989) and Second Reader John H. Lavely]; their signing of the approval page [was] only the culmination of a long series of most helpful acts of permanent value. The assistance of other teachers and those filling various positions in Boston University and in the other facilities for formal and informal education encountered earlier in life deserves to be remembered appreciatively.

The sources of information immediately relating to this study have been indispensable. The generosity and thoroughly delightful reception extended by the members of the Dresser family have been outstanding, and incidentally a tribute to the character of their forebears. The Evans and Quimby families, which have been subjected to less bother by this undertaking and hence have had less opportunity for response, also have been of great assistance. Important written and oral information, as well as exceptional courtesies and encouragement, have been found in, among others [some of the people have died and some of the institutions have had name changes or have become inactive or nonexistent], Boston University, the Library of Congress, Boston Public Library, Harvard University, Unity School of Christianity, New Church Theological School [Swedenborg School of Religion], Massachusetts New Church Union, First Unitarian Church of Brooklyn, New York, Carpenter Foundation, Society of Pragmatic Mysticism, Metaphysical Club of Boston, High Watch Fellowship, Church of the Truth [Ervin Seale], Boston Home of Truth, Erroll S. Collie, and Harold W. Lund.

To state a point so obvious that it may be in danger of being overlooked, a basic debt is to Quimby, Evans, and Dresser, as well as lesser and more remotely related lights. Taking note of this serves as a reminder that, with regard to both such people and those seen daily, much of one's debt--happily not viewed as such by one's benefactors--can be repaid only indirectly by helping others. Perhaps this is the most meaningful way of expressing gratitude. In spreading the fruits of past assistance that aid is given a continuing significance, and many who do not know of each other are united--a growing community of kindness. I hope that this volume will play a part in such a process.

CONTENTS

Page

PREFACE 1992 v

ACKNOWLEDGMENTS 1963 ix

Chapter

I. INTRODUCTION
   1. The Problem of the Study 3
   2. Definition 4
   3. Limitations 4
   4. Previous Research in the Field 5
   5. The Methodology of the Study 6

II. THE INTELLECTUAL SETTING OF NEW THOUGHT IN AMERICA
   1. Heritage of Early American Philosophy ... 9
   2. Nineteenth Century Utopianism 11
   3. Transcendentalism 13
   4. Oriental Thought 17
   5. Naturalism 21

III. FOUNDATIONS OF NEW THOUGHT
   1. Western Religious Healing
      before New Thought 23
   2. Magnetism and Mesmerism
      i. Introduction 27
      ii. John Bovee Dods 30
   3. Phineas Parkhurst Quimby 38
   4. Warren Felt Evans
      i. Introduction 41
      ii. Swedenborgian Background 42

xi

          iii. Development of the Evans
                Philosophy 46
    5. Summary............................. 63
IV. HORATIO WILLIS DRESSER
    1. His Parents
          i.   Their Early Lives, in Association with
               Quimby 65
          ii. Their Later Lives 92
    2. His Life
          i.   Early Years 95
          ii. Recollections of People Who Knew
               Dresser 101
          iii. Middle and Later Years 105
          iv. Summarizing Characterizations of
               Dresser 111
          v.   Dresser's Swedenborgian
               Activities 120
          vi. Summary 122
    3. His Constructive Idealism
          i.   Dresser's Approach to Philosophy   123
          ii. Dresser's Extrasensory Perception . 123
          iii. Dresser's Acknowledgment of Influence
               of Philosophers on Him 125
          iv. Dresser's Emphasis on Reason as Well as
               Experience
               (1) In General 126
               (2) In Regard to Mysticism 130
               (3) In Regard to Reason's Place in the
                    World 131
               (4) In Regard to Truth 135
          v.   Dresser's View of the World
               (1) His Philosophy of the Spirit . 140
               (2) His Views on Pantheism and its
                    Ethical Implications 148
          vi. Summary 157
    4. His Thought in Relation to New Thought
          i.   Dresser's Independence 158

ii.		Dresser's Relation to New Thought in the Light of its Nature
	(1)	New Thought's Development in General 160
	(2)	Unity 169
	(3)	Varying Views of New Thought 182
	(4)	Alliance Founding and Statements of New Thought 189
	(5)	Dresser Within New Thought 192
iii.		Summary 203

V.	SUMMARY--CONCLUSIONS 205
APPENDIX A:	QUIMBY'S EARLY KNOWLEDGE OF MESMERISM AND PHILOSOPHY 211
APPENDIX B:	H. W. DRESSER, "QUIMBY'S TECHNIQUE" 279
APPENDIX C:	EVANS BIOGRAPHICAL MATERIAL 305
APPENDIX D:	DRESSER'S EARLY BIOGRAPHICAL DATA 337
APPENDIX E:	DRESSER'S LETTER TO EL ON CHRISTIAN SCIENCE 341
APPENDIX F:	DRESSER'S LETTER TO MRS. BROWNE ON EXTRASENSORY PERCEPTION 345
APPENDIX G:	PARALLEL QUOTATIONS FROM BOTH EDITIONS OF DRESSER'S *THE POWER OF SILENCE* 355

APPENDIX H: SOME PERIODICALS RELATED TO NEW THOUGHT 361

APPENDIX I: LETTERS OF QUIMBY'S WIDOW . 365

APPENDIX J: "THE HEALING IDEALISM OF P. P. QUIMBY, W. F. EVANS, AND THE NEW THOUGHT MOVEMENT" .. 371

APPENDIX K: THE MARCH OF METAPHYSICS . 385

APPENDIX L: HIGHLIGHTS OF THE IMMEDIATE BACKGROUND AND NATURE OF PROCESS NEW THOUGHT 389

APPENDIX M: ANCIENT AND MEDIEVAL ANTECEDENTS OF NEW THOUGHT 401

APPENDIX N: MODERN WORLD AND NEW THOUGHT 407

APPENDIX O: PRACTICAL PROCESS PHILOSOPHY 413

APPENDIX P: SOME PATHS TO BOTH FORMS OF NEW THOUGHT 419

APPENDIX Q: THEMES AND THINKERS CONTRIBUTING TO NEW THOUGHT 423

APPENDIX R: COMPARISON OF SOME OLD AND NEW VIEWS................ 425

APPENDIX S: QUIMBY, "THE DIFFICULTY OF INTRODUCING MY IDEAS" 429

BIBLIOGRAPHY 433

SUPPLEMENTARY BIBLIOGRAPHICAL NOTES . 469

ABSTRACT 473

Phineas Parkhurst Quimby
Given by his granddaughter,
the late Elizabeth Pineo

Warren Felt Evans
Photograph at the start of the Leonard series of articles
in Sept.-Oct. 1905 *Practical Ideals*

Julius A. Dresser
Lent by Dorothea Reeves
Photograph by J. H. Kent, 24 State Street, Rochester, NY

Annetta G. Seabury Dresser
Lent by Dorothea Reves
Photograph by James Notman Studio, 270 Boylston Street, Boston

Horatio W. Dresser and his children, Dorothea and Malcolm
Lent by Dorothea Reeves

Alice M. Reed Dresser and Horatio W. Dresser
Lent by Dorothea Reeves
Photograph stamped "Macy's" and dated by hand 7-9-35

Healing Hypotheses

CHAPTER I

INTRODUCTION

1. The Problem of the Study

This book is a prolegomenon to the study of (1) the early philosophy of Horatio W. Dresser (1866-1954) as it relates to New Thought and of (2) the philosophical foundations of New Thought, especially as they relate to Dresser. New Thought is a philosophical-religious movement that originated in nineteenth century America and is dedicated in large measure to the remedying of illness and other human difficulties through nonphysical means.

Since both the thought of Dresser and New Thought have largely the same background, are concerned with the same problems, and--to an extent to be seen--overlap in classification, one cannot deal fully with either Dresser or New Thought without considering the other.

Part of the problem of this study is to indicate some of the complexity of the situation regarding Dresser and New Thought. Both Dresser and New Thought lie in a neglected area of the history of American philosophy. That this area is part of the history of American philosophy is a portion of what is to be shown below. The description of certain areas of thought makes it apparent that they have a place in that history. These areas include materialistic speculation of mesmerism, largely as seen in the thought of John Bovee Dods; the idealistic reaction of Phineas Parkhurst Quimby to such speculation; the originally Swedenborgian development of Quimby's insights by Warren Felt Evans; the pantheistic final development of the Evans thought, which, with similar thinking and the practice of it, came to be known as New

Thought; and the academically-guided Dresser philosophy, which was critical of New Thought yet sympathetic to it.

Inasmuch as one cannot find much of immediate help in this field of inquiry in histories of philosophy, a significant part of the present task is to provide background information. The whole study may be considered as a presentation of background information to serve as a foundation for any later investigations, so that they can take for granted what is given here.

While this study is all foundation, some of its material may be considered footings beneath the cellar walls. Such material is included largely in appendices, where it does not interfere with the presentation of the basic outline of philosophical history.

2. Definition

New Thought, already characterized in a preliminary way and to be dealt with at considerable length below, is used without intent wholly to exclude Dresser's thought from it, but as a matter of convenience is used, in connection with references to Dresser's thought, as a body of thought contrasted with Dresser's thought; it will be seen that his may be considered a minority (non-pantheistic) view within New Thought.

3. Limitations

With regard to New Thought and Dresser's thought, this study is not an exhaustive examination of either, but is a consideration of each in relation to the other, to the extent necessary to understand their common ground and differences.

With regard to Dresser, this limitation means that the study is centered on his early thought, of the closing years of the nineteenth century and the opening years of the twentieth century. However, to avoid an arbitrary cutting short of the bibliography and the summary of his life, these sections include years beyond the scope of this study. In these sections one sees something of Dresser's Swedenborgian and psychological interests.

The question of the genuineness of phenomena of healing and extrasensory perception is not examined. It simply is recognized here that claims of such happenings have been made and views developed on the basis of belief in the genuineness of such phenomena.

4. Previous Research in the Field

Research for this study has failed to disclose more than occasional brief references to the philosophy of Dresser. While New Thought has received some attention, it generally has been in connection with other varieties of thought. Reference to the bibliography should be of help to anyone seeking such material.

Here it seems worth mentioning Dresser's New Thought history.[1] This pioneering treatment of the topic will remain indispensable, especially for indicating Dresser's reaction to the matters with which he deals.

A forthcoming [1963] New Thought history by Charles S. Braden should be of immense value. Some parts of it that he has been so kind as to lend in an exchange of information are of great interest from the standpoint of the history of New Thought organizations. The extent to

---

[1]Horatio W. Dresser, *A History of the New Thought Movement* (New York: Thomas Y. Crowell Company, 1919).

which the book will deal with philosophy is not apparent from the parts read.

5. The Methodology of the Study

The procedure followed in preparing this study has been to rely primarily on writings of Dresser and the others treated here. In addition, this has been supplemented by personal interviews and letter writing.

The work is divided into parts that present (1, Chapter II) an introduction to American thought lying in the background of New Thought, (2, Chapter II) the immediate foundation of New Thought and (3, Chapter IV) Dresser's life, thought, and relationship to New Thought. The second and third of these may be summarized in terms of the following steps:

1. Religious healing that served at least as something of a continuing inspiration and reason for exploring possibilities of healing.

2. Mesmerism, which included phenomena of healing and extrasensory perception, and commonly was believed to be attributable to the flow of an invisible fluid from mesmerist to his subject. This was a materialistic explanation. John Bovee Dods is set forth as a man who followed this general line of thought, but at the same time emphasized the importance of mind and of consciously dealing with disease by mental methods.

3. The reaction against the fluidic explanation by Phineas Parkhurst Quimby, who maintained that "mind acts on mind" and that in his healing without use of mesmerism "the explanation is the cure."

4. The recognition by Warren Felt Evans of the importance of the Quimby views and of the ability of others to apply the Quimby method of healing. Evans proceeded to interpret the healing phenomena in terms of his own Swedenborgian beliefs. Gradually he grew away

Healing Hypotheses

from Swedenborgianism, and adopted a pantheistic philosophy that came to be known as New Thought.

    5. The carrying on of the Quimby views by the parents of Horatio Willis Dresser, and the differing views of Dresser and New Thought. Dresser began with pantheism, but became increasingly dualistic. By contrast, New Thought is seen to have been influenced little or none by Dresser's later views, and remains pantheistic.

CHAPTER II

THE INTELLECTUAL SETTING OF NEW THOUGHT IN AMERICA

1. Heritage of Early American Philosophy

Early New England thinking has been called "a twig on the Protestant branch of the Augustinian branch of the Mediaeval tree of knowledge."[1] In early colonial days this twig was almost the whole tree of American intellectual life.

The religious character of this thought is apparent, to the point of its often being neglected as a part of philosophy. Yet Jonathan Edwards has been judged "America's first real philosopher."[2]

While God was emphasized in Puritan thought, Nature was not ignored. It was believed that the study of Nature helps to reveal the truth about God, and that "whatever is helpful and brings results must have been intended by God."[3] Puritanism contained

---

[1] Walter G. Muelder and Laurence Sears, eds., *The Development of American Philosophy* (Cambridge, Mass.: Houghton Mifflin Company, 1940), p. 1.

[2] *Ibid.*, p. 2.

[3] W. H. Werkmeister, *A History of Philosophical Ideas in America* (New York: The Ronald Press Company, 1949), pp. 11-12.

not only the roots of Emerson's "pantheism" but also that basic practicality that contains the seeds of American pragmatism in its most general form."[1]

After the Puritan period came the period of the Enlightenment, when, incidentally, New England lost its early near monopoly in the field of philosophy.

The period of the Enlightenment coincided with that of the achievement of national independence. "There was no period in our history when the public interests of the people were so intimately linked to philosophic issues."[2] The philosophy of that time can be read in public documents.

Deistic, optimistic, this-worldly thinkers of the Enlightenment found much room for natural philosophy. In this a man of particular interest from the standpoint of this study is Benjamin Rush (1745-1813). This Philadelphia physician, medical teacher, and signer of the Declaration of Independence has been called "the father of American psychiatry."[3]

While his therapeutic approach called for treating mind by way of matter, contrary to the methods of those to whom this study is devoted, Rush's outlook is not entirely inconsistent with the views of those to be considered here.

---

[1]*Ibid.*, p. 12.

[2]Herbert W. Schneider, *A History of American Philosophy* (New York: Columbia University Press, 1946), p. 35.

[3]Walter Bromberg, *The Mind of Man: A History of Psychotherapy and Psychoanalysis* (New York: Harper & Brothers, 1959), p. 88.

> Rush's philosophical importance lies chiefly in the fact that he made an impressive scientific attempt to demonstrate the usnderlying unity of man's "excitability" and consequently of man's knowledge; he suggested, though he did not preach, that there was no radical separation possible between body and soul, medicine and morals, natural and social philosophy.[1]

"As a metaphysician he is at times weak, but as a physician he shows himself cognizant of such difficult discoveries as the cure of mental disorders by suggestion."[2] This is not to suggest that he influenced those dealt with here.

2. Nineteenth Century Utopianism

One of the most interesting outbursts of the romantic, youthful United States was a rash of perfectionist thought. All sorts of reforms were advocated.

> The abolitionists were clamoring for the end of slavery; temperance societies demanded the prohibition of alcohol and tobacco; the Oneida colony, established by John Noyes the Perfectionist, strove for a practical embodiment of the communist plan of life; and socialism, imported from France through Fourier, was to be based on

---

[1]Schneider, *op. cit.*, pp. 75-76.

[2]Woodbridge Riley, *American Thought from Puritanism to Pragmatism* (New York: Henry Holt and Company, 1915), p. 105.

"The Principles of a True Organization of Society.[1]

Perfectionism [was] a movement which marked the extreme expression of the new conscience, the most revolutionary of its aspirations, the apotheosis of ethical radicalism. Its want of literary skill narrowed its appeal and the archaic quality of its enthusiasm lessened its following; yet in spirit it was native to Puritan idealism, and it enlisted the active sympathy of many of the finer souls of New England. How greatly reform was furthered by the movement of perfectionism is not easily determined, but it is clear that its influence permeated much of the revolutionary activity of the times. Scratch an ardent Abolitionist and you were likely to find a potential perfectionist.[2]

Selecting more or less at random, and without any attempt at completeness, one would have to add Shakerism, Millerism, Mormonism, Spiritualism, and phrenology to the list in order to get an even remotely fair picture of the ferment that was abroad in the land during the first half of the nineteenth century.

Lest an impression of a national comic opera be giv-en, it should be observed that even the strangest of the enthusiasms were expressions of sincere and by no means irrational beliefs, as understood at that time.

---

[1]Bromberg, *op. cit.*, pp. 125-26.

[2]Vernon L. Parrington, *Main Currents in American Thought* (New York: Harcourt, Brace and Company, 1954), II, 334-35.

The foundation of this democratic faith was a frank supernaturalism derived from Christianity. The twentieth century student is often astonished at the extent to which supernaturalism permeated American thought of the nineteenth century. The basic postulate of the democratic faith affirmed that God, the creator of man, has also created a moral law for his government and has endowed him with a conscience with which to apprehend it. Underneath and supporting human society, as the basic rock supports the hills, is a moral order which is the abiding place of the eternal principles of truth and righteousness.[1]

For Christians the moral law was the will of God; for the small company of articulate free thinkers it was the natural law of eighteenth century Deism.[2]

One scarcely should be surprised by the various, essentially religious, reforms that were advocated in a land where everyone was free to approach perfection in his own way, reading God's law according to his own share of light.

3. Transcendentalism

The most noted intellectual movement that arose in the midst of this ferment was transcendentalism. It has

---

[1] Ralph H. Gabriel, *The Course of American Democratic Thought* (New York: The Ronald Press Company, 1940), p. 14.

[2] *Ibid.*, p. 15.

been traced to European sources[1] especially Kant, but it also has been maintained that

> this was largely a technical derivation for the American transcendentalists. The real animus of their activities was found in the local scene, where a rebellion took shape against the Unitarian synthesis of rationalism and Scriptural authoritarianism. In its reaction against all forms of evangelical piety, Unitarianism had hardened into a cold and formal creed. . . . The transcendentalists were Unitarians, mostly clergymen, who rebelled against their own denomination. It was at this point that the romantic movement in America came closest to making an open break with the past.[2]

Yet the transcendentalists were "Puritans to the core"[3] in dedication to "stern, unbending, uncompromising virtue."[4] Transcendentalism was

---

[1] See, for example, Octavius Brooks Frothingham, *Transcendentalism in New England* (New York: Harper & Brothers, 1959, originally G. P. Putnam's Sons, 1876), chapters 1-5.

[2] Stow Persons, *American Minds: A History of Ideas* (New York: Henry Holt and Company, 1958), p. 209.

[3] Harold Clarke Goddard, *Studies in New England Transcendentalism* (New York: Hillary House Publishers, Ltd., 1960, originally Columbia University Press, 1908), p. 188 (in italics in the original).

[4] *Ibid.*, p. 189.

the mingling of an old world and a new world element, the blending of an idealistic, Platonistic metaphysics and the Puritan spirit, the fusion--at a high, revolutionary temperature--of a philosophy and a character. The white heat of feeling brought out the noblest outlines of that character and touched into actuality the potential mysticism which that philosophy a hundred times has shown itself to hold.[1]

Whatever its origins were,

transcendentalism was, . . . first and foremost, a doctrine concerning the mind, its ways of acting and methods of getting knowledge. Upon this doctrine the New England transcendental philosophy as a whole was built.[2]

Despite some differences of Emerson, Parker, Alcott, and others,

there remains no possible doubt that in its large outlines they all held an identical philosophy. This philosophy teaches the unity of the world in God and the immanence of God in the world. Because of this indwelling of divinity, every part of the world, however small, is a microcosm, comprehending within itself, like Tennyson's flower in the crannied wall, all the laws and meaning of existence. The soul of each individual is identical with the soul of the world, and contains, latently, all which it contains. The normal life of man is a life of continuous

---

[1]*Ibid.*

[2]*Ibid.*, p. 4.

expansion, the making actual of the potential elements of his being. This may occur in two ways: either directly, in states which vary from the ordinary perception of truth to moments of mystical rapture in which there is a conscious influx of the divine into the human; or indirectly, through the instrumentality of nature. Nature is the embodiment of spirit in the world of sense--it is a great picture to be appreciated; a great book to be read; a great task to be performed. Through the beauty, truth, and goodness incarnate in the natural world, the individual soul comes in contact with and appropriates to itself the spirit and being of God. From these beliefs as a center radiate all those others, which, however differently emphasized and variously blended, are constantly met with among the transcendentalists, as, for example, the doctrine of self-reliance and individualism, the identity of moral and physical laws, the essential unity of all religions, complete tolerance, the negative nature of evil, absolute optimism, a disregard for all "external" authority and for tradition, even, indeed, some conceptions not wholly typical of New England transcendentalism, like Alcott's doctrine of creation by "lapse." But always, beneath the rest, is the fundamental belief in the identity of the individual soul with God, and--at the same time the source and the corollary of this belief--an unshakable faith in the divine authority of the intuitions of the soul. Insight, instinct, impulse, intuition--the trust of the transcendentalists in these was complete, and wherever they employ these words they must be understood not in the ordinary but in a highly technical sense.[1]

---

[1]*Ibid.*, pp. 4-5.

Healing Hypotheses 17

> [Emerson] makes this inner sense not merely a guide to conduct, but a diviner of spiritual truth.[1]

> Intuition--that is the method of the transcendental philosophy; no truth worth the knowing is susceptible of logical demonstration.[2]

4. Oriental Thought

In the United States "it was not until about Emerson's time that the Oriental was more than a heathen and his religious literature more than foolishness."[3]

> Emerson and his friends read the Hindus for their idealistic philosophy, a philosophy naturally congenial to the Transcendental mind. But they were also practical Yankees facing the demands of a work-a-day world; so they read Confucius, a sage as shrewd as any Yankee, and found in him effective precepts whereby to regulate their affairs with men. The Mohammedan Sufis provided poetry for their urbane and artistic needs. These three Oriental cultures were eclectically blended, despite their inherent contradictions, into a composite which in miniature is an excellent representation of that larger Transcendentalism composed of

---

[1] *Ibid.*, p. 142.

[2] *Ibid.*, p. 5.

[3] Arthur Christy, *The Orient in American Transcendentalism* (New York: Columbia University Press, 1932), p. vii.

borrowings from Greek, English, French, German and native thought.[1]

Since this is not a study of transcendentalism, the details of oriental influences on it will not be explored here, where the purpose is simply to show that Oriental thought was to be found in the United States.

The influence of Eastern thought did not cease with the decline of transcendentalism.

In 1875 the Theosophical Society was founded in New York.[2]

> Theosophy is clearly a syncretic system, a blending of Eastern and Western religious and philosophic thought and practice. It brings together elements from Hinduism, Buddhism, Christianity, Spiritualism, Egyptian Hermeticism, perhaps something from Jewish Kabbalism, and occultism generally.[3]

Perhaps the most significant influx of Oriental thought in "the return of the East upon the West"[4] came through the 1893 Columbian Exposition in Chicago. "For the first time on such an occasion, Religion . . . had due

---

[1]*Ibid.*, pp. xi-xii.

[2]Charles S. Braden, *These Also Believe: A Study of Modern American Cults and Minority Religious Movements* (New York: The Macmillan Company, 1949), p. 223.

[3]*Ibid.*, p. 243.

[4]Title of Chapter IX of Gaius Glenn Atkins, *Modern Religious Cults and Movements* (New York: Fleming H. Revell Company, 1923).

Healing Hypotheses

preeminence."[1] From September 11 through September 27 the World's Parliament of Religions met there, in the words of some of its objectives:

> To bring together in conference, for the first time in history, the leading representatives of the great Historic Religions of the world.
> To show to men, in the most impressive way, what and how many important truths the various Religions hold and teach in common.
> To promote and deepen the spirit of human brotherhood among religious men of diverse faiths, through friendly conference and mutual good understanding, while not seeking to foster indifferentism, and not striving to achieve any formal and outward unity.
> To secure from leading scholars, representing the Brahman, Buddhist, Confucian, Parsee, Mohammedan, Jewish and other Faiths, and from representatives of the various Churches of Christendom, full and accurate statements of the spiritual and other effects of the Religions which they hold upon the Literature, Art, Commerce, Government, Domestic and Social life of the peoples among whom these Faiths have prevailed.
> To inquire what light each Religion has afforded, or may afford, to the other Religions of the world.
> To discover, from competent men, what light Religion has to throw on the great problems of the present age, especially the important questions connected with Temperance, Labor, Education, Wealth and Poverty.

---

[1]John Henry Barrows (ed.), *The World's Parliament of Religions* (Chicago: The Parliament Publishing Company, 1893), I, 3.

To bring the nations of the earth into a more friendly fellowship, in the hope of securing permanent international peace.[1]

One of the speakers at the World's Parliament of Religions was Swami Vivekananda.[2] After the Parliament, he founded a movement that has placed Vedanta Societies in various cities. "The movement stresses the oneness of all religions, basing its teaching upon the Upanishads and the Bhagavad Gita."[3]

Another objective of the Parliament, which met at a world's fair that boasted "the first electric railway in the world"[4] and a Hall of Manufactures covering thirty acres,[5] was "to indicate the impregnable foundations of Theism, and the reasons for man's faith in Immortality, and thus to unite and strengthen the forces which are adverse to a materialistic philosophy of the universe."[6] Perhaps it was apparent that these forces were in need of greater support.

---

[1] *Ibid.*, I, 18.

[2] His opening remarks and paper on Hinduism are in *ibid.*, 102, and II, 968-78, as well as in (no editor listed) *The World's Congress of Religions* (Boston: Arena Publishing Company, 1893), pp. 43-44 and 187-98.

[3] Braden, *op. cit.*, p. 473.

[4] Kenneth W. Luckhurst, *The Story of Exhibitions* (London: and New York: The Studio Publications, 1951), p. 194.

[5] *Ibid.*, p. 190.

[6] Barrows, *op. cit.*, I, 18.

Healing Hypotheses

5. Naturalism

The most striking fact in the intellectual history of the last third of the nineteenth century was the blow to the historic doctrine of supernaturalism by new developments in the biological and physical sciences.[1]

About at the end of the approximately two decades' zenith of transcendentalism came Darwin's *The Origin of Species* in 1859. This "served as the final bell to summon the defenders of opposing views . . . for the battle which was to ensue."[2] Although

> stifled for a time in the United States because it had neither an organization nor a sufficient number of enthusiastic devotees to further it, naturalism was given new life through the development of evo-lutionary concepts.[3]

The United States was conquering a continent, and growing in wealth and population. While there were such developments as St. Louis Hegelianism, it scarcely can be denied that

> the economic and social transformation of the United States which culminated in the Gilded Age

---

[1] Merle Curti, *The Growth of American Thought* (2d ed., New York: Harper & Brothers, Publishers, 1951), p. 531.

[2] Paul Russell Anderson and Max Harold Fisch, *Philosophy in America from the Puritans to James* (New York: Appleton-Century-Crofts, 1939), p. 327.

[3] *Ibid.*, pp. 327-28.

was accompanied in the intellectual sphere by a new trend towards naturalism and materialism.[1]

While "at no time did the tenets of naturalism hold uncontested sway over American thinking,"[2] the naturalistic movement was something important that had to be dealt with by those to be considered here. Their existence, at least, has been recognized in some observations that will serve to conclude this sketch.

Idealism was driven underground during the latter part of the nineteenth century, to become the peculiar property of clergymen, professors, and women. But it could not be suppressed entirely, and it broke out in bizarre or partially disciplined forms, such as New Thought or Christian Science.[3]

---

[1] Werkmeister, *op. cit.*, p. 80.

[2] Persons, *op. cit.*, p. 217.

[3] *Ibid.*, p. 421. Persons continues with several pages devoted to Christian Science and the Emmanuel movement, but does not deal with New Thought beyond this reference to it, although he does treat Quimby briefly.

CHAPTER III

FOUNDATIONS OF NEW THOUGHT

1. Western Religious Healing before New Thought

"Nothing in the evolution of human thought appears more inevitable than the idea of supernatural intervention in producing and curing disease."[1] One finds

> power over disease claimed in Egypt by the priests of Osiris and Isis, in Assyria by the priests of Gibil, in Greece by the priests of Aesculapius, and in Judea by the priests and prophets of Jahveh.[2] The physicians were priests, or rather the priests were physicians, for the religious aspect did not preclude the use of drugs, medicinal springs, diet, and even surgery.[3]

The concern here is with the distinctively religious modes of healing.

---

[1] Andrew D. White, *A History of the Warfare of Science with Theology in Christendom* (New York: D. Appleton and Company, 1896), II, 1.

[2] *Ibid.*

[3] Paul Tillich, "The Relation of Religion and Health: Historical Considerations and Theoretical Questions," *The Review of Religion*, X (May, 1946), 358.

There is no doubt that Christianity began with an emphasis on faith healing. Jesus healed many, and told them that their faith had made them whole. When people had no faith, He was limited in His healing activities. His cures were not miraculous in the pagan sense, however. He always connected the patient's faith with God, and bade those, whom He cured, to give thanks to the Father for His love and mercy towards them.[1]

However, "in the first three centuries of our era the Church increasingly lost the gift of spiritual healing. . . ."[2] As more people became converted, or partly converted, to Christianity, the original faith became modified, as far as many understood it. "In many ways, the Church itself was captured by the paganism which it had attempted to destroy. . . ."[3] Magic crept into the Church's healing, and superstition took the place of symbolism in the interpretation of Church practices.[4]

---

[1] George Gordon Dawson, *Healing: Pagan and Christian* (London: Society for Promoting Christian Knowledge, 1935), p. 159.

[2] Leslie D. Weatherhead, *Psychology, Religion and Healing* (rev. ed.; New York: Abingdon Press, 1952), p. 79.

[3] Dawson, *op. cit.* p. 162.

[4] *Ibid.*

Healing Hypotheses 25

Obviously, much has to be omitted from this account. After 300, "spiritual healing languished for 1500 years."[1] However, it was not lost completely.

> Saints like St. Bernard of Clairvaux (1091-1153), St. Francis of Assisi (1182-1226), St. Catherine of Siena (1347-1380), Martin Luther (1483-1546), St. Francis Xavier (1506-1552), George Fox (1624-1691), John Wesley (1703-1791), Father Matthew (1790-1856), Pastor Blumhardt (1805-1880) and Father John of Cronstadt (1829-1908) were all healers.[2]

As this list shows, healing has not been confined to the Roman Catholic Church. "Healings have taken place in connection with almost every Protestant community."[3] Some of the most outstanding healings were those associated with an Irish Protestant, Valentine Greatrakes (1628-1683); his healings of such conditions as "grievous sores" and "cancerous knots" were authenticated by "the scientist and astronomer Flamsteed, the moralist Cudworth, and Bishops Patrick and Wilkins."[4]
Greatrakes is interesting not only as a layman in religious healing, but as a commoner. Before him,

> for generations the healing touch was regarded as the property of kings. . . . The practice of the

---

[1] Walter W. Dwyer, (ed. Florence M. Hehmeyer), *The Churches' Handbook for Spiritual Healing* (4th ed.; New York: Ascension Press, 1960), p. 2.

[2] Weatherhead, *op. cit.*, p. 86.

[3] Dawson, *op. cit.*, p. 260.

[4] *Ibid.*, p. 261.

king's touch faded with the removal of the Stuart line from the British throne. . . .[1]

After Greatrakes, "psychotherapy . . . could be dispensed by physicians and laymen as well as by kings and priests."[2]

It has been said that

in this transposition of faith from sovereign to subject, was a nodal point in the development of faith-healing. It was a visible phase in the investment of the psychotherapist with powers accepted almost universally as the attributes of divinity.[3]

In America, where there were less fixed lines of division of occupation and status, it may have been natural for healing to develop without much regard for the classification of those associated with it. Among religious groups with some relatively early American healing were the Shakers, Mormons, and Perfectionists.[4] However, it was outside of organized religion that the modern religious healing movement began, or at least was given an impetus that had waned within religion, as

---

[1] Bromberg, *op. cit.*, p. 36.

[2] *Ibid.*, p. 37.

[3] *Ibid.*, p. 37.

[4] Georgine Milmine, *The Life of Mary Baker G. Eddy and the History of Christian Science* (New York-Doubleday, Page & Company, 1909), Appendix C, and Charles Nordhoff, *The Communistic Societies of the United States* (New York: Hillary House Publishers, Ltd., 1961, originally 1875), pp. 289-99.

normally recognized. It was from mesmerism that there came the stimulus that led to the religious healing.

2. Magnetism and Mesmerism

i. Introduction

Since New Thought originated in the United States, it seems unnecessary to trace the long European history of its antecedent mesmerism in detail. However, a bit of this history may be helpful.

From at least the time of Thales, in the sixth century, B.C., there was speculation on the connection of magnetism and life. It came to be believed that there was a subtle magnetic fluid uniting all people with one another and with the heavenly bodies. It was maintained that one's life could be controlled through this field.

The most famous figure in the field that came to have his name was Franz or Friedrich Anton Mesmer (1734-1815). He made mesmerism fashionable and secured the attention of a French scientific committee. This group rejected the claims of a magnetic fluid, and attributed mesmeric phenomena to imagination. The importance of the production of physical effects by imagination was generally overlooked then. However, there was set up the question of fluid or imagination as the explanation of mesmerism. As the alternative name, animal magnetism, indicates, the nature of the subject was in doubt. Some upheld materialistic theories and others more idealistic ones. Recently discoveries regarding the importance of magnetism in relation to living systems and the recognition of nonmaterial fields as real in the realm of physics may leave the question unresolved, although in the twentieth century the fluid theory generally has been regarded as a thing of the past.[1]

Mesmerism reached the United States in the first half of the nineteenth century. This was before it received much medical recognition under the name of hypnotism. Some curative value was attributed to mesmerism, but this aspect of it was of less interest to many than the so-called higher phenomena of mesmerism; these were various parapsychological happenings brought about in connection with some mesmerized subjects. These phenomena included, it was reported, mind reading, sharing in the sensations of other people, seeing distant places or seeing through opaque materials wherever located, and, as part of this, diagnosing illnesses and prescribing remedies for them.

When Charles Poyen St. Sauveur came from France to the United States in the 1830's and spread the knowledge of mesmerism,[2] various people took up the practice of mesmerism and speculated on its nature. Perhaps because philosophical idealism had not recovered from the Enlightenment and because most mesmerizers probably had no very great knowledge of philosophy of any sort, the theory that a fluid was sent between operator and subject was the most popular view. Most speculation seemed to be a matter of variation on this theme. Perhaps because Franklin's electrical experimentation had gained

---

[1] See the recent issue of *Main Currents in Modern Thought* consisting of various articles relating to possible electrodynamic or psychodynamic fields, XIX Sept.-Oct. 1962), 3-28, and collection of articles, "The Magnetic Family," *Saturday Review* XIV (Feb. 3, 1962) 39-47.

[2] His account of himself may be found in introductory remarks in Charles Poyen, *Progress of Animal Magnetism in New England* (Boston: Weeks, Jordan & Co., 1837).

Healing Hypotheses

widespread recognition, little-understood electricity was offered as a characterization of the nature of the fluid. Poyen was one who turned to electricity as this fluid after a consideration of mesmerism or animal magnetism. In his defense of the fluid, finding no "loss of any sensible matter"[1] from the body when one sometimes becomes weakened, he suggests that there has been a loss of a

> substance, extremely subtile and nice, a fluid, running over all his body intimately and deeply connected with his organs--a fluid that can be accumulated or lost through peculiar circumstances.[2]

After considering animals that are known to generate electricity, he concludes "that the nervous agent is of the same nature as the electric fluid."[3]

---

[1] Charles Poyen introduction to *Report on the Magnetical Experiments* made by the Commission of the Royal Academy of Medicine, of Paris, read in the Meetings of June 21 and 28, 1831, by Mr. [Henri Marie is written in a Boston Public Library copy] Husson, the reporter, translated from the French, and preceded with an introduction, by Charles Poyen St. Sauver (Boston: D. K. Hitchcock, 1836), p. xxxi.

[2] *Ibid.*

[3] *Ibid.*, p. xxv.

ii. John Bovee Dods

A man who followed in this train of thought was John Bovee Dods (originally Beaufils) (1795-1872).[1] Probably he did not exert any significant influence on the development of New Thought, but Quimby knew of him and Dresser took note of his views.[2] His importance in this study is found in his concluding that there is an intermediate something between mind and matter; this something he called electricity. The reason for its importance here is its impressing Dresser as reasonable. While Dods produced a system that was essentially materialistic, it struck Dresser favorably because of its emphasis on the importance of mind, as conceived by Dods, in the scheme. This reaction of Dresser shows his commonsensical attitude, which finally could not accept the identity of thought and existence, which became the position of Evans, who is to be considered after taking note of Quimby.

The fundamental observation of the Dods philosophy is that not all things are self-moving. Matter without the power of self-motion is on all sides. The explanation of movement is ultimately to be found in something called mind or spirit, which by definition is

---

[1] H. W. Schneider and Ruth Redfield, "John Bovee Dods," *Dictionary of American Biography* V, 353-54.

[2] Horatio W. Dresser, *Health and the Inner Life* (New York: G. P. Putnam's Sons, 1906), pp. 21-22. See also Horatio W. Dresser note in Julius A. Dresser, *The True History of Mental Science* (rev. ed.; New York: The Alliance Publishing Co., 1899), p. 6 n. See also H. W. Dresser, *Voices of Freedom* New York: G. P. Putnam's Sons, 1899), pp. 68-69, and H. W. Dresser, "A Forerunner of the Mental Cure," *The Journal of Practical Metaphysics*, (May, 1897), 226-29.

Healing Hypotheses 31

self-moving. This seems to be dualism. However, he rejects "the *immateriality* of the spirit, because that which is positively and absolutely *immaterial*"[1] cannot have form and occupy space, an inconceivable situation for Dods, who maintains that

> to talk of a thing having existence, which, at the same time has no form, nor occupies space, is the most consummate nonsense. Hence an *immateriality* is a nonentity--a blank nothing."[2]

Yet form seems to have some sort of reality for Dods apart from its embodiment; he regards mind as "living and embodied form."[3]

Dods calls electricity an "emanation of God,"and also says that it is "co-eternal with spirit or mind,"[4] and "slumbered in the deep bosom of chaos."[5]

The existence of God is argued on the basis of "motion and the absolute perfection of the chain of elementary substances."[6] Each progressively lighter sort of matter is "nearer motion than its grosser neighbor."[7]

---

[1] John Bovee Dods, *The Philosophy of Electrical Psychology* (New York: Samuel R. Wells, 1870, originally 1850), p. 102.

[2] *Ibid.*

[3] *Ibid.*, p. 103, omitting italics.

[4] Dods, *The Philosophy of Electrical Psychology*, p. 54.

[5] *Ibid.*, p. 51.

[6] *Ibid.*, p. 103, omitting italics.

[7] *Ibid.*, p. 106.

Electricity is simply the something that is so rarified that it can be moved by mind. If mind is material, electricity is just the second highest form of matter. Both mind and electricity are imponderable, invisible, and coeternal.[1] However, electricity provides such valuable clues to the nature of God and the problems of evil and freedom that it may deserve special stress.

> If mind make use of electricity as its agent, then it must possess the voluntary and involuntary powers to meet the positive and negative forces in electricity. If this be not so, then the Infinite Mind cannot be the Creator and Governor of the universe; because it is by his *voluntary* power that he creates a universe, but it is by his *involuntary* power that he sustains and governs it.[2] If the voluntary power of the Creator governed the universe, then no possible contingencies could happen--and nothing once commenced could ever perish prematurely.[3]

---

[1] *Ibid.*, p. 108.

[2] *Ibid.*, p. 111. [*Cf.* the Troward-Holmes view of law, as in the Holmes definition of *law*: "The invisible mechanics of the universe pertaining to Mind, to Spirit or to physics. The Law of Mind in action used in mental treatment is intelligent but not volitional. The Law of Mind in action is a mechanical but intelligent reaction to the consciousness which sets it in motion." Ernest Holmes, *New Thought Terms and their Meanings*, (New York: Dodd, Mead & Company, 1942), pp. 74-75.]

[3] *Ibid.*

Dods calls electricity "primeval and eternal matter."[1] He also says that

> substances, in their infinite variety, pay a visit to time, assume visible forms, so as to manifest their intrinsic beauties for a moment to the eye of the beholder, and then step back into eternity, and resume their native invisibility in their own immortality.[2]

However, his eternity apparently is not timelessness, for, without reference to Kant, he says:

> There must be something eternal. God, duration, and space exist of philosophical necessity, and . . . space was eternally filled with primeval matter. When I say that they exist of necessity, I mean that the contrary of space and duration cannot possibly be conceived.[3]

> Matter would not be if it had not always been.[4]

Electricity

> is the body of God. All other bodies are therefore emanations from his body, and all other spirits are emanations from his spirit. Hence all things are of

---

[1] *Ibid.*, p. 123.

[2] *Ibid.*, p. 146.

[3] *Ibid.*, p. 123.

[4] *Ibid.*, p. 124.

God. He has poured himself throughout all his works.[1]

But "gross, inert matter cannot be transmuted into mind--cannot possibly secrete mind."[2]

Creation out of nothing is impossible.[3] The Hebrew word translated as create means "to gather together by concretion, or to form by consolidation."[4]

The Eternal Mind is not absolutely omnipresent, while his electrical body is because it pervades immensity of space.[5]

Although made of electricity, the world differs from it. "Electricity, being the uncreated substance, is the *positive* force, and the globe, being the created substance, is the *negative* force."[6]

The body of man is but an outshoot or manifestation of his mind. If I may be indulged the expression, it is the ultimate of his mind. Hence every creature in existence has a body which is the shape of its mind, admitting that the physical laws of the

---

[1]*Ibid.*

[2]*Ibid.*, p. 145.

[3]*Ibid.*, p. 121.

[4]*Ibid.*, pp. 122-23.

[5]*Ibid.*, p. 125.

[6]*Ibid.*, p. 130.

Healing Hypotheses 35

system were not interrupted in producing the natural form of the body from mind.[1]

"All feeling is in the mind."[2] The corresponding spiritual limb is the seat of the feeling experienced in relation to an amputated physical limb.

Mind resides in the brain, not all through the body; otherwise we should lose part of it with amputations, which seems inconsistent with the explanation just offered for feelings of amputated limbs; also separate parts of the body would think.[3] It is through the medulla oblongata that sensation comes, and it is there that "the royal monarch sits enthroned."[4] The cerebrum and cerebellum are "two distinct brains,"[5] dealing, respectively, with voluntary and involuntary nerves and powers. Half of the body's electricity (or nervous fluid or galvanism, for he means the same by them)[6] operates through the arteries and voluntary nerves and half operates through the veins and involuntary nerves.[7] The circulation of blood is magnetic, rather than hydraulic.[8]

---

[1] *Ibid.*, p. 125.

[2] *Ibid.*

[3] *Ibid.*, p. 58.

[4] *Ibid.*, p. 179.

[5] *Ibid.*, p. 170.

[6] *Ibid.*, p. 60.

[7] *Ibid.*, pp. 65, 66, 78, 84.

[8] *Ibid.*, p. 68.

"The one grand proximate cause of disease [is] the disturbing of the nervous fluid, or throwing the electricity of the system out of balance."[1] This throwing out of balance can be done by either physical or mental impressions.[2]

Here enters the great value of Electrical Psychology, which is "the doctrine of mental and physical impressions to cure the sick."[3] Dods distinguishes it from mesmerism by saying that although they use the same nervous fluid,[4] mesmerism is the doctrine of sympathy, in which magnetizer and subject are brought into such perfect sympathy that they see, hear, and feel what the magnetizer sees, hears, and feels, and there is somnambulism, which he identifies with mesmerism, whereas in the electro-psychological state one retains his senses and will and remembers what happens.[5]

Whatever the cause of a disease, "mind can, by its impressions, cause the nervous fluid to cure it, or at least to produce upon it a salutary influence,"[6] provided there be no organic destruction.[7]

---

[1] *Ibid.*, p. 71.

[2] *Ibid.*

[3] *Ibid.*, p. 188.

[4] *Ibid.*, p. 31.

[5] *Ibid.*, pp. 30-31.

[6] *Ibid.*, p. 84.

[7] *Ibid.*, p. 85.

"Medicine produces a physical impression on the system, but never heals a disease."[1]

> The sanative power is in the individual, and not in the medicine. Medicines and mental impressions only call that sanative principle to the right spot in the system so as to enable it to do its work.[2]

The electro-nervous fluid is able to heal for the following reason: "If all things were made out of electricity then it is certain that electricity contains all the healing properties of all things in being."[3]

Dods seems to want the best of all methods, and to be less than fully concerned with consistency of opposing means. He proposes to combine all healing methods into a grand Curopathy.[4]

Dods does indeed point toward later developments that constitute New Thought. He and it are alike in emphasizing the power of mind and in rejecting unconscious hypnotic influence, in favor of conscious redirection of thought. However, New Thought, to the extent that one can generalize about a broad group of writers, and Dods part company where he maintains a dualism of spirit and matter, or even a position of making spirit a form of matter, although his position on this seems unclear. His emphasis on the details by which operations of the body are carried on also is foreign to New Thought. His attempt to reason out the existence of God is

---

[1]*Ibid.*

[2]*Ibid.*

[3]*Ibid.*, p. 169.

[4]*Ibid.*, pp. 185, 188.

uncommon to New Thought, in which this is a point normally taken for granted.

Dresser's having written the article referred to in a recent footnote on Dods as a forerunner of the mental cure may be an indication that Dods was not well known to New Thought. This seems entirely possible. One cannot establish that he did have influence on the movement. But it has been seen that his ideas were available, and were in some degree symptomatic of the time in which he operated and out of which New Thought arose. Also, Dresser took note of him. Dresser's reaction will be mentioned in connection with Dresser's relation to New Thought.

While Dods may have been tending toward New Thought, the man to be considered next was the one whose career inspired the development of New Thought and whose insights pointed the way.

3. Phineas Parkhurst Quimby

Phineas Parkhurst ("Park") Quimby was born on February 16, 1802, in Lebanon, New Hampshire, and died on January 16, 1866, in Belfast, Maine. He lived practically all his life in Maine. Quimby received practically no formal education, but was intelligent and inventive.

Until becoming a mesmerist, as a result of visits of passing mesmerists, he was a clockmaker. In the early 1840's he gave mesmeric lectures and demonstrations. His writings show him to have been acquainted with some philosophy and a considerable amount of mesmeric writing.[1]

He discovered a youth, Lucius Burkmar, who had remarkable extrasensory abilities when mesmerized. Quimby used him in diagnosing illness and prescribing

---

[1] See Appendix A.

remedies. However, Quimby came to believe that the boy was reading minds, rather than doing more helpful work in healing, so he abandoned use of Lucius and somehow developed his own conscious extrasensory perception.

When thus equipped Quimby practiced a form of healing in which one's mind was not subjected to another human mind, as in mesmerism, but was allowed to attain its fullest freedom in relation to whatever divine dimension of reality there may be.[1]

The exact theory that underlay Quimby's practice is something that cannot be determined here, for the consideration of his large body of writing would be a task requiring a major study in its own right. However, for the purposes of considering Dresser and New Thought, it is not necessary to know with certainty what Quimby believed; what is most important here is that which will be seen in regard to Dresser's understanding of what he meant, and what Evans produced after becoming acquainted with Quimby. In one of his writings on Quimby, Dresser summarized Quimby's views as follows:

> Had Dr. [as he was called] Quimby systematized [his] writings, the development of his thought would have been somewhat as follows:--
>
> (1) The omnipresent Wisdom, the warm, loving, tender Father of us all, Creator of all the universe, whose works are good, whose substance is an invisible reality.

---

[1]See Appendix B, Horatio W. Dresser (ed.) *The Quimby Manuscripts* (New York: Thomas Y. Crowell Company; two editions published in 1921, the later one republished in 1961 by The Julian Press Inc., New York), and Ervin Seale (ed.) *Phineas Parkhurst Quimby[:] The Complete Writings*, 3 vols. (Marina del Rey, Calif: DeVorss & Company, Publishers, 1988).

(2) The real man, whose life is eternal in the invisible kingdom of God, whose senses are spiritual and function independently of matter.

(3) The visible world, which Dr. Quimby once characterized as "the shadow of Wisdom's amusements"; that is, nature is only the outward projection or manifestation of an inward activity far more real and enduring.

(4) Spiritual matter, or fine interpenetrating substance, directly responsive to thought and subconsciously embodying in the flesh the fears, beliefs, hopes, errors, and joys of the mind.

(5) Disease is due to false reasoning in regard to sensations, which man unwittingly develops by impressing wrong thoughts and mental pictures upon the subconscious spiritual matter.

(6) As disease is due to false reasoning, so health is due to knowledge of the truth. To remove disease permanently, it is necessary to know the cause, the error which led to it. "The explanation is the cure."

(7) To know the truth about life is therefore the sovereign remedy for all ills. This truth Jesus came to declare. Jesus knew how he cured and Dr. Quimby, without taking any credit to himself as a discoverer, believed that he understood and practiced the same great truth or science.[1]

---

[1] Unsigned but almost certainly Horatio W. Dresser, in whose publication it appeared, "A New Text-Book," review of *The Builder and the Plan* by Ursula N. Gestefeld, in *The Higher Law*, III (June, 1901), 148-149. See also Annetta G. Dresser, *The Philosophy of P. P. Quimby* (Boston: George H. Ellis, 1895), chapter IV, and Dresser, *Health and the Inner Life, passim*.

Quimby did not live to publish a book containing his views. But they served as an inspiration for writings of some who went to him as patients. The first one to publish was Warren Felt Evans.

4. Warren Felt Evans

i. Introduction

Evans (December 23, 1817-September 4, 1889)[1] was a Methodist minister who found in the writings of Swedenborg a message that he unsuccessfully sought to share with his congregation. He became a Swedenborgian and did some missionary work for the Swedenborgian New Church. But he turned to spiritual healing and writing about it as his full-time occupation.

Evans is of interest as a person with considerable knowledge of philosophy who worked into his system views of traditional philosophers, Quimby, Swedenborg, and others, eventually reaching a position that came to be known as New Thought. This is in contrast with Dresser's mature views relative to New Thought. Apparently Evans was not greatly concerned with reasoning out carefully the grounds for his outlook. He seems to have been satisfied to accept views of others that he intuitively took to be consistent with his own insights. However, he did seek to draw out of the philosophy that he accepted the practical consequences relating to healing.

---

[1]For biographical details see Appendix C.

ii. Swedenborgian Background

At the time of his going to Quimby, probably in 1863, Evans held Swedenborgian views. There can be no reasonable doubt of this, judging by the frequent references to Swedenborg in books by Evans and from the evaluation of him by Dresser as "an average exponent of Swedenborg's teachings"[1] whose "chief interest was to spread knowledge of Swedenborg's doctrines"[2] before he turned to healing.

While a full presentation of Swedenborgianism is beyond the scope of this study, some of the major aspects of it deserve mention. They show both the fertile ground that Quimby's thought found in Evans and also the perspective away from which Evans moved in later years.

Swedenborg adhered to a theism that he expressed in his own terms. He believed in a personal God of Love and Wisdom who created the universe. Creation is separated from God by a discontinuity known as discrete degrees. Pantheism thus is avoided. However, there is a relationship of correspondence of everything spiritual and material. In addition, God sustains the universe, his providential care being known as divine "influx." Thus Swedenborg has sharply separated realms, which nevertheless are in a state of correspondence and linked by influx of the divine into the natural world.

It may seem strange that with Swedenborg's views of close connection of the divine and the natural, the New Church did not promptly come to the fore in healing. However, it did not. But it did not wholly overlook the topic. One of its men wrote that the

---

[1] Dresser, *A History of the New Thought Movement*, p. 72.

[2] *Ibid.*, p. 73.

> mind-cure part of [its] doctrines [could] be summed up in this one sentence: All diseases are from the Spiritual world under the law of correspondences, and if their spiritual causes are removed, the diseases will disappear."[1]

In recent years that church's interest in healing has increased. A Dresser niece, Gwynne Dresser Mack, has contributed significantly to this present concern among Swedenborgians.[2]

After remarking that Evans "possessed the ability to grasp fundamental principles and think them out for himself," Dresser says:

> He had all the essentials, so far as spiritual principles were concerned; for the devotee of Swedenborg has a direct clue to the application of spiritual philosophy to life. What Mr. Evans lacked was the new impetus, to put two and two together. He lacked the method by which to apply his idealism and his theology to health. Mr. Quimby gave him this impetus. He [Quimby] possessed the method.[3]

---

[1] Charles H. Mann, *Healing through the Soul formerly called Psychiasis: Healing through the Soul* (Boston: Massachusetts New-Church Union, 1900, copyright date), pp. 127-28.

[2] For example, see Gwynne Dresser Mack, *Talking with God: The Healing Power of Prayer* (Pound Ridge, NY: New-Church Prayer Fellowship, 1960.

[3] Dresser, *A History of the New Thought Movement*, p. 72.

In his pre-Quimby writing Evans showed that he did have an outlook that was leading him in the direction of the Quimby thought, which made one's physical condition dependent on one's nonphysical state. However, Evans showed that he had not yet reached the view of Quimby. Evans at this time placed so much emphasis on the separation side of Swedenborgian closeness yet separation of physical and nonphysical worlds that the influence of mental states was decidedly limited:

> Our mental states here affect the appearance of the external world, and tend, in some degree, to adjust the outward universe in harmony, both in appearance and reality, with our spiritual condition. This important law of our spiritual nature operates but imperfectly in this world. In the next it will act without obstruction, so that the heaven in which we are placed, in its outward arrangements, will be the exact representative and correspondence of our interior state of mind and heart, or wisdom and love. . . . The outward world will be in correspondence with the world within, and will be the creation, as it were, of our spiritual state, just as the features of the face shape themselves in harmony with the varying emotions of the soul.[1]

He believes that "the earth is made of too gross a substance, too coarse a stuff, to express the spiritual and

---

[1] W. F. Evans, *The Celestial Dawn; or Connection of Earth and Heaven* (Boston: T. H. Carter and Company, 1864), p. 195.

celestial,"[1] although "outward nature is the shadow of heavenly realities":[2]

> The things in the natural world not only represent the realities of the celestial realms as words express ideas, but they exist from the spiritual world just as the body derives its life from the soul. The material universe is the region of effects; spirit is the only causal agent. Matter is dead and passive; all life in it is the result of an influx from the realm of spirit, which is the seat of causation. Thus the earth is conjoined to the heavens, as an effect is connected with the producing cause and made one with it. Before anything can exist in the natural world, it must first exist in the world of mind or the spiritual world, just as before an architect can construct an edifice, the plan or idea of it must pre-exist in his mind. The edifice when completed is the outward embodiment of the interior conception.[3]

Thus it is seen that while Evans must have found himself not immediately in agreement with Quimby, he was not so fundamentally out of agreement as to make appreciation difficult. Had Evans had no philosophy but that of Swedenborg at his disposal, perhaps he would have done as most Swedenborgians did—fail to incorporate the insights of Quimby into his own outlook. But Evans was interested in other philosophy also; this now is to be considered in connection with the development of the philosophy of Evans.

---

[1]*Ibid.*, p. 196-97.

[2]*Ibid.*, p. 203.

[3]*Ibid.*, pp. 203-204.

iii. Development of the Evans Philosophy

In the midst of an essentially Swedenborgian book of 1864 Evans gives a clue to the extra-Swedenborgian metaphysical content of his relatively early philosophy. He refers to the division of philosophy into forms of Sensualism, Idealism, Mysticism, and Skepticism by Victor Cousin in his "profound work on the History of Modern Philosophy."[1]

Presumably the work referred to is the three-volumes-in-two translation, constituting the second series of lectures, of the noted eclectic philosopher, who knew Hegel, Schelling, and Jacobi.[2] The fourth lecture of the second volume, "Classification of Philosophical Systems," especially seems to be referred to by Evans. Beyond this, it is worth noting that Cousin devotes the next two lectures to Indian philosophy and, as does Evans, pays his respects to the ancient Egyptians.[3] Numerous references to Oriental thought are scattered through the work. He also voices the belief that "nothing goes back-- everything advances!"[4] Evans must have welcomed Cousin's brief, but friendly, reference to Swedenborg.[5] Perhaps the most important fact about Cousin's history, in

---

[1] Evans, *The New Age and its Messenger* (Boston: T. H. Carter and Company, 1864), p. 81.

[2] Victor Cousin, *Course of the History of Modern Philosophy*, trans. 0. W. Wight (2 vols.; New York: D. Appleton & Company, 1852).

[3] *Ibid.*, I, 366.

[4] *Ibid.*, I, 46.

[5] *Ibid.*, II, 117.

relation to Evans, is that while he devotes his last eleven lectures to Locke, he says little about Berkeley, referring one to his first series of lectures, not contained in this history.[1]

Obviously this is no proof that Evans was poorly grounded in the idealism of Berkeley when he took note of Cousin. However, it is an interesting bit of information to add to other indications that Evans gradually grew into idealism. In his early Swedenborgian period Evans says that "the Spiritual world is entirely distinct from the natural world, being known by different properties and governed by other laws."[2] "The two realms have nothing in common as to their properties, yet they are not wholly disjoined and communication between the two is not closed."[3] By way of contrast, in his last published book, in which he still frequently refers to Swedenborg, Evans says that "thought and existence are absolutely identical and inseparable."[4]

Perhaps the simplest characterization of his later view is that given in his statement that "the highest development of religious thought and feeling is that of a *Christian Pantheism*, not the cold, intellectual system of Spinoza, but one nearer to that of the warm and loving Fichte, who exhibited the blessedness of a life in God."[5]

---

[1]*Ibid.*, II, 105.

[2]Evans, *The Celestial Dawn*, p. 67.

[3]*Ibid.*, p. 69.

[4]W. F. Evans, *Esoteric Christianity and Mental Therapeutics* (Boston: H. H. Carter & Karrick, Publishers, 1886), p. 37.

[5]W. F. Evans, *The Divine Law of Cure* (Boston: H. H. Carter & Co., Publishers, 1881), p. 15.

Obviously, when pantheism is used in such a way it does not mean the reduction of God to the totality of the universe as it is discoverable by means open to public verification, but includes all of that and all other realms of being, together called God.

It is on the issue of pantheism that New Thought was to follow Evans, and Dresser was to dissent. So this chapter and the next, on Dresser, are by no means mutually exclusive; they are divided chiefly in relation to emphasis on the thought of Evans and his predecessors in one and on Dresser in the other. Neither is to be considered in isolation from the other.

It was in his writings on healing that the philosophy of Evans assumed its final form, developing gradually over his years of writing on this subject. With regard to the first such book, *The Mental-Cure*, 1869, Dresser observes that this was "the first volume issued in our country on this subject,"[1] one that soon was read widely in this country and Europe, where it was translated into several languages.[2] He adds that in this work while

---

[1]Dresser, *A History of the New Thought Movement*, p.75.

[2]*Ibid*. In a January 26, 1915, letter to Rev. John Whitehead, H. H. Carter mentions that the next book, *Mental Medicine*, was published in five different languages. This letter is attached to a copy of the Leonard pamphlet in the library of the New Church Theological School, Cambridge, Massachusetts.

In part 3, p. 23, of the article on Evans, Leonard says that the fifth book of Evans, *The Primitive Mind-Cure*, which "reached the public early in the year 1885," was "perhaps, the most widely read work at the present day of the entire series. It was a popular treatise from the first. An English publisher issued it under the title of 'Healing by Faith.' This was due to the interest

Healing Hypotheses 49

Evans "branches out freely and expounds Swedenborg's views in his own fashion, he is still largely dependent on the teachings of the Swedish seer."[1]

This observation seems justified in light of an examination of *The Mental-Cure*. In this book Evans considers various possibilities with regard to what life may be.

Before turning to Evans in relation to Swedenborg in that volume, it is of interest to see with regard to Dods that Evans takes very brief note of the possibility that

---

taken in the book by an English truth-seeker, G. B. Finch, who was in America when it appeared and read it with delight." In the fall of 1962 Ervin Seale, minister of The Church of the Truth, in New York, offered a course called "Primitive Mind Cure," using this book as the text. The course had five sessions and was duplicated on Monday afternoons and Wednesday evenings. It was part of a three year series "arranged to cover such fields and areas of study as The Bible, The Science of Health by P. P. Quimby, Transcendentalism of Emerson and others, The Mental Science of Hudson, Troward, Evans, Modern Psychology and Techniques of Practice and Application." (*Autumn 1962-3 Announcements* of the church, which on October 7, 1962, moved its Sunday services from Carnegie Hall to the newly opened Philharmonic Hall of the Lincoln Center for the Performing Arts.)

William J. Leonard, "Warren Felt Evans, M.D.," part 3, *Practical Ideals*, X (December, 1905), 25, quotes English author Frances Lord in an unspecified 1888 book as saying of the Evans works, "In England these are the chief books which so far have attracted attention."

[1]Dresser, *A History of the New Thought Movement*, p. 75.

vital phenomena may be attributable to electricity.[1] However, he rejects this view; he believes that this would require the addition to one's stock of electricity from an electro-magnetic battery.[2] He remarks that there has been no demonstration of the existence of a nervous fluid.[3]

Turning to what Evans does believe life to be, he quotes Swedenborg as saying that "love is the life of man."[4] Apparently this assertion is its own proof for Evans. He says that it is "like the creative fiat, 'Let there be light.'"[5] For Evans it was light that needed no argument for support. He saw love as "the inmost life of the soul."[6] This being so, the rest of a human being, including thought, is the development of love.

Accepting a Swedenborgian dualism at this time, he assumed that there are "two distinct substances in the universe,"[7] mind or spirit and matter. After accepting this problem from Swedenborg, it is easy enough to accept the Swedenborgian solution of a divine influx to connect the two. Apparently not realizing that he could start with the view that love is both ultimate and the inherent property of the human being, Evans locates love in God and sees love as requiring transmission to human beings.

---

[1] W. F. Evans, (*The Mental-Cure* (Boston: H. H. & T. W. Carter, 1869), p. 199.

[2] *Ibid.*, pp. 199-200.

[3] *Ibid.*, p. 200.

[4] *Ibid.* p. 202.

[5] *Ibid.*

[6] *Ibid.*

[7] *Ibid.*, p. 27.

Healing Hypotheses

It is thought to be necessary for "our hearts to receive the influx of the divine and heavenly love."[1]

While maintaining a dualism at this time, he asserted that there is "only one Life, from which all in heaven and earth receive their being, but each in a different degree."[2] The differing degrees probably are the crux of the problem. He must have been too firmly embedded in Swedenborgianism to discard its dualism. Differing degrees of clarity of expression of divine life apparently suggested an essential difference between the human and the divine.

However, he managed to apply Quimby's healing technique within the bounds of Swedenborgian dualism. It was clear to Evans that whatever separation there might be between the material and the nonmaterial, the material was subject to the control of the nonmaterial.

He explained this on the basis of what he offered as a "general law--that influx is always into forms that are correspondences."[3] The divine life-love will be expressed in one in accordance with the sort of receptacle that he or she forms out of himself or herself. Since the nonintellectual side of one is basic in this view, the problem of providing the receptacle most appropriate to advancing the health and happiness of oneself becomes a matter of adopting the proper emotional attitude. This will provide the way for, or properly direct, the divine influx, allowing it to be expressed in the fullest, most healthful way possible. In short, it is for us to set out sails in such manner as to catch the divine wind.[4] This is not

---

[1] *Ibid.*

[2] *Ibid.*, pp. 76-77.

[3] *Ibid.*, p. 226, omitting italics of original.

[4] *Ibid.*, p. 230.

to say that one would be deprived of the divine influx in any case; however, the most fortunate relationship of human and divine is that of cooperation.

This is a religious outlook, much to the liking of Dresser. Dresser believed that Evans began his writing on healing at the peak of his spiritual insight and gradually declined. Dresser maintained that in *The Mental-Cure* Evans had a more spiritual view, including both cognitive and affectional aspects of human beings, emphasizing the importance of unselfish love in the pursuit of health, than was the case in later Evans writings.[1] As Evans further developed his thought, he gave increased emphasis to thought.

As Evans puts it, his next book, *Mental Medicine*, 1872, "is, in some degree, supplementary to the previous volume of the author on the mental aspect of disease and the psychological method of treatment."[2] In it he gives less evidence of traditional philosophical thought than of delving into medicine, mesmerism, and poetry. As in all his publications after finding Swedenborg, that thinker and seer occupies a place of importance. But the following Evans observation on Plato may indicate some turning away from Swedenborg.

In *The Mental-Cure* Evans refers to the futility of studying human nature from the standpoint of how it "was designed to be,"[3] as this yields only "an ideal model, like Plato's perfect man."[4] However, in *Mental Medicine* al-

---

[1] Dresser, *A History of the New Thought Movement*, p. 93.

[2] W. F. Evans, *Mental Medicine* (Boston: Carter & Pettee, 1873), p. 3.

[3] Evans, *The Mental Cure*, p. 25.

[4] *Ibid.*

though there is not a fully adequate basis of comparison with regard to his views on Plato, Evans shows appreciation of Plato's ideal forms. He observes that while Swedenborg is clearer than Plato, there is close resemblance between Plato's theory of Ideas and Swedenborg's doctrine of correspondence.[1] In both there is some unseen pattern that is the model of that which is apparent to us.

In the next book of Evans, *Soul and Body*, he continues with his view of spiritual supremacy, but still with matter as something having a reality of its own, at least in part of the book. He calls the matter that constitutes the body "passive and inert, having no life except that which is imparted to it by the all-pervading and animating spirit."[2] He does not make body a mode of apprehension of spirit, but says that the universe is a "crystallization or ultimation of spirit,"[3] and body the product of soul, with soul giving life to it by influx.[4] But he goes on to call body "only a reflection, a shadow, an outside boundary of the spirit."[5] He seems to waver here about what sort of reality he means to attribute to body. He has been referring to Swedenborg at this point.

However, he also turns to Berkeley and says that Berkeley brought to notice prominently the view that

---

[1] Evans, *Mental Medicine*, pp. 148-49.

[2] W. F. Evans, *Soul and Body* (Boston: H. H. Carter and Company, 1876), p. 9.

[3] *Ibid.*, p. 40.

[4] *Ibid.*

[5] *Ibid.*

matter's properties are "only sensations."[1] This follows the assertion by Evans that "the underlying reality in what we call matter is nothing but spirit. Material things, as they are only effects, can have no independent existence."[2]

Fortunately, it is not necessary to obtain a final view from *Soul and Body*. It may be taken as introductory to the next Evans book, *The Divine Law of Cure*, 1881.

In this work Evans returns to Berkeley and says that more than two score years before, he was converted to idealism by the attempt of Reid to refute Berkeley.[3] He adds that Berkeley's reasoning is logically impregnable. This dating places the start of his adherence to idealism as early as his college days or the start of his ministry, before his discovery of Swedenborg. It appears that for years after turning to Swedenborg that seer's writings tended to take the place of other thinkers. But by the time of this book Evans is well back into the reading of standard philosophers. This is not to say that he abandons Swedenborg; he thinks that Swedenborg's views will help to strengthen the growth of idealist influence, which he found then prevailing.[4]

In introducing *The Divine Law of Cure*, Evans lumps Berkeley, Fichte, Schelling, and Hegel together and says that in his philosophy, based on theirs, the "fundamental doctrine is that to think and to exist are one and the same, and that every disease is the translation into bodily expression of a fixed idea of the mind and a morbid way

---

[1] *Ibid.*, p. 67.

[2] *Ibid.*, omitting italics of original.

[3] W. F. Evans, *The Divine Law of Cure* (Boston: H. H. Carter & Co., Publishers, 1881), p. 154.

[4] *Ibid.*, p. 9.

of thinking."[1] He goes on to claim no originality except in the application of idealism to healing.

Although Evans here has indicated his stress on thinking, in contrast to his earlier emphasis on one's affectional nature, he proceeds to consider the nature of religion and to make it clear that religion is not merely intellectual, but calls for reunion of one's soul with God.[2] He would attempt not to prove God's existence, but to experience it.[3]

It is not always clear on the basis of what thought, or inspiration, Evans is writing, but sometimes he specifically says, as in the reference to Berkeley and in his statement that "Kant has clearly proved that space and time are not real entities, but subjective states, and the necessary conditions under which we conceive the existence of things external to ourselves."[4] Sometimes his references are so general as to make it uncertain whether he is writing from knowledge obtained from original or from secondary sources, but there are enough page references to works, especially of Fichte, Berkeley, and Hegel to make it almost certain that he must have read in their works to a considerable extent. Since his writing is more or less popular, or at least has the practical end of healing largely in view, he does not seem greatly concerned with presenting a philosophical system as such. Probably he is more concerned with offering such encouraging conclusions as the following, with an abundance of not very helpful general references:

---

[1] *Ibid.*

[2] *Ibid.*, p. 14.

[3] *Ibid.*, p. 22.

[4] *Ibid.*, p. 164.

There is truth in the old theory of an *Animus Mundi*, or Soul of the World, for God sustains to the material universe a relation analogous to that of mind and body in man. All of nature's action is God's action, and the uniform mode of the Divine activity and procedure is what we call a law of nature. All theological systems, and all religious philosophies, meet here and embrace,--Spinoza and Cudworth, Hegel and Schleiermacher, Berkeley and Locke, Renan and Neander, Fichte and Tholuch, Parker and Channing. They all believe, however cautiously they may express it, that nature is an apparition of the Deity,--God in a mask. This gives to this great truth, that God is the only Reality of nature, the character of an intuition, or inspiration, which means the same.[1]

In *The Divine Law of Cure*, Evans presents a fascinating chapter title in "The Creative Power of Thought, or Hegel's Philosophy as a Medicine." Here Evans gives his opinion that Hegel has expressed the gospel message of John in a philosophical statement, the essence of which is that "whatever *is* is thought."[2] He equates this with Berkeley's philosophy.[3] Evans seems not to be interested in reasoning out the position, but simply sets forth a view that can be applied practically.

In applying the philosophy to healing, Evans says that what is not in thought is not experienced, so cannot trouble one. This is basic to his healing method. He asserts that one can change the direction of his thinking.

---

[1] *Ibid.*, p. 48.

[2] *Ibid.*, p. 249.

[3] *Ibid.*

Healing Hypotheses 57

To switch one's attention from a difficulty is to provide relief for the time that the attention is switched. However, this is not a cure in itself. What is required is not simply to turn one's thought away from the trouble, but to turn to the height of thought that unites one with the divine healing power. This "divinely-intelligent force,"[1] which is found everywhere, is at work in healing and is given an easier job by one's conscious reception of it.

This is not essentially different from the practice advocated in the first Evans book on healing. However, there is more emphasis on thought in the present work and more emphasis on the nonintellectual side of man in the first book. Dresser in 1906 believed that all the books of Evans on healing were consistent with what Quimby would have said if he had possessed sufficient education.[2] However, by 1919 Dresser had become more familiar with Swedenborgianism and took a disapproving view of the later Evans views, which tended to depart from the Swedenborgian emphasis on divine life-love. Dresser now considered Quimby and the earlier Evans closer to each other. For Dresser, the later Evans view placed too much weight on thought, rather than on what Dresser considered more thoroughgoing reorientation of one's whole constitution. He recognized that for Evans thought was not superficial, but Dresser considered the later Evans message inadequate for guiding others into the most meaningful understanding of the divine nature of the healing process.[3] As will be seen in the next chapter, as Dresser progressed, he became increasingly dualistic, so it

---

[1]*Ibid.*, p. 261.

[2]Dresser, *Health and the Inner Life*, p. 119.

[3]Dresser, *A History of the New Thought Movement*, pp. 89-96.

was natural that he should find the Evans movement toward monism disheartening.

It is to the last two books of Evans that one should turn to see the fullest development of his outlook, which largely coincided with what would be called New Thought. Curiously, Dresser does not take note of these two books in his account of Evans in *A History of the New Thought Movement*.

These books were *The Primitive Mind Cure*, 1884, and *Esoteric Christianity*, 1886. In them one finds a rich mixture of Eastern and Western thought. They represent a movement away from standard philosophy into more occult pronouncements, essentially pantheistic

Evans believed that in this pantheism he found not only non-Christian Oriental thought, but also the essence of primitive Christianity. As indicated in Chapter II, Eastern thought was rather widely available in the United States late in the nineteenth century, so the extent to which Evans was responsible for its inclusion in New Thought is open to question. However, it may well be that especially before the 1890's the later writings of Evans were important sources of this sort of thought, at least for people primarily concerned with healing.

It scarcely can be doubted that Evans considered his last two books important. In *The Primitive Mind-Cure* he says that it "is intended to take the reader up where the last volume of the author, 'The Divine Law of Cure,' leaves him, and conduct him still further along the same path of inquiry."[1] Although the last two books published were "written in the interest of self-healing,"[2] they are

---

[1] W. F. Evans, *The Primitive Mind-Cure* (Boston: H. H. Carter & Co., Publishers, 1885), p. iii.

[2] W. F. Evans, *Esoteric Christianity and Mental Therapeutics* (Boston: H. H. Carter & Karrick, Publishers, 1886), p. 5.

essential to the appreciation of his completed philosophy. It is not strange that the theoretical and the practical should be found in the same works, for in his view they were one. In his final books Evans brings together all the strains that influenced him. He believed that they were united in original Christianity.

He says that the developing movement of mental healing was not new but simply the

> reappearance under the mask of another name of one of the fundamental principles of Christianity, *the doctrine of salvation by faith,* using the word *faith* in its primitive Christian and Platonic sense of higher form of knowledge."[1]

He goes on to observe that the cure of disease is really a matter of conversion. Obviously, this involves an act of will, but Evans adopts as adequate for bringing this about a Socratic identification of knowledge and virtue:

> It was a tenet of the Platonic philosophy, that no one ever desires or chooses evil *as* evil, but only under the mistaken conception of it as a good. According to the laws of the mind, evil viewed as such cannot be an object of desire. All deviation from right living is the result of an error of the understanding,--a sin,--and this must be corrected. It is to be also remarked, that to correct an error in ourselves is to come into the opposite truth. If it be an error, an illusion, that I, the immortal Ego and real self, am sick, if the error be removed, I must believe the opposite, that I am well. If my malady

---

[1] *Ibid.*, pp. 132-33.

is not my real self, it must be an unreal thing, a delusive appearance.[1]

In the primitive Christian system, sin and disease are the same. Sin is the mental, and disease the physical, side of the same thing. To cure disease and to *forgive* sin, in the fulness of meaning given to that expression by Jesus, are identical.[2]

Here is a religious outlook that might have pleased Dresser, but for the pantheism with which it is associated.

Evans also provides justification for his emphasis on thought in his later philosophy. It is seen to be not simply a pedestrian process of thinking, for "pure thought is the summit of our being."[3] It is spirit and governs us. It is the point of our appearance out of the unknown. Since thought and existence are one, any change of thought changes our conditions. To think a change in the condition of one's body, rather than just to think about it, will bring about the change.[4] Here Evans sums up the full depth of one's being in the name of thought. To be sure, this is no proof of what is claimed, but at least it is a possibility that Evans presumably believed that his healing practice confirmed. However, he humbly confessed that he had found no method of healing always successful.[5]

Evans continues to recognize something beyond the ordinary. While he speaks of it now in terms of intellect,

---

[1] *Ibid.*, p. 148.

[2] *Ibid.*, p. 145.

[3] Evans, *The Primitive Mind Cure*, p. 13.

[4] *Ibid.*

[5] *Ibid.*, p. 86.

Healing Hypotheses 61

rather than love, his meaning apparently remains essentially the same as it had been from his first writing on healing. Now using Platonic terminology, he writes of the necessity of receiving what he might have spoken of as divine influx:

> When we turn the receptive and passive intellect towards the realm of light, the "intelligible world," the light of truth will flow in according to our degree of receptivity. . . . This turning the receptive side of our mental nature towards the world of light is, in reality, the highest and most effectual form of prayer. The passive soul, with voiceless longing and in tranquil waiting, stands in silence as flowers turn toward the sun to receive its vivifying light and heat.[1]

He identifies this receptive nature with Plato's receptacle.[2] Of the references in the last book, none is of greater interest than those showing that he had discovered "that remarkable book, *The Perfect Way*."[3] Since he does not refer to its authors, it is probable that he did not know their identity. The book was issued anonymously in 1881. Later it appeared under the names of Anna Kingsford and Edward Maitland, with the preface dated Christmas, 1886, which was after the publication of *Esoteric Christianity and Mental Therapeutics*. The Evans references to *The Perfect Way* link the English seeress and eclectic thinker, Anna Kingsford, with New Thought [not only through Evans, but perhaps through Malinda E. Cramer, recent

---

[1] Evans, *Esoteric Christianity and Mental Therapeutics*, p. 11.

[2] *Ibid.*, pp. 12-13.

[3] *Ibid.*, p. 43.

research suggests, and more recently through Mildred Mann], and also show that Evans was exposed to some criticism of Swedenborg, especially if the edition read by Evans contained a footnote, to a Maitland paragraph, containing the following:

> [Swedenborg's] faculty ... extraordinary as it was, was allied to a temperament too cold and unsympathetic to generate the enthusiasm by which alone the topmost heights of perception can be attained. Nevertheless, despite his limitations, Swedenborg was beyond question the foremost herald and initiator of the new era opening the spiritual life of Christendom, and no student of religion can dispense with a knowledge of him. Only, he must be read with much discrimination and patience.[1]

Since Evans was more concerned with offering a practical approach to healing than with developing a philosophical system, he left no fully worked out philosophy. Perhaps his later outlook is summarized best simply by saying that he believed it to be both Christian, in the sense of primitive Christianity, and pantheistic.[2] He

---

[1] Anna Bonus Kingsford and Edward Maitland, *The Perfect Way; or the Finding of Christ* (5th ed.; London: John M. Watkins, 1923), p. 261 n.

[2] Evans, *The Divine Law of Cure*, p. 15. [Had Evans known the term *panentheism*, it is likely that he would have adopted it, but since it is not yet very well known, probably it was even less commonly used in the nineteenth century. It is attributed to Karl Christian Friedrich Krause, 1781-1832. When Evans says, as quoted above, "God sustains to the material universe a relation analogous to that of mind and body in man" he

moved from a Swedenborgian dualism to a view maintaining that thought and existence are one, and that thought, hence existence, is one with spirit. Thus, through thinking, one inevitably exerts some force in the only reality. Whatever its effects may be, and Evans confessed failure to apply his theory with full success, here he believed was at least the general formulation of the reason why there could be spiritual healing.

Others also encountered what they believed to be experiences to be accounted for on some rational basis. In the writings of Evans they found a possible explanation. As will be seen in the next chapter, the basic principles of Evans were given the name of New Thought. To what extent they were found in the writings of any other authors is a matter that is beyond the present inquiry. Clearly Evans was of great importance in the field, to say the very least. More significantly here, his development stands in contrast to that of the man to be considered next, Horatio W. Dresser--who moved from pantheism to dualism. [Perhaps it should be added that the dualism referred to in connection with all people associated with New Thought refers degrees of emphasis within idealistic outlooks; in none of them does it suggest a denial of dependence of both mind and matter on God.]

5. Summary

There is an ancient tradition of religious healing common to perhaps all people. One cannot well say how important this was in inspiring people to formulate what came to be known as New Thought, but it may have served at least as a general source of encouragement. A more immediately important part of the foundation for New

---

certainly appears to be a panentheist.]

Thought was provided by mesmerism. In this, both now usual hypnotic effects and "higher phenomena" of extrasensory perception were found. In seeking to explain mesmeric phenomena, the old magnetic and astrological theory of an invisible fluid linking people was employed. This hypothetical fluid came to be identified with electricity, which also was thought to be a fluid.

In the "electrical psychology" of John Bovee Dods (1795-1872) electricity is held to be the connecting medium between mind and matter. All three, connected and connector, are considered matter of varying densities by Dods.

Phineas Parkhurst Quimby (1802-1866), the healer who inspired New Thought, similarly suggested a "spiritual matter" between mind and matter. However, his view is considered an idealism by Dresser, whereas the Dods outlook was materialistic.

Warren Felt Evans (1817-1889), after a career in the ministry and after study of Swedenborg, turned to Quimby and to healing. He developed Quimby's insights into an idealistic philosophy. This philosophy was largely a collection of conclusions of idealistic philosophers, rather than a direct expression of the thought of Evans himself.

The Evans philosophy, as shown in his selection of views adopted as his own, went through a process of development. He began with Swedenborgian dualism, emphasizing the affectional side of life, but moved to a view that identified thought and existence. Thought is the nature of God; God is all. Hence thought has creative power for good or ill. This view came to be known as New Thought after the death of Evans. He considered his conclusions consistent with Christianity, a "Christian Pantheism."

CHAPTER IV

HORATIO WILLIS DRESSER

1. His Parents

i. Their Early Lives, in Association with Quimby

It has been said of Dresser,

> No one is so well qualified to deal with the [subject of Quimby's views and the teachings developed from them] as Mr. Dresser, for he has the distinction of being the only author in New Thought circles who was born and bread in the atmosphere of the new philosophy as it was imbibed directly from Dr. Quimby, and who is thoroughly acquainted with all of Dr. Quimby's writing.[1]

Perhaps it should be mentioned at this point that Dresser was not identified exclusively with New Thought, but more of that is to be seen later.

The parents of Dresser were Julius Alphonso Dresser (February 12, 1838-May 10, 1893) and Annetta Gertrude Seabury Dresser (May 7, 1843-December 5, 1935).

In a February 23, 1944, letter to his daughter Dresser identified as his father the man written about in the following quotation from a 1922 Dresser book.

> Two generations ago, in a small New England city, a promising young man of

---

[1]Leonard, *op. cit.*, part 1, X (Sept.-Oct., 1905), 3.

twenty-two lay apparently at the point of death. On both sides of his house the ancestors were physically weak, and all save two in a family of nine had already passed from this life when our record begins. The young man of whom we are speaking was frail in physique. There seemed to be little power of resistance to withstand the oncoming of a disease accounted fatal as matters go in this world of allegiance to material things. In type he was spiritually minded and highly intuitive, inclined to think for himself and exercise individual initiative. He was zealous in religion, devoted to the church, eager in fact to prepare himself for the ministry if his health should permit the completion of his college course. On the side of faith as conventionally understood nothing more could indeed have been asked.

He had joined the church at sixteen with a large measure of emotional enthusiasm. He regularly attended all services and was especially zealous in prayer-meeting. He was a Calvinist, however, in the thorough-going sense of the word. God to him was little more than a Man seated on a white throne of authority outside the world, a God to be admired with awesome reverence rather than a Father to be loved. Naturally our young man, devout as he was, had no idea of the power of divine love as an indwelling presence to be sought as one might turn to a friend. Christianity was a doctrine of salvation interpreted as a Baptist of the period understood it. Salvation as thus conceived by no means included the problems of bodily weakness and ill health. Prayer was for certain purposes. The observances decreed by the church were to be rigidly adhered to, leaving mundane matters for consideration in their proper place. Among these matters was the question of disease, and the physicians of the old school had apparently done their utmost to save this young man.

Healing Hypotheses 67

>Then there came from a wholly unexpected source marvelous change into this young life. This change not only meant that he was rescued from the abyss of death by spiritual means when material methods had failed, but that he was given a new impetus and an understanding of life which enabled him to live on this earth during many years of great usefulness. It will be worth while considering what wrought the change, why it could be so pronounced in the case of a man emphatically spiritual in type, genuinely a Christian as the Gospel was then understood.
>
>There came as if heaven-sent a man whose work among the sick had no place among therapeutic systems commonly known as scientific.[1]

This man, of course, was Quimby. Dresser says that the healing of his father

>was more than victory over death and the successful staying of a disease presumably fatal. It will hardly be possible to see the meaning of this profound turning of a young life from one channel into another if we look at it as a mental cure. The change was the equivalent of a conversion and much more, if by a conversion we mean the adoption of a creed which makes of a worldly man a follower of Christ. For this man had already given himself to Christ. Strange to relate, in adopting the teachings of the new therapeutist he renounced the church as an organization, together with all its observances, also his desire to become a

---

[1] Horatio W. Dresser, *Spiritual Health and Healing* (New York: Thomas Y. Crowell Company, 1922), pp. 1-3.

minister. Yet on the other hand he became more faithfully a follower of Christ than before.

The apparent paradox is resolved when we note that the transition was from the Calvinist deity to faith in God as immanent, loving, guiding Father, immediate and accessible, in a sense as intimate as that of our own self-consciousness when aware that there is an ideal self within us, when we will to have that self become actual in daily life. It meant the conviction that the true God is already present in our spirit to uplift and make us free as rapidly as we come to recognize and respond, admitting the divine life into all parts of our being. It signified the disclosure of the original gospel of health and freedom taught and proved by the Master. Sectarian Christianity no longer existed for him. He reacted against its limitations as against the faults of medical science and practice. Yet he did not in any sense cease to believe in Christ as the true Savior of the world.

That his was a genuine conversion in the practical sense of the word was shown by the fact that, once restored to active service, he began to live by what to him was a new gospel and to give his time to spreading this gospel in the world.[1]

This is not to say that he immediately set out on his own to spread the message. More will be seen on this point.

Later, our young man was fond of saying that one must set aside all preconceptions for the time being, to grasp the new point of view as a "spiritual science.". . .

---

[1]*Ibid.*, pp. 4-6.

This gospel involved the idea that Christ is not a Person in the sense in which orthodox believers associate the Son with the Father in the Trinity. The leading idea was that Christ was divine wisdom taught and exemplified by the historical personality, Jesus of Nazareth, whom we begin truly to understand when we make this discrimination. . . . .

Even our young man with all his Christian zeal was as one in a dream. To awaken him was to give him a different idea of what it means to be faithful to the Master, to believe in God and live by the divine wisdom. It was to start from within in the living present, the divine moment of his true selfhood. It was to concentrate upon what man is ideally, touched with the fulness of life by the quickening presence of Christ. . . .

Our young man began to reform the whole man--who needed it less in most respects than many men do. Or, rather the Spirit wrought such regeneration in him. The Spirit summoned him to live a consistent life in mind and body. He was still handicapped, with his frail physique and difficult inheritance. But he began anew to work on and up. He led a triumphant lift of the spirit. That is the great consideration.[1]

Elsewhere Dresser briefly summarized:

My father, Julius A. Dresser, was a patient and follower of Dr. Quimby, in Portland, Me., from June, 1860, and was in Portland when Mrs. Eddy, then Mrs. Patterson, came from Hill, N. H., to receive treatment. He owed the thirty-three years

---

[1]*Ibid.*, pp. 6-10.

of his life following 1860 to Dr. Quimby, whose ideas he ardently espoused and often explained to new patients, among them Mrs. Eddy. The first mention of Mrs. Eddy in my father's journal is October 17, 1862, and my mother, Annetta G. Dresser, who was cured by Dr. Quimby after six years of hopeless invalidism, was present when Mrs. Eddy was assisted up the steps to Dr. Quimby's office....

My father lent Mrs. Eddy his *copy* of the first volume of Dr. Quimby's manuscripts, which she may have copied for herself.[1]

The journal volume referred to has not been found in connection with the present study, but another still in the possession of the family covers the period November 1, 1861-April 7, 1862. During most of that time J. A. Dresser was at Waterville, Maine, studying in Colby College.[2] His journal entries show him as a sensitive, serious, not especially academic sort of person. He was much concerned about religion, and was trying to

---

[1] Horatio W. Dresser, "The Facts in the Case" section of "Christian Science and its Prophetess," *The Arena*, XXI (May, 1899), 539-40. The first volume of Quimby's manuscripts is published under the title "Christ or Science" as the fourteenth chapter of *The Quimby Manuscripts*. Mrs. Eddy is better known for her use of "Questions and Answers," chapter 13. See Milmine, *op. cit.*, chapter VIII, especially pp. 128-29; see also the Milmine *McClure's Magazine* fourth installment, April, 1907, p. 623.

[2] A February 6, 1962, letter from the college library, although the registrar was addressed, says that the only information available there "is that in a general catalog of 1920. It states only that he attended Colby 1861-62."

straighten out his thinking while influenced by both the new Quimby teachings and conventional religious thought. At this time he was maintaining his participation in the organized religious life of the community.

Something of his outlook is shown by a Christmas entry listing the presents that he gave:

> I gave (by hanging on the tree) to F. and H. [presumably his sister and brother, Frances and Horatio][1] "Hymns of the Ages," & "Lessons in Life," Kate Hawse, "Gold Foil," Amanda Bates, Tuppers Proverbial Philosophy, and bot. [sic] "Self Help" for myself. This morning I gave Abbie Hawse "Lessons in Life," by Timothy Titcomb. I gave, also, books to three of my class of little boys.

Fortunately, he recorded a look back to an earlier time. On November 8 he records:

> I got out my old journals--back books written in, to read what was recorded last fall, and observing a book among them in which I commenced a religious journal (i.e. strictly of a religious nature), I took that & read it. I find so many mistakes and strange notions in it that I think I'll burn it, as 'tis very short. But copy a few things.
> The first record is concerning my conviction of sin, which took place on my hearing a sermon, at the church where I attended service, in Lawrence, Mass.

---

[1] Their father, Asa Dresser, died February 21, 1854, at 47, and their mother, Nancy Smart Dresser, January 16, 1857, at 46. Some children died at early ages. Of the surviving ones, J. A. was the youngest and Frances (November 29, 1832-July 6, 1870) the eldest.

> That particular event happened on sunday [sic] evening Nov. 27th 1853. Then in my sixteenth year; sixteen the following Feb. On the friday [sic] evening following the sunday [sic] evening of conviction, I experienced a change--pardon, peace and acceptance into the fold of "our Lord and His Christ." Next evening I spoke a few words in prayer meeting, and on the second sunday [sic] following was baptized--immersed of course--by Elder Timothy Cole, of that church, & recd. into the church.
>
> I used to feel it my duty to take some part in nearly every meeting, and commenced very soon to feel it duty to pray. This duty I never faithfully performed, but experienced a great amount of trial with regard to it.

He goes on to lament his human shortcomings, but, as suggested above, he probably had less cause for concern than most people.

The next day he writes:

> I burned another journal yesterday, a regular account of life, while at work in the machine shop at Lawrence[,] Mass., which I read immediately after burning the religious journal. It contained an account beginning a few weeks before I met with a change of heart, and was continued for a few weeks after. Would like to have kept it, but I considered it too imperfect.

In addition to his recording conventional religious sentiments, including a desire for the conversion of his brother and sister, J. A. Dresser from time to time refers to Quimby and his teachings. A November 5 entry tells:

> This morning I experienced a clearness and command of the truth concerning disease &c, such

as I have not before had since I learned about it. Horatio & I both woke from sleep by four o'clock, and we had quite a talk about the source & location of pain. He brot. [sic] in disease also, but I knew it was not of any use to speak of that, so I would not talk upon that, but pain alone. ...
I could not convince him of anything nor he me. But I wonder if it was the opposition alone that gave me that exceedingly clear view of that truth that disease is in the mind, and also enabled me to see just how the temptations come, & how they effect, to make me fear & think in the old way, to distrust this. How much alike are the experiences in the Christian life and in this. But I took the most of that blessing (for it was truly a blessing) as an answer to my prayers. Oh, if I could maintain myself in that same state of mind, that I was in while dressing myself, all of the time, I would be proof against disease, and could conquer some lesser ails in others. I believe that is so!

The brief entries of the next two days do not give additional light on this matter. On the third day, Friday, November 8, 1861, he shows more of his thought in relation to customary religious activities:

Went to prayer-meeting at the Bapt. last night, and Congl. Tuesday night. Took no part (except to sing), though I tho't some of it, as I generally do. I enjoy some parts of a prayer meeting, for instance, Mr Pepper's very feeling address to us, (*remarks*) last night, and any time when I observe deep feeling in any one who takes a part. But Oh! the coldness & formality of prayer-meetings here I do not like. I expect that I am by far too exacting, and need to set myself right first before I demand anything dift. from others from what I may have given me.

I wish I knew myself, what & where I am!

Perhaps I should have gotten up last night & spoken, if Dr Champlin, & perhaps some other all-knowing (?) and educated (?) heads had not been there. But I dont [sic] like to be criticized. I rather get up to speak before a heart of charity than before a *head* of systems & rules.

But I should be better off, if I was in that state in which I would get up and say what might be beneficial (to either myself or others or both), always when I deemed it best, and without fear or hesitancy, whoever might be present.

Oh, hard is human nature! Blind & bigoted!

On December 11 he observes:

We had a most excellent meeting last night at the Congl. vestry. 'Twas the regular Congl. prayer-meeting and the best prayer-meeting I have been to in this place. The interest increases, bless God, Mr. Hawse appointed another for friday [sic] night.

I have for several days past been trying to work out the problem of anger, irritability, impatience, so that I may scientifically, as Dr. Q. says, avoid those evils; or, in other words, so I may see, not only its foolishness, in a clearer light, but may see just the source of the impatience, how it affects or moves, as I do in the case of many other evils, to which I am subject, as prejudice, dislike to anything; appetite, amativeness, love lying in bed in cold weather, &c, &c, and that I may guard against the anger and impatience as intelligently and successfully as in case of those others. Pride & vanity, thank God, I can command much better than I used to. These *diseases*, too, belong to the catalogue. But I have even better success with the diseases than with anger and impatience. The latter seem to be hard to detect, as I wish to see them. Yet I proved that, like the other evils, the source of them is *the flesh*. For, when I was angry I lost my clear view of the flesh and its influence, its temptations, looking from the spirit, or in other words, I departed from the spirit into the flesh, I lived no longer in the flesh. Hence the conclusion is plain, that the anger is in the flesh. Yet I cant [*sic*] detect its approach and ward it off so as in the case of the other evils.

On December 14 he reports without details, "Some firey trials come up, now-a-days, concerning anger and impatience; but I trust I am gradually working out the problem and becoming wiser." On the same day he says that

while at Mr Pepper's, . . . I got into a discussion upon scripture, which lasted about an hour, and then we took long walk, . . . all the while discussing theology, &c. He brought out of me about the whole theory of things, that that is so different from others views.

He really agreed with me much better than I had an idea of me, and . . . there was a great deal of truth in what I said, but that I carried it too far. Our talk before [referred to in his entry for the 9th] was a week ago tonight, and this time, as then, I got into a considerable of doubt and difficulty from hearing his views, although I tho't after we parted tonight that there was little reason for my being moved from my views this time, as came so near me, comparatively, But O, that is just my disposition. Oh! too weak to be described on paper!! But very likely I am not right in all I think. But I must be proved out of it. God will guide me! After coming home I felt a very unusual forbearance, mingled with love, towards my sister. Indeed I never felt so well disposed, and never talked so calmly, and patiently, as when we discussed so long [?], at tea time, our disagreements. And I could attribute the same to nothing except my talking and maintaining my ground upon what I did.

After mentioning academic and health difficulties on March 4, 1862, J. A. Dresser says,

> Frances has been thinking lately of going to see Dr Quimby, and I have been thinking it would, likely, do me good, so have both decided to go tomorrow, if pleasant.

The next entry, dated Wednesday, March 12, tells of being delayed a day by snow and of the trip, followed by:

> F. sat with Dr. Q. soon after getting there, & was benefitted. I sat with him, also, that afternoon, and recd. *great* benefit. I had been feeling debilitated, and he roused me up. Mr. Haines told me next day that the afternoon before he thot. I looked more like I did when he first saw me, in Sept. 1856 (when I was quite unwell . . .) than at any other time since then.
> I sat with Dr Q. twice & recd. much benefit, but it was difficult to keep my spirit up all the time. But the good I got still continues to benefit me. F. & I both stopped at the International Hotel, but I guess for the last time.
> I left on saturday [sic] noon & came back to Wat. . . .
> Recd. also a letter from F. last night. Said she went to Dr Qs room after I left & shed a "few briny tears, which Dr Q. said ought to be *bottled* as valuables."

On Friday, March 14, he rejoined F. in Portland. The following Tuesday his remarks include:

> I thot. some of going back to Waterville today, but wanted to talk more with Dr Q., so delayed....
> How much better I do feel & get along physically under the influence of the (as it *seems*) more sensible way of thinking!!

Back in Waterville he found renewed "inclination to sickness" and "disinclination to books," especially when not feeling well. He considered transferring to Bowdoin College.

The journal of Julius Dresser is most helpful, not only because of the information that it gives about his own difficulties in coming to accept the Quimby views that became his own, but because it shows something of the atmosphere prevailing at the time. From reading his forthright account one comes to appreciate the gap that it was necessary for one to bridge in moving from conventional religion to Quimby. One also learns something of the living conditions then prevailing. As an important record of that time and place, the closing pages of the journal are quoted at length below.

On Saturday, April 5, 1862, he wrote:

> Came to P[ortland] on Thursday [?]. Couldn't stop longer in Waterville. I am too susceptible to the influences that may exist around me, to live in so much error... in my present weak condition. So I have come to P. to stay until I can go away from here and accomplish something.
> Thought of bringing my books & making up this present college term, & last fall's term, but came away in a hurry, and had no convenient

trunk, nor room in my carpetbag, so left them. I guess it was just as well.

Frances has improved some since she has been here, but has set herself against Dr Q's views, and partly against him, (because he dont just exactly meet her sensitive nature), so she cant improve much yet, while she stands thus. She returns to W. on monday or tuesday. I found a pleasant boarding place yesterday, Mr. Chas. Farley's, at No. 3 Federal St. They are a fine family. Have four daughters & one son at home. Two or three sons away. Pay $3.50 per week for my board & have washing included. They are not so lively at least so far, as I wish they were. I am bound [?] for a good time now, like I had a year ago last fall. And I intend to get back where I was then in the possession of the truth. But Dr Q. has so many sick folks to attend to that I can get but little opportunity to speak with him. I brot. Robinson's flute with me from Waterville, and think some of taking lessons & learn to play it.

Monday 7th, 8 A.M. Heard Mr. Stebbins preach a doleful sermon on death yesterday morning, but heard some fine music there. They have the best choir that there is, likely, in the state (Stone church, Unitarian).

In the afternoon went to Dr. Quimby's room and discussed truth & error. Frances came in after meeting (knowing I was there), and stopped a while. She never listens to Dr Q. when she can keep her mind on something else, because he dont come to her requirements, so did not then, though three or four of us were listening (Mrs Q., Mrs Thacher, & I, also Miss Deering [presumably the one whose name appears on some Quimby writing that she once had in her possession; see *The Quimby Manuscripts*. 1st ed., p. 18, 2nd ed., p. 24]), all that were present beside F. After a while F. said to me that she wished I could have heard Mr Dwight, that he preached beautifully. That made me a little angry, though it ought not to have had that effect. But even if she did dislike Dr Q's talk, it did not follow that I disliked it also, and I was not to forbear hearing to assist her in her conceit. She irritates me strangely, and I her, though I wish it was not so, and dont like to be writing such a thing. I hope, however, after I learn more of *the truth* that I will be able to bear every such thing. I cant endure the thought of having to bear it by *self control*. I want to gain a free & willing forbearance. No, I mistake. It would not be forbearance, *that I know of*, if free & willing I want to learn to act *wisely* at all such times.

I wrote to Mrs Hawes, Abbie & Kate on saty, inviting a discussion of what I have been telling them, viz, *this truth*. Suppose Kate, only, will take it up. Wrote that I would like all the honest opposition that they could bring against me, by giving all their own objections, bible quotations, references to anything, & sayings and assertions of Mr Hawes (their minister. No relation). Said I would like it on several accounts, namely, it would be assistance to me, to give the answers, would bring up points that I might overlook (what help I wanted I should get from Dr Q.), and it might be instructive to them.

I see more and more now as time passes, the foolishness of the world's views of things, bible & nearly everything.

There has been a great deal more going on in my mind upon the subject of Dr. Q's views since I came to Pd. a month ago (with Fs.) and also was last fall when & after I came to Pd for a few days, & through the winter too, than I wrote in my journal. Indeed I have written but very little about those things since my first falling back into error a year ago last fall (when I unwisely talked so much with others that I found them too much for me. Some were smarter than I, & beat me), even when I was thinking a great deal, as was the case last fall, has been to some extent through the winter, and very much during the past month. I want now, and *intend to* get back where I was when I left Portland for Waterville, one year ago last August (28th). And in the future I'll know enough to keep my tongue still when I can't conquer, which would be often.

It was remarkable how easily I fell into this way of thinking, or theory, or truth, when I came again where I heard it talked, last Oct. For about a year (not *quite*) I had lived in disbelief of it, having, about the last of the Oct. previous closed, through the conquering influence of others, I being away from any one who knew the truth, my very earnest &, to me, *bright* career in believing & preaching (and partly *living--in joy--*) this noble, liberal, high and holy truth (not holy in that very hypocritical, sanctimonious sense). I even thought of meeting Dr Q. as an opposer, some day; intending to fortify myself and expecting to present some knock-down arguments to him, such is the natural conceit I have, which is illustrated also in the case of my pitching into everybody, right & left, upon the *truth*, when I went to Waterville in Oct. '60, thinking I was going to conquer. But a part of that, though, may be over-confidence. But when I came to see Dr Q. last fall, without my consent, and almost unawares [?] to myself I fell, into the upright way, in spite of my boasted (to myself) ability to meet & oppose Dr Q. Then I met that Mr Carter here also, who had a great deal of influence over me. I went home, at that time, not knowing just what to think. Mr Carter told me to remain in the church & to pray,

& so I did. After a while I got interested, with some others, in helping others to become religious, and gave much attention to that all through the winter. I spoke in the prayer meetings, and perhaps I say not wrong if I say that, I was one of the principle [sic] getters up of the late revival there. I took my letter from the Yth. [Yarmouth?] church & joined the Waterville Baptist church in Oct., and was one of their most active members.

I had some hesitancy, in Oct., after leaving Pd., to having an outward form of prayer, but I yielded to what seemed best, and took the form. But never, during the last year & a half, have I regularly had more than one kneeling prayer, which seemed enough. And in all this time I have had some difficulty in asking forgiveness of sin.

It did not seem *necessary* to ask forgiveness, tho' I could not account for that, but wanted to acct. [?] full [?] [act free ?] [add faith?] During the winter I thought sometimes about those common exhortations in the meetings, & wished I knew just what was right. But I wanted to do good & thinking that that was the best way I knew, I took hold on [in?] the old form, & was active. When I was home this last time they (the church brethren) noticed my apparent coldness, and some spoke with me. But now I may expect a warm time with them at some time in the future.

In one of Dresser's later writings, quoted in Appendix B in relation to Quimby, he tells of "a man [J. A. Dresser, no doubt] of frail physique who was suffering from typhoid pneumonia" who was removed from the critical phase of his illness by [Quimby's] silent treatment before being told the explanation for his disease, including the statement "Your religion is killing you."[1] Dresser continued undoubtedly about his mother, with an account of a

> case [in which] the chief bondage was not doctrinal, although this patient was also very religious; it was with regard to the patient's physician. This was a young woman of nineteen who had been an invalid for five years and had been given up as hopeless by several physicians, the disease being known rather vaguely as "spinal complaint." Despite the fact that these physicians had tried to find a cure, and had inflicted painfully exacting methods of bodily treatment, including cauterizing over the supposed vital spot in the spine, the patient still believed in the old-school practice and was devotedly attached to the family physician. In fact she was taken to Quimby amidst protestations that he was an "old humbug." Still loyal to her doctor, sustaining her loyalty by belief in his medicines and methods, her attitude was partly sustained by her religious faith. Moreover the mode of life to which she had been subject since her health broke down when she was a schoolgirl of fourteen had tended to reinforce her allegiance to everything pertaining to old-time methods. Her emotional life was greatly repressed. She had been deprived of all opportunities for physical exercise and social contacts. During the major part of the time she had been confined to her room, if not to her bed, hampered in every respect by physical weaknesses; still more by nervous disability and mental disturbances. Hence the force of Quimby's remark when he said "I am going to make you mad with your doctor today." Proceeding to carry out what he said during the

---

[1] Horatio W. Dresser, "Quimby's Technique," p. 25.

silent part of the treatment, the treatment had the effect of transferring her allegiance so that she reacted as forcefully against her doctors as the young man above mentioned against his Calvinism. The major servitude to old-time patterns once broken, the secondary bondages were broken more readily. In all this it is not a question of "influence" as if to compel a person to change allegiances. The patient must "get the picture," in line with what the therapeutist is accomplishing spiritually, so that the whole chain of adverse relationships shall fall. This done, re-education can begin. Quimby's work for these two people was as great as anything that can be accomplished for the human soul.

Was Quimby's technique always as efficacious? No, because some people resisted almost from the start. Some were healed in part, as in the case of a patient [Mary Baker Eddy?] who became an enthusiastic follower for a time only, and then branched out for herself, the deeper issues of her life being left unresolved. Now and then a patient was unwilling to face vital issues, but still clung to self-love, to pride, or whatever may have been the chief deterrent, such as an attempt at serving two masters. The patient who followed part way usually demurred when it became a question of the ruling love. If however a patient was willing to make any needed change, while also interiorly receptive, Quimby could apply his technique to the full.[1]

There is scarcely any doubt that Dresser was writing of his parents, probably about seventy years after

---

[1]*Ibid.*, pp. 26-27.

their healings, but at a time when his mother still was available to check the information, if Dresser thought that necessary.

Her own remarks are of equal interest as Dresser history and as information about Quimby:

> It was some time in 1860 that I first heard of Dr. Quimby. He was then practising his method of curing the sick in Portland, where he had been located about a year. My home was a few miles from that city, and we often heard of the wonderful work he was doing.[1]

Mrs. Dresser continued after telling of her own case.

> The most vivid remembrance I have of Dr. Quimby is his appearance as he came out of his private office ready for the next patient. That indescribable sense of conviction, of clear-sightedness, of energetic action,--that something that made one feel that it would be useless to attempt to cover up or hide anything from him,-- made an impression never to be forgotten. Even now in recalling it; after thirty-three years, I can feel the thrill of new life which came with his presence and his look. There was something about him that gave one a sense of perfect confidence and ease in his presence,--a feeling that immediately banished all doubts and prejudices, and put one in sympathy with that quiet strength or power by which he wrought his cures.
>
> We took our turns in order, as we happened to come to the office; and, consequently, the reception room was usually full of people waiting their turn. People were coming to Dr. Quimby from

---

[1] A. G. Dresser, *op. cit.*, p. 43.

all parts of New England, usually those who had been given up by the best practitioners, and who had been persuaded to try this new mode of treatment as a last resort. Many of these came on crutches or were assisted into the office by some friend; and it was most interesting to note their progress day by day, or the remarkable-change produced by a single sitting with the doctor. I remember one lady who used crutches for twenty years, who walked without them after a few weeks.

Among those in waiting were usually several friends or pupils of Dr. Quimby, who often met in his rooms to talk over the truths he was teaching them. It was a rare privilege for those who were waiting their turn for treatment to listen to those discussions between the strangers and these disciples of his, also to get a sentence now and then from the doctor himself, who would often express some thought that would set us to thinking deeply or talking earnestly.

In this way Dr. Quimby did considerable teaching; and this was his only opportunity to make his ideas known. He did not teach his philosophy in a systematic way in classes or lectures. His personal explanations to each patient, and his readiness to explain his ideas to all who were interested, brought him in close sympathy with all who went to him for help. But further than that he had no time for teaching, as he was always overrun with patients, although it was his intention to revise his writings and publish them.[1]

Perhaps overlooking Evans or considering his early work in healing only experimental, she says of Quimby that

---

[1]*Ibid.*, pp. 47-49.

if any one evinced any particular interest in his theory, he would lend his manuscripts and allow his early writings to be copied. Those interested would in turn write articles about his "theory" or the Truth," as he called it, and bring them to him for his criticism. But no one thought of making any use of these articles while he lived, nor even to try his mode of treatment in a public way; for all looked up to him as the master whose works so far surpassed anything they could do that they dared not try.

Among the more devoted followers were the daughters of Judge Ware . . . and Mr. Julius A. Dresser, also of Portland, who spent much of his time for several years in the endeavor to spread Dr. Quimby's ideas.

It was also at this time, 1862, that Mrs. Eddy, author of "Science and Health," was associated with Dr. Quimby; and I well remember the very day when she was helped up the steps to his office on the occasion of her first visit. She was cured by him, and afterwards became very much interested in his theory. But she put her own construction on much of his teaching, and developed a system of thought which differed radically from it.

This does not seem strange when one considers how much there was to learn from a man as original as Dr. Quimby, and one who had so long investigated the human mind. Unless one had passed through a similar experience, and penetrated to the very centre of things as he had, one could not appreciate his explanations sufficiently to carry out his particular line of thought. Hence none of the systems that have sprung up since Dr. Quimby's death, although originating in his researches and practice, have justly represented his philosophy....[1]

Information concerning Mrs. Eddy introduces a fact of interest concerning J. A. Dresser; at some time he was at a water cure establishment, whether as a patient it is not clear. A quotation from his journal entry apparently of October 17, 1862, says:

> The most peculiar person I have seen of late is Mrs. Patterson, the authoress, who came last Friday, a week ago today, from Vail's Water Cure in Hill, N. H., where Melville, Fanny Bass, and I were, and is now under Dr. Quimby, and boarding also at Mrs. Hunter's. She was only able to get here, and no one else thought she could live to travel so far, but today she, with Mrs. Hunter and sister, Nettie [a footnote explains: Annetta Seabury, later Mrs. Julius Dresser] and I went up into the dome of the "New City Building" up seven flights of stairs, or 182 steps. So much for Dr. Quimby's doings.[2]

This quotation is of considerable worth here for its showing that J. A. Dresser and his future wife apparently were well by that time. It also suggests that he did not know the future Mrs. Eddy before she went to Quimby. One might get a contrary impression from the following:

> When Mary reached Doctor Vail's Sanatorium [during the summer of 1862], she found that Doctor Quimby of Portland and his work were one of the

---

[1] *Ibid.*, pp. 49-51.

[2] Ernest Sutherland Bates and John V. Dittemore, *Mary Baker Eddy[:] The Truth and the Tradition* (New York: Alfred A. Knopf, 1932), p. 88.

main topics of conversation. The whole Sanatorium seemed to be in a state of vague unrest and expectancy. Several of the patients had actually been to Portland and seen Quimby. One Julius Dresser--afterwards to figure so prominently in Mary Patterson's life and story--returned to the Sanatorium from such a visit shortly after Mary got there. He was much improved in health and quite enthusiastic about Quimby's work and methods.

Mary [who previously had tried to get Quimby's help] was more than ever satisfied that she must get to Portland at all costs.[1]

Perhaps she heard of J. A. Dresser, but did not meet him then. Whatever the facts about these matters may be, they do not seem to be of great consequence.

It is said that when she reached Portland, she "was received by Julius A. Dresser and introduced to Dr. Quimby."[2]

While most details of Mrs. Eddy's story cannot be dealt with here, the reactions of people to her when she visited Quimby may be of some importance in relation to the later relations between her and J. A. Dresser. It is reported that Quimby told another patient that she was "not so quick to perceive the Truth as Mrs. Patterson,"[3]

---

[1]Hugh A. Studdert-Kennedy, *Mrs. Eddy[:] Her Life, Her Work and Her Place in History* (San Francisco: The Farallon Press, 1947), pp. 110-11; see also pp. 132 and 305 for assertions that it was J. A. Dresser's reports that were instrumental in causing her to call on Quimby.

[2]Milmine, *op. cit.*, p. 56.

[3]Bates and Dittemore, *op. cit.*, p. 95. Milmine, *op. cit.*, p. 62; installment 2, XXVIII (February, 1907), 349.

and that "Quimby at first took a decided liking to her. 'She's a devilish bright woman,' he frequently said."[1] It is reported that some around Quimby were

> doubtful, not of Mrs. Patterson's intelligence, but of her character. Annetta Seabury suspected her of being too ambitious, George Quimby warned his father that she would steal his ideas, and Quimby himself admitted that she lacked "identity" or integrity. [A footnote adds: On the authority of Horatio Dresser, who received this information from his parents and from Mrs. McKay, formerly Sarah Ware.] It is significant that she never was asked to join George Quimby and the Misses Ware in copying Quimby's manuscripts and never saw any of them save two [mentioned above] . . .[2]

Just how long J. A. Dresser continued to devote much of his time to explaining Quimby's views to new patients seems not to be known. Nor does it seem to be known whether he ever spent his full time at it. It seems unlikely that Quimby could have afforded to hire him for the purpose. The Dressers were married in September, 1863, and after that J. A. Dresser "took up newspaper work in Portland."[3]

---

[1] Milmine, *op. cit.*, pp. 57-58; *McClure's Magazine* installment 2, XXVIII (February, 1907), 347-48.

[2] Bates and Dittemore, *op. cit.*, p. 95. That Quimby believed that she had "no identity in truth" was the way that Dresser once put it in a letter. See Appendix E, his letter to El. Compare Quimby on identity in Appendix A.

[3] Milmine, *op. cit.*, p. 79 n, installment 2, p. 509 n.

On January 16, 1866, Quimby died. On February 1, 1866, Mrs. Eddy had the historic fall on the ice, which it is claimed was followed on the third day by the revelation[1] on which Christian Science is supposed to be founded. On February 14, or 15, 1866, she wrote to J. A. Dresser appealing for help, and urging him to step into the place left by Quimby, as she considered him the one best qualified.[2] However, he

> was now engaged in newspaper work in Portland and was at the moment in no mood to take up the task of becoming Quimby's successor. Knowing Mrs. Patterson well, he was not particularly alarmed over her condition. From the tone of his reply it is evident that he assumed that she had exaggerated the seriousness of her plight.
> "I am sorry to hear of your misfortune, and hope that with courage and patience neither the prediction of the doctor nor your own fears will prove true, and I think they won't. That is my prediction. . . . You say you have not, in your troubles, placed your intelligence in matter, and yet you are slowly failing. If you believe you are

---

[1] Sibyl Wilbur, *The Life of Mary Baker Eddy* (Boston: The Christian Science Publishing Society, 1923, originally 1907), p. 130.

[2] Both dates are given. See *The Quimby Manuscripts* 1st ed., p. 163; Bates and Dittemore, *op. cit.*, p. 109; Studdert-Kennedy, *op. cit.*, p. 132; Fleta Campbell Springer. *According to the Flesh[:] A Biography of Mary Baker Eddy* (New York: Coward-McCann, Inc., 1930), p. 133; Milmine, *op. cit.*, pp. 69-70, correcting the February 1 date given in installment 2, p. 354; and Edwin Franden Dakin, *Mrs.Eddy: The Biography of a Virginal Mind* (New York: Charles Scribner & Sons 1930), p. 60.

failing, then your intelligence is placed in matter. But if you can really place your intelligence outside of matter then do so, and let the Devil take the hindmost or what he can get. Be assured he can't get *you*, nor any part of you. Keep your intelligence, which is yourself, out of your matter, and the Devil or death won't get you, for he is in matter, and that's what's the matter."

With regard to the vacant throne of Quimby, the following words of Dresser must have been pondered long and seriously by Mrs. Patterson, for she later turned them to good account.

"As to turning doctor myself, and undertaking to fill Dr. Quimby's place and carry on his work, it is not to be thought of for a minute. Can an infant do a strong man's work?" To be sure he did a great work, but what will avail in fifty years from now, if his theory does not come out, and if he and his ideas pass among the things that were, to be forgotten? He did work some change in the minds of the people, which will grow with the development and progress in the world. He helped to make them progress. They will progress faster for his having lived and done his work. So with Jesus. He had an effect that was lasting and still exists. He did not succeed nor has Dr. Quimby succeeded in establishing the science he aimed to do. The true way to establish it is, as I look at it, to lecture and by a paper and make that the means, rather more than the curing, to introduce the truth. To be sure faith without works is dead, but Dr. Quimby's work killed him, whereas if he had spared himself from his curing, and given himself partly and as considerately, to getting out his theory, he would then have, at least, come nearer success in this great aim than he did." [Footnote: Julius Dresser to Mrs. Patterson, March 2, 1866.][1]

ii. Their Later Lives

Possibly his turning to newspaper work was related to his idea of publishing Quimby's ideas. He may have sought publishing experience and perhaps even a plant. In 1866 he "moved to Webster, Mass., where he edited and published the Webster *Times*."[2]

The death of Quimby was a great shock to Mr. and Mrs. Dresser. It was generally expected by Quimby's followers that Mr. Dresser would take up the work as Quimby's successor. Mrs. Dresser hesitated to attempt it publicly, knowing her own and her husband's sensitiveness, and after consideration they decided not to undertake it at that time. "This," says Mr. Horatio W. Dresser, "was a fundamentally decisive action, and much stress should be placed upon it. For Mrs. Eddy naturally looked to father as the probable successor, and when she learned from father that he had no thought of taking up the public work, *the field became free for her*. I am convinced that she had no desire previous to that time to make any claims for herself. Her letters give evidence of this."

Mr. Dresser's health again weakened from overwork, and after living in the West for a time he returned to Massachusetts and began his public

---

[1]Bates and Dittemore, *op.cit.*, pp. 109-10, ellipsis there.

[2]Milmine, *op.cit.*, p. 79n., installment 3, March, 1907, p. 509.

work as mental teacher and healer. In Boston Mr. Dresser found that Mrs. Eddy's pupils and rejected pupils were practising with the sick, and he believed that their work was inferior to Quimby's. This gave him confidence to begin. In 1882 Mr. and Mrs. Dresser began to practice in Boston, and in 1883 they were holding class lectures, teaching from the Quimby manuscripts and practising the Quimby method.

From this the facts with regard to Mrs. Eddy and Mr. Quimby spread, and this was this beginning of the Quimby controversy.[1]

It may be that the Dressers began their public healing before moving to Boston. In a biography of Mrs. Eddy by a Christian Scientist who resigned from tho church, but wrote "a reverent, eminently appreciative work [that, however,] failed to win official approval,"[2] it is reported:

> Shortly after Quimby's death, Dresser, who had married, went west, and for some years he and his wife practised a form of mental healing out there. By 1881-1882, word of the new system being taught in Boston reached him, and when he found that the Mrs. Eddy who was identified with the movement was the Mary Patterson he had known in Portland, he determined to make his way east again and see what was going forward.
>
> His first impression, before he set out, was possibly that Mrs. Eddy was making a success of

---

[1]*Ibid.*

[2]Charles S. Braden, *Christian Science Today: Power, Policy, Practice* (Dallas: Southern Methodist University Press, 1958), p. 12.

"Quimbyism," and, remembering her regard for himself and the appeal she had made to him for help, he may have thought that he might as well have his share in any success that was being achieved.

He did not approach Mrs. Eddy directly after his arrival in Boston. He decided to have all the facts before he made any move, and these facts when he discovered them were not at all to his liking. As the result of judicious enquiry and sundry visits to Hawthorne Hall, all he could see in Mrs. Eddy's teaching was something very like an "apostasy" from Quimby. As George Quimby was to write several years later, "the teaching was all too evidently her own," but it ought to be the teaching of Quimby.

The possibility that what Mrs. Eddy was teaching was something she herself had evolved never occurred to him apparently. Mrs. Eddy, the Mary Patterson who for four years had been associated with Quimby and himself, ought to be teaching Quimbyism and that was all there was about it as far as Julius Dresser was concerned. If she was not teaching Quimbyism, then she must be teaching something fraudulent and in any event was clearly guilty, in some inexplicable way, plagiarism.[1]

Without entering into the details of the controversy, it can be said that it was maintained that although Mrs. Eddy had various thoughts of her own, the basic insights and even terminology came from Quimby. Supporters of Quimby could disown Christian Science because of its Eddy elements and at the same time attribute to Quimby its "grain of wisdom . . . mixed with

---

[1] Studdert-Kennedy, *op. cit.*, pp. 305-306.

a great quantity of chaff,"[1] as it was put in the opening letter of the controversy, published in the Boston *Post* on February 8, 1883, giving some of J. A. Dresser's information. Had Mrs. Eddy granted what Quimby's supporters claimed for him and proceeded to assert the superiority of the features of her thought that differed from Quimby's substantially, the present situation promptly could have been reached: the recognition of Christian Science as one interpretation of what it means for existence be spiritual. Presumably it would have been with Mrs. Eddy as it was with Evans, who worked out a system that Dresser believed finally differed considerably from Quimby's but brought about no personal disputes. There would have been philosophical competition but not the resentment that followers of Quimby understandably felt over misrepresentations of his views, which were offered apparently to make Christian Science seem wholly different from the thought of Quimby.

In addition to writing to newspapers, and producing *The True History of Mental Science* in 1887, J. A. Dresser did some writing for healing periodicals that came to be established, and with his wife remained in practice in Boston. In the teaching that they did they were joined by Horatio W. Dresser. His life, in connection with which some additional details of the life of his father will be seen, is to be considered next.

2. His Life

i. Early Years

The day before Quimby died, Horatio Willis Dresser was born. This was at seven o'clock in the

---

[1]Bates and Dittemore, *op. cit.*, p. 233.

morning on January 15, 1866, in Yarmouth, Maine. He was the first child of Julius and Annetta Dresser. He was followed by Ralph Howard (1872-1873), Jean Paul (1877-1935), who found his career in the New Church [Swedenborgian] ministry, and Philip Seabury (1885-1960), who took the name David Seabury, dropping Dresser, and was best known as a writer of books and articles in a New Thought vein.

Dresser lived in various places as a boy, for his father edited newspapers in Dansville, New York; Denver, Colorado; and Oakland, California.[1]

> Financial necessities compelled him to leave school at the age of thirteen and to learn a trade, and having chosen telegraphy, he at the age of sixteen, took charge of a railroad station at Pinole, Cal., on the Central Pacific. Removing to Boston, Mass., in 1882, he became a reporter, and later business manager of the "New England Farmer," meanwhile giving as much time as possible to general reading. He fitted himself for Harvard, though he had never attended a high school, and matriculated there in 1891; but owing to the death of his father he left college during his junior year, and took up the work of writing and lecturing. He has been a serious student of Emerson since the age of seventeen, and intensely fond of philosophy.[2] [He took part in the founding of a New Thought organization called the Metaphysical Club of

---

[1]*National Cyclopaedia of American Biography*, XI (1901), 110.

[2]This is dealt with below.

Boston in 1895,[1] an organization not to be confused with the informal, more academic "Metaphysical Club" of some years before then.][2] In October, 1896, he founded the "Journal of Practical Metaphysics," and this periodical he edited until 1898, when it was consolidated with "The Arena," of which Mr. Dresser was for a time associate editor. In December, 1899, he founded "The Higher Law," a periodical of advanced ideals. ...[3]

This publication ceased in 1902, at which time he was conducting a correspondence course in "practical spiritual philosophy"[4] and, with Warren A. Rodman, an Institute of Metaphysics.[5]

From 1896 to 1898 he was the proprietor of the Philosophical Publishing Company.[6]

---

[1]Dresser, *A History of the New Thought Movement*, pp. 181-82.

[2]Schneider, *op. cit.*, pp. 519-20.

[3]*National Cyclopaedia of American Biography*, XI (1901), 110.

[4]Advertisement in *The Higher Law*, V (August-September, 1902), 228, if the pages of advertisements were numbered.

[5]Advertisement in *The Higher Law*, V (February, 1902), iii-iv, if numbered.

[6]Dresser entry in *The Twentieth Century Biographical Dictionary of Notable Americans*, the pages of which are not numbered.

On March 17, 1898, he married Alice Mae (originally Mattice) Reed (March 7, 1870-August 19, 1961), whom he met the previous summer at a Greenacre New Thought session, at which her brother, Frederick Reed, was a manager and Dresser a lecturer.[1] She had received her A.B. degree from Wellesley College in 1893, and was a teacher of Latin and history in Natick, Massachusetts, High School.

Some details of his life are best left for mention in consideration with his thought, as distinguished from this account primarily of the "external" side of his life. Here it is enough to say that in Harvard he received his Ph.D. degree in philosophy in 1907, and served as an assistant in philosophy from 1903 to 1911.

As he went on in his academic work, he became less closely identified with New Thought. A 1902 article says that "he has recently resigned from all organizations, desiring to be identified only with his own interpretation of Christ's teaching."[2]

The reports of the Harvard College Class of 1895 provide valuable information given by Dresser. In the 1902 (second) *Report* he says, "My residence since leaving college has been Boston, and my occupation, author, lecturer and editor." (p. 129) After listing his publications and marriage he mentions that he "travelled in Holland, Switzerland and England in summers of 1898 and 1899." (p. 130)

The 1905 *Report*, which contains a warning that the sketches of the men may not be exact quotations, finds

---

[1]Dresser, *A History of the New Thought Movement*, pp. 177-78 and conversation with Mrs. Dresser, August 30, 1960.

[2]Paul Tyner, "The Metaphysical Movement," *The American Monthly Review of Reviews*, XXV (March, 1902), 314.

Dresser reporting more writing, the birth of his daughter Dorothea, now Mrs. Charles H. Reeves, on December 18, 1901 [still living in 1992], and:

> In 1902 I returned to Cambridge to complete my philosophical training, and have now nearly finished the requirements for a Ph.D. in philosophy at Harvard. Since September, 1903, I have been assistant in philosophy at Harvard and Radcliffe, and in 1904 I was Professor Royce's assistant in the Summer School. With the publication of "Man and the Divine Order" my work as a popular writer and lecturer was completed, and I am now fitting for a professorship in the history of philosophy and ethics. (p. 47)

The publication of that book in 1903 did not close that phase of his career. In the fourth *Report*, in 1910, Dresser adds word of the birth of his son, Malcolm, on October 14, 1905 [died August 15, 1985], and the completion of his academic degrees. In part he says:

> My time has been devoted to teaching, lecturing, and writing, and there is little of importance to tell apart from this work in the philosophical field. I have undertaken to establish vital connections between philosophy and practice by giving a part of my time to technical studies, and all the rest to individual and practical needs. Accordingly, I have held a position as assistant in philosophy ... and published books from year to year on the topics that have grown out of my private teaching outside of the university. "The Philosophy of the Spirit," published in 1908, is the book into which I have put most time and thought. Appended to this volume is my doctor's thesis on Hegel's Logic. ... I have lectured before various societies round about, and served a short term as professor of applied psy-

chology in the Massachusetts College of Osteopathy. I am a member of the Old South Club, of Boston, and president of the Harvard Philosophical Club. (p. 61)

By the time of the fifth *Report* in 1915, he was living at 139 Mason Terrace, Brookline, Massachusetts, but the move was not directly from Cambridge. He mentions lecturing in "Hartford, New York, Philadelphia, Atlanta, London, and other cities," and after referring to assisting Professor Palmer in the history of philosophy and ethics, continues:

In 1911 I went to Philadelphia for a few months, and taught philosophy for a term in Ursinus College, Collegeville, Pa. In 1912 I was appointed professor of philosophy at this college, but resigned in 1913 to return to Massachusetts and resume literary work. In 1911 I established a permanent summer home in Gray, Maine. (p. 80)

At Ursinus he was so well liked that the yearbook, *The Ruby*, prepared by the junior class, was dedicated to him. Written on a part of that volume in the possession of his family is:

In appreciation of kindly advice and inspiration in the higher things of life, this book is lovingly inscribed to our teacher, Dr. Horatio Willis Dresser, by the Class of 1914, Ursinus College.

In concluding a biographical sketch printed in the book, it is said:

Since coming to Ursinus, Dr. Dresser has gained the respect and esteem of the entire student body. His department is one of the best in the college. Not only is he esteemed as a teacher, but

Healing Hypotheses

> his courteous treatment to all, and his wise counsel have won for him a place in the hearts of the students which could not be easily filled by another.[1]

The briefer account of him in the preceding year's yearbook includes the information that

> In 1912, he was elected Professor of Philosophy and Education in Ursinus College, where by reason of putting his personality into his subjects and giving them vital interpretation, he is at this early date meeting with success.

John W. Clawson, in a letter of December 9, 1961, says, "I believe that Dr. Dresser was teaching Education in addition to Philosophy." *The Ruby* of 1913 refers to him as "Professor of Philosophy." It also says that he received his A.B. degree "with honorable mention three times in philosophy, Magna Cum Laude."

ii. Recollections of People Who Knew Dresser.

Dr. Clawson, professor of mathematics and later dean of the college, indicated that the 1912 date of Dresser's election is incorrect, the faculty being that of 1911-1912. He also says:

> I remember him quite well. But he was only with us for two years, 1911 to 1913, and I was not intimate with him. I remember being impressed by his wide interests and information about many things as exhibited in the meetings of a Faculty Men's Club which met from time to time during the academic year.

---

[1] *The Ruby*, 1913, p. 9.

He adds that he has "no information as to the reason for his leaving Ursinus."

Some who studied under Dresser at Ursinus have been located. Without exception, they expressed high opinions of him. In the words of Robert L. Matz, "Dr. Dresser was loved by all of us."

Rev. E. Bruce Jacobs recalls, in a letter of January 5, 1962:

> I can see him slowly wandering towards his class room, early for class, then seating himself on a log or tree stump, for a period of meditation. This act reveals part of his philosophy of life. He would do it repeatedly.
>
> In his class room, I remember most distinctly his fine English diction. One word which I will always remember as being associated with him was, or is, "awareness." He spoke of awareness with an earnestness and emphasis, quite distinctive.

He also tells of a time two years after his graduation:

> I spent a summer in a small town in Ohio, and became quite well acquainted with an eighty year old Quaker citizen of that town. This eighty year old citizen was the leader of a remnant of Quakers in that community, and when he learned that I had been a pupil of Dresser's, I became highly exalted in his opinion.

Apparently Dresser did not make a practice of referring to his books, for until then, "I did not realize the eminence of Dr. Dresser as a lecturer and writer."

In reply to more questioning, Mr. Jacobs wrote on January 27, 1962,

> As I suggested previously, I knew nothing of his religious connections. To me he was a teacher of philosophy, and just what courses he taught I do not know. I know he taught no courses in religion. I have no recollection that he ever referred to Phineas Quimby, Swedenborg, New Thought or Christian Science.

Chester Robbins wrote on December 18, 1961:

> I recall Dr. Dresser with great appreciation. I have no recollection, however, that he ever mentioned Swedenborg or New Thought. It seems to me that he was careful not to attempt in any way to indoctrinate his students with his own beliefs. Rather it was his constant endeavor to stimulate his students to think for themselves and encourage them to have the confidence and courage to express their own beliefs.
>
> I remember Dr. Dresser for what he stood for and his approach to teaching rather than for anything he taught. He was one of the most stimulating teachers in whose classes I ever sat. We students had been accustomed to mastering subject matter in text books and reproducing the material in examinations in order to satisfy our instructors. Dr. Dresser insisted on original thinking by the student rather than on reproduction of the views of a text book writer. Perhaps a personal anecdote will illustrate: One of the college "grinds" who had a passion for high marks, dutifully mastered his textbook in preparation for an examination. On the other hand, I read widely and made no attempt to master the text. In response to Dr. Dresser's questions, I gave my own thoughts as a result of my reading. When the marks were given, I received an

"A" and my classmate a "C." He was outraged and thought it unjust that he received a lower mark than I when he had followed and I had ignored the conventional way of preparing for an examination. He protested to Dr. Dresser who told him very quietly that he was interested in the student's thinking and not in the memorized views of a textbook writer.

Dr. Dresser believed in freedom of thought and the right to express it. While he was in no way an agitator, it was hearsay about the campus that he never hesitated to express his views forthrightly in faculty meetings regardless of the views of his colleagues and the college administration.

Writing under the date January 6, 1962, Walter R. Douthett, says:

> I recall that in the year Dr. Dresser was at Ursinus I had one course with him. Not only was he a great and popular teacher but a friend of students on the campus. My outstanding recollection of him was his defense of [a fellow student].
>
> In English Bible Class he was assigned the paper topic "Did Jesus Rise." After very thorough research he arrived at the conclusion that such a person never lived. For this the bible teacher and most of the faculty wanted to expel him. Dr. Dresser came to his defense and saved him.

The fellow student has confirmed the essentials of this incident, with the addition that he was not expressing his own views, but was doing an assigned term paper in relation to an author whose name he does not recall, on "Did Jesus Rise from a Lawyer's Point of View."

iii. Middle and Later Years

Something omitted from Dresser's account in the Class of 1895 *Report* may help to explain why he left Ursinus. The records of the New Church Theological School in Cambridge [now in Newton], Massachusetts, indicate that he was both a student and instructor in church history there 1913-1914. It is not clear whether he ever intended to devote his life to the New Church ministry, but he did not do a great deal of preaching

In the sixth Class of 1895 *Report*, in 1920, he observes that since leaving college he had

> taken no part in political or commercial life, or have engaged in any kind of activity on a large scale such as we single out for special mention when it is a question of success. My time has been devoted for the most part to the life of thought, in preparation for the twenty-five volumes I have written during this period. My interests have centered mainly about the inner life, on the problems of self-knowledge and self-control and human efficiency in general. My contacts have been chiefly with people in quest of light in these days of restless inquiry and uncertainty, of dissatisfaction with the teachings of conventional institutions.
> I did not give up teaching in college in 1913 because I disliked it, or because of any reaction against philosophy as I was able to expound it, but because it seemed to me that there were men enough who could teach philosophy in the usual way, and my part was to do what others were not doing. Nor am I reactionary so far as the organized church as a whole is concerned: It came my way to associate rather with people who were

exploring and thinking for themselves, and for whom I seemed to have a message.

At this point he could have added that in the April, 1915, through August, 1917, issues of *Home Progress* magazine, he edited a "Home History Circle" feature.

>The only radical departure from this plan of life came when I enlisted with the Y.M.C.A. for service overseas during the last year of the War. I was fortunate enough to be transferred to a position under the auspices of the Fourth French Army, as director of a Foyer du Soldat, where I had uncommon opportunity to know officers and men, and to realize my main interest in connection with the War, that is, in its human side, its effect upon the men and upon their faith. I came back with increased faith in the principles of thought and life I have acquired in the course of the years. It seemed to me eminently worth while to have this privilege of serving among men who were doing their part so splendidly to win the War, and I would enlist earlier if I were to live over the last three years again. [The editor adds: Dresser received a bronze medal from the *Foyer du Soldat*, in recognition of his services with the French Army.]
>I should find it rather difficult in looking over the twenty-five years to say what ought to have been different, what I would change another time. For life seems to exercise a kind of selection over us all, and our part is to do as well as we may under the destiny assigned to us. I have grown rather naturally into a kind of spiritual empiricism as the best working philosophy of life. It does not seem to matter especially whether one is conversing with people here at home who are troubled, or a French officer in the moonlight amid the dangers

of air-raids and other ominous events. Everywhere the great interest is life. after all, and one's part is to help people where they are, into a better understanding, a more affirmative faith.

And so my twenty-five years have been divided between more or less interrupted college work and teaching, in conversations with individuals and lectures to small audiences, and the writing of books growing out of these lines of interest and work. The world has used me as well as I deserve meanwhile. I have no complaints to utter. What I would like most to see is the world working as steadily and unitedly for ends worth pursuing in times of peace as I found the Allies and the "civiles" working in France during the War. That was the greatest event of the twenty-five years-- that human contact with united peoples working together as brothers for a noble end.

Aside from these personal matters, I have to report concerning my family life only that which is most pleasant to hear, since the family group remains unbroken. I have had the pleasure of seeing my wife engaged in public service in war time [she did graduate work in dietetics and institutional management in Teachers College, Columbia, University, was associated with the United States Department of Agriculture Home Economics Extension Service, and in the First World War organized and directed the Food Economy Kitchen in Boston's North End] and my children developing in school and daily life. My home has been in or near Boston all this time, save in 1911-13, when I was teaching in Pennsylvania. We have a summer home in Gray, Maine, on the shore of the little [Sebago] lake; and if I have any hobby it is in cutting trees and other rural work during the three months of "the simple life," when we turn to as a family and cultivate soil. (pp. 114-116)

Of considerable interest in connection with considering his relationship with New Thought is the listing of "clubs and societies": "International New Thought Alliance (Honorary Pres. and Field Sec.)." Perhaps this is to be explained by his having written *A History of the New Thought Movement*, which was published in 1919.

By the time of the seventh *Report*, of 1925, he had moved to South Hadley, Massachusetts, as his wife headed a dormitory at Mount Holyoke College from 1923 until 1945. The editor says that Dresser has retired from lecturing since the last *Report*, and Dresser adds:

> I live such a quiet life that ordinarily nothing happens of interest outside of a small group of friends. About four years ago I began work on a series of textbooks for the Crowell Company, in connection with their social science series. The first of these came out in 1924, "Psychology in Theory and Application," a book which undertakes to coordinate all branches of psychology. The second one, "Ethics in Theory and Application," is now being put into type.
>
> Meanwhile I am taking the place of a professor of philosophy in Mount Holyoke College. My daughter, Dorothea, graduated from Radcliffe last June, and my son, Malcolm, is a freshman in Massachusetts Agricultural College.
>
> I wish there were something else to say. It is absorbing work, writing and reading to keep up to date on philosophical subjects, but I have done nothing worth recording since our Twenty-fifth. (p. 75)

The eighth *Report*, of 1930, finds him saying:

All my time is absorbed in literary work. Nothing else of any importance has happened to me.

> My son was graduated from Massachusetts Agricultural College in 1928 and received his Master's degree from Columbia in 1929. My daughter has presented the family with a fine boy, who is now two and one-half years old. (p. 29)

In the ninth *Report*, 1935, he refers to his textbook writing and continues:

> For four years I have been connected with churches in Brooklyn, [New York,] doing part-time work there in personal problems of all sorts, chiefly by the aid of applied psychology. I use the term "Consultant in Personal Research" to distinguish this work from psychiatry and psychoanalysis. Last year I published a book about this work, "Knowing and Helping People," issued by The Beacon Press, Boston. Meanwhile, I have made my home in South Hadley, Mass., and during the summer I still go to Gray, Maine. (p. 31)

The birth of a granddaughter also was noted.

The fiftieth anniversary, tenth, *Report* in 1945 republishes some of the earlier material and adds:

> Strange to say, some of us may have nothing momentous to report even in war-time. That is my case exactly. Since neither my son nor my son-in-law has been called into service, not my wife and not my daughter, everything has continued as usual. So have I, in my work as consulting psychologist in the clinic in Brooklyn. I have written no more books because when paper is short and printing is costly, I could not produce a book that would appeal to a publisher as a first-rate seller. Sometimes, however,

business as usual is good news. For if we keep the even tenor of our way we can be of some small service at least to those who find the sledding difficult. Still agreeing with my great teacher, William James [who was like a father to him, Mrs. Dresser said] that there will always be war as long as there are warring passions in the human breast, I find it possible to put people on the right track when increased self-knowledge may lead to better self-control, thus to a victory over inward conflicts. The advance from inwardness to overt social expression may seem slow indeed when one thus advises individuals only, leaving each to make a better adjustment to his group. But that at least is my province until after the duration, "continuance in well doing" being an excellent motto for those whose pathways lie in fairly pleasant places, such as my summer home in Gray, Maine, where I still spend three months each year, cutting our season's wood, and beautifying our pine-clad acres. (pp. 152-53)

At some time he went to Europe to study with Jung and Adler, but details of this are lacking.

Dresser continued his work with the Associated Clinic of Religion and Medicine, later known as the Associated Counseling Service, from 1931 to 1953. This marked the continuance of an old friendship, for the minister of the First Unitarian Church, associated with the clinic, was John Howland Lathrop; they met as Harvard students. It was he who suggested Dresser as the spiritual advisor to succeed Elwood Worcester, who was much better known for his pioneering work in the

Healing Hypotheses 111

Emmanuel Movement. Both of these undertakings were cooperative endeavors of clergymen and physicians.[1]

About a year after he retired from this work, Dresser suffered a heart attack, and died in the Osteopathic Hospital in Boston at four o'clock in the morning on March 30, 1954. Since Mrs. Dresser's retirement in 1945 they had been living first with their son and his family in Hartsdale, New York, for eight years and thereafter with their daughter and her family in Marshfield, Massachusetts. He continued his writing and might have published another book if he had lived longer.[2]

iv. Summarizing Characterizations of Dresser

After making numerous inquiries about Dresser, one is struck by the similarity of reactions to him. Although a considerable proportion of inquiries went to people whose names were suggested by others who had no knowledge of Dresser except what reference works might reveal, the only opinion that might be considered unfavorable was one indirectly transmitted from a person unwilling to be identified, so who could not be questioned about it. This person saw him in connection with his residence at Mount Holyoke College and considered him a "rather sad and ineffectual figure." The following reactions are more representative.

Some very interesting glimpses of her "dear and revered friend, Horatio Dresser," are given in an August 4, 1962, letter of Mrs. Ruth Ricciardi:

---

[1]Part of this information was obtained in a conversation with Dr. Lathrop on October 24, 1960.

[2]Correspondence in the Swedenborg School of Religion shows that he was exploring this possibility until nearly the end of his life.

Our acquaintance began in June 1913 when we met on the station platform where the New York-Portland express had left me. It had been arranged through my college adviser for me to spend the summer with the Dressers as a "mother's helper" at their cottage at Gray, Maine, where people came as paying guests to consult Mr. Dresser. Mr. Dresser's tall, stately figure and fine face, with his slightly greying beard (tho' he was only 47), instantly made me feel confident that I had fallen into good hands.

On our slow trip out to Camp Content [a name it had even before Dresser acquired the place] Mr. Dresser talked gently of his family, whom I had never seen, and incidental things, putting the heart and mind of a shy, timid young stranger at rest.

During my summer's stay with the Dressers I never once saw Mr. Dresser in any but a calm and peaceful frame of mind; when his children misbehaved he talked to them quietly, pointing out the error of their ways in a gentle voice; there were no loud scoldings and spankings.

He had long talks with the people who came to stay with us for the purpose of seeking his advice and help in their mental and spiritual problems, and they went away helped and encouraged.

He had long talks with me under the stars. ... In the evenings he often read to the assembled family beside the crackling fire--for Maine evenings are chilly.

Mr. Dresser had a strong belief in the mental healing of physical ills; he told me of the parlor meetings which his parents had conducted in his youth in an endeavor to help people to help themselves. Mrs. Dresser told me of an incident which had occurred one summer while they were at their cottage; Mr. Dresser had been taken ill with a serious intestinal disease for which he refused to have any treatment. By the end of the summer he had cured himself without recourse to medicine, simply by his belief in his mental and spiritual powers.

Mr. Dresser was a deeply religious man but there was very little formal observance of religion in the household; sometimes on Sundays we had an informal gathering in a little clearing among the tall pines and Mr. Dresser would give a little talk, too informal to be called a sermon yet with a serious purpose. He was more inclined to the Quaker form of religious observance than to any other.

His love of nature was immense; when not writing in his upstairs study he was usually in his beloved woods, clearing out underbrush, making paths, cutting down trees which needed to be removed.

I made other visits to Camp Content and always came away feeling better for my association with a truly great man, one of the finest persons I have ever known.

The last time I met him and Mrs. Dresser in New York he was in his eighties and he made a rather sad remark--"We have lived too long." I think he felt that his usefulness had come to an end, and that from then on he might be a burden to his family, though as far as I know he retained his mental faculties and his physical health until a few weeks before his death. [On April 19, 1962, his daughter said that he was sick about a month until his death.]

After his death Mrs. Dresser wrote me that he had been confident that he would meet his parents who were "waiting for him on the other shore." . . .

There was perfect love between Mr. & Mrs. Dresser, and perfect harmony; I never heard cross or angry words exchanged.

His spiritual counsels, in his daily living as well as in his speeches and his books, must have influenced thousands toward a bettor life.

In an August 17, 1962, letter she continues:

> I don't remember ever seeing Mr. Dresser hurry, nor even move fast; he was a large and calm man who planned his work thoughtfully and achieved results with efficiency and economy of movement. He studied and wrote in his upstairs study, we could hear the rattle of his typewriter in the kitchen below. This type of work was done largely in bad weather when he could not work in the woods, or when some thought which had come to him needed to be put down immediately.
>
> In good weather he spent much time in his beloved woods, felling superfluous trees and keeping the wood shed stocked with wood cut for the kitchen stove and the livingroom fireplace, and improving the picturesque, winding path down the hill to the lake. Often we had a beach picnic, sometimes a supper picnic, sometimes an early morning one Mr. Dresser brought kindling and enough odd pieces of wood for the fire which he built and kept going so that Mrs. Dresser could cook our bacon on it. He was very careful to see that the cinders and ashes remaining when we were ready to leave were wet with lake water and covered with sand.
>
> These delightful open-air meals were often finished off with a row on the lake, Mr. Dresser pulling at the oars; he was as good a boatman as he was woodman. In addition to these short boat trips, there was one long one, the highlight of the summer, our trip to Raymond, a town and tourist resort on Big Sebago, a few miles from Little Sebago Lake where the Dressers' summer home was situated. We started early in the morning, taking

our lunch with us. Mr. Dresser rowed us across the lake with long powerful strokes; after eating our lunch in the woods on the west side of our lake we made sure the boat was securely fastened and then climbed the hill and went down to Raymond on western slope. There we wandered the streets, licking our ice cream cones, Mr. Dresser enjoying the novelty of the trip and the cones as much as the children and I did--he retained his boyish enjoyment of any variation in our everyday living--then we returned home late in the afternoon, Mr. Dresser eager to share the day's exploits with Mrs. Dresser, who had not felt like taking the long trip with us.

Once or twice during the summer he went to visit his mother at Yarmouth, about 15 miles away. As there was no means of transportation he walked--he enjoyed walking--and he had a better view of the scenery than he would have had from a fast-moving vehicle. After spending a night or two with his mother he walked back. Another summer he took the two children and a family friend to see the President Range; they climbed Mt. Washington and one of the children left the family's precious binoculars on a rock there, but when they reached home the incident was closed, there were no lamentations and no unpleasant reminders from Mr. Dresser.

At their urgent invitation I visited Mr. & Mrs. Dresser at camp one summer years later when their children were married and gone and my own were pretty nearly grown up. I went because not only did I want to see them but I had the mistaken idea that they were a lonely old couple in need of company from the outside. How wrong I was! They welcomed me gladly but it was obvious they were perfectly self-sufficient unto each other, they shared the same interests, they laughed at the same jokes, Mr. Dresser teased his wife because he had found a gift for him in the morning mail, but she had received none. They read the now defunct Boston Transcript with a good deal of interest, there were trips to town for supplies, and ice cream cones. Mr. Dresser still worked in the woods but not as hard as in his younger days, and we read the Atlantic Monthly by the fire in the evenings.

I have many memory pictures of Mr. Dresser: pushing the wheelbarrow loaded with logs which he had cut up the hill from the woods to be piled neatly in the woodshed; sitting at our long outdoor dining table eating Mrs. Dresser's good New England baked beans--in a bean pot--with gusto, and enjoying apple dumplings with boiled molasses sauce which she made often, "because Horatio is so fond of them"; sitting at the south side of the woodshed in a comfortable old chair, listening to the outpourings of a troubled guest, and giving her strength to go on with her life. And walking up the hill with me in the evenings, talking to me under the stars, before I went to bed.

During the winters when they lived in a small house on their son's property in Hartsdale N.Y. Mr. Dresser was accustomed to spending several days a week at a church in Brooklyn, I believe as a psychologist. . . .

I have barely mentioned Mrs. Dresser because I knew that your chief interest was in Mr. Dresser, but I do want to pay tribute to her--she was a very fine woman and the perfect helpmate for Horatio, to whom she always looked up and loved with a perfect love.

Mrs. Jessie M. Hamilton, in a letter of May 31, 1962, says:

I first knew Dr. Dresser slightly when I was a student at Radcliffe and he was in the Philosophy Department. Later, probably 1916, I came across one of his books, "Living By the Spirit," and found his thought very congenial. On the jacket of the book was the information that the author gave a correspondence course on the subject, and I made arrangements to take the course. Since I lived in the Boston area Dr. Dresser suggested I come to his home in Brookline for discussions, and thus I became quite well acquainted with the family.

In the latter part of World War I Dr. Dresser went to France under the War Work Council of the Y.M.C.A., where because of his knowledge of the French language he was assigned to a French camp. Since my family was also temporarily disrupted by the war I went to live with Mrs. Dresser and the children, and remained something over two years after Dr. Dresser's return from France.

It was a real privilege to live in the Dresser home, with two highly intelligent adults and two interesting children. It was a very happy home. It was a very hospitable home, where parents complemented each other well. Mrs. Dresser was more objective than her husband though with a great appreciation for his depth of insight.[1] I suspect that it was necessary that she work outside the home at her profession of dietician, for Dr. Dresser's work during that period could not have been very remunerative. He was writing, doing some speaking and some counseling, both by correspondence and in person.

---

[1] On August 30, 1960, in a conversation with Mrs. Dresser, she called herself a good "balance" to her husband; she considering herself "a very practical person." She also said that Dresser was practical, that his philosophy was not just up in the air. But she had a more external approach to things.

> As to my impressions of Dr. Dresser as I look back more than forty years, I remember him as a quiet, scholarly man, a very thorough and logical thinker, an able writer. He was rather retiring; was not active in any group such as a church, or community or other groups. At the same time, in the small, intimate gatherings in his home he talked freely and displayed a good sense of humor.
>
> My impression is that his influence during that period reached a rather small, select group, as you would probably expect because of his retiring personality and because of the profundity of his thought. I think he probably got closer to people in general later on when he worked at counseling in cooperation with doctors in a clinic in Brooklyn, N.Y. I have no detailed knowledge of his work there.

In a letter of July 15, 1962, Mrs. Hamilton elaborates on some points, the most relevant for this study being the following:

> Dr. Dresser was instructor in a course in the History of Mediaeval Philosophy which I took at Radcliffe. The professor was Ralph Barton Perry, now deceased. The only time I remember seeing Dr. Dresser was once when Professor Perry was not able to meet the class and Dr. Dresser gave the lecture. He also assisted George Herbert Palmer in his course Philosophy IV, a course in Ethics. He told me once that Professor Palmer told him that he should have remained in teaching. So far as I know none of my classmates knew Dr. Dresser at that time. I didn't until later.
>
> As to the correspondence course, I do not know how many people took advantage of it. It was advertised in some of his books and I suspect

others like myself were brought in touch with him through this means.

Dr. Dresser was decidedly not in sympathy with Christian Science. You probably have learned about a man named Quimby, who was a spiritual healer. Both Mary Baker Eddy and Dr. Dresser's father were disciples of this man Quimby and the elder Dresser seems to have practised spiritual healing. Dr. Dresser said that Mrs. Eddy got her ideas in the beginning from Quimby and claimed that they originated with her. She developed these ideas further herself and in ways that Quimby would not have approved. For example, the denial of disease was not his conception at all. But the fundamental ideas with which she started were not hers though she claimed them.

Of course Dr. Dresser was himself influenced in his thought by his father and indirectly by Quimby. However, he acquired a thorough education in philosophy and psychology to supplement and perhaps correct these early ideas. His thought as expressed in his books was quite original. I do not think he can be classified with any group such as New Thought or New Church. During the period I knew him I think most of his lecturing was before New Thought groups, though I do not think he identified himself as one of them. His teaching was all his own.

His brother ... was a Swedenborgian minister. During the period with which I am familiar he, Dr. Dresser, was ordained in the ministry of that church but again I do not think he can be classified as a Swedenborgian, though he seemed to be well acquainted with Swedenborg's teachings. Frankly, I think the reason he went into this ministry at this time was that it was a means of gaining a little income at a time when he must have needed it sorely. He substituted in Swedenborgian pulpits for a while and that was about all there was to it. It didn't seem to be very strong "call." I do not know why he discontinued this association.

v. Dresser's Swedenborgian Activities

A memorial adopted by the General Convention of the New Jerusalem after his death says:

> Ordained in 1919, Dr. Dresser had withdrawn from our ministry in 1929, that the Church would not seem to be responsible for his secular work, but was reinstated at his own request in 1942. His only pastorate was in Portland, Maine, for a short time following his ordination.[1]

Dresser did not see fit to tell of his Swedenborgian activities in his reports to his classmates. Little seems to be known of his attachment to the New Church. From time to time articles by him were published in New Church Journals, and shortly before his death he became a regular columnist in *The New-Church Messenger*, with a feature called "With the Consulting Psychologist."

How Dresser learned of Swedenborg and what influence his writings exerted on Dresser early in his life are not known. He could have learned of Swedenborg from Emerson, or from a family physician who was a Swedenborgian, or from reading Evans. As will be seen, Dresser's earliest writing does not suggest that Dresser would become a Swedenborgian.

That little or nothing was known of Swedenborg in the Dresser family, so presumably also in Quimby circles, during the nineteenth century is shown by Annetta G. Dresser's saying that Quimby's

---

[1] *Journal of the General Convention of the New Jerusalem in the United States of America for 1954*, p. 57.

method was to me a good working theory for many years, but it was not until some years after my husband's death that I felt that I understood the reasons why the theory worked. The light came to me in the writings of Emmanuel Swedenborg. Here I found the science I had been seeking.[1]

She adds that she wrote to Quimby's son to inquire whether "his father had been acquainted with Swedenborg's writings, and he replied that his father had read some of them before Mr. Dresser and I had known him."[2] If Quimby was influenced by Swedenborg, what seems most significant is the failure of this to come out clearly in his writings or his discussions with his followers.

The Dresser family has a copy of Swedenborg's *Divine Love and Wisdom* marked "Horatio W. Dresser with cordial regard from John Worcester Feb. 1896," possibly his first work of Swedenborg.

However Dresser learned of Swedenborg, he eventually became a Swedenborgian, but most of his Swedenborgian career lies beyond the period covered in connection with his philosophy in this study. [Some

---

[1] Annetta G. Dresser, *The Future for the New Thought* (Boston: a pamphlet originally available from the author, 1914), p. 10.

[2] *Ibid.*, pp. 11-12. John Whitehead received from George Quimby the statement, "Father was at one time quite interested in Swedenborg's ideas." The New Church Theological School, Cambridge, Massachusetts, has the letter from which this is taken, not otherwise relating to Quimby's seemingly passing interest in Swedenborg. The sentence also is found in John Whitehead, *The Illusions of Christian Science* (Boston: The Garden Press, 1907), p. 224.

correspondence at the Swedenborg School of Religion suggests that his mother may have been important in prompting him to his going to that school.]

vi. Summary

Dresser's was a frontier life. In some degree this was so in regard to his early Western life, although the area may not have been so wild as it had been a few decades earlier. Dresser's yearly return to his Maine woods also has something of a frontier flavor.

More significantly, it was a frontier life with respect to Dresser's place in the forefront of movements seeking to advance the welfare of humankind. Early in his life this meant helping his parents to spread the teachings of Quimby in their home meetings. A little later he was helping to establish New Thought organizations. Toward the end of his life he was serving in a clinic of religion and medicine.

Dresser had a gentle, calm strength. His very appearance and attitude helped people. Dresser did not seek controversy, but would not avoid it when the occasion arose, as when his sense of justice called for the defense of anyone, whether Quimby or a student who had written an unpopular paper.

What might be called a frontier practicality and suspicion of rigid formulation of beliefs remained with Dresser, despite his Harvard education. His approach to life was marked by tentativeness, yet with trust in an abiding divine source of guidance and support.

Dresser's life was a quiet center in the midst of controversial history and theoretical disputes over the healing gospels being advocated in various ways by competing groups. It could be said that he rose above disputes of all sorts in his love for people and his desire to help them.

3. His Constructive Idealism

i. Dresser's Approach to Philosophy

Dresser was not primarily a philosopher. Most of his writing was in the field of popular spiritual uplift. Eventually he used the title psychologist. No doubt, he meant his writing to be consistent with what he considered sound philosophy, but he was little concerned with offering a complete philosophical system. He wanted to help people; to the extent that he found philosophy useful in this aim, he used it.

Philosophy could be considered a natural interest of Dresser, or at least one that he acquired at an early age. Partly this interest may have grown out of a search for understanding of his own abilities.

ii. Dresser's Extrasensory Perception

In addition to ordinary perception, Dresser had some degree of extrasensory perception. He wrote of his boyhood "spontaneous impressions regarding things mislaid or lost,"[1] as well as of later experiences. In a letter of February 8, 1943, he says:

> The telepathic experiences have been the most numerous. . . . I have had comparatively few experiences of clairvoyance that are outstanding, but a sufficient number to discriminate the type in contrast with telepathy. I have heard words from a distance as if uttered in my ear when there was

---

[1] Horatio W. Dresser, *The Open Vision: A Study of Psychic Phenomena* (New York: Thomas Y. Crowell Company, 1920), p. 172.

no clairvoyance and no telepathy otherwise than that of this limited experience. I was near enough to mediumship for two years, 20 to 22, to fear that I might succumb to it.[1]

Quimby's teachings helped to keep him from turning to spiritism,[2] and provided a home atmosphere recognizing "the spiritual world as near at hand."[3] Undoubtedly Quimby's method of intuitively approaching each patient individually, rather than as a case for the application of rigidly fixed principles, was of great importance in developing Dresser's empirical attitude. It was Quimby's technique that he upheld in preference to the employment of more formalized mental treatment. However, it will be seen that despite Dresser's own extrasensory abilities and beliefs about those of others, he was far from uncritical of these abilities.

Looking back to his childhood, he recalled "spending delightful hours by myself supposedly under punishment but really at home in my own world of imagination."[4] This may indicate an early introspective tendency. It, or the native capacities that it may have represented, seems to have aided both in laying a foundation for the extrasensory experiences that he believed indicated the awakening of powers latent in everyone, the awakening of which "came naturally, in my

---

[1]This letter, containing valuable biographical information, as well as comments on extrasensory perception, is given fully in Appendix F.

[2]Dresser, *The Open Vision*, p. 180.

[3]*Ibid.*, p. 172.

[4]Horatio W. Dresser, "True Punishment," *Home Progress*, III (February, 1914), p. 288.

case in connection with therapeutic interests in helping people from the time I was about 17,"[1] and in encouraging the development of an inclination to subject all experiences to critical examination. Dresser says, "I deliberately trained my mind to the limit in philosophy at Harvard to be as critical as the best of them...."[2]

iii. Dresser's Acknowledgment of Influence of Philosophers on Him

Turning to the influence of standard thinkers on Dresser, it will be recalled that his early interest in Emerson was noted in a biographical entry. Eleven Emerson volumes of Dresser, in the possession of the family, contain dates ranging from Christmas, 1883, to 1888. Emerson apparently reinforced the approach of Quimby. Dresser says:

> Emerson's method was always to let the inspirations of the Spirit lead the way, instead of inflicting one's hypotheses and presuppositions upon the Spirit.[3]

Later he summarizes:

> Emerson was for years the writer who most directly guided the way to the interpretation of inner experience. Then a time came when one turned rather to Professor Royce, to Plato, Hegel,

---

[1]February 8, 1943, letter, in Appendix F.

[2]*Ibid.*

[3]Horatio W. Dresser, *Man and the Divine Order* (New York: G. P. Putnam's Sons, 1903), p. 272.

and other idealists, in quest of the system Emerson failed to supply. Meanwhile it was the stimulating instruction of William James which strengthened the empirical tendency. . . .[1]

iv. Dresser's Emphasis on Reason as Well as Experience

(1) *In General.* From his association with spiritual healing, extrasensory perception, and various religious groups emphasizing mysticism, Dresser could have developed a view of life disparaging reason. Or he might have reacted so strongly against his background as to overemphasize reason. However, he did neither. Throughout his life he sought to exercise discrimination, a term that he liked, in trying to achieve a proper balance among the various sides of life.

Dresser set the tone for all his writings in his first book, *The Power of Silence*, 1895, when he wrote:

> This book does not . . . advise rigorous self-analysis of the personal self alone. It seeks a way of escape from narrowing introspection and self-consciousness. It seeks the Origin of all consciousness and all life. It proceeds on the principle that man cannot fully understand himself without constant reference to the omnipresent Spirit in whom he lives, and that in this profoundest wisdom is to be found the one unfailing resource in every moment of need.[2]

---

[1]Horatio W. Dresser, *The Religion of the Spirit in Modern Life* (New York: G. P. Putnam's Sons, 1914), pp. ix-x.

[2]Horatio W. Dresser, *The Power of Silence*, (1st ed., Boston: Geo. H. Ellis, 1895), p. 11.

He did not fail to give much attention to the practical end of fuller, healthier--in all ways--life to be attained, but he would not pursue any course that he considered inconsistent with his reasoning. He was ever critical of those who were less concerned with having a solid intellectual foundation for actions. His criticism was summed up succinctly. "What is the greatest need of the New Thought movement?--Scholarship."[1]

In *The Power of Silence* he shows concern about experience, as in saying:

> No formula seems large enough to cover all we know and feel. There is an element in experience that always eludes us. Some experiences can never be told. They are part of us. They are sacred, and one hesitates to speak of them. Yet one can suggest them, or at least let it be known that in these rarest moments of existence one seemed most truly to live.[2]

But his approach in this work is shown by his observation that "experience is best explained by its immediate environment."[3] This led to ontological considerations that are best left for the next section. Although Dresser's second book, *The Perfect Whole*, came the next year, its epistemology may be considered essentially a final statement of his epistemology. This is not to say that much thought and writing after it did nothing to refine and add to Dresser's outlook. However, the basic views are to be found in 1896.

---

[1] Untitled section of "Editor's Study," *The Higher Law*, VI (August-September, 1902), 219.

[2] Dresser, *The Power of Silence*, 1st ed., p. 12.

[3] *Ibid.*, p. 14.

In this book Dresser devotes his first chapter to experience. He points out that "experience is both direct and indirect."[1] One simply awakes at some point to the awareness of "things, beings, and events without, and of a continuous stream of thought within."[2] One might think that he would consider what is purely "within" to be the direct experience and that relating to the "without" to be indirect, but this is not the way that he puts it. He says:

> Direct or immediate experience originates in the world of qualities and relations. Indirect experience is our own mental reaction upon the world, the attempt to comprehend it by means of ideas. . . . The former is the concrete, the substantive, the realm of immediate feeling or intuition. The latter is the abstract, the adjective, the secondary.[3]

It is the indirect that gives meaning to the direct. He turns to the baby's state of being "simply conscious"[4] of an "indiscriminate whole"[5] that cannot well be meaningful.

> Yet the infant ego is already in its first instant of conscious life in the presence of a whole of experience which, through its future

---

[1] Horatio W. Dresser, *The Perfect Whole* (Boston: Geo. H. Ellis, 1896), p. 40.

[2] *Ibid*, p. 11.

[3] *Ibid*., pp. 33-34.

[4] *Ibid*., p. 41.

[5] *Ibid*.

> development, is to constitute the sole reality of its entire life. It unwittingly knows the fact that something real exists in receiving its first sensation. Its consciousness is a part, an inseparable part, of the great whole of immediate experience. Although it is utterly ignorant of this first experience and removed by years of patient thought from the reality which the philosopher distinguishes from appearance, the absolute and eternal Reality is nevertheless there in that highly important first moment of consciousness,--if it is ever to be present at all.[1]

Obviously one cannot say what, if anything, the baby thinks, but Dresser here is not concerned to say what the baby's outlook may be. He simply is making the point that the whole is present to the baby, although not sorted out into its elements and made meaningful by reflection. Here again Dresser's chief concerns are ontological, but he is paying increasing attention to epistemological matters. A little later he remarks:

> The second moment of experience possesses increased value to the degree only that it enriches or throws light upon the first. Could the infant know all that is related to that first moment, as an inseparable part of the infinite series of relations and qualities finding their ground in the ultimate All, the infant would be omniscient. An omniscient Self or God would possess all this at once. The finite self, just because it is finite, must develop these relations bit by bit through temporal and spatial experience.[2]

---

[1] *Ibid.*

[2] *Ibid.*, pp. 41-42.

Dresser goes on to say that "the finite ego is made aware of itself in relation to an 'other,'"[1] but this takes one to at least the border of his ontology, so at this point one turns to perhaps the most significant area in which immediate experience may be upheld most strongly--mysticism.

(2) *In Regard to Mysticism.* Turning to Plotinus as "the father of Western mysticism,"[2] Dresser takes mysticism to be "the belief that God may be known face to face, without anything intermediate."[3] Having established what he means by mysticism, he expresses his respect for such "surely sublime and in the highest degree spiritual"[4] experience, but proceeds to stress that it *is* experience, of a primary or immediate sort.[5] As such, it "needs to be reflectively interpreted."[6]
He observes that

> the mystical transport of itself gives no immediate and unquestionable certainty; for there is no assurance, until one doubts, that one is not merely contemplating one's self, or some imagined Absolute, instead of the pure being of love and wisdom whom we call God.[7]

---

[1]*Ibid.*, p. 43.

[2]*Ibid.*, p. 103.

[3]*Ibid.*

[4]*Ibid.*, p. 104.

[5]*Ibid.*

[6]*Ibid.*

[7]*Ibid.*, pp. 104-105.

Dresser could well refer back to the baby, for mere experience is empty of meaning. The mystic has to interpret his experience. Thus Dresser says:

> the mystic in accepting his transport as genuine ... does so for *reasons*.--[namely] because believes all reasoning to be vain. This in itself is a flat contradiction of his whole theory that the intellect is "the language of contradiction"; for this is an intellectual conclusion arrived at by a process of rapid reasoning.[1]

Dresser of course is operating within the bounds of reason, but is saying that the mystic has no cause for objection, since the mystic himself has to do the same.

(3) *In Regard to Reason's Place in the World.* Dresser sees reason as

> the necessary unfoldment or interpretation of immediate experience in all its phases. It is the faculty [seemingly the term is used simply as a matter of convenience, rather than a deviation from his rejection of faculty psychology] which examines itself, and seeks the cause and meaning of things. Intuition deals with wholes, of whose parts we are for the time unaware. . . . Reason is that closer scrutiny which reveals what we mean by beauty [when we view a distant scene without being aware of its elements], how its essentials are combined, and its ultimate basis of reality. It [reason] is emotion, experience, intuition, rendered explicit. Intuition oftentimes permits us but a glimpse of truth, like the flash of lightning on the darkest night, which illumines all our surroundings for a moment, and then dies out before we grasp

---

[1]*Ibid.*, p. 107.

their relationship. Reason is that measured and law-governed evolution by which all the mysteries of nature are gradually spread out before us. It is the essential and necessary verification of insight, without which truth is not truth at all.[1]

It is apparent that Dresser was very much concerned with the whole at this time, as the very title of this book indicates. The immediate and the mediate were seen to be indispensable to each other, and ultimately simply different stages of the same process or different perspective, separated by the form of time in our apprehension of them. It may be doubted that he could start with epistemology and work to ontology even when, as in the second book, he approached his task that way. His vision, if such it may be called, of the whole could not fail to shape his epistemology.

While the question of Dresser's conception of the nature of the world is left for the next section, it may be noted here, as his devotion to evolution suggests, that he tended to accept scientific judgments as valuable, although not final in an overall interpretation of reality. He went so far in a book published the next year as to suggest something at least approaching materialism:

> Thought . . . by means of motor images or mental pictures, probably blends by insensible gradations with neutral action and the nerves, muscles, and tissues of the entire physical system.[2]

This, of course, does not say what the ultimate nature of the body is. Whatever it may be, Dresser

---

[1] *Ibid.*

[2] Horatio W. Dresser, *In Search of a Soul* (Boston: Geo. H. Ellis, 1897), p. 46.

emphasizes the "directive power of mind."[1] Ever close to practical problems of use of our abilities, and helped in his theorizing by clues derived from spiritual healing, Dresser says:

> The real problem of mind-matter relationship... becomes the problem of motion and the power that directs it. Here we seem to have the question in its lowest terms, but terms in which mind and matter have become incidents in a larger whole. The field of the mind is literally the field of the universe with all its mysteries. Within this field you and I gather ourselves as much of all this as a finite mind can grasp, and the act of grasping we call consciousness. The thought of the moment is the emerging and entering point of consciousness. Round this centre cluster the associated sensations or vibrations of light, heat, color, sound, hardness, etc., which constitute the borders of consciousness.[2]

While he has been seen to criticize the Evans final view that identifies thought and existence, Dresser here seems close to the same outlook. Certainly his emphasis on wholeness makes any separation of the two realms only relative.

While there is no way of knowing what led Dresser to particular aspects of his thought, except in the most general terms, it can be seen that his reference to motion and its direction and the relatedness of a whole, while not accepting the Evans identification of thought and existence, came about the time when he also took note of the thought of Dods. It may be that Dods provided for

---

[1] *Ibid.*

[2] *Ibid.*, pp. 19-20.

Dresser either a preface to Swedenborg or a supplement to Swedenborg. The notion of degrees is similar to the system of gradations found in Dods.

In summarizing Dods, Dresser says:

> According to this theory, electricity is the creative agent of God, the ultimate energy out of which all chemical and physical forces and substances have been evolved, and by which all planetary and stellar relationships are sustained. The will of God gives direction to electricity, sets up motion, whereupon all development proceeds; and all life is maintained by the involuntary or subconscious results of the creative fiat or divine volition. By a similar process, the mind or will of man commands and uses the body through the gradual transmission from will, or mental energy, electric action, nerve vibration, and muscular contraction, to movement. *All action is fundamentally mental* and electricity is the agent of transfer.[1]

It is apparent that the attitudes of Dresser and Evans were sufficiently related that Evans could ignore distinctions between epistemology and ontology, and Dresser at a time when he had growing epistemological concern could view Dods and pass over the Dods recognition of both physical and mental impressions, and find in Dods a fundamental mental action, but with real "gradation of forces... evident from all our knowledge of

---

[1] Dresser, *Voices of Freedom* (New York: G. P. Putnam's Sons, 1899) p. 68.

Healing Hypotheses 135

nature."[1] Yet Dresser called "consciousness and activity ... two aspects of spirit."[2]

(4) *In Regard to Truth.* It is not surprising that when Dresser turned to a chapter on "The Criteria of Truth"[3] he should emerge with a conclusion recognizing "consistency and practicality."[4] He observes:

> The philosopher delights in the construction of a theoretically perfect system of metaphysics--which convinces only himself. But as surely as metaphysics originated in the two-fold motive of truth for its own sake and truth for the sake of utility, so surely must the practical tendency be the critic of the speculative. The chief point of this chapter is that no wholly sound, merely speculative system of philosophy is possible. All speculative metaphysics must be supplemented by the higher spiritual insights and spontaneous experiences of the soul.
>
> It has been argued again and again that reason is the only test of truth. But one may prove anything by argument and make it reasonable. Your logic may prove an event impossible: the next moment you may experience that which was declared impossible....

---

[1] Dresser, *Voices of Freedom* (New York: G. P. Putnam's Sons, 1899), p. 68.

[2] *Ibid.*, p. 69.

[3] Horatio W. Dresser, *Education and the Philosophical Ideal* (New York: G. P. Putnam's Sons, 1900), chapter XII.

[4] *Ibid.*, p. 183.

> Experience contradicts, verifies, or modifies and enlarges reason; reason must interpret and test experience.[1]

While Dresser here is concerned more with "higher" experiences, there is nothing to indicate that he would consider ordinary experience as of less importance.

In summarizing his view of truth Dresser reveals that he apparently considers it more than a characteristic of propositions. While recognizing the necessity of empirical coherence in testing truth, the nature of truth takes him into metaphysics. Although Dresser purports to "sum up the criteria of truth as follows,"[2] he appears to get into the nature of truth:

> Philosophic truth in its ultimate sense is self-consistent, but this self-consistency often lies far below the surface which it apparently contradicts. It meets the reasonable, mutually supplementary demands of realism and idealism, the head and the heart, intellect and intuition, and is at once valuable for its own sake and because of its utility. Reason is its most useful criterion, yet experience is its most important corrective. It must never overlook the distinctive revelations of individuality, yet must be equally faithful to the universal. It is an organic totality to which all phases of thought and life contribute their share; in its pursuit every man must give play to the highest side of his nature. It is progressive, and can only be progressively revealed. It is eternal and

---

[1] *Ibid.*, pp. 186-87.

[2] Dresser, *Education and the Philosophical Ideal*, p. 193.

Healing Hypotheses

> may, happily, for ever be sought without permitting itself to be fully grasped.[1]

Here Dresser seems to be adopting the common practice of New Thought[2] and Christian Science[3] of calling truth, meaning the content rather than a judgment, one of the aspects or synonyms for God, although Dresser does not quite put it that way.

More than a decade later, after receiving his doctorate in philosophy, Dresser produced a chapter, "What Is Truth?,"[4] in which he answered his question:

> Truth is not first a human judgment, looking outward to nature, and referring upward to God; but an imbuing life entering into man by the heart and later revealing its substance through insight, and the clarification of the pathway of experience.[5]

This identification of truth and life, another commonly attributed aspect of God, continues the thought

---

[1] *Ibid.*

[2] "What We Believe," published on the back of [now inside] the quarterly *New Thought*. See also Emmet Fox, *Alter Your Life* (New York: Harper & Brothers, 1931), p. 126.

[3] Mary Baker Eddy, *Science and Health with Key to the Scriptures* (Boston: Trustees under the will of Mary Baker G. Eddy, 1934), p. 465.

[4] Horatio W. Dresser, *The Religion of the Spirit in Modern Life*, Chapter XII.

[5] *Ibid.*, p. 245.

just referred to. However, in the same chapter Dresser maintains, presumably consistently with his saying that truth is not *first* a human judgment, that truth

> is a statement or explicit relation concerning life. It is really true if your statement conform to real experience when further comparisons are made.[1]

This may sound like correspondence theory, but the correspondence is within the broad field of coherence. He continues:

> Truth expresses the law of being, that is the order or system. It is exact, satisfactory, if it correctly represent the vital order, our supreme interest. Hence we know its import by seeing what lies beyond it. Our chief interest is not the report of experience, not even the formulated purpose or ideal; but the life which gives truth its being and inspires us to perennial accomplishment.[2]

Again this points toward ontology. Indeed Dresser says that once one becomes "thoroughly loyal to truth"[3] he pushes "past all discouragement and all doubt, past mere argument to that eternal region where heart and head are one."[4]

On this point elsewhere he says that reason is "simply a later phase of mentality within the same group

---

[1] *Ibid.*, p. 253.

[2] *Ibid.*

[3] *Ibid.*, p. 254.

[4] *Ibid.*

Healing Hypotheses 139

of processes"[1] as "instincts, desires, emotions, and the will,"[2] all of which are dependent on experience. Reason is distinguished from the others by its not simply "taking experience as it comes,"[3] but analyzing, comparing, bringing order, and restating in terms of law, thus bringing new results.[4]

All of Dresser's writing appears to have been intended to be helpful, most of it in immediately practical ways, such as offering suggestions for living happier, healthier lives. Because of this, much of his philosophy has to be culled from pages not primarily intended as philosophical argument, although Dresser tried to hue closer to the line of technical philosophy than usually is the case with popular inspirational writers. He seems never to have attempted to bring together his thoughts into one exhaustive statement of his system. But he could not do this consistently with his basic belief that, as quoted above, "no wholly sound, merely speculative system of philosophy is possible." Any attempt at completeness would have to fail.

However, he did write one book that, while also offering practical guidance, deserves to be put into a somewhat different class from that of most of his books, which were largely practical or were historical surveys or other sorts of essentially second-hand treatments of various matters. This book is *The Philosophy of the Spirit*, which he singled out for special mention in the 1910 class report quoted above. That work is not essential to his

---

[1] Horatio W. Dresser, *Human Efficiency* (New York: G. P. Putnam's Sons, 1912), p. 302.

[2] *Ibid.*, p. 301.

[3] *Ibid.*, p. 302.

[4] *Ibid.*

philosophy, for the other writings already quoted offer its essentials. *The Philosophy of the Spirit*, however, serves as a good point for summing up Dresser's epistemology and turning to his ontology, and more broadly to a consideration of his place in relation to New Thought.

v. Dresser's View of the World

(1) *His Philosophy of the Spirit.* The *Philosophy of the Spirit*, which appeared in 1908, was the culmination of thought aided by "studies in the concept of immediacy carried on a number of years [earlier] in the logical seminary at Harvard."[1] With the aid of Royce's criticism, he developed "the problem of the relationship of immediate experience to the religious and idealistic interests of [Dresser's] earlier volumes."[2] This book includes as a "Supplementary Essay" his doctoral thesis, *The Element of Irrationality in the Hegelian Dialectic*. This was begun with advice of Royce, but "did not receive the criticism of [him], nor have those who passed judgment upon it communicated their opinions."[3] The copy in the archives of Harvard University bears the signatures of William James, Hugo Munsterberg, and G. H. Palmer. It has the date May 1, 1906, and the deposit date June 27, 1907.

The Philosophy of the Spirit may be taken as a restatement and development of essentials of Dresser's doctoral thesis, as Dresser's own views, not unlike his earlier ones. Since this is the case, and since Dresser's

---

[1] Horatio W. Dresser, *The Philosophy of the Spirit* (New York: G. P. Putnam's Sons, 1908), p. ix.

[2] *Ibid.*

[3] *Ibid.*, p. 387.

treatment of Hegel could be the subject of a study in its own right, it is enough to say here that Dresser presents Hegel's empirical approach in opposition to the commonly accepted view that Hegel was purely, and unrealistically, a rationalist. Dresser does not purport to undertake a sweeping study of Hegel, but seeks to present data for consideration in anyone's interpretation of Hegel.

The fruits of Dresser's Hegelian explorations are seen best in his chapter called "The Import of Immediacy."[1] Before reaching this chapter he engages in what might be called preliminary consideration; in light of what has been seen of other works by him, it scarcely seems necessary to go into these.

The importance of immediacy is indicated in Dresser's remark that

> philosophy begins with the discovery that the immediate is not self-explanatory, but gives rise to clues which are susceptible of various interpretations, and is a quest for universally valid principles of mediation. . "[2]

After considering definitions of immediacy, he says,

> For our purposes the term immediacy practically resolves itself into a matter of sentiency. The immediate is the psychical element as it exists for the subject of an experience when the experience occurs.[3]

---

[1] *Ibid.*, chapter XI.

[2] *Ibid.*, p. 240.

[3] *Ibid.*, p. 246.

He likens immediacy's apprehension to the creation of frictional heat, and adds that "immediacy is a joint product, due to relatedness"[1] and that "experience reveals nothing that is not related."[2] Even description is relating, and the same is the case with psychophysical explanation and philosophical interpretation.

Citing James, Dresser maintains that there is no such thing as simple sensation, or that we cannot experience it.

> What we mean by [sensation] is some sort of unexperienced union or pre-experienced immediacy. . . . What is immediately given is not sensation, but a complex stream of consciousness in which manifold characteristics are distinguishable."[3]

This stream is "empirically verifiable by everybody, while 'sensation' is a psychological construction."[4]

One cannot fail in careful inspection to find both subject and object.

> Even the self, regarded as immediate, proves to be an interchanging relationship of subject and object. There is no ground for believing that it is a bare unity, intuitively known as such; it is rather a ground of multiform differences. The same is

---

[1] *Ibid.*

[2] *Ibid.*

[3] *Ibid.*, p. 252.

[4] *Ibid.*

true of God, regarded as the ground of all differences in the universe.[1]

At this point these observations are not metaphysical conclusions, but simply certain cases of the general principle stated with regard to any experience.

Continuing one's examination, it is found that introspection discovers "the moment that is just now passing,"[2] rather than the present. The first instant of awareness can provide only "a mere 'that' without a 'what.'"[3] An attempt to capture it is a reconstruction, for it is already past. Yet the attempt is an admission of the importance of immediacy, which is the grist for the mental mill. There is a feeling of the immediate, but it cannot be called knowledge, which must come with thought. There is knowledge of immediacy also. Thus one distinguishes between "immediacy as (1) just now presented and involving change, and (2) as it exists for reflection, as a concept."[4] There is not a hopeless gulf between the immediate and the mediate; their dependence on each other for our fullest functioning is indication of a kinship. There is an "inherent rationality of the immediate which thought endeavours to make explicit. Mediate thought, when complete, enters into full possession of the truth which immediacy implicitly meant."[5] Indeed, Dresser defines thought as "that power

---

[1] *Ibid.*, p. 250.

[2] *Ibid.*, p. 253.

[3] *Ibid.*, p. 255.

[4] *Ibid.*, p. 257.

[5] *Ibid*, p. 260.

in us which makes the empirically implicit intelligibly explicit."[1]

But there must be a continuing process of clarification. Referring to Hegel, Dresser says that the truth "is found neither in the immediate nor in mere mediacy, but in a higher moment."[2] This third moment resolves the rivalry of immediate and mediate, for in it

> experience is conceptually given back enriched, immediacy has lost its innocence and its independence, yet it retains a value which thought can never take away.[3]

Out of this examination come two foundations of Dresser's metaphysics: the conviction of an other-than-ourselves emerging from a consideration of immediacy and the transitivity or becoming exhibited in the dialectical process.

Dresser calls immediacy the "point of contact" of two streams, "one flowing from the environing field of our mental life, and the other meeting it from the depths of the self."[4] He finds a perceiver to be a necessity for immediacy.[5] The other necessities for it are something given, which he believes implies a giver; and a "state of union between perceived and perceiver."[6] The perceiver

---

[1] *Ibid*, p. 268.

[2] *Ibid*.

[3] *Ibid*., p. 270.

[4] *Ibid*., p. 256.

[5] *Ibid*., p. 263.

[6] *Ibid*.

Healing Hypotheses 145

or self required is one that "possesses some sort of cognitive constitution; the self on its part brings those principles to the experience which enable it to enter into the union."[1]

As to the second, transitivity, this in the epistemological realm is, presumably, reflective of the whole evolutionary movement accepted by Dresser as essential to the world at large. He believes everything to be developing.

It would be contrary to Dresser's tentative approach to expect a system worked out from any one basic statement. He freely admits that in his consideration of immediacy there are "many assumptions."[2] But he offers what he calls the "general presupposition":

> The self is able, through mediate thought, to grasp the meaning of immediacy; reason is competent to complete its task; immediacy and the mediate belong to one system; thought and corrected feeling apprehend the same Reality.[3]

Having said this, one is well into a metaphysical system. However, there remains to be established the nature of the Reality, other than its being something capable of apprehension by thought and its including the mediate and immediate. Dresser calls his investigation of the nature of reality (not capitalized this time) incomplete in concluding *The Philosophy of the Spirit*.[4] Most of his writing from that time onward was less systematic, in

---

[1] *Ibid.*

[2] *Ibid.*, p. 265.

[3] *Ibid.*

[4] *Ibid.*, p. 374.

terms of his own thought. He gave greater attention to means of self-help in living a better life. However, this may be taken as the chief conclusion of his philosophy, that reality will support such efforts. However, it is not necessary to leave his metaphysics that vague.

The discovery of the agreement of feeling and reason gives ground for suspecting that there is an ultimate unity. The becoming nature of the dialectical process suggests that the ultimately real also is of this becoming nature. Unity and development may be said to be Dresser's cornerstones. With the aid of them it is easy enough to take the common stock of religious insights and philosophical hypotheses and construct a metaphysics that is at least adequate for purposes of testing. The test, of course, is living.

Taking the term "spirit" in a manner that cannot well be called either personal or nonpersonal, Dresser fits it in with his cornerstones as

> God made concrete. Thus conceived, Spirit may be said to possess both cosmological and human significance. Regarded as a cosmological power, Spirit is the creative life which proceeds from the Godhead as the orderly, continuously active, centralising life of the natural universe. Spirit is the essence, the uniting ground of all physical forces, all modes of physical life, the ultimately efficient energy of all natural evolution. That is, Spirit is the universal power, while natural energy in its various forms is the cosmological phase which Spirit assumes. Spirit is not the mere sum of all natural energy, and should not be identified with the totality of physical modes of motion. For Spirit has other modes of manifesting itself. Spirit

is also the central principle in mental life, in moral and religious experience.[1]

Dresser admits that for some there is no reason for calling by the name of Spirit what may be explained in much more ordinary terms. But here there enters what immediacy can provide. Although immediacy has been shorn of direct knowledge-giving properties, it remains as something to be united with thought. Immediacies are of various qualities, which become recognizable to those who are receptive enough to cultivate them. There is a witness of the Spirit, which when reflected on is seen to justify belief in a higher, value-giving something entitled to be called Spirit.

Somehow the world that we see came about. Dresser is unwilling to try to explain this. He says:

> It hardly seems profitable to attempt to assign a motive for the manifestation of the Spirit in the world. There may never have been a beginning of such manifestation. The universe may well be the eternal expression, outpouring, externalisation of the Spirit. At any rate it is not conceivable apart from the divine consciousness.[2]

It is this divine consciousness that is the highest limit of being, yet we scarcely are entitled to say that it is forever fixed. There could not well be any notion of it if it were entirely unlike our consciousness, but Dresser is careful not to identify God and man. He continues,

> Not, I insist, that it [the universe] is "in" that consciousness, not that it is like a dream or vision,

---

[1]*Ibid.*, p. 41.

[2]*Ibid.*, p. 52.

but that it exists *for*, is present to; manifests the mind of God. That mind may be in a measure unlike our own, hence its objects may not be in any sense remote but possessed as one whole. But the conception of an all-inclusive consciousness at least suggests the intimacy of relationship between God and His universe. Since the universe exists, we may safely assume that it fulfils the divine nature. Since you and I exist as dwellers in this divine universe, we may with equal assurance assume that we meet some need in the life of God. Whether or not we or any other beings save God have had a life without beginning in the past, here we are, members one of another in the great universe which reveals the majesty and wisdom, the beauty and love of God.[1]

In these various assertions Dresser may be correct or incorrect in whole or in part. He could easily assume otherwise, many would say, but presumably he would call on the "witness of the Spirit" to uphold his assumptions.

(2) *His Views on Pantheism and its Ethical Implications.* The central problem here is the identity or not of God, human beings, and the universe. This is the great point of difference between Evans, the "Christian pantheist," and Dresser. [Neither was clearly aware of panentheism as an alternative to both pantheism and conventional theism.]

In seeking the reasons for this split between two men both of whom were strongly influenced by Quimby and Swedenborg, as well as by what they found in their own experience in connection with spiritual healing, at least three differences, in addition to their differing amounts of formal education, stand out as possibly significant. Evans came first to Swedenborg and only

---

[1]*Ibid.*

later to Quimby and what grew into New Thought. As he progressed in thought, he tended to grow away from Swedenborg. Dresser was born into the Quimby influence, and probably was growing in appreciation of Swedenborg as he pursued his philosophical studies.

Evans had essentially mystical experiences. Although he did not undertake such epistemological searchings as Dresser did, it seems fair to say that he may well have placed greater emphasis on the alleged knowledge-giving quality of immediate experience. Dresser's extrasensory experience seems to have been of a more "finite" sort, dealing with limited situations, some of which could be checked by normal means, in confirming certain information given to him.

Evans apparently was concerned preeminently with metaphysics, especially as it was relevant to the healing of individual patients. Dresser had a strong concern for ethics and social life. It may well be that this concern was the primary source of his rejection of pantheism.

Dresser says:

> Usually that part of our nature which is dissatisfied with a pantheistic or fatalistic scheme is the moral or spiritual self, which wills to triumph, to play an individual part in universal evolution. Or, to put it more clearly, I think all would agree that human existence has no satisfactory meaning unless the soul is self-active, an agent, with probabilities of success in the realization of ideals.[1]

For Dresser there can be no freedom, no loving interrelationships in which the involved parties are parts of another entity that makes them only apparently separate and free.

---

[1] Horatio W. Dresser, *Voices of Freedom*, p. 54.

In discussing the pantheism of the Vedanta, Dresser does not so much argue as express his inability to conceive of a loss of multiplicity. He observes:

> It is . . . the absolute identification of subject and object, with no room for the splendidly elaborate system of nature as the realm of divine manifestation. It endeavors to put off the creation of the world upon man, but he proves unreal. It tries to put it upon Brahman, but cannot, because that would imply imperfection.[1]
>
> It is absurd . . . to say, "Do not tell a lie," if you are really telling a lie to yourself. You, of course, know the truth, and therefore cannot lie to yourself. A lie becomes such only when told to another who is deceived by it. Is not this fact of ethical separateness worth more than all the speculation in the world.[2]

From the time of the writing of his first book Dresser was concerned with evil and suffering, which needed to be reconciled with a good God. Presumably the problem seemed all the more difficult if all were God. If God were everything, the need of evolution also might be questioned. As it was, Dresser found in evolution an answer to evil. He says:

> The meaning of much of our moral suffering and evil is . . . to teach the right use of our powers. . . . All cases of sickness, misery, evil, wrong, demand better self-comprehension. If there be one general meaning which applies to them all,

---

[1] *Ibid.*, p. 114.

[2] *Ibid.*, p. 120.

it is, in one word, progress,--the effort of the Spirit to give us freedom.[1]

It is not clear in what sense this is conceived. He spoke of this as "the evolutionary origin of evil."[2]

Dresser did not consider himself a pantheist, and he never failed to draw some distinction between God and human beings. However, he changed his views considerably in the decade 1894-1904, as seen by a comparison of some of the wording of one of the chapters of *The Power of Silence*. It may be significant that this chapter was published originally as a pamphlet "at the request of many who have found it helpful"[3] and that its reception led to the publishing of it and other lectures given in 1894 in the form of Dresser's first book.[4] In the Preface of the second edition of the book, Dresser says that the lectures were changed little and the chapter in question not changed in incorporating it into the book. He attributes the "defects" of the first edition to its being a

---

[1]Dresser, *The Power of Silence*, 1st ed., pp. 124-25.

[2]Dresser, *Education and the Philosophical Ideal*, p. 12.

[3]Horatio W. Dresser, *The Immanent God: An Essay* (Boston: "Published by the Author" Geo. H. Ellis, Printer, 1895). Preface: The following essay was the second in a course of lectures delivered in Boston during the past year under the general title, "Talks on Life in its Relation to Health," and given in co-operation with Mrs. A. G. Dresser. Like the others in the series, this paper was designed to emphasize certain great truths of the inner life on their practical side. It is now revised and published at the request of many who have found it helpful.

[4]*The Power of Silence*, 1st ed., p. 6.

first book, compiled from lecture notes. However, it is obvious that the changes to be noted below are changes of thought, rather than merely of style.

In the first edition, Dresser says that God, if he be at all, "put forth his own being as the world,"[1] and in the second that God "put forth His own life in the world." In the first, God is "not only immanent, but is that in which he dwells," while in the second, God is "not only immanent, but . . . is also independent of that in which He dwells." Similarly, we are "a part of the one omnipresent Reality," as contrasted with "intimately related to the Father." However, much of the writing remains unchanged. There is a warmer, more theistic tone to the second edition, but the attitude could be called the same. Nevertheless, these philosophical changes are important. However, they may not be such a great change as would seem to be the case. Dresser never apparently lost human beings in God, but this was in terms of his own satisfaction rather than philosophical argument. On the basis of the incomprehensibility of a beginning of a series of causes and effects, he makes activity a quality of God. He goes on, apparently using eternal in the sense of everlasting, rather than timeless:

> Continuity of motion is one of the attributes of . . . Reality, the activity of which originates within itself, and is never self-destructive. Eternal self-interaction is the cause of eternal self-manifestation. The Reality has therefore never been without manifestation. Although it is the One, it must ever have been the Many: it must ever have been at once finite and infinite, since it is not simply an undivided whole, but is the sum of all its parts, each of which . . . is

---

[1] For page references see the extended quotations in Appendix G.

finite. Motion could not spring suddenly out of a perfectly simple, inert unit. . . .

The One is the sum total of all possibilities: it is eternally the Many, either actually or potentially.[1]

That he had early pantheistic [or perhaps panentheistic] tendencies was shown in February, 1898, when he gave in Boston's Church of the Higher Life an address in which he maintained "the absolute necessity of the presence of the creative power in every detail of life's minutest changes"[2] and the absence of any "opposing force in the universe, since a universe to exist must ultimately be a harmony."[3] This means that we have no power, no life, of our own. He goes on to ask:

> But are you and I identical? Is this mere pantheism, this profoundest of all philosophical conclusions? Once more, let us remember the only means of revelation; namely, experience. Experience tells us that you and I are different; that we are finite selves, possessing the power of choice. This is just as truly a fact as the existence of an immutable law superior to our wills. The nature of the one life must then be such that it can exist or manifest itself through distinct centres of

---

[1] Dresser, *The Power of Silence*, 1st ed., pp. 32-33. In the second edition he abandons the attempt to prove God's existence in relation to cause.

[2] Horatio W. Dresser, "The Omnipresent Spirit," *The Journal of Practical Metaphysics*, II (April, 1898), 199.

[3] *Ibid.*, p. 200.

consciousness. I am just as truly myself as I am a part of God.[1]

In answer to the question of how this can be, Dresser says that it is a miracle.[2] Presumably this is to be interpreted as being a fundamental basis for reasoning, behind which one cannot go. He has chosen to consider, or has thought it necessary to believe, that God must be omnipotent, and has had to conclude that any power must be part of God. Granted the premise, the conclusion is inescapable. However, he does not consider this pantheism.

By 1903, undoubtedly influenced by his old belief in evolution, his dissatisfaction with Vedanta, his epistemological studies, and perhaps his presumably growing knowledge of Swedenborgian views, Dresser is saying that his

> conception differs from the merely immanental theory, since it reserves room for God unmanifested. That is, God does not exhaust Himself in His world-activity; He is not merely the life or substance of the universe. He also transcends, is larger than, the world. ... It does not assert that God *is* the world, either viewed as nature, as consciousness, or as the spiritual unity of nature and consciousness. The world *reveals* God, is part of God's activity; but it is not all of God, therefore is *not the same* as God. Yet one would like to bring God as near as pantheism does when it worships nature as God, or identifies the mystical experience with Him. ...

---

[1] *Ibid.*, p. 201.

[2] *Ibid.*

> The present theory may for convenience be called organic theism [this name reminds one of the "philosophy of organism" that would be developed by Alfred North Whitehead, who also appreciated William James], that is, God is regarded as Father-Spirit amid many son-spirits or moral individuals. He is a Being whom one can love and worship.
> In a theistic world, the distinctions between souls and the world are real, continuous. The sons of God, while not separated from God, do not become God, any more than a human father absorbs his child.... To say that God is resident in the world of our consciousness, that He is the Life of our life is not ... to maintain that the life that is immanent in us is all there is in the human life.[1]

The start of this statement would not have to lead to the end of it. The statement that God includes more than the universe that we know removes Dresser from pantheism as he has used the term; but not from the usual philosophical use of the term. But to go on, as he does, to say that God is not the world, or to say, as he also does, that people as set off from the world are not only God, does remove him from any sense of pantheism. Presumably his desire for "bringing God as close as pantheism does" is an appeal for meaningful worship. Beyond the mere words that he uses, one may be left wondering whether Dresser did not want both pantheism and theism [perhaps panentheism]. His remark about bringing God that close could be an indication of dissatisfaction with the theistic position. Perhaps the following about his choice of a name for his views indicates some such attitude:

---

[1] Horatio W. Dresser, *Man and the Divine Order*, pp. 410-11.

The first name chosen for the present system was "organic empiricism." The term "organic" was employed to denote the many-sidedness of experience,--the fact that no one department of life is the source of all truth, but truth must be a co-operative product; and "empiricism" denoted the tentative, changing, promising character of our many-sided experience. But "empirical idealism" is a better term, since experience, although many-sided, is of *one general type*; it is an experience in terms of ideas. The term "constructive idealism" carries the definition a stage farther; for, however varied experience may be, and however much allowance one must make for future experience of other types, the final work of philosophy is to recast the data of experience in terms of constructive thought.[1]

In view of his emphasis on empiricism, it is not strange that Dresser went on to give more attention to epistemology, as has been seen above, and that thereafter his efforts were devoted primarily to practical help, rather than to attempts to work out a complete system. He concluded his career calling himself a psychologist and writing for Swedenborgian publications, it will be recalled. He apparently did not care to identify himself with Swedenborgianism in his writings meant for the general public. Swedenborgian influence in his general writing is a matter of conjecture. However, it is not a matter of great importance, for as far as it makes any difference in this study, Swedenborgianism may be taken as simply another theism. It may be that the doctrine of discrete degrees, for example, was a reason for Dresser's finding theism acceptable, but idle speculation on the matter is of no use. The more distinctly religious matters,

---

[1] *Ibid.*, pp. 419-20.

such as interpretation of scripture according to Swedenborg's correspondences, is not a matter of consideration here.

vi. Summary

While Dresser does not purport to give a complete philosophical system, nor even a fully clarified statement of constituents for such a system, his analysis of experience does produce the tentative outlines for some of the more important parts of a system.

On analyzing the complex stream of consciousness, Dresser resolves it into two streams. The first stream, reason, renders explicit all that is implicit in the other stream. The second stream, experience, reveals our environing fields. The point of contact of the two streams is one's self, the finite person, which is the perceiving unifier of both streams.

Having found the nature of the thought process to be moving--becoming--and capable of being understood as a unified whole, Dresser suggests that reality as a whole has these characteristics of unity and becoming. This makes reality a progressing whole, but not numerically one, since Dresser finds the experience of a finite self inconsistent with pantheism. Dresser does not presume to explain the origin nor full nature of the world, but he turns to the divine Spirit that his experience reveals, and suggests that God is in meaningful communication with people in the world.

In rejecting pantheism, after his early acceptance of it, Dresser asserts that it denies one's essential, free, responsible action. He also emphasizes the importance of the cooperative relationship of love, which the unity of pantheism would eliminate.

In emphasizing love as of primary worth, Dresser differs from the final Evans position, seeming to stress thought above love. Dresser is in agreement with Swedenborg in his conclusions regarding God, humankind, and the world, but Dresser differs from Swedenborg in reaching them on rational grounds, rather than from the acceptance of purported messages from discarnate beings, relied on by Swedenborg. But Dresser agrees with Evans, and diverges from Swedenborg, in emphasizing the possibility of divine healing. The acceptance of such healing of course provides the great common ground of Dresser and New Thought.

4. His Thought in Relation to New Thought

i. Dresser's Independence

The question of pantheism takes one to the heart of New Thought. It has been said that "the sharp, clearly drawn distinction between God and man and the world, characteristic of most Christian thought, is never found in New Thought."[1]

Inasmuch as Dresser devoted a considerable amount of his writing to New Thought, this may seem rather strange. Certainly Dresser after his earliest years of writing drew such distinctions with insistence. Moreover, he has been included among "the 'New Thought' writers whose vogue rivals that of the popular novelist."[2] This characterization was published in 1902, so must have been based on his early writings. References to such writings, especially the first edition of *The Power of Silence*, show that Dresser may well have helped to promote a pantheistic trend in New Thought.

---

[1]Braden, *These Also Believe*, p. 138.

[2]Tyner, *op. cit.*, p. 314.

After this early period, if not before, Dresser probably was reluctant to be associated very strongly with New Thought. However, he did help to organize the Metaphysical Club of Boston, which was a New Thought organization, and later he held office in the International New Thought Alliance, as has been seen above. Nevertheless, from at least as early as 1899, in writing on New Thought, he took pains to identify himself as

> an independent truth seeker, not . . . a mere follower of the New Thought, but one who believes the doctrine has made an important contribution to the knowledge and practice, the life and thought, of our time."[1]

In his *Handbook of the New Thought*, published in 1917, Dresser says that he "stands a measure apart from any branch of the mental healing movement."[2] He gives perhaps his most helpful statement on this matter in 1910:

> As a student of these popular movements of thought, I write from a very general point of view, not as a partisan of any therapeutic cult. . . . My own position here as elsewhere is that of the teacher of philosophy who aims to reach people

---

[1] Dresser, *Voices of Freedom*, p. 54. The original, slightly different, statement is in Dresser, "What is the New Thought?," *The Arena*, XXI (January, 1899), 29; here he omits "Not as a mere follower of the New Thought." In the early years of the movement it was common to insert *the* before *New Thought*, as the term was becoming more clearly a special name, rather than simply a reference to thought that was new.

[2] Horatio W. Dresser, *Handbook of the New Thought* (New York: G. P. Putnam's Sons, 1917), p. iv.

where they are, and help them to know their powers of self-mastery. Hence from my point of view any one of the therapeutic doctrines now in vogue may serve an intermediate purpose.[1]

He considered his books dealing with healing "independent volumes, without any direct connection with the therapeutisms of the day."[2]

There can be little or no doubt that Dresser wished to remain independent. However, this does not mean that one can exclude him from New Thought by virtue of whatever desire he had to be excluded. His classification should be determined by what he said and by the way that others have classified him. It has been seen already that he has been linked with others as a New Thought writer. If others considered him part of New Thought, to that extent he was. In considering the matter of classification, it is necessary to take note of some of the history of New Thought beyond the contributions of those persons already seen.

Fortunately, much of this was presented by Dresser and can be given to some extent in his own words. Observations of others who also have surveyed New Thought to an extent beyond what is possible in this study also are to be seen. With such aids it is possible to obtain a considerable knowledge of what New Thought is.

ii. Dresser's Relation to New Thought in Light of its Nature.

(1) *New Thought's Development in General.* The New Thought movement might have developed out of the

---

[1]Dresser, *Health and the Inner Life*, p. iv.

[2]*Ibid.*

teachings of Quimby, as given some circulation by J. A. Dresser and the Misses Ware and given more by Evans.[1] However, the efforts of these people did not excite great public interest. What might have been developed if they had been the only ones to offer views in the general area of their concern cannot be said, for another factor entered the situation in which they operated. In the opinion of Dresser,

> What was needed, perhaps, was a more radical and less reasonable statement of the principles underlying the new therapeutism. For the general public is more apt to respond to radical views. Oftentimes the less reasonable view is needed to give sufficient contrast and provoke controversy.
> This impetus was given ... by the launching of Mrs. Eddy's radical propositions in *Science and Health*, published in 1875. If we are to see any purpose at all in the publication of that book, we may venture to say that it had value in arousing people out of their materialism. The results of the past forty years [up to 1919] apparently justify this statement, for to those of us who have known former Christian scientists [lower case in original] as they came out of their radical into more reasonable views it has been plain that something like *Science and Health* was needed to set matters in motion.[2]

After the appearance of *Science and Health*

---

[1]Dresser, *A History of the New Thought Movement*, pp. 126-27.

[2]*Ibid.*, pp. 127-28.

there was a tendency to read both Evans and Eddy, and [there] was a commingling of ideas gathered from these two sources and from teachings of those who, like Mr. Julius Dresser, had held to Quimby's teaching in its original form. The term "mental science," introduced by Mr. Evans, with reference to the psychological aspect of the new therapeutism, began to be used in 1882-3 for the whole teaching. It was used in preference to the term Christian Science because the latter term had become identified with the hypothesis of a "revelation." The term "mental" was spiritualized by those who adhered to Quimby's teaching. Thus Mr. Dresser employed it when responding to the request to narrate "the true history" of the therapeutic movement. The term "mental" was almost a synonym for "Christian," as used by those who believed that the new healing was wrought by spiritual means. For others it was a convenient expression for their faith that health is mental rather than physical, that causality is in the realm of thought, and that true science is the opposite of medical materialism.[1]

Mrs. Eddy, who believed that it followed from God's being all, that matter was nothing, rather than some sort of expression of God, is characterized by Dresser as having "taught an idealism akin to Berkeley's view, as Berkeley is misunderstood. Readers untrained in philosophy easily found the two interpretations [of Mrs. Eddy and of Evans in *The Divine Law of Cure*] identical."[2]

Probably Dresser's 1882-1883 dating of the term *mental science* is to be taken in connection with his later

---

[1] *Ibid.*, pp. 128-29.

[2] *Ibid.*, p. 129.

statement indicating that "the first groups of people assembled to discuss these matters in Boston in 1882 and 1883."[1]

The term *mental science* continues to have some prominence in New Thought, especially through the Edinburgh Lecture Series of books on mental science by Thomas Troward (1847-1916). Dating from 1904 to those published after his death, these books remain in print. He had been a British divisional judge in India[2] and brought Eastern and Western thought together in his writings. Troward's views are reminiscent of the later ones of Evans, and are important in relation to American New Thought both from the circulation of his books here and from his association with the young Emmet Fox, who later moved from England to the United States and became one of the most popular New Thought writers and speakers.[3] [Troward's views also are important because of the continuing use of his writings by Religious Science.] Gaze was another link.

In addition to the name *mental science*, the new movement was given the name *mind-cure* and *the Boston craze*.[4]

As the mental scientists had no authoritative textbook, no leader accepted as a revelator, and no

---

[1]*Ibid.*, p. 131.

[2]Harry Gaze, *My Personal Recollections of Thomas Troward* (no publication information except 1958), booklet 1 (of 3), p. 19.

[3]Harry Gaze, *Emmet Fox: The Man and His Work* (New York: Harper & Brothers, 1952), p. 32.

[4]Dresser, *A History of the New Thought Movement*, p. 132.

organization maintaining a hold upon its followers, the tendency was for each healer to branch out freely, say nothing about the origin of the ideas in question; but to set them forth as if they had just been acquired.[1]

In the early days "no one ... thought of supporting the teachings . . . by associating them with transcendentalism and the writings of Emerson."[2] As early as 1881 Evans says, "There may be much of truth in the saying of Emerson that 'the history of Jesus is the history of every man written large,'"[3] and quotes him on the "Over-Soul" in *The Primitive Mind-Cure* in 1884.[4] Without referring to Evans, who did not live to see New Thought by that name, Dresser says that "the beginning of interest in Emerson on the part of those who later became known as New Thought leaders"[5] began with the publication of *Facts and Fictions of Mental Healing* by Charles M. Barrows in 1887. Unless he means to restrict his statement to leaders who carried their activity over into the period of New Thought under that name, Dresser is incorrect in saying that "none of the therapeutic leaders had until then noted the resemblance."[6] Barrows,

---

[1]*Ibid.*, p. 133.

[2]*Ibid.*, p. 127.

[3]Evans, *The Divine Law of Cure*, p. 72.

[4]Evans, *The Primitive Mind-Cure*, p. 20. See also, for example, pp. 83 and 138.

[5]Dresser, *A History of the New Thought Movement*, pp. 135-36.

[6]*Ibid.*, p. 135.

Healing Hypotheses 165

however, did devote a full chapter to Emerson and another to Indian views.[1] He had pointed out the long background of healing and something of the philosophy related to the new movement two years earlier in *Bread-Pills: A Study of Mind-Cure*, which he concluded by quoting at length from Emerson.[2] If he were to be credited for being the first to notice Emerson in relation to mind-cure, it would seem to be advisable to cite the earlier work. However, in all of this, his publications were later than those of Evans.

William James, ignoring Quimby, says:

> One of the doctrinal sources of Mind-cure is the four Gospels; another is Emersonianism or New England transcendentalism; another is Berkeleyan idealism; another is spiritism, with its message of "law" and "progress" and "development"; another the optimistic popular science evolutionism . . . ; and, finally, Hinduism has contributed a strain.[3]

---

[1] Charles M. Barrows, *Facts and Fictions of Mental Healing* (Boston: H. H. Carter & Karrick, 1887), chapters XIII and XII, respectively, "Emerson's Idealism" and "Help from Ind." [*sic*].

[2] C. M. Barrows, *Bread-Pills: A Study of Mind-Cure* (Boston: Deland and Barta, Printers; Mutual News Company, Agents, 1885), pp. 85-88.

[3] William James, *The Varieties of Religious Experience* (New York: The Modern Library, n.d., originally Longmans, Green and Company, 1902), p. 93. James recognized Dresser as a leading mind-cure writer. pp. 94n, 97, 284. [At p. 94 James says: To the importance of mind-cure the medical and clerical professions in the United States are beginning, though with much recalcitrancy and protesting, to open their eyes. It is

Taking

> their clue from Mr. Evans's book [various people] began to trace out the ideas in the philosophies of the past which resembled mental science. Thus after a time the term "metaphysics" came into vogue to indicate that the fundamental principles of the new movement were akin to the great idealisms of the past.[1]

Dresser cautions that "metaphysics," strictly speaking, applies to a technical system of philosophy, and only by explanation is it to be understood as the name of a practical movement."[2] He also says of the term *metaphysical healing*,

> Many disciples of mental science used this term as synonymous with "mental science" and applied idealism. Mrs. Eddy also employed the term "metaphysical" as the name of her school in Boston. The term "metaphysics" as thus employed need not be understood in the philosophical sense as a complete system of first principles. It means a practical idealism emphasizing mental or spiritual causality in contrast with the prevalent

---

evidently bound to develop still farther, both speculatively and practically, and its latest writers are far and away the ablest of the group. Footnote: I refer to Mr. Horatio W. Dresser and Mr. Henry Wood, especially the former....]

[1] Dresser, *A History of the New Thought Movement*, p. 135.

[2] *Ibid.*, p. 156.

materialism, or the assumption that matter possesses independent life and intelligence.[1]

In the so-called metaphysical movement's development one of the most important figures was Emma Curtis Hopkins. After serving as an editor of the *Christian Science Journal* she turned to independent dissemination of her views in 1885.[2] Her writings, now [1962] being published by the High Watch Fellowship, Cornwall Bridge, Connecticut, show much Bible interpretation. She drew on Eastern and Western religious views.

She established the Illinois Metaphysical College. It published *The Christian Metaphysician*. The January-February, 1891, number includes the following announcement:

> The next class at the college will be organized Thursday, Jan. 29th. A class will also meet on the 4th of February, and another on the 9th of March. Fifteen lectures, usually four per week, constitute first course. Students, when prepared to heal, will receive Diploma, conferring

---

[1]*Ibid.*, pp. 141-42. See also pp. 136-38.

[2]Mrs. Hopkins cannot be dealt with here except by way of pointing her out as a link between Christian Science and New Thought and as a teacher in her own right. Many facts about her life seem to be in doubt. Even the date of her birth is given from 1849 to 1854. She came from Killingly, Connecticut, and died there. The Registrar of vital statistics in a letter of January 9, 1962, reports that no birth record is found, but that the death certificate gives September 2, 1854, as her date of birth and April 8, 1925, as her date of death. On her relations with Mrs. Eddy, see Bates and Dittemore, *op. cit.*, p. 265, and Wilbur, *op. cit.*, p. 294

title of "*Christian Metaphysician*." The college is the oldest of the kind in the State, and the lecturers are prominent educators as well as being experienced Metaphysicians.

All moral people, who desire increased usefulness and happiness, are invited to call upon or correspond with the President of the college, relative to instruction in the Science of Christian Healing.

Some of the topics considered in the course, are:

Metaphysics, Ancient and Modern; as a Science and an Art; principle and application.

Christian Metaphysics are [sic] adopted to the wants of humanity. The idea of God; and God considered as Life.

Substance, not matter, but Spirit. What matter is and is not. God considered as Intelligence and Wisdom. God as Truth and Rightness, or Perfection. God as Goodness and Love. The Creation, Spiritual, not Material. The "Word," as the Universal Christ or God Revealer. Man in Christ and Christ in God. St. John, i, 1-14. Man from the standpoint of the human and the Divine, Jesus as Man; his relation to God and to man. Material Sense and Spiritual Sense. Man's Fall, Disease, Death, the Law of Deliverance. Closing lectures give practical instruction for healing the sick; and show the highest harmonies of Truth.

Tuition payable in advance. Primary course, thirty dollars; review same, ten dollars. Normal course, twelve lessons, twenty-five dollars. Graduation fee, two dollars. Consultation free. We are prepared to supply all kinds of standard metaphysical literature.

Correspondence solicited. Address, Illinois Metaphysical College.

Central Music Hall, Chicago, Ill.[1]

This issue of the magazine contains quotations from, among others, Emerson, Luther, Phillips Brooks, and a fairly lengthy one from the Jowett translation of Plato's "Charmedes" [sic], 156-157, on the folly of treating the body without considering the soul. It also presents the concluding installment, of how many it is not indicated, of some writing on "Desire, Will and Faith," "From Dr. W. F. Evans' unpublished manuscripts, furnished by Mrs. Evans."[2] It is only a page in length, and includes the following:

> Persons of a weak character content themselves with feebly *desiring* a thing as a state of health and usefulness, persons of a strong character *will it*, which expresses itself outwardly in efforts to attain it; persons of a still stronger character *believe* it, and thus make it a present and living reality.[3]

(2) *Unity.* Before turning to what calls itself New Thought, it is appropriate to observe that Mrs. Hopkins was important in leading to the formation of one of the most outstanding religious groups in the world today, Unity. This group published some Dresser articles. In

---

[1]"College Classes," *The Christian Metaphysician*, V (January and February, 1891), 24.

[2]The same issue, p. 9.

[3]*Ibid.*

relation to Mrs. Hopkins, a Unity history says that in the spring of 1886[1]

> a lecturer named Dr. E[ugene]. B. Weeks came to Kansas City and delivered a series of talks. . . . Doctor Weeks was sent to Kansas City from Chicago as a representative of the Illinois Metaphysical College, which had been founded shortly before by Emma Curtis Hopkins.
> Emma Curtis Hopkins was one of the most unusual figures that has appeared in the whole metaphysical movement. Originally she had been associated with Mary Baker Eddy as an editor of the Christian Science Journal, but as the two had not seen eye to eye on many questions, Mrs. Hopkins left the Eddy School of Christian Science. From Boston, she went to Chicago where she founded a school of her own, which was probably the most influential school of its kind at the time. Emma Curtis Hopkins was a teacher of teachers. Many founders of metaphysical movements learned their fundamental principles from her. Besides [Charles Fillmore (1854-1948) and his wife, Myrtle Page Fillmore (1845-1931), who were the founders of Unity] there were: Charles and Josephine Barton, who published the magazine "The Life" in Kansas City and had a Truth movement of their own; Malinda Cramer, the first president of the International Divine Science Association; Dr. D. L. Sullivan, who taught Truth classes in St. Louis and Kansas City; Helen Wilmans, editor of "Wilmans Express" and a very influential New Thought teacher at the turn of the century; the popular

---

[1] James Dillet Freeman, *The Household of Faith: The Story of Unity* (Lee's Summit, Mo.: Unity School of Christianity, 1951), p. 44.

> writer, Ella Wheeler Wilcox; Paul Militz and Annie Rix Militz [teacher of Eleanor Mel, who has led the Boston Home of Truth for more than forty years], who founded the Homes of Truth on the West Coast; Mrs. Bingham, who taught Nona Brooks, founder of the Divine Science movement in Denver; C. E. Burnell, a popular lecturer throughout the country for many years; H. Emilie Cady, who studied under Mrs. Hopkins on one of her trips to New York; and many others.
> Charles and Myrtle Fillmore took several courses of study under Mrs. Hopkins and became her fast friends.[1]

After adopting these teachings, the Fillmores experienced healings. In 1889 Charles Fillmore began the publication of a magazine originally called *Modern Thought*.[2] The following year its name was changed to *Christian Science Thought* after Mrs. Hopkins changed the name of her school to Christian Science Theological Seminary.[3] It is added that in neither case did the name mean "that they were teaching the doctrine taught by Mrs. Eddy." After a year the name was changed to *Thought*, for

> Mrs. Eddy made it known that she felt that the name *Christian Science* was her exclusive property and if the Fillmores wanted to use it they must also follow her teaching.[4]

---

[1] *Ibid.*, pp. 42-43.

[2] *Ibid.*, p. 55.

[3] *Ibid.*, p. 60.

[4] *Ibid.*

In 1891 Charles Fillmore received an inspiration to name their work Unity,[1] and the magazine of that name was started as the organ of the prayer group called the Society of Silent Unity, which had come into existence some months earlier as the Society of Silent Help.[2] In 1895 the two periodicals were consolidated.[3] In 1914 the publishing and prayer branches were incorporated together as Unity School of Christianity.[4]

---

[1] *Ibid.*, p. 61.

[2] *Ibid.*, pp. 67 and 88.

[3] *Ibid.*, p. 69.

[4] *Ibid.*, p. 71. Now Unity has a Unity Village with a farm, ministerial school, correspondence school, publishing plant, and facilities for Silent Unity, retreats, and the production of radio and television programs.
> Unity produces 50 million pieces of printed material annually, including 18 million magazines. More than a million people read Unity periodicals, titles of which are [in 1962, since which time some have been discontinued] *Wee Wisdom* for children, *Progress* and Unity Sunday School Leaflet for teenagers, *Weekly Unity*, *Unity*, *Good Business*, and *Daily Word* for young and old.
> *Daily Word* is . . . the most popular. It is published in ten languages besides English: Afrikans, Dutch, Finnish, French, German, Gujarati, Japanese, Portuguese, Sinhala, and Spanish. . . .
> Five publications are printed in Braille and distributed free to the blind. . . .
> Unity publishes more than fifty books, including a Bible dictionary, histories of Unity and its founders, a vegetarian cookbook, inspirational

Since the 1890's Unity has published writings of H. Emilie Cady, a homeopathic physician who studied with Mrs. Hopkins. Of the primary Unity text it is said:

> *Lessons in Truth* is the most famous Cady book and is the subject of intensive study and review by Unity friends all over the world during Lessons in Truth week that is held annually. Translations of Lessons in Truth appear in Spanish, French, Russian, Dutch, German, Greek, Italian, Japanese, Portuguese and English, and the book is also available in Braille.[1]

Among the teachings in this work one finds a basic pantheism typical of New Thought. The book says

---

and metaphysical books, a songbook, children's books, and pamphlets and tracts. The sales of books and magazines cannot begin to cover the huge printing cost or meet the expense of Unity's benevolent services. Every month, tens of thousands of magazines, books, and other literature are distributed free of charge to charitable institutions, religious groups, and needy individuals. Therefore, the work is financed mostly by love offerings sent in by friends. [Marcus Bach, *The Unity Way of Life* (Englewood Cliffs, N.J.: Prentice-Hall, Inc., 1962), pp. 60-61. De Witt John's *The Christian Science Way of Life*, of the same publisher, came in the spring and this book in the fall of the same year.] There are 260 more or less independent local Unity centers. [Bach, pp. 68 and 81.]

[1]Advertisement in *Unity*, CXXXVII (Nov., 1962), 87.

that the real substance within everything we see is God; that all things are one and the same Spirit in different degrees of manifestation; that all the various forms of life are just the same as one life[1]

---

[1]Formerly "life" was capitalized, at this point. *Lessons in Truth*, 1958 printing, p. 2, contains a notice that the book was published first in 1894 and was revised in 1953. However, a comparison of 1919 and 1939 versions of this quotation shows that essentially the 1958 version was used as early as 1939, but that it differs considerably from the 1919 version, which is the one referred to in the footnotes here. Probably the 1953 revision chiefly was the placing of the former twelfth lesson at the beginning as the first lesson, and the omission of some material from the lesson formerly called "Definitions of Terms Used in Metaphysical Teachings" and renaming it "Personality and Individuality," the definitions of which were retained and are quoted below. By 1939, paragraph numbers, still used, had been inserted. References here are to current lesson numbers, followed by paragraph numbers, followed by current page numbers, with 1919 page numbers in parentheses. Varying "Question Helps" are found in 1939 and 1958 editions. This feature is not found in the 1919 edition. According to a 1957 copy of *The Lessons in Truth Study Guide*, pp. 4-5,

> The first contact of Charles and Myrtle Fillmore with Doctor Cady was through Mrs. Fillmore's receiving a copy of the booklet *Finding the Christ in Ourselves* [now one of the many five-cent publications of Unity]. The Fillmores recognized in this booklet so much spiritual discernment and such remarkable ability to present Truth in a lucid, forceful manner that they immediately invited Doctor Cady to contribute to *Unity* magazine.

come forth out of the invisible into visible forms; that all the intelligence and all the[1] wisdom[2] in the world are[3] God as Wisdom[4] in various degrees of manifestation; that all the love which people feel and express toward[5] others is just a little, so

---

The first of several articles in *Unity* by Doctor Cady appeared in January, 1892. Her articles met with the instant approval of *Unity* readers, many of whom requested more of her writings, asking especially to have her write a simple course of lessons on the principles of divine healing.

Doctor Cady was at first doubtful about undertaking the task. Finally she consented. From the appearance of the first lesson (in *Unity* in October, 1894), these lessons met with an extraordinary response. Continued demand for extra copies of the magazines in which the lessons were printed led Mr. Fillmore to have them reprinted in three booklets, four lessons in each booklet.

Lessons in Truth is now printed and bound in one volume, in lots of sixty thousand or more at one time.

[1] In 1919 (the edition referred to below also) "all the" not used.

[2] Followed by "there is"

[3] "is"

[4] Capitalized.

[5] "to"

to speak, of God as love[1] come into visibility through[2] human form.[3]

There is in reality only one Mind (or Spirit, which is life, intelligence, and so forth[4]) in the universe and yet there is a sense in which we are individual, or separate, a sense in which we are free wills and not puppets.

Man is made up of Spirit,[5] soul, and body. Spirit is the central unchanging "I" of us, the part that since infancy has never changed, and to all eternity never will change. That which some persons[6] call "mortal mind" is the region of the intellect[7] where we do conscious thinking and are free wills. This part of our being is in constant process of changing.

---

[1]Capitalized

[2]Followed by "the"

[3]H. Emilie Cady, *Lessons in Truth: A Course of Twelve Lessons in Practical Christianity*, fortieth printing (Lee's Summit, Mo., 1958), 3, 1. p. 24 (p. 13).

[4]"etc."

[5]Not capitalized.

[6]Not "some persons" but "Christian Scientists"

[7]Followed by a comma. Not all such seemingly minor changes are noted here, but this comma could change the meaning greatly.

Healing Hypotheses

In our outspringing[1] from God into the material world, Spirit[2] is inner--one with[3] God; soul is the clothing, as it were, of the Spirit;[4] body is[5] the external clothing of the soul. Yet[6] all are in reality one, the composite man--as steam, water, and ice are one,[7] only in different degrees of condensation. In thinking of ourselves, we must not separate Spirit,[8] soul, and body, but rather hold all as one, if we would be strong and powerful. Man originally lived consciously in the spiritual part of himself. He fell by descending in his consciousness to the external or more material part of himself.

"Mortal mind," the term so much used and so distracting to many, is the error consciousness,

---

[1] "descent or outspringing"

[2] Not capitalized

[3] Not "one with" but "next to"

[4] Not capitalized.

[5] Followed by "yet"

[6] Preceded by "And"

[7] Not "the composite ... ice are one," but "which makes up the man--as steam at the center, water next, and ice as an external, all one,"

[8] Not capitalized.

which gathers its information[1] from the outside world through the five senses.[2]

Personality applies to the human[3] part of you--the person, the external. It belongs to the region governed by the intellect.... It is the outer, changeable man, in contradistinction to the inner or real man.

Individuality is the term used to denote the real man. The more God comes into visibility through a person the more individualized he becomes.[4]

Obviously these quotations leave much unsaid about the "Unity viewpoint," which is an accepted way of referring to it, but enough has been seen to show a basic outlook. A recent Unity summary provides additional information.

Charles Fillmore studied many teachings. "More than forty," he wrote. There are elements of Christian Science in Unity, but there are also elements of the Methodism of Myrtle's early life, and of many other teachings. Charles Fillmore

---

[1] Followed by "through the five senses from the outside world."

[2] Cady, *Lessons in Truth*, 3, 5-8, pp. 25-26 (pp. 14-15).

[3] Not "human" but "mortal"

[4] *Ibid.*, 7, 5-6, p. 72 (p. 73).

fused many teachings and his own personal contact with God into the teaching that is now Unity.[1]

With regard to the results of this fusion, it is summarized:

> Go within.
> This is the great instruction of Unity. Go within--seek, ask, knock, meditate, pray--and you cannot miss God.
> This is why in Unity's magazines and prayer ministry, doctrine plays a minor role. . . . Unity is not so much a set of descriptions as it is a set of directions.
> Unity has some very specific teachings.
> Metaphysically, it is a mysticism, but a practical mysticism. Unity is practical Christianity. Also, it has elements of objective idealism. We teach that reality is of the nature of mind. Unity uses the Bible constantly. We feel that the Bible is God's Word, actually intended for people to live by. So we help people interpret the Bible that they can apply its message to their daily lives. . . .
> This is the central teaching of Unity. Jesus Christ is the Way, the truth and the Life. He came to show us how to do what He did. . . . He told us that if we follow Him, we shall learn how to overcome every limiting mortal condition, even death. So we teach the infinite perfectibility. . . .
> We believe that life is an eternal unfoldment. . . .

---

[1]James Dillet Freeman, *What is Unity?* (Lee's Summit, Mo.: Unity School of Christianity, n.d. [1961], from a *Christian Herald* article), p. 4.

We suggest reincarnation as a possible explanation as to how this unfoldment may take place, but we do not insist that this idea be accepted. As a matter of fact, Unity is almost entirely concerned with the here-and-now rather than with the hereafter. What is important is what we are making of the present moment. God has brought us this far; we can trust Him for the rest.

About God, we use the familiar terms and we accept the Trinity. But we emphasize His impersonal aspect. We do not believe that God is a person sitting on a throne over us in an arbitrary manner. God is principle. God is not separate and far away and hard to reach. God is in you. In you! God is part of you, as you are part of Him. God is right where you are. You have constant, instant access to Him.

God is Love.... God's will is good.... Thus, we do not pray in order to change God. How would we change the wholly good? It is not God, it is we who need to change. The purpose of prayer is to change *our* thinking.

This is why we use, not supplication, but affirmative statements in prayer....

But though the purpose of prayer is to change thinking, it is not to thought itself that we ascribe power. All power is God's. Thinking--mind--is the connecting link between man and God. We cannot heal through our thought. But God can heal through our thought when we align ourselves in thought with His healing love and power. God can meet every need through our thought; He can pour His rich ideas into our mind; He can give us every needful thing.

We do not teach that God gives a man everything he wants. But we do teach that a man should take everything he wants to God.

No thing should be made the object of existence, but all things necessary to a happy, full life will be ours if we trust God's love and let ourselves be used by His wisdom.[1]

This summary forms a good introduction to New Thought, for it seems unlikely that many New Thoughters would object to it.[2] However, Unity does not consider itself part of New Thought. In the early days of Unity, the Fillmores were close to other leaders of what was growing into New Thought. Unity was a member of the alliance of New Thought groups, but left it twice, most recently in 1922.[3] The primary difference between Charles Fillmore and some others seems to have been that he considered his teachings more fully in accord with those of primitive Christianity.[4] Although Unity as a whole is not a formal part of New Thought, an examination of the directories in each issue of *Unity* and

---

[1]*Ibid.*, pp. 6-11.

[2]If I were to write the book again, almost certainly I should say much more about the views of such groups as Divine Science and Religious Science, but I still believe, in 1992, that this fairly lengthy presentation of Unity gives a good first look at New Thought as a whole.

[3]Freeman, *The Household of Faith*, p. 105. [The Association of Unity Churches belongs to the International New Thought Alliance, although the school as such does not. It seems doubtful that many Unity people who are aware of New Thought as a whole would say that Unity is not part of New Thought, in teaching if not fully in organization.]

[4]*Ibid.*, pp. 102-105, and Braden, *These Also Believe*, pp. 153-56.

of *New Thought* shows some local leaders listed in both. Braden has said of Unity that "its genius is essentially that of the New Thought movement in general,"[1] and

> Whether or not Unity and New Thought will ever again unite in any organization, cannot be predicted, but as, probably, the largest and strongest, numerically and institutionally, of any of the New Thought groups, Unity does not feel so keenly the need of association that lesser groups may be inclined to feel.[2]

(3) *Varying Views of New Thought.* It may be that in the past several decades there has been even less reason than formerly for distinguishing one branch of New Thought from another. Since there is little or no stress on formal membership in any group, and followers are free to work out their views from as many sources as they can find, it is all but impossible to say what significance there is to organizational boundaries, or even to whatever bounds there may be for New Thought.

Dresser saw New Thought in a broad perspective as

> a phase or tendency within a growing movement of our time which has for its object the full emancipation of our fellowmen. The main characteristics of this larger movement are, the belief that every man may go to the sources of power, that he can and should prove their worth through practice. This means for the New Thought a profound belief in the immediate presence of God, and the sufficiency of that presence in every

---

[1] Braden, *These Also Believe*, p. 140.

[2] *Ibid.*, p. 156.

moment of need. There is no barrier, and need be no intermediary between the finite soul and God. ... God is still supreme Father over all, the source of all life, wisdom and love, and none is good save through God. But all men are God's children, all may commune with the Father. Man is by nature such that he is able to enter into conscious relation with the divine presence, he is good. What is needed is conscious realization of that presence in a manner so practical that we shall find freedom from every bondage, help for every ill, a solution for every problem.

The cardinal principle of the New Thought with reference to this spiritual realization is the belief that all life is one. The old-time distinctions between the natural and the supernatural, the profane and the sacred, are broken down. The entire cosmos is a revelation of God, every force active within it is from God, and all experience is meant for our good.[1]

It would seem that all or considerable parts of the "growing movement of our time" has been called New Thought by some writers.

"New Thought" is used as both a generic and a specific term. As a generic term it denotes the idealistic thought patterns usually associated with transcendentalism of the Concord School, which has close affinities with Plato, Neoplatonism, and the Vedanta philosophy of India.[2]

---

[1]Horatio W. Dresser, "Swedenborg," part V, *Practical Ideals*, XXIII (February, 1912), 12-13.

[2]F. E. Mayer, *The Religious Bodies of America* (3d ed.; St. Louis, Mo.: Concordia Publishing House, 1958), p. 542.

In this view the "specific term" is applied to "about a score of metaphysical cults"[1] associated with a formal alliance of New Thought groups. This writer distinguishes New Thought from Christian Science and Unity (the Unity School of Christianity).

In another opinion, "New Thought ranges from simple interest in the advice of Norman Vincent Peale and his 'positive thinking' to subtle touches of ancient Hindu beliefs."[2]

A history of psychotherapy, while apparently excluding Christian Science and Unity from New Thought,[3] differs from most by including Theosophy[4] and the Emmanuel Movement[5] in New Thought.

One classification groups Christian Science, Unity, and some clearly New Thought organizations together as "egocentric or 'New Thought' bodies" (apparently alternative terms for the same thing), while placing such entities as Theosophy and Vedanta in "esoteric or mystical

---

[1]*Ibid.* [See the reference to Sydney E. Ahlstrom's use of the term *harmonial religion* in Appendix J.]

[2]Richard Mathison, *Faiths, Cults and Sects of America from Atheism to Zen* (Indianapolis: The Bobbs-Merrill Company, Inc., 1960), p. 72. [In recent years Robert H. Schuller's "possibility thinking" has taken its place alongside the "positive thinking" of his mentor, Norman Vincent Peale, both outlooks derived at least in part from New Thought.]

[3]Bromberg, *op. cit.*, p. 137.

[4]*Ibid.*, p. 138.

[5]*Ibid.*, p. 138.

Healing Hypotheses

bodies."[1] Christian Science, Unity, and New Thought have been termed three "branches on the same tree."[2]

New Thought has been termed both a cult and an attitude of mind.[3] "It represents a general point of view held by a multitude of people, organized into numerous smaller or larger groups,"[4] and, it could be added, held by many without organizations.

> New Thought has never had an apostolic succession or a rigid discipline or a centralized organic form. This has given it a baffling looseness in every direction, but has, on the other hand, given it a pervasive quality which Christian Science does not possess. It has a vast and diffuse literature of contemporaneous thought as to make it difficult to find anywhere a distinct demarcation of channels.
> New Thought is either a theology with a philosophic basis or a philosophy with a theological bias. It is centrally and quite distinctly an attempt to give a religious content to the present trend of science and philosophy, a reaction against old theologies and perhaps a kind of nebula out of which future theologies will be organized.[5]

---

[1]Elmer T. Clark, *The Small Sects in America* (rev. ed.; Nashville: Abingdon Press, 1949), p. 234.

[2]Jan Karel Van Baalen, *The Chaos of Cults: A Study of Present-Day Isms* (5th ed.; Grand Rapids, Mich.: Wm. B. Eerdmans Publishing Co., 1946), p. 182.

[3]Atkins, *op. cit.*, p. 210.

[4]Braden, *These Also Believe*, p. 128.

[5]Atkins, *op. cit.*, pp. 210-11.

It has been said that

> New Thought presents two ideas as supremely fundamental and important in man's development: (1) that he is a divine soul, and hence has within himself unlimited potentialities, slumbering perhaps and waiting to be called into expression; and (2) that he is under the dominion of universal law--the law of cause and effect; that he is punished by every wrong and rewarded by every virtue. Until we grasp the true significance of these truths, we shall never find a true religion or the pathway of spiritual progress. This philosophy conceives of evil as only a misdirected energy. All forces are good; only as they are misdirected do they produce harm. . . . True teaching exalts the good and replaces negative with constructive thoughts. To teach man to come into the conscious realization of the divinity within, the unity of God and man, so that out of the sublimity of his own soul he can say with the Gentle Seer of Galilee, "The Father and I are One," is the supreme voice and meaning of New Thought.[1]

A more recent characterization of New Thought in terms of trends in theology probably would note that throughout the vogue of Neo-Orthodoxy in recent decades, New Thought has retained its Liberalism, which always has differed from most theological Liberalisms in

---

[1] Abel Leighton Allen, "New Thought," *Encyclopaedia of Religion and Ethics*, ed. James Hastings, IX (1917), 360-61. See also John Benjamin Anderson, *New Thought Its Lights and Shadows: An Appreciation and a Criticism* (Boston: Sherman, French & Company, 1911) and Henry C. Sheldon, *Theosophy and New Thought* (New York and Cincinnati: the Abingdon Press, 1916), *passim*.

emphasizing the "miraculous." Most New Thought people have little or no interest in any very formal theology.

A self-professing New Thought dictionary defines:

> New Thought: A system of thought which affirms the
>> unity of God with man, the perfection of all life and the immortality and eternality of the individual soul forever expanding.
>
> new thought applied: The conscious use of the laws of thought for the purpose of producing betterment in one's life or in the lives of others.
>
> New Thought Movement: Groups, societies, religious
>> and spiritual organizations built upon the New Thought philosophy, leaving room for ample independent individualism. The principles governing the New Thought Movement are universal but individually and independently applied.[1]

The introduction to a book published for the International New Thought Alliance asserts that the metaphysics of the New Thought movement is

> a practical idealism, which emphasizes spiritual causation and the accessibility of spiritual mind

---

[1] Ernest Holmes, *New Thought Terms and Their Meanings* (Los Angeles: Institute of Religious Science and Philosophy, 1953), pp. 15-16. Varying capitalization in original.

power, acting in accord with law and available to all people.[1]

The term "New Thought" requires some explanation:

> The term New Thought is more comprehensive than any other that has been applied to the mental-healing movement. The term itself has often been criticized, and some attempts have been made to give it up. It has come to stay, however, and may well be accepted in the widely representative sense in which it is at present employed. Like other terms, it had a natural history implying changes in human interests. From the first the mental-healing movement was a protest against old beliefs and methods, particularly the old-school medical practice and the old theology. . . .
> Dr. Holcombe . . . was the first writer in the mental-science period to employ the term "New Thought," capitalized, to designate the new teaching in the sense in which the term is now used. In his pamphlet, *Condensed Thoughts about Christian Science*, 1889, Dr. Holcombe says, "New Thought always excites combat in the mind with old thought, which refuses to retire."
> There is no line of demarcation, then, between the earlier terms and "New Thought." Nor can one say that mental science abruptly ceases and New Thought begins. After 1890, devotees of

---

[1] Ernest Holmes and Maude Allison Lathem (eds.), *Mind Remakes Your World* (New York: Dodd, Mead & Company, 1941), p. xi. This quotation follows the statement, "The New Thought Movement is metaphysical, but not in a strict philosophical sense."

Healing Hypotheses 189

mental healing acquired the habit of speaking of the new teaching as "this thought" in contrast with the old theology. Thus in time the term came into vogue in place of mental science, and writers like Dr. Holcombe began to give up using the term "Christian Science" when they wished to show that they did not mean Eddyism. Then in 1894 the name "New Thought" was chosen as the title of a little magazine devoted to mental healing, published in Melrose, Mass. The term became current in Boston through the organization of the Metaphysical Club, in 1895. At about the same time it was used by Mr. C. B. Patterson in his magazine *Mind*, New York, and in the titles of two of his books, [and by others in their books and magazines.][1]

(4) *Alliance Founding and Statements of New Thought*. On the invitation of the Metaphysical Club, "the first New Thought convention under that name ... was held in Lorimer Hall, Tremont Temple, Boston, October 24-26, 1899."[2] However, the name of the organization that emerged from the convention was The International Metaphysical League.[3] This organization was reorganized in 1908 as the National New Thought Alliance, which became the present International New Thought Alliance in 1914.[4]

In 1916 it adopted

---

[1] Dresser, *A History of the New Thought Movement*, pp. 152-54.

[2] *Ibid.*, p. 195.

[3] *Ibid.*, pp. 195-96.

[4] *Ibid.*, p. 202.

a declaration of purpose [that] ... read: "To teach the infinitude of the Supreme one, the Divinity of Man and his infinite possibilities through the creative power of constructive thinking and obedience to the voice of the Indwelling Presence which is our source of Inspiration, Power, Health and Prosperity."[1]

Each issue of the Alliance's quarterly, *New Thought*, includes the Declaration of Principles adopted by the 42nd Congress on July 25, 1957:

We affirm the inseparable oneness of God and man, the realization of which comes through spiritual intuition, the implications of which are that man can reproduce the Divine perfection in his body, emotions, and in all his external affairs.

We affirm the freedom of each person in matters of belief.

We affirm the Good to be supreme, universal, and eternal.

We affirm that the Kingdom of Heaven is within us, that we are one with the Father, that we should love one another, and return good for evil.

We affirm that we should heal the sick through prayer and that we should endeavor to manifest perfection "even as our Father in Heaven is perfect."

---

[1] Braden, *These Also Believe*, p. 136.

We affirm our belief in God as the Universal Wisdom, Love, Life, Truth, Power, Peace, Beauty, and Joy, "in whom we live, move, and have our being."

We affirm that man's mental states are carried forward into manifestation and become his experience through the Creative Law of Cause and Effect.

We affirm that the Divine Nature expressing Itself through man manifests Itself as health, supply, wisdom, love, life, truth, power, peace, beauty, and joy.

We affirm that man is an invisible spiritual dweller within a human body, continuing and unfolding as a spiritual being beyond the change called physical death.

We affirm that the universe is the body of God, spiritual in essence, governed by God through laws which are spiritual in reality even when material in appearance.

This appears to be a more concise form of a Declaration of Principles adopted in 1917.[1] It may well be that it represents no change of view, but it also is possible that it is the expression of a slightly more

---

[1] Quoted in full in Braden, *Ibid.*, pp 136-37 and extensively in Atkins, *op. cit.*, pp. 228-29 and Mayer, *op. cit.*, pp 543-44; Atkins and Mayer omit parts stressing the Alliance's belief that it is carrying on the Christ teaching, that "the universe is spiritual and we are spiritual beings." The 1957 declaration also omits an explicitly Christian name for the teaching.

orthodox outlook. At least its language may be somewhat more meaningful to those not familiar with New Thought. The 1917 declaration includes the affirmation of

> Heaven here and now, the life everlasting that becomes conscious immortality, the communion of mind with mind throughout the universe of thoughts, the nothingness of all error and negation, including death, the variety in unity that produces the individual expressions of the One-Life, and the quickened realization of the indwelling God in each soul that is making a new heaven and a new earth.[1]

It also speaks of "the vision and mission of the Alliance" in connection with "the opportunity to form a real Christ Movement."[2] The general tone of the earlier declaration seems somewhat more crusading than the one adopted by an Alliance that had survived two world wars and other sobering events. However, New Thought shows no essential change in its optimism. It now may make less use of obviously Christian terminology, but this may be to avoid confusing people with terms that it seldom did use in the same ways that most Christians did. It still believes that its views are closer to those of Jesus than are those of the churches.

(5) *Dresser Within New Thought.* After seeing these characterizations of New Thought, one might wonder how Dresser could be classified as a New Thought writer. Certainly New Thought now may be called a form of pantheism [or increasingly, perhaps, panentheism], and Dresser became increasingly opposed to pantheism. However, there are other criteria for classification.

---

[1]Braden, *These Also Believe*, p. 137.

[2]*Ibid.*

The broadly inclusive nature of New Thought is such as to make it almost impossible to exclude anyone who considers God and people to be in meaningful communication and cooperative endeavor, in considerable degree under the control of the human mind. However, this makes the term *New Thought* of little use.

The progressive, evolutionary attitude of Dresser is consistent with the drive toward the realization of perfection on the part of New Thought.

Certainly the aim of helping people to realize their greatest mental and spiritual abilities in the most practical ways, including bodily healing, is common to both Dresser and New Thought.

The respect for Quimby and the attempt to make use of his insights are found in Dresser and in New Thought.

Perhaps the strongest ground for including Dresser among New Thought writers is his intention to write for the New Thought audience, attempting to influence the beliefs of his readers to what he considered better views than those more commonly found, but without the attempt to get them to leave New Thought. The most important part of his writing, from the standpoint of his classification as a New Thought writer, is his defining of New Thought in ways acceptable to his views at the time of writing. During his more pantheistic period he found the "fundamental principle" of New Thought philosophy to be

> the belief that the reality lying beyond phenomena is ultimately spiritual Being, absolute Self, or omniscient Life.... As known by us, Being is the living God, the source of the tendencies which stream through us, and make for righteousness; the

resident force of nature and of cosmic evolution, the life of the universe at large.[1]

The "real man," as he believed then that New Thought saw the "real man," is "an original individuation of ultimate Being, existing in the environment of Being's outgoing life, or the immanent Spirit."[2]

By 1920, in a statement given in response to a request for "a brief account of the teaching" of New Thought, he offered a statement that was not pantheistic, and that was sufficiently illustrative of his later views to merit full quotation:

WHAT THE NEW THOUGHT STANDS FOR

> The New Thought is a practical philosophy of the inner life in relation to health, happiness, social welfare, and success. Man as a spiritual being is living an essentially spiritual life, for the sake of the soul. His life proceeds from within outward, and makes for harmony, health, freedom, efficiency, service. He needs to realize the spiritual truth of his being, that he may rise--above all ills and all obstacles into fullness of power. Every resource he could ask for is at hand, in the omnipresent divine wisdom. Every individual can learn to draw upon divine resources. The special methods of New Thought grow out of this central spiritual principle. Much stress is put upon inner or spiritual concentration and inner control, because each of us needs to become still to learn how to be affirmative, optimistic. Suggestion or

---

[1]Dresser, *Voices of Freedom*, pp. 27-28. *In Search of a Soul*, pp. 223-24 is similar.

[2]Dresser, *Voices of Freedom*, p. 28.

affirmation is employed to banish ills and errors and establish spiritual truth in their place. Silent or mental treatment is employed to overcome disease and secure freedom and success. The New Thought then is not a substitute for Christianity, but an inspired return to the original teaching and practice of the gospels. It is not hostile to science but wishes to spiritualize all facts and laws. It encourages each man to begin wherever he is, however conditioned, whatever he may find to occupy his hands; and to learn the great spiritual lessons taught by this present experience.[1]

This appears in a book that refers to Dresser as "the most prominent leader and teacher"[2] of New Thought. This characterization of Dresser is quoted above a publisher's list of some of his books opposite the title page of *Spiritual Health and Healing*.

That book was intended by Dresser to complete his work dealing with the subject,[3] and indeed it was his last book that reasonably is a candidate for inclusion within New Thought, and hence within this study.

He does not present the book as a work on New Thought, but refers to unspecified criticism of New Thought and Christian Science largely because of their failure to distinguish God and humankind.[4] He believes that removal of cause for criticism would require

---

[1] James H. Snowden, *The Truth About Christian Science* (Philadelphia: The Westminster Press, 1920), pp. 282-83.

[2] *Ibid.*, p. 281.

[3] Dresser, *Spiritual Health and Healing*, p. xii.

[4] *Ibid.*, p. ix.

discriminations [that] point the way beyond mysticism and pantheism in all its forms, beyond self-centeredness and mere thought to the ideal of constancy of love for God and man in frank recognition of our sonship.[1]

Clearly Dresser believed that he was distinguishing "God and man" adequately. However, he said that "there is but one Wisdom and all spiritual truth comes from this source,"[2] and "there is no opposing power."[3] By this he could not well have meant that there are no conditions contrary to the ideal situation; that there are such is obvious to everyone. This point is clarified when he says in relation to healing:

> It is not primarily a question of supremacy over the flesh as if the body contained nothing friendly to the spirit. The body contains nothing unfriendly save what man himself has generated in it. It needs regeneration with man's own spiritual rebirth. It needs to be purified with the purification that is thorough.[4]

In Dresser's view, accepting "Swedenborg's statement,"[5]

---

[1]*Ibid.*

[2]*Ibid.*, p. 23.

[3]*Ibid.*, p. 54.

[4]*Ibid.*, p. 85.

[5]*Ibid*, p. 99.

> there is an influx into the soul ... which not only sustains us but protects and guides us, withholding man by a "very strong force" from influences that tend to his injury. That is to say, this heavenly or divine influx really "rules every one" whatever the appearances to the contrary and despite man's failure to give recognition to it.[1]

This shows Dresser's tendency toward dualism. Even after saying that there is only one Wisdom and no opposing power, he does not follow through with a pantheistic conclusion. It seems probable that this is because of his belief in the need of regeneration.

Dresser maintains, with favorable reference to Swedenborg, that love is prior to thought.[2] Hence regeneration must come first, before argument or affirmation of what is desired but not yet present. Dresser asserts:

> Man will not change his thoughts or outward life until his love changes. When he begins to love spiritual things with devoted or constant love he will find every helpful influence in the world coming to him.[3]

Here Dresser is fully in the New Thought spirit of optimism, and of confidence in a law of action and reaction. Once we do our part, God will respond, or as it also is put, God already has done his part and we need only accept what has been done.

---

[1] *Ibid.*

[2] *Ibid.*, p. 171.

[3] *Ibid.*, p. 166.

When one sees that Dresser's opposition to New Thought's pantheism is in order to uphold the need for regeneration, for change of direction of affection, for coming into broader, fuller communion with the divine, one finds strong similarity with the New Thought approach.

It has been seen already that Evans spoke of healing as conversion. Perhaps the most popular New Thought writer of recent years, Emmet Fox, was similar. In justifying prayer for oneself and others he says:

> We worship God by believing in Him, trusting Him, and loving Him wholeheartedly--and we can attain to that only through prayer.
>
> The sole object of our being here is that we may grow like Him--and we can do that only through prayer.[1]

From this quotation it might be thought that Fox was not a pantheist. Indeed in his own terminology he was not. In describing metaphysics, in the sense of New Thought, he says that it is not pantheism, but proceeds to state that

> pantheism, as generally understood, gives the outer world a separate and substantial existence and says that it is part of God--including all the evil and cruelty to be found in it. The truth is that God is the only Presence and the only Power, that He is entirely good, that evil is a false belief about the Truth; and that the outer world is the outpicturing of our own minds.[2]

---

[1] Emmet Fox, *Make Your Life Worthwhile* (New York: Harper & Brothers, 1942), p. 195.

[2] *Ibid.*, pp. 228-29.

Certainly his assertions about God qualify him as a pantheist according to the more usual understanding of the term. Elsewhere he recommends as an aid to realizing the Presence of God the saying of "there is nothing but God."[1] Yet, within this pantheistic framework, he has no difficulty in taking human beings as "individualizations" of God. He says, "You are the presence of God at the point where you are."[2] Fox likens people to electric light bulbs giving visible expression to invisible electricity.

It seems to be as obvious to Fox that there can be a reality that is all, but includes realities that are not all, as it is obvious to Dresser that such a relationship of something to itself is unreal. Unfortunately, neither was sufficiently concerned with the philosophical expression of the problem to bring out clearly the grounds of the rival beliefs. What is significant here is that with such differing outlooks in metaphysics they could be so close in their devotional views. But it should be added that they did differ on the amount of emphasis to be placed on thought, Fox stressing it as the means of reaching realization of the presence of God, and Dresser emphasizing a loving attitude as necessary before thought could be changed. In reality, it appears that they were giving their attention to differing stages in the same process. As Dresser in his epistemology recognized, immediate feeling and mediate thought correct each other.

Another difference of approach between Dresser and definitely New Thought writers was Dresser's accent on spontaneous action guided by the spirit, as contrasted with New Thought's reliance on what could be called formulas, such as the affirmation of God's sole being offered by Fox. Perhaps Dresser's attitude with regard to

---

[1] Emmet Fox, *Stake Your Claim* (New York: Harper & Brothers, 1952), p. 74.

[2] Emmet Fox, *Alter Your Life*, p. 136.

this grew out of his recognition of the dialectical becoming process in his epistemology and from his acceptance of evolution. It could well be that these prepared him for the acceptance of the Swedenborgian doctrine of divine influx, which is believed to overcome the Swedenborgian difficulty set up by the doctrine of discrete degrees. Once accept the view that there cannot be pantheism, and the Swedenborgian twin doctrines offer at least a verbal explanation of the state of affairs existing without pantheism and of the bridge across the gulf between God and humankind. Pantheism can imply a static outlook; if all is God, there may not be need for development, for influx, for loving response. If there is such a flowing system, it seems appropriate that one should not attempt to work out the final answers, but rather join the flow, in loving trust of whatever guides the flow.

From this expression, which may be taken as an approximation of Dresser's position, it would seem that New Thought must differ considerably. However, this is not the case. Despite the widespread use of affirmations and formulations that are given to certainty of expression of ultimate truth, one finds considerable tentativeness and humility in New Thought. Fox warns against "outlining," the attempt to "think out in advance what the solution of your difficulty will probably turn out to be."[1] He advocates giving one's attention to God and leaving "the question of ways and means strictly to God."[2]

As suggested by Dresser's appreciative reference to "the warm, loving, tender Father of us all" in his summary of Quimby's views in the last chapter, Dresser placed much value on the personality of God, although, curiously,

---

[1] Emmet Fox, *Power Through Constructive Thinking* (New York: Harper & Brothers, 1932), p. 140.

[2] *Ibid.*

Dresser did not seem to care to consider himself a Personalist. Perhaps the Swedenborgian discrete degrees kept him from attempting to explain all reality in terms of personality, for to do so would be to overcome the discontinuousness of creation.

One of the most important attempts of New Thought is to consider God both personal and impersonal. Fox believes in a personal God,[1] but says that "God is not a person in the usual sense of the word. *God has every quality of personality except its limitation.*"[2] But God also is principle[3] or law.

Perhaps the most interesting New Thought explanation of the relation of the personal and the impersonal is that of Thomas Troward. He finds his solution in God as undifferentiated originating life that progresses by generic evolution to the stage of there being both law and personality discernible to evolved units sufficiently high in the developed scale of existence to be self-conscious. Progress beyond the point at which self-consciousness is attained is dependent on the many's conception of what the one is. Because God remains undifferentiated, He or it, supposedly, can be called both personal and impersonal. Troward says:

> If we see that the Eternal Life, by reason of its non-differentiation in itself, must needs become to each of us *exactly what we take it to be*, then it follows that in order to realize it on our own plane

---

[1] Fox, *Alter Your Life*, p. 133.

[2] *Ibid.*, p. 132.

[3] *Ibid.*, p. 143.

of Personality we must see it *through the medium of Personality....*[1]

There is a humility akin to Dresser's in the recognition that "Principle is not limited by Precedent."[2] Troward observes that God has the power, and it is for us to make ourselves suitable receptacles for it. No doubt, Dresser would consider this an inadequate substitute for his conception of devotion, but at least it is not the exalting of oneself that would be even more unacceptable to him.

Taking these various resemblances and differences of Dresser and New Thought apart from him into consideration, one finds that the way is open for classifying him on reasonable grounds either within or without New Thought with respect to the period with which this study is concerned.

If one were to take only his nineteenth-century writing, there would be little or no hesitation, except for his protestations of independence, to group him firmly with New Thought. Of his writing covering approximately the first two decades of the twentieth century, one can decide about as easily one way as the other. He opposed the prevalent pantheism of New Thought, but remained essentially in agreement with New Thought's healing aims, tolerant attitude, and optimism. Perhaps the best classification for Dresser at that time is a friend of New Thought.

What influence Dresser had on New Thought it is impossible to say. Judging by the official platform of the International New Thought Alliance seen above, he seems to have had little. However, it already has been pointed

---

[1] T. Troward, *The Law and the Word* (New York: Dodd, Mead & Company, 1950, originally 1917), p. 207.

[2] *Ibid.*, p. 113.

out that his earliest writing could well have contributed to the pantheistic position that he later opposed. His books must have been read to a considerable extent, but certainly did not sell so well as to make him financially well-off.

What influence his writings may have in the future cannot be told. From the prevalence of pantheism in the movement for its now many years of existence, it seems extremely doubtful that any future reading of his works could bring about any great doctrinal change. However, it may be that his devotional attitude interpreted within the bounds of pantheism [or panentheism] could have, and may have had, some influence. Beyond this, his plea for scholarship could be heeded, and may have been of some importance in making New Thought as open as it is to scholarship. From experience in preparing this study it can be said that New Thought welcomes investigation. From the existence of classes such as those of Ervin Seale, mentioned above, it is seen that New Thought is taking account of the intellectual world apart from its own writings. In this respect New Thought, knowingly or unknowingly with regard to Dresser, is following some of his advice. As a teacher, he probably would consider it some of his most basic advice.

iii. Summary

New Thought arose [however directly or indirectly] primarily out of Quimby's healing practice and his philosophical speculation about phenomena of healing and extrasensory perception produced by mesmerism and by Quimby without use of mesmerism.

Evans and others developed the Quimby thought in various ways having the common denominator of pantheism. Among the influences contributing to this was Oriental thought, introduced partly through American Transcendentalism. New Thought differed from other forms of pantheism in emphasizing that the allness of God provided the ground for healing, if one were to become sufficiently aware of this possibility.

Various New Thought organizations arose. Soon they began to hold conventions, and most groups became members of what now is the International New Thought Alliance. The most notable organization of the general New Thought type that is not a member of the Alliance is Unity. This group may well be the most important disseminator of New Thought teaching.

New Thought proceeded in a rather doctrinaire manner, assuming pantheism and the healing effects possible from an appreciation of the implications of pantheism. However, Dresser preferred to consider New Thought to be not necessarily pantheistic, but part of a broad movement of varying theological and philosophical positions aiming toward the full self-development of humankind. Dresser considered recognition of the closeness of God necessary, but pantheism to be an overstatement of the case. Dresser saw the loving relationship of the presence of God as capable of opening a channel that could result in healing. He was wary of attempts to put God into a formula; instead he believed in simply turning to God in humility and awaiting whatever spiritual leadings and healing might be provided in God's grace.

CHAPTER V

SUMMARY--CONCLUSIONS

Early American philosophy, in both Puritanism and Deism, paid attention to Nature and had a practical outlook encouraging one to get on in the world. In the first half of the nineteenth century in the United States, hopes were high and all sorts of utopian schemes were put forth. If demands for publicly observable reforms were impressive, the upward-looking changes of thought and affection called for by utopians and transcendentalists were no less significant. In the latter part of the century, Oriental thought became more apparent in the American philosophical scene. Naturalism also played its part, especially after the appearance of Darwinian evolution. This addition served to further the optimistic American belief in progress. Hence there were favorable conditions for there to arise an optimistic, progressive, eclectic, philosophical-religious movement.

There was an ancient tradition of religious healing, as well as speculation on the nature of magnetism and the influence of heavenly bodies. Against this background, mesmerism came to the fore. It was explained variously as due to imagination or to the influence of a subtle fluid flowing from the mesmerist to his subject. Little-understood electricity was thought by some to be a fluid, perhaps the same as the magnetic fluid of mesmerism (animal magnetism). Although mesmerism early was seen to have some healing properties, perhaps greater attention was given to the "higher phenomena" of extrasensory perception that mesmerism was reported to awaken in some people. This was the situation when mesmerism was spread abroad in the United States in the 1830's, largely at first by Charles Poyen.

Some of those who took mesmeric phenomena seriously sought to find the most adequate philosophical framework into which to fit their observations. They seemed to know little of philosophy, but engaged in their own speculation. A mesmeric thinker later recognized by Dresser was John Bovee Dods.

Dods saw that not everything seemed to be self-moving. He called what is self-moving, mind or spirit. But he rejected its immateriality, on the belief that existence requires form, which in turn requires materiality. He found that mind cannot move and called it electricity; he also proposed a gradation of material, each grade of which could be moved by the next more refined. At one point he called electricity an emanation of God, but later called it coeternal with mind or spirit. Since both were material, the distinction seems questionable. Despite this, Dresser stressed the Dods emphasis on mind as the originator of motion. Dresser admired the gradation from mind to matter. Dods considered healing the restoration of proper electrical balance of the body. As New Thought was to do, Dods believed in keeping the patient conscious, rather than putting him or her into a mesmeric state.

While the views of Dods may have exerted some influence on Dresser, those of another man who investigated mesmerism were of great importance in the lives of Dresser and his parents, Julius A. Dresser and Annetta G. S. Dresser. This man was Phineas P. Quimby. He gave mesmeric demonstrations and used a mesmerized subject, Lucius Burkmar, to diagnose and prescribe for sickness. After observing this process for some time, Quimby concluded that the results were due to beliefs held by patients. He abandoned his subject and mesmerism, developed his own extrasensory perception, and worked out a system of spiritual healing. Dresser stressed Quimby's theistic attitude, intuitive method of diagnosis, and discovery of "spiritual matter" similar to the "electricity" of Dods as a link between mind and matter. The spiritual matter was believed to be impressed by beliefs and to bring forth the physical conditions corresponding to the beliefs. In Quimby's view, disease was real, but was in the form of false belief, which could be changed by a realization of divine Wisdom. Quimby identified one's true self with the parapsychological senses revealed in mesmerism but not dependent on mesmerism once one learns to use them consciously.

Quimby did not live to publish a book of his views, but they were interpreted in Swedenborgian terms by Warren F. Evans, who published several books. The Swedenborgian philosophy came to be adopted by Dresser, but Evans moved farther away from it as his thought developed subsequent to his learning from Quimby. The hallmark of the Swedenborgian outlook was the supremacy of God, with correspondence of the spiritual and material, but with a doctrine of discrete degrees of existence according to which there could not be pantheism, and divine influx uniting the spiritual and material worlds.

Evans grew into pantheism, and in doing so produced a system that substantially was taken over as the content of New Thought [which is not to say how many New Thoughters got it from Evans, inasmuch as there were parallel tracks of development]. Evans was less original with regard to his fundamental thought than those considered thus far. He was willing to accept the standard philosophical idealists for his system, but sought to connect them with healing. He also turned to occult writers of East and West in producing his "Christian Pantheism." His ultimate view was one of the identification of thought and existence, thus eliminating the need of any sort for gradation between mind and matter or any gulf to be bridged between mind and matter.

Turning to Dresser, one does not find him presenting a system purporting to be complete, nor even careful attention to such distinctions as soul and self or the nature of personality. His outlook was primarily practical, in wishing to try to help those in search of more meaningful, healthful life. Undoubtedly he must have been influenced by the association of his parents with Quimby before his birth.

Both parents came from conventional religious groups and were skeptical of Quimby at first. J. A. Dresser's journal shows a falling away from Quimby and a return. The elder Dressers did not seek to carry on the work of Quimby at the time of his death, but moved to the western part of the United States. There Dresser early found himself in non-philosophical work. However, he managed to get a Harvard education, through the Ph.D. degree in philosophy, after the family moved to Boston.

Dresser was gifted with extrasensory perception, but did not allow this to sway him away from critical thought. Before completing his formal education he began publishing books, mostly of a self-help, inspirational sort. The earlier ones, at least, were entitled to be considered part of New Thought. Throughout his life, his writing, along with counseling and lecturing, constituted his major occupation, although he taught college for some years until 1913. He was ordained as a Swedenborgian clergyman in 1919, and did a little preaching.

Dresser begins his writing with largely an acceptance of pantheism, although he does not call it that, believing that the reserving of some of God unmanifested in the world saves him from pantheism. As he progresses in his philosophical studies, Dresser becomes increasingly concerned with epistemology. He finds that one begins with an indiscriminate whole of experience and that one gradually becomes aware of himself or herself in relation to another. He discovers no knowledge in the uninterpreted immediate. Hence, he rejects any claim of knowledge from unreflective mysticism. Nevertheless, he recognizes the necessity of the immediate as the content for reflection. He accepts the newer psychology that excludes separate faculties. His study of Hegel confirms his epistemological observation, and serves to stress the aspect of motion in the dialectical process. This probably reinforces his Quimbian reliance on a particularistic approach to life, doubting the adequacy of any formulation satisfactorily to represent reality as a whole. The becoming nature of the knowing process suggests the unfinished nature of the reality, something already offered by the theory of evolution, which he accepts. The Swedenborgian influx also may tend to stress motion, rather than a static system.

While the whole could not be compressed into one's understanding, Dresser retains faith in a meaningful whole, and makes his test for truth a consistency including all experience. This, and life itself, is the nature of truth for Dresser. He has a common-sense acceptance of a practical dualism of mind and matter, which leads him to appreciate the Dods gradation of matter and the Quimby "spiritual matter." This attitude probably is aided by his extrasensory perception, which he characterizes as operating in an intermediate realm neither visible in the ordinary way nor more divine than the commonly known world. Hence, stressing the details of the world, in whatever way revealed, Dresser finds no solution to the mind-body problem in the Evans identification of thought and existence. Both Evans and Dresser recognize the importance of non-intellectual experience, but where the mystical nature of Evans sweeps away distinctions of mind and matter, and of God and humankind, the more analytical Dresser rejects any solution that he considers lacking in discrimination. Both Evans and Dresser preserve the reality of the world as a divine expression, but Dresser believes that the Evans view does not adequately preserve the common-sense reality of the world.

Dresser remained optimistic, but in the exercise of his discrimination could not go so far as to call everything good. He wished to preserve the meaningfulness of finite ethical effort. Yet he held evil to be only an incident in the evolutionary process, a consequence of the freedom necessary for ethical value. Presumably, eventually all would become wise enough to want to do what is for the common good. While he stressed freedom, he remained an advocate of essentially divine guidance, presumably part of the Swedenborgian influx. In the period beyond that covered in this study Dresser became rather closely identified with Swedenborgianism, at least in his writing.

Turning to Dresser and New Thought, Dresser participated in early activities of the movement, in helping to organize it and in his writing and lecturing. However, he maintained an independent attitude. This was increasingly the case as he moved away from pantheism and as New Thought showed an insufficient amount of scholarship, in his opinion.

New Thought is seen to have a strong pantheistic bent. Indeed, pantheism is the central doctrine for most of New Thought. Yet Dresser defined New Thought as not requiring pantheism, accepted at least honorary New Thought office, shared New Thought's open-minded, optimistic outlook, its healing aims, and to a considerable extent advocated its technique, to the extent that it recognized something beyond mere thought. On the basis of these facts, it is possible to classify him as a New Thought writer throughout the period here in question. At the very least, he was a friend of New Thought, if a critical one. In a movement as broad as New Thought one cannot very well exclude differing attitudes and internal criticism. At the present time, New Thought is showing some interest in thought beyond its own borders, and in doing so it is following advice given by Dresser, regardless of whether it has taken it from him. But on the side of doctrine, the prevailing pantheism indicates that the non-pantheistic views of Dresser made little headway in influencing New Thought.

APPENDIX A

QUIMBY'S EARLY KNOWLEDGE OF MESMERISM AND PHILOSOPHY

The manuscript being quoted here is what Dresser referred to[1] as Quimby's "lecture-notes" of the period 1843-1847. Since this name has been used, it is continued here, although it appears that Quimby may have considered publishing these well written-out "notes," especially as he refers to them as this "work," as one might to a book, and as "this volume,"[2] as well as addressing "our

---

[1]*The Quimby Manuscripts*, 1st ed., pp. 47-52, 2nd ed., pp. 53-58. Dresser does not mention the lecture notes in his list of material at 1st ed., pp. 17-18, 2nd ed., pp. 23-24, but he may have included them under the first item, "Original manuscripts of articles and letters in P. P. Quimby's handwriting...."

[2]Quimby, lecture notes, VII, 3. The manuscript is neither titled nor provided with page numbers, except for two dozen pages with penciled page numbers seemingly by Dresser. It is contained in seven booklets bearing the apparently trade name Ames. The page numbers used here are derived by counting the written pages, generally on only one side of a sheet. In addition, there is an extra copy of part of the first volume. At this time [1962] all are in the possession of the Quimby family [in 1992 in the Special Collections of the Mugar Memorial Library of Boston University].

reader."[1] Dresser did not indicate that it contains 153 pages. In part, he says:

> Referring to Mr. Quimby's lecture-notes, used during the period of his public exhibitions with Lucius, we find that he very gradually came to [certain] conclusions when he saw that no other explanation would suffice. He not only read all the books on mesmerism he could find but familiarized himself with various theories of matter, such as Berkeley's, and with different hypotheses in explanation of the mesmeric sleep. Convinced that there was no "mesmeric influence" as such, no "fluid" passing from body to body but simply the direct action of mind on mind without any medium, he had also become convinced that the states perceived by the subject were not due to imagination. He found, for example, that by creating a state in his own mind and vividly feeling it, Lucius felt the same and exhibited signs of its effect in the body. "Real cold" was felt by Lucius in response to certain suggestions. If imaginary, the subject would not have acted upon the ideas in question. Thus when Mr. Quimby handed Lucius a six-inch rule and pictured it in his own mind as a twelve-inch rule, Lucius would proceed to count out the twelve inches, and to him it was literally a twelve-inch rule. That is to say, the impressions received by the subject were real, not "imaginary," as real as would have been the actual things in question. An impression might

---

[1] *Ibid.*, V, 25.

indeed be produced on a subject's mind from a false cause, but the cause would then be real.[1]

Presumably, George Quimby used this manuscript in writing his article on his father.[2] It was available to Collie, cited below; however, with Quimby's later material in mind, he looked at it without thinking that it was written by Quimby. Probably no other writers than the three, including Dresser, just mentioned have consulted this writing until now.

The manuscript seems to be just as it left Quimby's hand, except for such obviously recent additions as now somewhat yellowed cellophane tape, and some insignificant changes of wording apparently of approximately the same time as the original writing; but there is nothing to call into question Quimby's authorshlp.

At this period Quimby used orthodox terminology in relation to the mind. This suggests that his later language was not that of one who had no usual terms to use, but was employed to deal with something not yet discovered in his earlier period. The framework on which his later thought was built is shown in the lecture notes.

With regard to the coming of mesmerism Quimby says:

---

[1] *The Quimby Manuscripts*, 1st ed., p. 47, 2nd ed., p. 53. The ruler incident is in the lecture notes at III, 17. Later, 1st ed., p. 51, 2nd ed., p. 57, he says that Quimby "had heard something about Berkeley's views," but does not mention Berkeley after the period of the lecture notes. Quimby's references to Berkeley, not quoted by Dresser, are quoted below.

[2] Now published in Ervin Seale (ed.) *Phineas Parkhurst Quimby[:] The Complete Writings* (Marina del Rey, Calif.: De Vorss & Company, 1988) I, 19-27.

Mesmerism was introduced into the U State [*sic*] by M. Charles Poyen, a French gentleman, who did not appear to be highly blest with the powers of magnetising to the satisfaction of his audience in his public lectures. I had the pleasure of listening to one of his lectures, & pronounced it a humbug as a matter of course. And that his remarkable experiments, which were related, were, in my belief, equally true with witch craft--I had never been a convert to witch craft, nor had even had any personal interviews [?] with ghosts or hobgoblins & therefore considered all stories bordering on the marvelous as delusive--

Next came Dr Collyer,[1] who perhaps did more to excite a spirit of enquirey [*sic*] throughout the community than any, who have succeeded him. But the community were still incredulous & the general excentricity [*sic*] of his character no doubt contributed much to prejudice the minds of his audience against his science--He, however, like all those who had preceded him on both sides of the water, must have a *long handle to his science* namely, a subtle fluid of the nature of electricity-- So contrary to all experience did all the facts, elicited from his experiments appear, in connection with the laws wich [*sic*] govern electricity, that almost every man of science would reject both theory & facts without a moments [*sic*]

---

[1]For information showing that this probably was Robert H. Collyer, judging by his dates of learnlng of mesmerism and his travels, see Robert H. Collyer, *Mysteries of the Vital Element in Connexion with Dreams, Somnambulism, Trance, Vital Photography, Faith and Will, Anaesthesia, Nervous Congestion and Creative Function. Modern Spiritualism Explained* (2nd ed.; London: Henry Renshaw, 1871, originally Bruges, 1868), *passim*.

consideration. However, the perseverance of the Dr. overcame, in part some of the prejudices & he at last drew out of a committee in the city of Boston an acknowledgement of the facts, altho' they refrained from any expression of their opinion as to their occasion--

Collyer was, like all others, satisfied as to the *fluid*--& nothing could be accomplished without producing a current upon the subject or surcharging him with a quantity of the electric fluid--In a work published by him in 1843 altho' he is still the advocate of the fluid, yet he rejects the doctrine of Phreno Magnetism, neurology &c as introduced & defended by Dr Buchanan & LeRoy [sic] Sunderland. The same course, which enabled him to detect the fallacy of their theories would have led him, upon pursuing the subject a little further, to have rejected entirely his whole theory of a fluid. He would have looked to another cause of all this phenomenon. From testimony, now before the community, there is no doubt that Collyer performed the first phreno magnetic experiments[1] in this country & that the honor, if there be any, of the discovery should be yielded to him. It is a matter of little consequence to the community, who shall wear the wreath of honor, but we prefer to see the peacock dressed in his own plumage, & not bear the shame of a naked plucking by his neighboring fowle [sic].[2]

---

[1] On the next page Quimby refers to these as "the exciting of particular organs in the brain by the nervous fluid or by electricity." This was to produce the state of mind believed by phrenologists to be brought about by such supposed organs.

[2] Quimby, lecture notes, IV, 6-7.

It will be seen that Quimby does not say where he heard Poyen's lecture, seemingly only one, and whether he heard Collyer; however, it seems likely that Belfast was the place and that he heard both of them.

In the manuscript under examination Quimby offers general philosophical observations before getting to mesmerism.[1] The first nine pages follow in their entirety, except for the omission of various alternative wordings rejected by Quimby in his corrections and of no significance for the meaning of what he was saying. As far as possible, his spelling, dashes (sometimes used in place of periods), and other characteristics are kept. Difficulty of reading the writing may have resulted in slight inaccuracies, but probably very few.

Primary Truths

What are primary truths? According to Mr. Stewart, "they are such & such only, as can neither be proved nor refuted by other propositions of greater perspicuity." They are self-evident--not borrowing the powers of reasoning to shed light upon themselves.

We are naturally inclined, to consider the reality of our *personal existence*. That we exist is the great basis upon which we build everything. It is the foundation of all *knowledge*. Without *self-existence* nothing could result in the progress of the understanding. If any man questions the fact of his own existence, that very process, by which he doubts, proves to a demonstration, that an *existing, dowting* [or doubting] power must have been precident, [sic] must have had a creation. The

---

[1] A brief account relating to philosophical works referred to by Quimby may be found in Schneider, *op. cit.* (*A History of American Philosophy*), pp. 238-41.

first internal thought is immediately followed with an undoubting conviction of personal self-existence. It is a primary truth in nature, and requires no further explanation.

Personal Identity

Another primary truth is *personal identity*. This is the knowledge of ourselves. The idetifying [*sic*] of ourselves with our self-exietence.

We know that we exist, and in that existence we recognise our personality.

Man is composed of *matter* and mind, by some mysterious combination united; and we may divide our identity with *mental* and *bodily*.

Mental identity is the continuance and oneness of the thinking & reasoning principle. It is not divisible in length, breadth & dimentions [*sic*]--composed of particles &c. like matter, nor does it change or cease to exist. It remains as it was originally with all its eternal powes [*sic*]--its eternal principles

Bodily identity is the sameness of the bodily organisation--the man in figure, as we behold him with our natural eyes. The particles of matter of which the body is composed may change, but its shape and structure and its physical creation are the same. Professor Upham, in his work on Intellectual Philosophy, in reference to this subject, uses the following language. "It was a saying of Seneca, that no man bathes twice in the same river and still we call it the same, altho' the water within its banks is constantly passing away. And in like manner we identify the human body, although it constantly changes."

Personal identity, then, comprehends the man as we behold him, in his bodily & mental nature, mysteriously & wonderfully made!

The old soldier, who has fought the battles of his country in the days of the American Rovolution, will recount his deeds of valor & his heroic sufferings to his youthful listeners, not doubting that he is really the same old soldier, who was in his country's service some sixty years since. The early settlers of our country, as they look abroad over the cultivated plain, never doubt, that they are really the same individuals, who some forty years felled the trees of the forest & turned the wilderness into a fruitful garden!

So is man constituted, that his own identity is one of the first primary truths[.]

We are so constituted that we believe, or rather there seems to be an authorative principle within us of giving confidence or credence to certain propositions and truths, which are presented to our minds. Among the first things, which the mind admits, is *that there* is no beginning or change without a cause--that nothing could not create *something*. When any new principle is discovered, man immediately seeks out the cause, looks for some moving power; as tho' it could not be self-creative & self-acting.

In contemplating the material universe, in beholding the beautiful planetary system, the sun, the moon & the stars regulated & controlled by undeviating laws, who does not say, "these are the results of some mighty creative intelligence." That the power of their existences & harmonious motions was originated beyond themselves.

Thus it is that we attribute to every effect a cause--to every result a motive power.

Matter & Mind have uniform, undeviating & fixed laws. And they are always subject to, & controlled by them. We are not to suppose otherwise, unless we give up our belief, that any object is governed or directs. Yet we are not to suppose, that the same laws apply both to matter & mind. Each has it peculiar governing principle, & in as much as mind, in its nature, deviates from matter, so may its laws deviate.

We all believe, that the earth will continue to revolve on its axis & perform its anual [sic] orbit around the sun; that summer & winter, seed-time & harvest, will continue to succeed each dother; "that the decaying plants of autumn will revive again in spring."

This belief does not arise in the mind at once; but has its origin now in one instance & then in another, untill [sic] it becomes *universal*.

Immateriality of the Soul

It is a conceded principle, that mind does not possess, or rather, we fail to detect the same qualities in mind as in matter. No sect of philosophers, I believe, have ever pretended that mind is destinguished [sic] by extension, divisibility, impenetrability, color &c--& therefore most have [originally "all are"] agreed to use *immateriality* as applied to the soul, in destinction [sic] from *materiality* as applied to the body--that the soul is destitute of those qualities, which appear in matter, having its own peculiar atributes [sic], such as *thought, feeling, remembrance & passion*.

The mind as it exists in man, & deveops [sic] itself thro' the bodily organs, no doubt, has a close connection with matter, the physical system & particularly the brain. Yet we are not to suppose, that mind is dependent for its existence upon the organs of the body, nor is it subject to the controll [sic] of matter, altho' influenced & impressed by it. Mind rather exercises a direction to matter, producing certain results. If mind was any portion of the materiality of the body, a destruction of any portion of [originally "any injury done to" instead of "a destruction of any portion of"] this, would destroy a portion of [originally "effect" instead of "destroy a portion of"] that. But this is not the fact. Individuals, deprived of some of their limbs, do not exhibit any degree of loss of mind. How often has it appeared far more active & energetic, in the last moments of desolving [sic] nature, than when the physical powers were in full health & vigor. Men, upon the battlefield, mutilated & wounded & suffering the intensest pain, have displayed, amid all this disaster of the body, the highest powers of intellectual action. So that, altho' *mind* to us appears at first view to have an inseperable [sic] connection with the body, yet, for its energies, its full unqualified powers of action, does not rely upon bodily health & vigor.

The works of genius, as displayed in the various branches of science, literature & law, bear the character of a higher order of creation, than matter. Memory & imagination, do not appear to have resulted from ponderous substances. The powers of *Judgment & Reasoning* must have originated in something higher & nobler than divisible bodies. To what cause can you attribute the origin & perfection of the demonstrations of *Euclid*? What constituted the authorship of the wise laws of Solon & the political institutions of Lycurgus & those of modern Europe; and the greatest concentration of wisdom ever embodied into one human work; I mean the *American Constitution*? What gave almost intellectual inspiration to the *Iliad & Oddessa* [sic]. What gave berth [sic] to the wonderful productions of Tasso & Spencer & Milton? Where shall we look for the origin of the phillipics [sic] of the Ancients; or in more modern days, for the speeches of a Fox and the Orations of a Webster?

Where human genius has wrought its highest triumphs & achieved transcendent greatness, who can say, its creative cause, its fountain light is in powerless & innert [sic] matter! To ascribe the qualities of matter to the soul would erase forever, the ideas of a future, & eternal existence. But we have no direct evidence of the soul's dissolution & discontinuance at death. The death of the body is only the removal of the souls [sic] sphere of action from our natural view; & no doubt gives a long world of spiritual action, in its new distination [sic]. And have we not every reason to suppose, that the soul will exist after the dissolution of the body? "Death," in the language of Dr. Stewart, "only lifts up the veil, which conceals from our eyes the invisable world. In annihilates the material universe to our senses, & prepares our minds for some new & unknown state of being."

We have already stated, that belief is a simple state of the mind & consequently cannot be made plainer by any process of reasoning.

It is always the same in its nautre altho' it admits of different degrees, which we express in the language of *presumpsion* [sic], *probability* & *certainty*, &c.

It is on the principle of belief that the mind is operated upon in the various exhibitions of its power. For, without confidence, what can we accomplish. With a belief in our ability to accomplish, what would be the result? It is a principle, which comes into every department of reasoning; & testimony is only so operative upon the mind, as it effects [sic] our *belief*.

The Soul

[Marked "strike out," presumably meaning the section marked by a marginal line. Only the first paragraph is given here.]

Those, who style themselves phylosophers [sic] & have written upon the subject of the mind, have always considered the soul as constituting a nature, which is one & indevisable [sic]; yet for the purpouse [sic] of more fully understanding its various stages of action, they have given it three parts or views, in which it may be contemplated expressed in the *Intellect, Sensibilities* & the *Will. Intellictual* [sic], *sensative* [sic] & *voluntary* states of the mind.[1]

In part of the next section, "Origin of Knowledge," Quimby says:

"The mind" says Professor Upham in his work on Mental Philosophy "appears at its creation, to be merely an existence, involving certain principles & endowed with certain powers; but dependent for the first & original developement [sic] of those principles & the exercise of those powers, on the condition of an outward *impression*. But after it has been once brought into action, it finds new sources of thought & feeling in itself."

Having, therefor, all these inherent powers to acquire, its knowledge is in proportion to the impressions [originally "& thoughts" followed "impressions"] it has received from external objects & internal operations. If you present a subject of conversation to a well trained mind, stored with impressions or knowledge, you have started a point,

---

[1] Quimby, lecture notes, I, 1-9.

which sets in motion the whole ocean of mind, educated from the past, & leads to endless discussions. But should you present the same topic to an untaught or [originally "uneducated" followed "or"] partially disciplined mind you would start the current of thought, it is true, but that current would soon cease, or rather could not be very extended; because the subjects of thought or the whole amount of knowledge [originally "or impressions" followed "knowledge"] possessed by the individual, is limited.

I have spoken of the natural mind and the way of acquiring knowledge thro' the bodily senses only. But there are other means of communication, by which impression are conveyed to the mind.

If the spiritual being be independent of matter, why cannot we communicate with it, without aid of the bodily senses? It is to this subject I would now call your attention. The mind itself obeys the laws which its Creator first laid down, & we are not to suppose any strange anomily [sic], in its outward exhibition is contrary to the original design. The great *Law-giver* posseses [sic] all wisdom, & is the fountain head of all perfection. The mind is not a creative experiment of his, himself being ignorant of what results will follow. If these strange phenomana [sic] of the mind, which are exhibited in the different states of excitement are exceptions to the common rule, we must attribute to the *Great Mind* imperfection & humanity or a direct interposition [?] to stay the great laws which were first given, to supprise [sic] & bewilder ignorant & dependent man. But to my mind, it does not appear consistent with the wisdom[1] of God, that so extended an interference would be personnally [sic] made to counteract first principles which are dsplayed [sic] in this age of mesmeric light-- It must be that all these strange appearance are reconcileable [sic] with eternal laws. And we are to look to these alone for a probable and clear solution. The same laws govern the mind, when in its natural state & susceptible of impression thro' the five senses as when its excited & unnatural condition or under the influence of Nervaric [?], Phreno-magnetic, mesmeric or somnambulic influence [originally "state"]. The only difference is this. In the method of conveying impressions to the mind. Give the impression, whether thro' the senses or otherwise & the same correspondent results follow. If I make an impression upon the mind, of a beautiful landscape by pointing it out to the natural eye, it is the same as tho' I made the same impression upon that mind while in an excited or mesmeric state. The view is real & pleasing in one case as in the other, to the mind that beholds it. It is as much an existence before the mind, when the impression, without the material object, is made, as when the impression, with a presentation of the real landscape to the natural eye, is given.

We shall here give a brief ouline [sic] [originally "synopsis"] of what appears to be the condition of mind, when in an excited or mesmeric state. Susciptibility [sic] is in its highest state of action & the operator sems [sic] to controll [sic] the direction of thought if he choses [sic] or can so impress the mind with influences as to govern its

---

[1] A word of great importance in Quimby's later thought; here it is associated with God; there it is identified with God.

action in a measure. This point is, no doubt gained by some powerful impression produced by the operator upon the mind of the subject. This condition can be produced by other influences than an individual mind. A fright by suddenly coming upon some external object, will often produce a similar state of mind. Intense thought & excrutiating [sic] [originally "writhing"] pains produce this excited state & some times sets the mind in action, when it is enabled to exhibit the same phenomana [sic] as when induced by an individual operator. We shall have occasion in the progress of our work to refer to cases which arise from unknown impressions upon the mind, producing hallucination, insanity, dreaming, somnambulism, spectral illusions &c.

This excited state of the mind, called by some, the magnetic, mesmeric & congestive is no doubt produced by a powerful impression of the operator upon the mind of the subject, concentrating or drawing the whole attention to one influence. No set rules can be given by which this influence can be exercised; because the same efforts will produce different results upon different minds; yet no doubt overy mind has its portal of access & could we know where that is, or the way & manner of approaching it, we could produce impressions so powerful upon every mind as to subdue the action of the bodily senses & communicate directly with it [originally "mind"]. The doctrine, therefore, of "powful [sic] magnitisers" [sic] (as they call themselves) that only a more powerful capacity or higher order of intellectual vigor can subdue a weaker mind & produce the excited or mesmeric state is idle as the wind. These higher orders of intellects with strong sensibilities are *more* capable of being brought to the contemplation of one individual subject &

receiving the most powerful impressions, if you can discover the accessable road to their sensibilities. If you can produce an impression upon such a mind as will overcome all his prejudices, towards you or your S[s]cience [originally "subject"][1] acquire his individual confidence, you will then excite the mind into this spiritual state of action & he will readily read your own thoughts. Indeed I have been lead [sic] to the conclusion, that the highest powers of genius have been the results of excited minds, upon the principles I have laid down--that they are but the inspiration of this spiritual action. What is it that contributes so much to destinguish [sic] Homer & Demostenese [sic], Vergil & Cicero, Milton, Tasso, Shakspear [sic] & the whole host of great men, who lived in ancient & modern times! It must have been this excited state during which poetry & eloquence & the highest achievements of mind were left [or "lift"?], lights of their genius, to live through all coming time. Eloquence which holds the multitude in breathless silence or sways them hither & thither, produces the controlling impression upon each mind which in its turn impress & influence the other exciting a low degree of the mesmeric state. It is, in fact, a principle, by which we are all more or lesss governed in all our pursuits.

The high degree of excitement called clairvoyant gives the mind freedom of action, placing it in close contact with every thing. There

---

[1] In this word and some others it is not clear whether the first letter is capitalized. This suggests the somewhat amusing possibility that the practice of capitalizing "science" and some other words originated in handwriting style, rather than in original intent to capitalize.

Healing Hypotheses 227

is nothIng remote or distant past or future; everything is present & discoverable. It only requires direction, & the subject is before it.

It is enabled to discover & discribe [*sic*] countries & cities, mountains & plains, rivers & oceans, inhabitants & animals on distant parts of the globe. The mind will pass into the depths of the earth or rather looks through all matter, all space & all time, giving its charactor, its condition & its result. Call its attention to any subject however remote & it is present to the mind. These ideas, I have thrown out in relation to mind in its highest state of excitement, are not the result of a vivid imagination or the producions [*sic*] of a speculating mind, but the effect of experiments, repeated at different times & on various occasions--They are facts, which stand out beyond all contradiction--all cavil! And we are not to pass them as freak of nature or as the result of contradictory laws. It must be the highest state of action, to which the mind has arrived, giving testemony [*sic*] of the great powers with which it is created, yet controlled by its natural laws. We must not, therefore, account for this wonderful developement [*sic*] upon the suposition [*sic*] of exceptions to general rules; but upon the continuation of great & undiviating [*sic*] principles.[1]

In the next section[2] Quimby continues with some

---

[1]*Ibid.*, I, 17-23.

[2]This section is the first of the remaining, non-mutually-exclusive sections following the heading "The different degrees of excitement of Mind--taken up in their order & discussed." (II, 1) The titles and the

remarks that may point toward his later discovery of an additional level of mind.

> We have witnessed a great number of experiments upon subjects in the excited or mesmeric state, which demonstrate what I have advanced in regard to impressions. Every subject can be so powerfully impressed as to recall the thought, in his waking moments while, of ordinary transactions, no idea is retained. These experiments prove both the similarity of states of mind in the dreaming & mesmeric; & also, that our powers of mind are never at rest.[1] [He has given examples such as recovering information in one's sleep.]

In words similar to some used above, illuminating Quimby's early views on mind, time, and space, he says that in the excited or mesmeric

> state the mind may be said to be before a map, on which is written the past, present & future--only needs direction to some deffinite [sic] point, to disclose every act of our lives.[2]

---

pages at which they begin are "Dreams & their Causes" (II, 1), "Mesmerism" (III, 14), "Clairvoyance" (V, 7), and "Insanity" (VI, 23). "Insanity" includes remarks on illness in general, as well as a page on the ancient mysteries, which may well not have been intended to fall within the title, especially since it is begun "We now enter upon another branch of of subject . . . " (VII, 6). Untitled subdivisions are not listed here.

[1] *Ibid.*, II, 14.

[2] *Ibid.*, II. 8.

It may be that he considered space unreal, but time real, or more likely both real, but space subject to mind.

> I have frequently alluded to the capacities of mind, acting in its excited state, independent of matter.
> This can be clearly proved by a subject under the mesmeric influence. The mind is then present with all things & needs only to be directed & the object is before it. Distance & space are nothing, & therefore, no time is required to pass the mind from one object to another. It is so in our waking thoughts. The mind is occupied with only one thing at a time & when it is directed to a new object of thought, the direction & the attention pass at the same instant. Nor does it require any longer time or any further effort to think of an object in the Chinese Empire than those nearest us. But the mind in our natural state depends upon the five senses for its external information & forms all its ideas of things thro' them. But in the excited state, it receives no impressions thro' the organs of sense, but every object, which acts at all, acts directly upon the mind or is presented by the influence of another mind.[1]

At some times Quimby can be taken as denying the reality of both space and time, at least for the mind in a mesmerized condition. In the excited or mesmeric state "the bodily sense cease to act--impressions are now conveyed directly to the mind. All space & time, in this state, is annihilated."[2]

---

[1]*Ibid.*, III, 1.

[2]*Ibid.*, II, 19.

We believe that experiments have proved that to a mind in its excited or dreaming state, when its bodily senses are dormant or inactive, & impressions are conveyed to it, by direct influences upon itself, all space, time, distance & matter are no obstacles to its action. In the cases above named, let us assume the fact, that there is no such thing as time with the mind, that the past, present & future are all present & displaid [sic] before it as upon a map & which are all visible & the explanation of the dreams which occurred previous to the actual occurrence are simple & readily understood.

The mind in this state looks forward & beholds occurrences, which have not yet transpired, but are reserved for a future event; yet it is not able to distinguish at what hour of time it will transpire. It, in fact, appears to the mind precisely like all other events, whether past or present & probably would not be remembered unless connected with some powerful emotion.[1]

The stories of second sight are also explainable upon the same principle laid down in our preceding work. Anxiety & constant thought upon subjects connected with our interests will sometimes lull us into a mesmeric or dreaming state, in which we can behold many scenes, sometimes real & sometimes fictitious.

The mind is excited into the clairvoyant state & is then enabled to perceive objects without bodily senses. The principle of sight is in the mind, & in our natural state, that principle developes [sic] itself thro' the eye. In the excited state it is

---

[1] *Ibid.*, II, 15-16.

developed independent of the eye; acting directly upon the object.[1]

What we dream will not always come to pass. This does not militate against the doctrine we have laid down, but will only confirm, what we have before declared in relation to the power of impression to regulate our thoughts--We will illustrate our subject in this manner. Suppose an individual, whose mind has been long upon one subject in which he finds himself deeply interested. While having his mind intently fixed under ordinary excitement with all his external faculties in action, he arrives at certain conclusions, which he believes to be correct & a strong impression is made governing the further actions of the mind in relation to the subject. Now this conclusion may not be correct, yet the individual would be firm in his position. A wrong impression, arising somewhere in the process of reasoning, has led to a wrong conclusion. Now if the individual could detect the first false step, he would correct the conclusion & vindicate truth. This is the natural operation of mind under ordinary excitement--Now place a subject in the dreaming or mesmeric state, & it become far more susceptible of impressions than before. It is, therefore, even more liable to receive a wrong impression, from some external cause or internal emotion, than in its natural state; & therefore, all of these false dreams passing into this excited state, may have, in his waking moments impressed upon his mind, something as having actually taken place which had not & did not transpire, with such power, as that the impression would controll [sic] the mind; & be led to an endless number of false conclusions which the facts in the case did not

---

[1]*Ibid.*, II, 20.

warrant--This is when the mind is led astray & does not receive impressions from facts but from preceding impressions. And the mind cannot distinguish the *false*, from the *true* cause, unless in the course of its progress, it is led to reconsider or review the whole scene with the idea of getting the facts & giving a true statement. The mind can act from facts, or rather receive its impressions from facts & when this is the case will always develope [*sic*] true results.[1]

There still remained a material world for Quimby. The mind simply was able to encompass it much better than most were aware. Even mind required time, in some sense. In the following he may have meant that time is relative, that there are different kinds of time in different kinds of experiences.

These experiments all confirm the doctrine of the rapidity of thought, that no time, as we are accustomed to measure it, is required for transactions which would occupy months & years in their performance. Yet the mind lives in these short periods required to pass upon such scenes apparently the whole time it would require to perform them. The mind in its dreaming or excited state, will pass from country to country, from shore to shore, mountain to mountain in rapid succession, feeling that it has actually past [*sic*] over a space of time sufficient to have accomplished all these distances. Under such influences, the mind would perform a pilgrimage to Mecca, experience all the particulars of the passage of the Rubicon, visit St. Petersburg & Moscow & be engaged in a whaling voyge [*sic*] in the Pacific Ocean all in rapid

---

[1]*Ibid.*, II, 21-22.

succession. Impression follows impression & results & conclusion follow as rapidly as they are produced. It is true that the mind compares every transaction of thought with its knowledge, previously attained. And it is thus deceived in the measure of time, when it does not through the organized body, perform its thoughts--It has no other method by which to calculate than such as is derived from previous knowledge.[1]

Despite his evidence of the remarkable abilities of mind, Quimby at this time did not question the independent existence of the material world, whatever its relations with mind might be. Mind somehow contacts it, for he maintains that

in the excited, dreaming or somnambulic subject, impressions are conveyed to the mind without the aid of the bodily organs; & that the faculties of the mind are acting in direct communication with objects--that the mind sees, hears, tasts [sic] & smells & feels, without the eyes, ears, tongue, nose & hands. And that precisely the same impressions may be conveyed to the mind directly without these organs as could be with them--[2]

Summarizing this area of Quimby's early thought:

We say then that the mind is capable of such excitement or of attaining to a state in which it may see without bodily eyes & also be present with all things at the same [time ?]--In other words, that to the mind, independent of the body, there is no

---

[1]*Ibid.*, III, 3-4.

[2]*Ibid.*, III, 11.

such impediment as time, space, distance & materiality, but that it only requires direction--& all its inherent faculties are in operation, giving its attention to the object to which it has been directed--The eye, ear, nose, sense of touch or the tongue is nothing except as they convey in our natural state certain sensations to the mind, from which a peculiar state of emotions arise. The faculty of sight, hearing, taste smell & touch exists in the mind independent of the organs by which objects are communicated to these faculties. Cut off these organs or appendages, & then, mind acts direct or receives its impressions directly from external & internal objects. If then, you institute a peculiar state of the mind, called mesmeric [originally "clairvoyant"] & close up the bodily eyes, the faculty of the mind does not cease to act. It is rather, in part, freeing the soul from its narrow confinement in the sphere of acquiring knowledge thro' the limited means of the eye, & giving it a range of sight limited only by the laws of mind & not the laws of matter. It returns more like itself, when it shall have been entirely divested of [originally "freed from"] man's materiality & left free, not to roam thruought [sic] the ranges of thought, but to be existent, with all its original faculties in full display, with all the creations of the Great First Cause.

We have given experiments to show the position we have taken--experiments which we challenge the world to gainsay, & which we cannot explain by any other principles than those we have laid down as governing the mind at all times under similar [originally "all"] circumstances. We say, conclusive proofs are given in these facts of the mind's capacity to see thro' all space or to be present with all things in the universe & behold them, independent of the knowledge of the operator.[1] [He gives such examples as a clairvoyant subject's describing a distant place in what the person who requested that he describe the place considered an inaccurate description, only to discover later that the place had been changed to the appearance described by clairvoyance without the knowledge of the one requesting the description.]

Perhaps because he was guarding against dismissing anything as merely imaginary without good cause, and quite possibly without more than some brief reference to Berkeley at his disposal, Quimby at this period apparently failed to appreciate Berkeley. From absence of reference to Berkeley later, it is not known whether Quimby ever gave him any thought later in life. In connection with the fluid theory, which will be taken up shortly, Quimby observes that "the fluid which really exists, is in the mind of the operator, being like Berkley's [sic] composition of matter, made up of ideas, impressions &c--"[2] He drops the matter and gives his remarks about Poyen and Collyer quoted above. After discussing the French committee's rejection of Mesmer's views, as contrasted with imagination, Quimby goes on:

If I direct my subject to do a certain thing at such a time, informing him what that is, & the result I wish to produce; & nothing further is said or thought about the direction untill [sic] the time arrives; & should the subject by his own voluntary act do according to my direction, is it the result of

---

[1] *Ibid.*, V, 14-15.

[2] *Ibid.*, IV, 6.

his imagination? If on the other hand, I desire him to do something at a certain time, but do not communicate to him my desires & he should without further cause, perform the very act, I wished, would it be the power of his imagination? If these are all the result of imagination, every thing which surrounds us exists only in imagery-- the world is ideal. The system of Berkley [sic] concerning the non existence of matter might well be adopted: & to carry up the science a little further, Hume, with his creations of images & impressions, would be the patern [sic] philosopher of the *images* of men!

We are rather disposed to confine the use of the word imagination to its proper difinition [sic] & not to confound it with realities. We must therefor [sic] reject both the "*magnetic fluid*" & the "*imagination*" as being the cause of the phenomena [sic, but perhaps referring to various phenomena combined] called mesmerism. We embrace a doctrine which both the committee & the followers of Mesmer do not deny, namely, the influence of mind over mind; not through the medium of a "*fluid*" or of the "*Imagination*" but by the direct contact with & action upon mind.[1]

Apparently Quimby was not much concerned with Berkeley or Hume. No commentator until now seems to have remarked on Quimby's reference to Hume, but the handwriting scarcely leaves any doubt that the name written is Hume. He was, however, very much concerned with the question of a fluid in mesmerism. This might be said to be the equivalent of the question of the ultimate nature of reality as seen from within the perspective of mesmerism. In part of his lecture notes Quimby answers

---

[1] *Ibid.*, III, 20-21.

Healing Hypotheses 237

Chauncey Hare Townsend's *Dispassionate Inquiry into Mesmerism*, quoted by Quimby from page 276, in part as follows:

> "Standing at some yards distant from a person, who is in the mesmeric state, (that person being perfectly stationary, & with his back to me), I, by a slight motion of my hand (far too slight to be felt by the patient thro' any distance of the air) draw him towards me as if I actually grasped him.
>
> "What is the chain of facts, which is here presented to me? First, an action of my mind, without which I could not have moved my hand; secondly, my hand's motion; thirdly, motion produced in a body altogether external to, & distant from myself. But it will at once be perceived, that, in the chain of events, as thus stated, there is a deficient link. The communication between me & the distant body is not accounted for. How could an act of my mind, originate an effect so unusual?" Here then follows the explanation. "That which is immaterial, can not, by its very definition, move masses of matter. It is only when mysteriously united to a body that spirit is brought into relationship with place or extention [sic], & under such a condition alone, & only thro' such a medium, can it propagate motion. Now, in some wondrous way spirit is in us incorporate. Our bodies are its medium of action. By them & only by them, as far as our experience reaches are we enabled to move masses of foreign matter. I may sit & will forever that yonder chair come to me, but without the direct agency of my body, it must remain where it is. All the willing in the world cannot stir it an inch. I must bring myself into absolute contact with the body which I desire to move. But in the case before us, I will, I extend my hands; I move them hither & thither &

I see the body of another person--a mass of matter external to myself, yet not in apparent contact with me--moved & swayed by the same action which stirs my own body. Am I thence to conclude that a miracle has been performed; that the laws of nature have been reversed; that I can move foreign matter without contact or intermediate agency. Or Must I not rather be certain, that, if I am able to sway a distant body, it is by means of some unseen lever; that volition is employing some thing which is equal to a body; something which may be likened to an extended corporeity, which has become the organ of my will?"[1]

Quimby replies:

Now if electricity or any other fluid can so connect mind & matter, I do not see why we may not connect ourselves with the chair in the supposition above & mind with its [?] organ of contact will cause the chair to move, on the same principle of connection as the body of the patient. Mind, no doubt, has equal power to connect itself with a chair as with any other material body by the agency of electricity. The body of the patient, without his mind, or acting independent of his own will, as it must, if it were moved by the mind of the operator, would be like every other material thing, & susceptible of action upon it by another mind to the same degree, as the chair, being no more or less. And if he proves to you that the motion of the patients' hands is frome [sic]the same mind as the motion of the operator's, thro' the agency of electricity, I will as conclusively prove that by the same agent your minds may be in

---

[1]*Ibid*., III, 23-24 and IV, 1.

"absolute contact" with any, or all, material bodies & that you can as easily move the universe of matter by the mind, as the body of one man. But, was not the experiment really performed? We answer, yes; without electricity or any other fluid. Not by the mind of the operator acting on the body of the patient, but upon his mind. It was mindacting upon mind. The proposition laid down by the Rev. gentleman that immateriality cannot move masses of materiality does not apply to destroy the influence or action of mind, being immaterial.over immaterial mind. We trust we have shown, by such experiments as have been introduced into the former part of this work, the great laws by which such facts are produced. That mind in the excited or mesmeric state is present with everything--that space, distance & material objects are no impediments to its action--that it is susceptible of impressions from other minds & will act under such impressions as it receives. Suppose, then, the operator is impressed to extend his hand; that impression is immediately made upon the mind of his patient & all the organs of his body, being under this controll [sic] of his mind, act in conformity to the impression. The distance from the patient is no obstacle because, mind acting directly without the medium of the bodily senses, knows nothing of space & distances--It only requires direction & it is present with the object--If electricety [sic] be the "lever" by which the operator moved the arm of the patient, as asserted by the Rev. Mr. Townsend, we would ask where the fulcrum rests, by which he gets his power. It might be answered, that it rests where the fulcrum of the globe's foundation, was supposed to--upon the "back of an enormous tortoise."

  We will say further, that the experiment above, could have been performed, without the motion of the hand of the operator, by his willing the patient or impresing [sic] his mind to extend the hand. So that all, that is necessary to be done in such experiments, is to give an impression to do an act upon the mind of the subject--the result immediately follows.[1]

Quimby comments on Dods:

> The Rev. Mr Dodds [sic] of Boston Mass--we believe, deals more extensively in the Magnetic Fluid than any other magnetiser. We have examined his book upon the subject of Mesmerism & can but smile at proofs so conclusively drawn in support of his theory--A careful reading of the whole work is a comfortable electuring [?] into a talkative sleep ending in ethereal & sublime explanatio[n]s, above the capacity of ordinary men. We were at a loss to determine whether the Rev. gentleman was most profuse in his language or his fluid! We do not doubt his sincerity in support of his fluid [originally "theory"], but must wonder at his credulity. It is a strong proof of the wanderings of an excited mind connected with a strong belief of the means by which wonderful results are produced.
> If we were to take up all the points in his theory & discuss them, we fear our pages would be too voluminous for ordinary purposes & that few would be inclined to peruse the investigation. [This is another indication that Quimby thought of this writing as something to be read by othors, not exclusively--at any rate--something for him to present in lectures.] Dodds [sic], like all others who

---

[1] *Ibid.*, IV, 1-3.

believe in the fluid-theory, supposed that something must be the medium of communication between mind & mind & between mind & matter separate from the bodily senses, & he has at once brought in the aid of a subtle fluid, which pervades all nature.[1]

"To introduce the whole [fluid] theory as it is contended for by most of those who have gone before me"[2] he makes a note to copy the fourth chapter of "a pamphlet published in the City of Boston AD 1843 entitled 'The History & Philosophy of Animal Magnstism' and dedicated by the Author to Robt H Collyer M D &c--" His failure to distinguish Robert H. Collyer from the often mentioned Dr. Collyer may add weight to the supposition that they are the same. He continues:

And who, after such an array of distinguished names would differ from their established [originally "sage"] theory! All these men were powerful magnetisers, & many of them of the first order of talent but we fear a little inclined to speculate upon a theory, rather than to elicit facts aside from theory. We are satisfied that they all believed in the Fluid, but what its character is, remains to be settled among them; as it seems no two agree to alow [sic] it the same name or character. If this "elastic, invisible ether pervaiding [sic] all Nature" causes all these phenomena it is a god-like power, second only to its Author. That it should operate so mysteriously, sometimes magnetising individuals by contact & at others, passes thro' the space of one hundred miles

---

[1] *Ibid.*, IV, 12-13.

[2] *Ibid.*, IV, 13.

& surcharges the patient & induces the mesmeric state; now made to reside in a letter, & again concealing itself in a tumbler of water, passing to the trunk of a tree; & from all these passing out upon a perticular [sic] individual & inducing the magnetic sleep. If I could possibly believe in the "Fluid Theory" it would be far more marvelous and astonishing, to trace out such laws as must govern [?] this "*invisible ether*" than the experiments which follow. Or perhaps it may be a principle without the pale of the law, governing itself under the direction of the operator, in part, at some times & at others, entirely at its own controll [sic].

Some of the theories of the old Philosophers who wrote upon the subject of the Soul appear to us rather speculative [?]--Fire & other imponderable agents so called were made not the connecting link of Soul & body, but Soul itself. Tracing the analogy of their ideas down to those of the Fluid system, we cannot see, why this Fluid might not be the Soul itself. It is the means we are taught thro' which the mind acts & we are to suppose of course that it cannot act at all, except thro', the fluid, when the bodily senses are closed. It may then be either the soul itself or a necessary appendage, without which altho, Soul might exist, it could not act or give any evidence of its existence.

The same Author, from whom we have quoted the "Fluid Theory," makes the following remarks in defence of his Theory against the powers of Imagination. "We disapprove this charge at once," (that it is all the work of the imagination)" by the fact that a person who has been magnetised several times, can be thrown into the magnetic sleep by the magnetiser, when he is at a distance of half a mile, and at a moment, when the person to be acted upon shall not even suspect it. This has been done successfully by a person who did not even know where the subject of his operations was at the time he made the attempt." Now upon the principle of a Fluid to be "directed upon the brain of the subject" how is it possible that direction can be given, when the operator is ignorant of the location of his subject; & how is it possible that this fluid can be made to pass thro' so great a distance? If the experiment above aluded [sic] to has been performed, could it have been done by the "Fluid"? If by a "Fluid" how could the operator so direct it as to strike upon the brain of the subject, when he was ignorant of his situation. How could he give effectual direction without knowing where to direct! And then the "Fluid" is to pass thro' the space of half a mile before it can act upon the subject. If such an experiment as the above, can be performed (& we know personally it can) with the fluid & not without it, we certainly must assign the power of intelligence to the "Fluid" & it being commanded by the mind of the operator, to go in search of his subject & induce sleep &c-- obeys its master. Such experiments as the above prove one of two things; namely, either, that there is no Fluid by which a communication is effected between mesmeriser & mesmerised, or that this Fluid is an intelligent being, capable of thought itself. We contend that there is no Fluid in the case. If others believe there is, & that it is capable of receiving intelligence & obeying commands, we are not accountable for such belief; but we leave the community who read & think the sole [?] of judging, which Theory, Fluid or no Fluid appears the most consistent.

I have performed a similar experiment upon my subject, Lucius, at a distance, sometimes knowing where he was and some times not knowing--Yet I did not use any fluid to my knowledge. We have, in another part of this work alluded to the experiment of the magnetised trees-- the experiments before the Committee at Paris, France in proof that no Fluid was in the tree & communicated to the subject. I will again repeat the experiment in substance. The subject was blindfold & led up to a magnetised tree & immediately fell into the magnetic sleep. Being again blindfold, was without his knowledge, led up to a tree not magnetised & also fell into the magnetic sleep. Proving conclusively that there was the same virtue in the magnetised & the natural tree.

There is another class of subjects introduced by magnetisers in proof of a magnetic fluid. Some are in the habit of giving their subjects a magnet by which they are thrown into the magnetic sleep. This experiment is explained by attributing the power to the magnet of communicating the Fluid to the subject &c--I have repeatedly magnetised subjects by any little metalic [sic] article presenting it to them, often having imbued it with the "Fluid." I have also performed the same experiment by passing to them a similar article not imbued with my Fluid & it produced the same results. I took two combs belonging to two ladies present & magnetised one of them, that is went thro' all the ceremony of magnetising it & the other I only took & past [sic] back to the lady without any operation upon it & both ladies were thrown into the magnetic sleep by these combs. The lady who received the comb not magnetised, was ignorant of that fact; & on the contrary believed it magnetised. Perkin's metalic [sic] points, are celebrated among mesmerisers & were considered sacred proffs [sic] of the fluid Theory. Yet after they had their run, some curious [?] wag introduced wooden points so neatly counterfeiting the metalic [sic] in their appearance that they would effect the same results upon a patient as the genuine points--I recollect a young man who in company with Dr. Cutter, the famed lecturer in this part of Maine, visited this place & being an easy subject to mesmerise, as a matter of defence, against the influence of powerful magnetisers, carried with him a magnet, believing it to be a safe preventive against all magnetic power. When armed with his magnet, no one could magnetise him, but without it, almost any one could induce sleep.

If, by some artful management we could have induced him to believe his magnet absent, altho' it might have been concealed about him, we venture to say that he would have been quite as easily operated upon--as if his magnet had really been absent. The truth is, that it was a matter of belief with the subject & he governed himself accordingly. If I could induce him to believe that magnetism or the magnet had nothing to do with mesmerism, or the excited state of mind called mesmeric, then the charm of the magnet would be broken. The Rev. Mr. Dodds [sic] has become so confident of a fluid medium of mind & its similarity to electricity that he has found it convenient & perhaps companionable to cary [sic] about with him when upon his tours of Lecturing, an Electric Machine & I believe he makes it an associate or assistant in throwing subjects into the magnetic state. If this Fluid be electricity, we do not see why Mr. Dodds [sic] could not with his machine surcharge a whole audience with a few turns of the handle by placing them in contact with its power.

We have witnessed the experiments of persons standing upon a glass stool & receiving a surcharge of electricity so that sparks might be seen to emit from various parts of their body, yet we saw no signs of magnetic sleep. Now if this Fluid be electricity, it does appear to me that the Electric Machine would be the very [?] first power by which subjects could be magnetised.

While in the City of Boston about one year since, I met with a friend, who began to question me as to the tricks I was [or "am" ?] playing in Magnetism & as we continued our conversation some time, he suddenly turned his head & after a few moments pause, charged me with an attempt to magnetise him! I did not let him know, but it was so in truth however, I did not think of it untill [sic] after he named it. I state this experiment to show, that I did not designedly use any fluid, indeed, could not have given direction to any; but the result upon my friend was just the same, no doubt, as though I had really sat down with the intention of performing an operation. This was the belief which he exercised in his mind, that I was trying my powers upon him & he became excited--& partially yielded. I do not think I exerted any power to controll [sic] him, yet he felt a power which he believed proceeded from me & it began to induce the mesmeric state, into which he was passing.

A friend of mine, a powerful magnetiser, who called on me not long since, operated upon a young lady in my family & threw her into the mesmeric sleep. He was a firm believer in the Magnetic Fluid & every thing was done according to the laws supposed to govern it. I began to exercise the power of my mind over his subject & she would readily obey me--Desiring her to come to me, she immediately turned her head & was about to rise when her operator observing the movement, began to cut off the fluid with his hand, so as to shut out the power. I was gaining over her. I ceased trying to impress her mind with the desire of coming to me & she turned back--During the same sleep I exercised a controll [*sic*] over her which was observed by the operation, & when he discovered it, awoke her saying it was very dangerous mixing up the fluids of diferent [*sic*] magnetisers upon the subject at the same time. I could not induce him to go on with his experiments, & was obliged to do what I could to show, that there was no danger from mixing up fluids &c--or that all the danger arising in the case would be from the fear & belief of the mesmeriser. I then performed a few experiments & requested him to exercise all his fluid power to counteract them. I am unable to say, whether the fear of "*disturbing the fluid*" did not prevent him from making an effort, for all my experiments succeeded.

Steel and various kinds of matter are supposed to have powerful influence over subjects in the mesmeric sleep. Experiments have been introduced to prove the suposition [*sic*]. Some operators cannot exercise their magnetic powers, if they have about them steel or silver. This is also a matter of belief. If an operator believes he cannot make an impression upon his subject, while this or that metalic [*sic*] substance is about him, then as a matter of course, he will not; but remove what he thinks is the difficulty & then mind acts in full faith & produces a full & decided expression.

I recollect, that when I first began to magnetise, I had all this horrid fear about the influence of mettle [*sic*], steel, silver &c upon the subjects & being a full believer then in the Fluid Theory, supposed some strange connection in all metalic [*sic*] substances, with the magnetised subjects. Having on a certain occasion put my subject into sleep often surcharging him with the fluid, a young lady present held the scissors pointing directly towards the head of the subject. Upon my first observing it, I was excited fearing some bad result. The impression was conveyed to the mind of the subject & all the consequences I feared would result, followed. This to my mind, at that time, was conclusive proof of the power of certain metalic [sic] substances, highly magnetic, upon a subject.

I have had very many excellent experiments in Phreno Magnetism exciting the organs by pointing a steel rod pointed at one end ["& blunt at the other" crossed out] to the supposed location, believing the fluid past [sic] out of myself thro' this rod into the organ. When I held the sharp point of the rod towards the organ the subject would immediately arouse & answer to the direction; but if I held the blunt end, ["towards any organ" crossed out] it would not effect him [her?]. This to me, as I was trying my experiments to prove whether there was any fluid or not, was strong testimony in favor of the fluid system. I had supposed there must be some agent to bring out such results & immediately embraced the theory adopted by most magnetisers, for want of something better. Having adopted, as a matter of belief, an agent by which I could bring about this excited state of mind, I had as[s]ign[e]d it certain laws as I knew to govern electricity. I had all the faith to produce a result when I directed the pointed end to the organ I wished to excite; but when I reversed the point & presented the blunt end I did not suppose for an instant that the excitement would follow. So the results corresponded with my own feelings. I have witnessed the same experiments performed by other mesmerists & they always advance such facts as I have named as conclusive proofs of a fluid Theory. Since I have abandoned the fluid Theory,

Healing Hypotheses

I find no difficulty in using either end of the steel rod or use no rod at all & placing myself at a respectable distance from the subject, can produce the same results as I did when the steel rod & fluid Theory were the only means of my operation.

When in the City of Boston with my subject, one of the most powerful magnetisers put my subject into the magnetic sleep & proceded [*sic*] with his experiments in phreno-magnetism [originally and finally this wording, but with a seemingly second version crossed out: "proceded to experiment upon my subject in his waking state"] to convince me that the organs were excited by a fluid. He remained in contact with the subject & directed his fluid with the points of his fingers. I was sitting in the room some distance from the scene [seemingly "scenen"] of operation & exerted myself to counteract ["reverse" is crossed out] the impression given by the operator [originally exerted "all my powers to make a counter impression to the operator's design, & produced results opposite to the direction of the organs excited"]. The operators [*sic*] experiments all failed altho' he was in contact with the subject and as he supposed was filling up his head with the electric or magnetic fluid.

I also entertained the same idea with other magnetisers about the condition of the atmosphere as being favorable or unfavorable to successful experiments. I could always, under this belief, succeed better in fine clear weather. Indeed, my experiments seldom succeeded in a dull and cloudy atmosphere. I had been giving some very interesting experiments ["at Bath, Maine," crossed out] during one evening & did not know but the atmosphere was clear & bright as when I entered the hall. At the close of the experiments I was astonished to learn that, for the last two hours, during the time of my best experiments, the atmosphere had been cloudy & that rain had been falling. This circumstance was one of the first, which led to the rejection of the fluid theory.

I believed in the power to mesmerise a tumbler of water which, upon being drunk, would throw the patient into the magnetic sleep, & have often amused my audience by this simple experiment. I supposed, I did imbue the water with some new virtue & this was also the belief of the subject, & the results followed as I had anticipated. The experiment of the silk handkerchief has been one ["of mine" crossed out] I have performed repeatedly. I would magnetise the handkerchief & pass it to the subject & it would induce the mesmeric sleep. I was so confident in the fluid theory & that silk would effect [sic] its operation, that on one occasion when I had put my subject to sleep & a lady was sitting [or setting] near by [sic] dressed in silk his hands & feet were extended towards her dress. These simple facts all went to confirm me in the belief of the fluid theory. Yet I have been compelled to reject them all & I find there is no difficulty in producing the same results with a tumbler of clear water as when I have surcharged it with magnetic fluid; or with a silk handkerchief in its natural state as when magnetised. And I can with all safety allow ladies to sit near my subject in silk aparrells [sic] without fear of distracting his slumber.

I have magnetised a ceder [sic] twig & given it to my subject & he would immediately pass into the magnetic State. I have also given him other articles & told him I had magnitised them, altho, I had not, yet he would pass into sleep as before. We might multiply simple cases of this class to a very great number but all of them would terminate as those I have mentioned. I have performed them with the fluid & have done the same without it.[1]

Undoubtedly when Quimby refers to his use of fluid, he means that he made use of whatever passes or other procedures were supposed to impart fluid to objects.

From some of these observations it might be thought that Quimby simply discovered such susceptibility to suggestion as now generally is recognized, due entirely to the subject's awareness of suggestions given to him in an ordinary manner. However, Quimby found more than this. Some of his most important experiments dealt with the waking state.

It has sometimes been supposed that subjects are not susceptible of influence from the operator only in the sleeping state. This is not so. Dr. Buchanan, altho a devoted advocate of the fluid, has given many experiments, in proof of a controlling power, which the operator may have, over the subject. It is, with me, my daily practice to perform most of my experiments, when the subject could not know in his waking moments, my wishes, while to all appearance he is not influenced by any one. I have frequently exerted my power to impress upon the mind of some person in my presence a wish to do something, keeping distinctly in mind, what I would have him do. And the subject would soon do the very act, which I had wished to bring about. I have frequently operated upon a subject in his waking state producing, certain feelings in him corresponding to my own. I have relieved [originally "extracted"] pain in hundred[s] of instances to the benefit & happiness of persons under my influence; have releaved [sic]

---

[1]*Ibid*, IV, 14-24.

headache, pain in any part of the body. As I was writing a few sentences above, an individual called on me & stated that his foot was very painful to him; & if I could ease the pain, & adding that he did not believe I could, that he would not deny the fact & should be a believer in Mesmerism! I operated upon his foot & released the pain. He acknowledged the fact & began, he said, to be a little more serious.

Another individual present, who began to ridicule the fact & made some strong remarks against any power I might exercise over him, desired me to make a simple experiment upon his foot & leg--I immediately wrote upon a piece of paper not letting any one know the writing & laid it down upon the table & told him I had written upon that paper what kind of a sensation I would produce upon his foot & leg. I commenced the operation & in about two minutes, he said his foot & leg began to prickle & felt as tho' it was going to sleep. I handed him the paper & he read just wat [sic] he had felt. Some have replied to similar experiments above, that they were the results of Imagination. We reply that the subject did not know what kind of a sensation we should produce & therefore could not imagine in the case. To him it was a reality, because he felt the prickling sensation & did not imagine [Quimby's spelling of the word may be "immgine"] that I was going to produce it. I have frequently taken persons & endeavored to produced [this is the way that the sentence apparently started originally. and the word was not changed when inserting "endeavored to"] a warm or cold sensation upon their limbs

Healing Hypotheses 253

without their knowledge & have succeded [*sic*] in bringing about my wishes.[1]

An experiment of interest in itself and also from its probably relating to the Dods subject mentioned by Lucius Burkmar, in his journal,[2] in relation to Skowhegan, is related to Quimby. If this was on the same occasion, it dates the manuscript, or at least this part of it, as not earlier than 1844, as references already seen do also.

In the town of Skowhegan on the banks of the Kennebec, I met with a young man deaf & dumb, but was a very sensitive subject & easily operated upon in his waking moments. I requested to sit down & place his hand upon the table & count by raising his hand up & down. I then asked some one to direct me to stop him when he had made a certain number of counts naming to me the number. When he had made the particular counts I willed him to stop & he did so. I then impressed his mind with the desire to walk back & forth upon the floor, & he arose & commenced walking. A gentleman asked me to stop him when he arrived at a certain point & I exercised my power upon his mind & he stopped instantly at the very point. I then desired him to speak to me & he made a noise--I made a stronger impression upon his mind to speake [*sic*] louder & he made a stronger effort to talk ["speak" crossed out], graduating his effort, & raising his voice or noise with my thoughts impressing him to speak louder or softer. Some one then asked him in writing, if he heard me speak ["to him" crossed out] & he answered "that his mind

---

[1]*Ibid.*, IV, 24 and V, 1.

[2]Seale (ed.), *The Complete Writings*, I, 32-52.

heared" [sic]. And so it is. The mind hears sees, feels & causes every action of the body. And impressions are conveyed directly upon the mind, when the attention is given to the operator in such a manner as to shut out all other influences. And to produce these impressions & sensations, when the mind of the subject is thus prepared, the operator must produce in himself the same sensation which he could communicate to the subject [following "must" the sentence originally read "feel in himself just as he would have the subject"]. The experiments last mentioned upon the deaf & dumb young man were performed without the subject knowing, by any of his outward senses, what I could design. I was behind the subject & out of his sight, during the most of the experiments. I took every precaution in this case as I have done repeatedly, to place the experiments upon such a basis that no one could attribute these to the imagination.[1]
It is necessary to draw the attention of the subject to myself in order to receive the impression: because no one could receive the impressions from external objects unless he should give his attention to them. . . . So in mesmerism, some powerful impression must be produced to draw the attention of the subject & exclude other external influences & then the mind is prepared for further action.[2]

It may not be clear whether the initial impression need be made by conventional means, such as a spoken or written request for one's attention, or perhaps just being noticed by one to be impressed.

---

[1] *Ibid.*, v, 2-4.

[2] *Ibid.*, v. 2.

It might be a question in regard to all the experiments we have presented in this volume whether it is really the strong intellectual power of a mind, which may gain the ascendncy [sic] over another, & hold it in complete submission. . . . We answer that, we do not think it is great intellectual power; but the capacity or power of arresting the attention & producing a strong impression. And this faculty may be cultivated & enlarge its power to produce impressions & arrest the attention of mind to the exclusion of surrounding influences. We have mentioned the fact in another page, that the idea of magnetising or mesmerising only those persons who are dull & enjoy poor health & weak minds is exploded. The more intelligent the mind, if the attention can be fixed & drawn away from surrounding influences, the more certain you are of producing the excited or mesmeric state in the highest degree--A bright, intelligent & thoughtful person, enjoying good health always makes the best subject.

We do not therefore claim a more powerful intellect by which we can produce such results upon mind, but attribute it to a natural & cultivated power in this capacity which I am enabled to exercise & produce such experiments as are called mesmeric, magnetic &c--The fact, that the community have always laid it down as a general principle that only a more powerful mind can operate & controll [sic] a weaker, has retarded the progress of this branch of intellectual philosophy--The idea, no doubt, arose from some self-conceited personage, or perhaps a numerous class of those who were public magnetisers, desirous of claiming all the intellect, which is really worth having--It is in fact we are compelled to acknowledge, that some of my predecessors in this branch of science, seem to have possessed no other intellectual faculty than that of mesmerising; & the consequence was that they would be desirous of instructing the world to believe, that the power they exercise is indeed [originally "purely"] that of a great mind--to be surpassed by no other power. All we have to remark upon this class of philosopher is, that whatever discoveries & advances they have made in the progress of human knowledge should be thankfully received. And the follies & egotisms, which have been interwoven with their progress, should be rejected, as the consoling food for the vanity & self-esteem of its projectors. No man would be justified in rejecting the whole Copurnican [sic] system because some *wandering* genius, desirous of making himself greater than the rest, should have advanced the idea & proceded [sic] to prove it, that the earth is spherical & turns on its axis every twenty four hours & is kept in motion on the constant tramping of an enormous meamouth [sic] upon the equator. "Retain the good & reject the evil." Then will science advance--[1]

Except for some writing about the mysteries, perhaps an afterthought inspried by Collyer's dealing with the subject, this is the conclusion of the "lecture notes." However, some other parts of the "lecture notes" are to be noted here.

At one point Quimby says:

> We have . . . given examples, proving to a demonstration that there are such states of mind as Clairvoyant, Thought Reading & that arising from association. That the mind some times acts in one of these capacities & sometimes in another & is also

---

[1]*Ibid.*, VII, 3-5.

governed at other times by the principle of association.[1] Now the difficulty in a clairvoyant subject is this. The mesmerised mind is liable to be under the partial controll [sic] of all these conditions at the same time & would describe an object partly from actual independent sight, partly from thought reading & partly from association; & the result always is, *a total factum in all.* We are not able, in this early stage of our science, to give definite rules by which one can tell how far the subject may be led astray from independent sight by these two other principles [We have no standard] by which to ascertain how much weight our own thoughts, or associations of the subject, may have over the mesmerised mind. In the progress of future advancement, this mystery may be solved; & subjects, under proper regulations, may discover to the operator, the true action of his mind, whether it be *Seeing, Thought-reading* or *Association.*

When mesmerism has attained this hight [sic] in the march of its discoveries, a new & brighter era in the history of the world will have dawned upon humanity--the ["grave of" crossed out] ignorance of the past will be entombed in the light ["forgetfulness" crossed out] of the future, & truth, disrobed of superstition will govern paramount, the universe of immortal [?] thought.

Our remarks have thus far been confined to what we are pleased to call the ["metaphysical" crossed out in favor of use later in the sentence]

---

[1]In speaking of ordinary knowledge, Quimby says, "a succession of objects presented, multiplies the number of impressions, which follow, in a ten fold ratio. The principle of association, which is a successive train of impressions is set in operation—keeps the mind ever on the stretch." *Ibid.*, I, 14.

development of the metaphysical mysteries of our subject (mesmerism). We have sought to select that system which appears to be most consistent with the facts we have offered--that system only by which we can explain satisfactorily the wonderful phenomena of mind. We have thought our course thus far justifiable upon the ground, that a complete knowledge of the development of mesmerism is necessary to a good understanding of the practical part of our science. We protest against a mere knowledge of results without cause. We should know rather the *cause* & we may then produce or prevent results. Our course has been to introduce such explanation as appears consistent with all experiments given & as far as we had the power, to enlighten the understanding rather than to mystify what already has been too mysterious. How far we have succeeded, an intelligent community will act as our tribunal & we shall rest satisfied with their candid decision. We now come to the useful-practical part of our subject. It is to this part of our work we would solicit the attention of our reader. The study of the philosophy of science is entertaining & instructive, but the utility of science, is often all the great point to be attended in its advances--We shall procede [*sic*] to show what connection mesmerism as we understand it, has with the relief of suffering humanity & consequently its necessary connection with medical science.[1]

---

[1]*Ibid.*, VI, 24-25.

Even at this relatively early period, Quimby says, "We lay it down as a principle, that all medical remedies effect [sic] the body only through the mind."[1]

Quimby says of competing schools of medicine:

The different Theories of practice . . . no doubt grew out of the uncertainty of medicine. And the uncertainty of medicine was the necessary result of a want of a knowledge of those laws by which the animal economy of man is sustained. It all procedes [sic] from the mistaken notion, that medicine operates upon the organs which constitute the body without any reference to the impressions which it conveys to the mind. [This might be taken to mean a direct action by the drug or it might mean the patient's belief about the drug, or perhaps the physician's. If there were such action of drugs, it might be something like the Dods belief, expressed later, in physical impressions.] Medicine upon [?] the organs of the body, if it were to act upon them alone, would always produce the same results upon the same organisations. . . .
And the same medicines do not affect different individuals in the same manner; because they, upon being taken, convey to these minds different impressions & the mind exercises a controll [sic] over the body & answeres [sic] to the impressions, by a result upon the functions of the body, either good or bad. Every intelligent physician with whom I have conversed has always acknowledged that mind has much to do with the taking of medicine, if good results follow. That no physician could probably do his patient much good, unless he should possess the confidence of such patient.

---

[1] *Ibid.*, VI, 11.

Intelligent physicians, altho, they have full faith in medical remedies & believe that these, with the mental emotions of the patient are the only restoratives of health, yet do not often all consider that remedies possess such astonishing powers as is supposed by the quacks. I believe that there is a virtue in medicine, which, when taken by the patient, conveys impressions to the mind & that these impressions often result in the entire restoration of health. [Possibly it is significant that Quimby says "taken by" rather than "given to" or some other expression of passivity on the part of the patient, this perhaps implying that the medicine itself is powerless.] The mind of man is generally taken up with surrounding objects & seldom is attracted to contemplate the body to which it is attached [a significant, but not surprising, view of mind].

If however by any attraction it should be turned upon the body, a war [?] seems to arise, between the body & mind, & the mind appears to be unwilling to abide its confinement--Diseas [sic] then begins to pray upon the body & continues to increase untill [sic] the soul departs & leaves matter to return to its original dust. We think we have abundant proof of the power of the mind to controll [sic] the health of the body. Patients are advised to travel in pleasant countries & visit watering places, to bathe in sea water, & mineral water, to spend the cold season in milder climates, engage more in the pleasantries of society or even do anything by which the mind may be led off from its old habits of working [?] with the body. But why should we enumerate perticular [sic] methods of restoring the health of a patient without a dose of medicine. All these methods are medicines for the mind, they leave lasting impressions & they restore the health. So is every

> remedy taken into the stomach or externally applied to the body, a medicine for the mind--And it is only so far effectual to the end designed as it impresses the mind. We do not then discard the use of medicines, but rather recommend them; but we protest against such use, unless he who prescribes knows the laws by which his remedy is governed.
> The true design of all medicine is to lead the mind to certain results & then it, the mind, will restore the body. No matter what this medicine is, if it accomplishes all the physician designs. [The next sentence appears to be the conclusion of the last one.] It will effect a cure if it produces a healthy state of the mind. Thus it is that very small doses, under the direction of the Homeopathic practice, effect such astonishing cures--Thus it is that so many drops of pure water taken under the direction of a skillful physician, will restore health--Thus it is that a change of scenery gives new & pleasant impressions to the mind of a patient & results in a perfect restoration of the bodily health.[1]

After illustrating his view, Quimby says that

> it is really the mind upon which an impression is to be made & ... the medicine has nothing to do in the matter only so far as it induces a state of feeling antecedent to a restoration.[2]

Since the physician is unaware that "mind acts upon mind" (which might be taken as the motto of Quimby's early

---

[1] *Ibid.*, VI, 1-4. *Cf.* the observations about the nature of all healing (and other) influence in Apendix L, no. 14.

[2] *Ibid.*, VI, 5.

period, as "the explanation is the cure" is of his later period),

> the quack may effect more than the intelligent physician, because he has more confidence in the remedies he applies. He, however, believes the great remedy is really in the medicine & has full confidence in administering it to the patient, & thereby impresses his mind with the restorative powers of his balsam. Perhaps, the quack might not understand the composition of his medicine, yet he knows the results & is so firm in his belief that he would almost bring about the result if the medicine had by mistake been omitted. The intelligent physician knowing the properties of his medicine & having seen much practice does not attribute an almighty charm to his antidote & therefore manifests less confidence in his skill. His mind influences directly that of his patient & he too will place but little confidence in the medicine. The result is that the patient becomes worse. Now had the physician understood or rather had he brought into his practice the great law that "mind acts upon mind" he might have remedied the whole evil. He would then have commanded all the influence which his powerful mind, could exert over the mind of his patient & thus with the powerful or gentle action of the medicine directed a healthful result. In some instances, a powerful medicine taken under the impression of a good influence may do much & indeed in some instances entirely restore the patient. But it acts far more healthfully upon the patient when the mind is rightly directed.
>
> This principle of making deep impressions upon patients by a medicinal [?] or other process seems to have been well understood by Hippocrates, the great father of cures [originally "medicine"]. [Quimby cites an example of the technique of

Hippocrates of] employing external agents to impress deeply the mind with the idea of effectual remidy [sic]. We might enumerate other instances, where the great cause of success in a particular treatment of disease, was similar in principle to the above; but history is full of such examples & daily observation of every student of human nature confirms its records. Every action which results to the benefit or injury of the patient, is direct upon the mind which immediately answers the impression, upon the disease of the body. Matter, in itself, is ["nothing" is crossed out] capable of no action, except by chemical process [originally "action"], unless connected with a mind or spirituality. [This sentence is a very interesting possible indication of his early ontology, in which he may have started to say that matter is nothing, but backed away from that view.] The health & vigor of the body depends solely upon the condition & action of the mind--; because the immaterial part of man governs the material-- matter or body connected with mind is under the immediate controll [sic] of ["mind" crossed out] this spirituality. [This sentence not only emphasizes Quimby's basic point here, but raises the question of the difference between mind and spirit; it may be that here he simply wished to avoid repeating the word mind, but it may be a foreshadowing of his later fuller recognition of the divine dimension of reality beyond the mental; however, spiritual with Swedenborg and various others can mean simply the invisible, rather than the divine, which sometimes is called the celestial. Again, in this sentence, it is not clear whether the s of spirituality is capitalized.] If, then the mind by external or internal influences has received impressions to destroy the health & vigor of the body & the impressions cannot be removed, then the body follows that state of mind & readily submits. If the mind of a patient does not feel some confidence in the restorative powers of a medicine taken, there is a probable chance that it will do the patient no good. His mind counteracts the impression usually conveyed to the minds of most patients, by a strong [or stray ?] impression that it could do no good.[1]

After dealing with the reducing of medical effectiveness by competition among physicians, Quimby continues:

> We return to an expression we have before uttered, that we have full confidence in the power of certain medicines to produce healthful results; but further assert, that the mind of the patient or physician may so controll [sic] this power as to produce disasterous [sic] results. We protest against this pretended ignorance of the physician upon the causes of the uncertainty of medicine. He should or ought to know what they result from or the great governing principle by which a failure follows. We exclaim against the daring & lawless courage of a physician, who marches up, blindfold [sic] to the battleground of disease strugling [sic] with nature, often failing in his efforts to effect a reconciliation, raises a war club & strikes at random. If he luckily hits disease, the patient is restored & if not, the patient dies.
> Our remarks thus far go to show that the mind has much to do with the practice of medicine & that results are from impressions conveyed to it by some process. We now procede [sic] to illustrate by experiments, what mesmerism has to do with

---

[1] *Ibid.*, VI, 6-8.

Healing Hypotheses 265

> diseases & shall at the same time show the influence of mind acting upon mind.
> By the action of my mind upon my patient in his waking state, I can produce the same results which flow from the taking of medicine. I can produce an emetic or cathartic, a disiness [sic] or pain in the head, relieve pain in any part of the system & restore patients by acting directly upon their minds [originally "restore any patient who could be restored by medicine"].[1]

After reporting various healings and mesmeric anesthesia for a surgical operation,[2] Quimby turns to the topic of insanity. In part, he observes:

> This disease among physicians is not usually attributed to flow from the same sources as what they term those of the body & therefore they do not resort to the same remedies--Physicians, generally call Insanity a disease of the mind while fever & other similar states are diseases of the body--I maintain that all diseases are only known to exist as they effect [sic] the mind of the patient-- that is, there would be no disease which could effect [sic] an individual provided it could not make a sensation upon his mind. If he did not feel sick, he would not probably be sick.[3]

In discussing a dislocated elbow, Quimby says that

---

[1] *Ibid.*, VI, 10.

[2] *Ibid.*, VI, 22-23.

[3] *Ibid.*, VI, 26.

all the pain which was the result of the falling from the horse was in the mind, being the only part of man susceptible of sensation--that the mere blow or contusion would not produce any pain unless there was a mind which could feel the blow; because matter is not supposed to have the power of sensation--We might bring many facts, as we trust we have in the former part of this work, to show when disease is to be remedied--where of course it must flow from to effect [sic] the person & when [where?] an impression is produced from which follows all the phenomena of disease both of body & mind--But alude [sic] to the subject, here to illustrate our ideas upon Insanity--And by the results we have affected [sic] upon diseases by operating upon mind, we think the argument is conclusive, that all diseases including insanity flow from the impressions upon the mind as their first cause.[1]

In insanity

The mind is governed & controlled by the same laws in this state as in the natural or dreaming state--It acts from real impressions under the full belief of the real causes of such impressions--This state is no doubt induced by some powerful impression upon the mind which cannot be removed by slight impressions produced upon the mind from common & every day objects. If this state is removed at all, it must be done by inducing some counteracting impression, which will lead the mind into a different channel of thought. This state of mind often exhibits in the individual more acuteness of intelligence in almost every subject

---

[1] *Ibid.*, VI, 27.

than when in its natural condition. He will reason correctly altho' from unsound [originally "wrong"] data & return answers justifying his conduct, which would display a thoughtful & premeditating mind--[1]

In less than two decades Quimby's views changed to the extent that a patient could ask and he could reply as follows in perhaps the best known of his writings, "Questions and Answers," of 1862. This writing used to be loaned to patients, including the future Mary Baker Eddy, for study. Dresser considered this question, the eighth, to be "obscure," and observes that Quimby does not characterize God this way elsewhere, and does so here to bring meaning from the question.[2] However, the question and answer here serve as an interesting transition from his earlier period to his later one. Little is known of his years between them. In the following quotation the major variations among the three copies of the writing known to exist are indicated by parentheses.[3]

---

[1] *Ibid.*, VI, 24.

[2] *The Quimby Manuscripts*, both eds., p. 175n.

[3] *The Quimby Manuscripts*, both eds, pp. 174-75, contains the question and answer quoted, slightly edited by Dresser, who notes at the start of "Questions and Answers" that "it is printed as originally written, with a few changes in punctuation and capitalization to conform to writings of the same year." (p. 165) The three written copies are parts of the 1947 addition to the Library of Congress Quimby collection. They are titled "Questions and Answers," "Answers to questions asked by one of my patients," and "Answers to questions asked me by patients." Apparently these are the three copies listed by Dresser at 1st ed., p. 18, 2nd ed., p. 24 as being in the

Suppose a person (was) kept in a mesmeric state (a long time), what would be the result? Would he act independently if allowed? If not, is it not an exact illustration of the condition we are in, in order to have matter (,) which is only an idea (,) seem real to us, for we act independently?

I think I understand your question. God is the great mesmeriser or magnet,[1] (&) he speaks man or the idea into existence, & attaches his sense to the idea & (so) we are to ourselves just what we think we are. So is a mesmerised (-ism) subject, they are to themselves matter. You may have as many subjects as you will & they are all in the same relation to each other as they would be in the state we call waking. So this is proof that we are affected by (each other) one another, sometimes independent & sometimes governed by others, but always retaining our own identity, with all our ideas of matter and subject to all its changes, as real as it is in the natural or waking state (after "ideas of matter": as real as it is to you in your state, subject to all its changes).

Although undoubtedly Quimby developed his views largely from his own experimentation both with mesmerism and with his abilities of a higher sort after his mesmeric period, in developing his thought he probably had more (which is not necessarily to say very much) knowledge of the views of philosophers to stimulate his

---

collection from which *The Quimby Manuscripts* was published.

[1]*Cf.* Whitehead's view of the lure of God through the initial aim of an occasion of experience. See Appendix L, no. 6, and Whitehead quotations from PR 522 and 526 in that appendix.

Healing Hypotheses

thought than has been supposed by most people, especially those who have limited their study of his writings to those contained in *The Quimby Manuscripts.* Yet one finds there:

> Are our senses mind? I answer, no. This was the problem ancient philosophers sought to solve. Most of them believed the soul, senses, and every intellectual faculty of man to be mind, therefore our senses must be mind. The translator of Lucretius says Lucretius attacks the ancient academics who held the mind to be the sole arbiter and judge of things, and establishes the senses to be the arbitrators. For, says he, "whatever can correct and confute what is false, must of necessity be the criterion of truth, and this is done by the senses only." This difference is true in part. Both were right. But they confused mind and senses into one, like the modern philosophers who make wisdom and knowledge, mind and senses, Jesus and Christ, synonymous. Now mind and senses are as distinct as light and darkness, and the same distinction holds good in wisdom and knowledge, Jesus and Christ. Christ, Wisdom and spiritual senses are synonymous. So likewise are Jesus, knowledge and mind. Our life is in our senses: and if our wisdom is in our mind, we attach our life and senses to matter. But if our wisdom is attached to Science, our life and senses are in God, not in matter; for there is no matter in God or Wisdom; matter is the medium of Wisdom.
>
> This difference has been overlooked by the ancients. And modern philosophers have put mind and soul in matter, thus making a distinction without a difference. Now according to modern philosophy, the soul, mind, life and senses are all liable to die; but according to this truth mind is spiritual matter, and all matter must be dissolved. Wisdom is not [physical] life. Our senses are not

life. But all of these are solid and eternal; and to know them is life and life eternal. Life is in the knowledge of this wisdom, and death is in the destruction of your opinions or matter.

I will give some experiments of a man of wisdom acting through and dissolving the man of matter so the man of wisdom can escape. This process is Science. Take for example two persons, or you and myself. One wishes to communicate to the other some fact. You feel a pain, I also feel it. Now the sympathy of our minds mingling is spiritual matter. But there is no wisdom in it, for wisdom is outside of matter. If we both feel the same pain, we each call it our own; for we are devoid of that wisdom which would make us know we were affecting each other. Each one has his own identity and wants sympathy, and the ignorance of each is the vacuum that is between us. So we are drawn together by this invisible action called sympathy. Now make man wise enough to know that he can feel the pains of another, and then you get him outside of matter. The wisdom that knows this has eternal life, for life is in the knowledge of this wisdom. This the world is unacquainted with.

Now Jesus had more of this life or truth than any other person, and to teach it to another is a science.... There are a great many kinds of life. The natural man begins at his birth. Animal life is not vegetable, and vegetable is not animal life. And there is another kind of life that is not understood, and that is the life that follows the knowledge of this great truth. The word "life" cannot be applied to Wisdom, for that has no beginning and life has. The word death is applied to everything that has life. All motion or action produces life, for where there is no motion there is no life. Matter in motion is called life. Life is the action of matter, and to know it is a truth, and to know how to produce it is Wisdom. This Wisdom was possessed by Jesus, for He says: "My sheep hear my voice and I give unto them eternal life." "I (Christ) and my Father are one."[1]

More on philosophers is found in Collie's presensation of Quimby writings. The following is dated 1864:

> Disease is as old as man's existence but the causes of it have never been explained. Various causes have been given. The ancients admitted disease and then tried to show that it arose from the people's habits of living. The Epicurean philosophers tried to show that man by his own acts caused his disease. Lucretius one of the pupils of Epicurus contended that man is the cause of his own misery by his own belief. He does not use these words but I shall show that that was what he meant and being so misrepresented, his ideas have never found their way into the minds of the Christians of our day because he showed that the religion of his day was the cause of all the disease, and trouble that men suffered. To show this was his labor in his poem that has never been understood. The reader will see by going back one hundred years before Jesus how the people were excited by the religion of that time. To see what Lucretius had to contend with is to know what the people believed in. The effect of religion on the people Lucretius showed in his poem. I will give

---

[1] *The Quimby Manuscripts*, both eds., pp. 244-45; "physical" in brackets added by Dresser. This article apparently was written in January, 1861; see 249n., 430, and 230.

some extracts. [He quotes from the first few pages of *De Rerum Natura*.]

"Indeed mankind in wretched bondage held and lay groveling on the ground galled by the yoke of what is called religion. From the sky, this tyrant showed her head and with grim looks hung over us poor mortals here below until a man of Greece with stea[dy] eye dared look her in the face and first opposed her power. Here not the fear of Gods or thundrous roar kept back, nor threatening tumults of the sky, but still the more they roused the active virtue of his aspiring soul as he pressed forward to break through nature's scanty bounds, his mind's quick force prevailed. And so he passed by far the flaming portals of this world and wandered with his comprehensive soul all over the mighty spaces. From thence returned triumphant, told us what things may have being and what may not and how a finite power is fixed to earth, a bond it cannot break. And religion which we feared before by him subdued, we tread upon in turn. His conquest makes us equal to the Gods." It is generally believed that the writers of the Epicurean philosophy were men who opposed everything that was good, but they are misrepresented. They opposed the errors and superstitions of their day and to do this was to show that the heathen mythology was based on nothing but a belief. So he shows the absurdity of their religion. The Pythagoreans held to the transmigration of souls. A poet who lived about a hundred years before Lucretius affirmed that the "Soul of Homer was in his body, but that he might not injure Pluto, he bequeathed to the infernal mansion not the soul nor the body, but the ghost which the ancients held to be a third nature of which together with the body and soul the whole man consisted." Speaking of this class of philosophers, Lucretius says "And yet the nature of the soul we know not whether formed with the body or at the birth infused and then by death cut off she perishes as bodies do or whether she descends to the dark caves and dreadful lakes of hell, or after death inspired with heavenly instinct, she returns into the brutes as our great Ennius sang, who first a crown of laurels ever grew brought down from Helicon, describes the stately palaces of Acheron where neither our souls nor bodies ever come, but certain spectres strange and wondrous pale." But then he goes on to say that "He shall search into the soul what her nature is and what meets our wakeful eyes and fights the mind and how by sickness and by sleep oppressed, we think we see or hear the voice of those who died long since, whose mouldering bones rot in the cold embrace of the grave." "These terrors of the mind, this darkness, these not the sun's beams nor the light ray of day can we dispel, but nature's light and reason whose first principles shall be my guide." This taught him that nothing was by nothing made, therefore could not produce something and every effect had a cause. Now these strange ghosts and spirits are all the inventions of man not of God, yet to man they are something. But ask where they come from and how they got here, then comes the mystery. Now Lucretius shows that man is matter dissolved and like all other matter passed into space, and the matter was seen by those who believed in spirits. Here was where he failed. He proved that every effect had a cause and as these spirits are nothing they have no cause or beginning.

His theory was that matter, like seeds, dissolves and each seed retains the element of the whole lump. This reasoning he carried into man, so that man like all nature dissolves and passes into space and each particle or seed contains the whole of man's life. This was the cause of their strange spectres being seen that the people called spirits and ghosts. Their fear produced it by their imagination. This was his theory, and as far as he reasoned, cannot be refuted. His starting point was light and reason. This taught that nothing cannot produce something, for if a thing could spring from nothing, what need is there for bodies to grow. And if nothing could produce something, then man might spring up out of the ground, grain from the sea, and fish live on the land. But, everything shows that all things have their causes and all phenomena must come from something. This shows that imagination is either something or nothing, and if a person imagines a thing and the thing appears, it shows that it has a cause outside of the thing seen. Now all these things have been seen and thousands more and there is proof to show that spirits, ghosts, spectres and strange delusions are matter moved without the aid of the natural man and all these phenomena are so well attested that it is folly in anyone to deny the fact. Among the strange phenomena are diseases, for disease is one of the great proofs that these things are among the things believed.

  The ancient philosophers were promulgating certain truths as they thought and to live up to them was their religion. They did not have creeds as the people of our day but a sort of philosophy that governed their lives according to the science of philosophy. The Pythian [Pythagorean?] philosophy consisted of searching into the laws of mathematics. This would teach them causes and effects, so all their acts were governed by their wisdom and their happiness was the fruit of their religious philosophy. Plato believed in one great cause and matter in an invisible state subject to a power. Here he like all the rest of the philosophers loses man. Now according to my own experience, matter is a substance to the one that believes it but to suppose that matter exists independent of wisdom, it is not in the power of man to prove. So, if matter is an idea, it is very easy to see that it is entirely under the control either of our belief or our wisdom. Now here are the two powers--one wisdom and the other belief. Now belief admits matter as a substance, wisdom admits it as a belief. Wisdom speaks it into existence and to belief it is a reality. I will now show how a belief can create matter and yet to wisdom it is nothing. To do this, I must assume to know what I am going to do. So, if I can make a person believe a thing, I impart to him a sort of wisdom (I call it wisdom because it is the highest he has) and he thinks it wisdom and I know it is not wisdom but an error. Now to the person, it is wisdom after I convince him of its truth so I must prove it to the person to establish the fact. So I will take a person and perform a mesmeric experiment and satisfy the person that it is performed. Now he knows that I have done it. This to him is true, but he believes he cannot do it. I tell him he can do the same, so he tries and I produce the phenomenon myself but he thinks he does it. In this way he gets confidence and does it himself. Now he, in his belief, does the very thing I do. Now I am in his belief and he knows it not and thinks it is himself, so now he uses the wisdom he gets from me to perform his experiments. . . . Matter supposes distance between like our senses, that is one chair must be not as another chair, so our senses are divided into five. Now with wisdom there is no division only as wisdom makes it. Senses are swallowed up in wisdom and there can be no space. So everything is present. The difference between wisdom and belief is this-- Wisdom is never deceived, belief is never certain, but always changes. Man is like a town. The inhabitants are the intelligence and the identity of the town is the same. The locality is the same always although the intelligence is always changing, yet every person admits the identity of the town but its inhabitants or intelligence are always changing and improvements are going on showing the growth of the intelligence, not of the town nor the ground on which the town is built.

So God makes the ground or identity called body and gave it an identity called man. This is under the wisdom of man until it is able to act of itself when man's body like a city or town is governed by the inhabitants or wisdom of the town. As a town is made up of different talent, so man is made up of different ideas and sometimes one set of rules and sometimes another. Man is not a unit but is governed by a city or nation and is liable to be deceived by false ideas into a belief that gets up a sort of rebellion.[1] All this is the working of matter. So diseases and revolutions take place and sometimes the inhabitants flee from their enemies but this is the working of matter. There seems to be a sort of inconsistency in regard to God. If God knows and rules all things, how should there be another power that seems to be contradictory to what we call God's wisdom? Now according to my theory that mind is matter, it looks very plain to me that there should be a conflict going on in man as in nations, for there is a regular grade of matter from the mineral to the animal creation and there is a regular grade of intelligence that corresponds to the matter. Now as the matter of vegetables and animals are connected, it is not strange that every person should partake of the elements of each, yet we all admit that the mineral and vegetable life

---

[1] *Cf.* the process panpsychist view of Hartshorne in Appendix L.

acts just as it was intended by God but when man steps in, he reasons that God isn't quite up to the intelligence of man and we try to reconcile God to man, not man to God. This is natural as our breath. Man wants to rule his fellow man and even dictate to God what is best for mankind....

So if you trade the working of the mind in man, you will find that man is now largely identified with the brute and is not to be condemned for his brutal feeling. Once admitted as such, you don't keep a dog that growls at you in excitement (he may) like to bite you but you don't expect anything better. Now that intellect which is nearly on a level with the brute shows itself opposing everything that goes to restrain its acts but at the same time shows its brutal instinct by fighting down everything that will not bow to its own will, showing no wisdom of doing to another as you would have another to do you. This is the point where the man ceases or breaks the link between the brute and the human species. This step taken opens the door to reason which the brutal man never does. His reason is all on one side, that he is the lord and his will is law. And, if he cannot have his own way he goes for destroying them. With man or brute, it is rule or ruin. Now this is all as God intended and man as I said, is like a new country unexplored, full of every kind of ideas that is embraced in the world.[1]

---

[1] E. S. Collie (ed.), *The Science of Health and Happiness* (2nd ed.; privately processed), II, 164-68; Seale (ed.), *The Complete Writings*, I, 430-36.

APPENDIX B

H. W. DRESSER, "QUIMBY'S TECHNIQUE"

Dresser calls Quimby

an unlettered empiricist in attitude and outlook: to this end he followed the clues of inner experience in contrast with theories which limit our horizon by authority or through bondage to material things, as if man were merely a body.[1]

Quimby

possessed a remarkable native equipment in his exceptional powers of concentration, his keenly reflective observant mind. In these respects he owed his training solely to the use to which he put his powers when intent upon solving a problem such as the alleged mystery of mesmerism. He seems to have been unaware of his exceptional ability to concentrate upon a mental image or idea,

---

[1] Horatio W. Dresser, "Quimby's Technique," p. 5. This is a typed copy of what appears to be a revision of an article of the same title in printed form pasted onto pieces of paper, without printed page numbers or clear indication of the publication from which clipped; it may be *Christian Victory*. A 1929 book is referred to as if recently published. Unless otherwise indicated, references here are to the page numbers of the typed revision; both versions are in the possession of the New Church Theological School, Cambridge [now Swedenborg School of Religion, Newton], Massachusetts.

and he certainly did not know at first that he was in high degree intuitive, with unusual powers of envisaging the inner world. These powers he discovered through use, first by attributing over-much to his "subject," and then learning by experience what abilities he possessed apart from the cooperation of Lucius....

It is also important to note that Quimby was not at first interested in therapy. The fact that as his experiments went on people in his audience came forward to request a diagnosis by Lucius was an unforeseen development of his investigations. Quimby's own recovery of health[1] in connection with the later period of his [perhaps four years[2] of] work with Lucius was a surprise to him, for he did not know that he too had been a victim of an erroneous view of disease.[3]

Dresser says that "it is significant that Quimby had no theory concerning the human mind, but was free to follow wherever his investigations might lead."[4] Dresser does not take note of the various mesmeric philosophies available to Quimby, except to point out that little was known of mesmerism when Quimby began to experiment

---

[1]*The Quimby Manuscripts*, 1st ed., pp. 27-29, 2nd ed., pp. 33-35. It may have been reenforced by the memory of a premesmeric period healing of Quimby when excited by driving a horse when sick; see *The Quimby Manuscripts*, 1st ed., p. 22, 2nd ed., p. 28.

[2]1843-1847, *Ibid.*, 1st ed., p. 10, 2nd ed., p. 16.

[3]Dresser, "Quimby's Technique," p. 6.

[4]*Ibid.*

Healing Hypotheses 281

with it.[1] It is not clear how much Dresser knew of relatively early mesmeric speculation, except that elsewhere he refers to Dods, which may not indicate that he was aware of his early work, although the probable reference to Dods in the Burkmar journal[2] and the references to various mesmerists in Quimby's "lecture notes" must have been seen by him at least a decade or so before writing this article. Apparently Dresser did not consider the work before Braid's very important; he says:

> It was not until 1845, in England, that Braid introduced the term hypnotism, and began the studies which eventually prepared the way for scientific understanding as explained by the French and German psychologists of a later period.[3]

Dresser observes that

> Quimby had that rare opportunity which is open to the pioneer who makes the first trail into a hitherto unknown land. Quimby did not blaze his trail in the direction followed by Braid and the French specialists who investigated the phenomena

---

[1] *Ibid.*, pp. 3-4.

[2] See *The Quimby Manuscripts*, 1st. ed., pp. 37-40, 2nd ed., pp. 43-46; in the journal itself see p. 6 [Seale (ed.), I, 34; contrary to the Seale statement at I, 32, the original is in the Library of Congress; the error is understandable, since the journal probably is the only part of the collection that Mrs. Charles Pineo sent to the Library of Congress, rather than to Boston University] on Doods. [*sic*].

[3] *Ibid.*, p. 3.

of hysteria. His interest never became scientific in the traditional sense. He followed a practical clue because he was practical in type, ready to adopt any principle which might prove serviceable even if it conflicted with established theories.[1]

Quimby was fortunate in finding his subject and the degree of mesmerism employed. He apparently managed to bring about

light sleep or partial hypnosis, during which the subject cooperates more or less with the operator. The "rapport" is not then complete. This state does not involve the entire domination of the subject by hypnotic suggestions, for the subject is left in a measure of freedom for following his initiatives.[2]

Lucius was "psychically alert under Quimby's commands but intellectually almost passive."[3] Lucius

was free to utilize cooperative hypnosis to the limit, while seeing the mental and bodily states of those who came forward for diagnosis, without claiming to contact disembodied souls.... And he talked about his apparent bodily journeyings [while his physical body remained where this experiment was being conducted] ..., describing tangible objects as he apparently saw them. Possibly he would have developed a secondary personality ... with secondary memories to match, and so on, if Quimby had learned or wished to

---

[1] Dresser, "Quimby's Technique," p. 5.

[2] *Ibid.*, pp. 4-5.

[3] *Ibid.*, p. 7.

produce "deep sleep." Then the question of dissociated memory would have been a salient fact. But dissociation did not occur. Lucius was not in any sense abnormal, if we hold that it is normal to exercise clairvoyance.[1]

Unless we note the fact that Quimby did not exercise and did not wish to exercise complete control over the mind of Lucius, but desired to *follow* the reports which Lucius gave wherever the phenomena in question might lead, we will not appreciate Quimby's readiness to accept clairvoyance as a basic experience. Many psychologists would begin by discounting as illusory (or impossible) precisely those matters which to Quimby were to prove most productive when he gave up Lucius as subject and ceased to experiment with hypnotism. He was ready to accept all the evidences at their face value because he was not deterred by the assumption that the bodily senses are the only sources of contact with worlds. Again he was free because he did not hold that all mental states are caused by states of the brain. What he needed, to carry the evidences through to complete orientation was not physiological psychology or any spiritualistic theory; but Myers' conception of the subliminal self, with the hypothesis that beyond the margin of consciousness the self has wider points of contact, with possibilities of increased knowledge of the self's relationships, including direct contacts between mind and mind. Lacking the theory that was not yet formulated in terms of what we now call extra-sensory perception, Quimby simply assumed that when the physical senses were

---

[1] *Ibid.*

quiescent Lucius *saw* with an inner eye, his vision being spontaneous. Quimby was free to "listen in," so to speak, to whatever Lucius might say, the mind of Lucius being in that case the leader. Nor was he deterred from accepting outright the fact that telepathy was a regular means of communication between mind and mind long before the existence of thought transference became a problem. Rapport between minds having been accepted as a fact, other matters easily followed, including the transfer of an activity such that mental pictures were set up in the mind of Lucius, side by side with processes which belonged more directly with Lucius' clairvoyance. Lucius could listen to Quimby mentally, receive suggestions, and see the mental picture which Quimby desired him to see, while also discerning clairvoyantly as freely as if Quimby were not communicating with him. Plainly, then, telepathy and clairvoyance are not identical. As surely, both operator and subject are most likely to apprehend the phenomena in question if undeterred by previous assumptions. We have then a remarkable record of sheer experience.

Since Lucius' experiences were not abnormal, but implied powers which all people possess potentially, Quimby was freed to conclude that these powers became active without such intermediaries as those in which spiritists believe. As neither mediumship nor spirit-guides are necessary, what is essential is a type of openness on any person's part, with freedom to utilize any activity that may disclose itself, unhampered by notions concerning the human mind. This openness implies the existence of an inner world in each of us, thus a point of view from within outward, from the interiors of the mind to the interiors of another, and from these interiors to a higher mental world if experience leads to such a conclusion. So the usual point of approach, from externals (the natural world) to internals (the spiritual world) is exchanged for this inwardness as central in all instances. Granted this outlook from inwardness in any direction, whether into the minds of people or into the regions of a psychical journey, we see why Quimby came to believe in the existence of "spiritual senses," not as mere counterparts of bodily senses, but as involving activities of their own (not determined by brain-states). The human spirit is so constituted, then, that spirit can talk with spirit, each of us in his own little world, with sensibilities enabling us to detect what Quimby called mental atmospheres. By our inner sensibilities we function more directly (in telepathy, clairvoyance, etc.) than when we speak and otherwise express ourselves through the circuitous means of sounds, facial changes and gestures. These higher abilities are dormant in most of us because we are absorbed in external circumstances and events. . . . When Quimby realized the very great potentiality of all people as spiritual beings, he knew that a hypnotic subject was no longer necessary, that there was no reason for even partly controlling another's mind.[1]

In these experiments a considerable measure of the success was due to Quimby's habit of depending on mental communications when telling Lucius what to do in contrast with spoken commands. Thus Quimby became convinced that the whole process was mental, not attributable to "magnetism" or to mysterious passes around a subject's head as in alleged instances of "animal magnetism." Hence the whole problem was

---

[1] *Ibid.*, pp. 8-10.

simplified.[1]

While employing Lucius, Quimby received considerable evidence of the concrete effects attributable to the formative power of mind impressed by imagery. But

> there was much more... than could be clarified by continuing to put Lucius under hypnosis. [So Quimby gave up Lucius] and, after an interval for reconsideration [started] afresh into the relatively unknown world which the phenomena in question disclosed. This step was also the right one for Quimby to take because his experiments had convinced him that he too was clairvoyant, possessed spiritual senses and other abilities that could be trusted to lead the way by following the deliverances of his own mind without depending on anybody else. Few people would have sufficient self-reliance to make such a venture as this, since, for one thing, nobody is said to be perceptive enough to acquire the requisite power of introspective analysis while also penetrating into the little known world of psychical phenomena. Here in any case was the most significant turning point in Quimby's explorations.[2]

This turning point was

> Quimby's advance from the psychological to the spiritual stage of his career. In the first stage, covering the epoch of his study of hypnotism, with his dependence on hypnosis and suggestion, thus on

---

[1] *Ibid.*, p. 11.

[2] *Ibid.*, p. 13.

his "subject," Quimby was solely concerned with the human mind as highly susceptible to mental atmospheres, "errors of mind," adverse emotions like fear, and subconscious reproductions of this mass of conflicting activities. The most fruitful result of the psychological period was the conclusion that he too (as well as Lucius) possessed clairvoyance, the ability to transmit thought and to travel psychically. His departure from the psychological to the spiritual phase of his career signalized the rejection of hypnosis in favor of the method of spiritual healing as his own deepest inner experiences had brought it to light. While he still made use of his mental equipment, notably his unusual powers of concentration, this equipment became instrumental only. He did not now transmit a mental picture as if efficient in itself. He did not depend on an idea or mental process set up in another's mind, although ideas in line with his realization were aids. Instead, his spiritual relation with patients centered about the conviction that man is spirit, created into the image and likeness of Wisdom, with an unchanging true identity to be summoned into activity. . . . Thus the creative phase of his work was outstanding. He had a *true* religion to offer to his patients, displacing the "false identifications" of the old order of things in the churches.[1]

In introducing the spiritual phase of Quimby's work, Dresser observes that Quimby did not consider disease imaginary or matter

> unreal or non-existent. What especially interested him in the experiments with Lucius was the fact

---

[1] *Ibid.*, p. 33.

that Lucius could *see through matter*, penetrating the surfaces of the body and discerning the internal conditions of the organ in the region where there was an "obstruction." Apparently, then, so Quimby reasoned, matter is less solid than had been supposed. Meanwhile condensed thought is more real in its effect on the body than anybody would suspect who lacks clairvoyance in its active modes, noting the stages through which such thought passes in causing trouble.[1]

Elsewhere Dresser says that Quimby "was in possession of the facts we now call 'subconscious,' but could not readily name them."[2] Here Dresser says:

> Unwittingly we create formative images always at hand when condensing our thoughts into an efficacious opinion. Thus our beliefs are followed by results even though we are unaware of all the factors at work, notably those that are chiefly subconscious. Quimby's discoveries in such connections led him to compare mind to a fertile soil as "spiritual matter," seed-thoughts having the potency of suggestion, as he might have added had he possessed the term. That is to say "spiritual matter" resembles tangible substances, symbolically speaking, but is more nearly akin to mental

---

[1] *Ibid.*, p. 14.

[2] *The Quimby Manuscripts*, 1st ed., p. 63, 2nd ed., p. 69. In a probably late manuscript, "Outline of the Teachings and Methods of P. P. Quimby," p. 6, he says, "Quimby discovered the subconscious long before Freud was said to have discovered the 'unconscious.'"

products. Prentice Mulford[1] seems to have been groping after the same idea in saying "Thoughts are things." What signifies, however, is not the apparent substantiality but the mental life which utilizes what we are intent upon and projects inner states that are precisely what we take them to be, as hell to a Calvinist was what Calvin said it was.[2]

The recognition of intuitive sensitivity within himself put Quimby in possession of possibilities far exceeding any results that might have come from any further efforts in trying to control another mind, as he controlled Lucius. Hypnotism would have been a hindrance to the development of his method of spiritual healing, the object of which was to *persuade* people of the Truth, whereas through opinion people had been subject to "error" as a subject is regulated by an operator. Quimby gave up Lucius once for all by giving up the mesmerism which had first aroused his interest. This was several years before he began his therapeutic practice in Portland. For he needed time to assimilate his conclusions and develop a radically different method from his work as a hypnotist.

It became clear that Lucius in performing what passed as a cure by aid of what he told a sick person was no further along towards mastery than the victim of a disease-pattern such as heart-disease. For the recipients did not realize in either case that they had been influence[d] by

---

[1] 1834-1891, journalist, miner, etc., author of a series known at the White Cross Library; his autobiography is *Prentice Mulford's Story* (New York: F. J. Needham, 1889); it mostly ignores his philosophy.

[2] Dresser, "Quimby's Technique," p. 14.

suggestion. Obviously, nobody had ever consciously thought himself into disease. There must be a hidden activity between consciousness as we ordinarily know it and the disturbing result, with a part played by the amenability to suggestion about which the medical world was ignorant in Quimby's day. Step by step the whole process had become so clear to Quimby that he could begin to reduce it to a science. . . .[1]

As Lucius had once explored a person's mind by casting about to whatever might be discovered merely because Quimby asked him to look and then to report on what he saw, so Quimby began at first by penetrating the inner life of this or that person to note what he found on the basis of experience not regulated by prior conceptions concerning what is real or true. This directive search is unlike what we call reason, thought or imagination. It does not proceed by inferences, after certain premises have been adopted. The searcher has a willingness to be led, to *learn*, without any desire to impose or dictate, and is entirely free from any desire to control. This is what marks off Quimby's silent treatment from hypnotism in all its guises. To see its import is to understand why, in the beginning with person after person, Quimby did not ask for faith in him or in his methods, and did not even require a measure of receptivity. This may seem strange at first thought, until we realize that he was directly concerned, not with the person as a conscious being, but with the whole personality as mostly subconscious at any given moment. Coming in touch with the *mental atmosphere*, Quimby knew

---

[1] *Ibid.*, p. 15.

from this the inner "quality," whether or not there was an inner point of contact or clue, what the *attitude* was to this or that in relation to persons and things, and what the prospect was for reaching deeply into the selfhood as a whole in so far forth as resistances might be disclosed. In brief, Quimby put himself *within* this selfhood in readiness to detect whatever his intuition brought to attention.

While it might seem at first glance that the factors at work in spiritual healing are the same as those functioning in hypnotism, marked differences come into view when we look at these matters more closely. In hypnosis there is an emotional subservience to the suggestions of the operator, the intellect of the "subject" being quiescent, the will in abeyance. Hypnosis takes away from the subject for the time being any resistance to the operator. While hypnosis might be said to resemble the possible receptivity on the part of the patient, in the latter case there is no emotional subservience, no intellectual abeyance and no yielding of the will; the "silence" is for therapeutic purposes only, and is akin to worship or prayer. . . . The patient is not infatuated, is not asleep. Will is now appealed to, not put into abeyance. Intellect is quickened, not stilled. In short, the whole personality is welcomed and construed by spiritual standards, as in the worship in which the communicant listens for the voice of the Spirit. Thus the silence differs in both motive and objective, as a verifiable *inner* experience.

Quimby arrived at this point of *qualitative difference* between hypnosis and therapeutic receptivity because he found that by sitting near a person mentally disturbed, and by rendering his mind receptive, he could detect the inner life at its center, with its atmosphere. The atmosphere thus given off discloses the state of worry, fear, excitement, depression, suppression, or what not. To discern it is to trace it to disease-patterns, medical opinions, religious dogmas, and any other bondage that may have held the patient's mind in subjection. No device like "free association" was called for, because Quimby was not interested in what the patient could conjure up from the depths. Any analysis of dream-states would have been of minor importance. The resulting experience in the mind of the patient was to be far from the "control" brought about by hypnosis, for control spells quiescence on the part of the very qualities which under receptivity are to be brought into action through a cure. It was less necessary for Quimby to know the past history in detail in proportion to his discernment of the heart of the trouble. So his first remark to the patient, when the conversational part of the treatment began, might hit the very center of the whole inner life-history to the point of its earliest bondage.

The sequence of inner causes leading to the present trouble proved to be less significant than the discernment of the *meaning* of the patient's bondages, although in the "explanation" which was to be the "cure" [this being Quimby's way of putting it] in its final aspect it was indeed important to show that the patient had been held in subjection as if the soul were little more than a prisoner of the flesh. The patient needed to see that the imprisoning patterns had held the mind almost with the power of truth, and also to learn that the whole mass of associates in the subconscious had been favorable to the development of trouble. More important still, the patient needed to know that by identifying with the factors of his trouble he had helped to create it. For Quimby had found that the mind of the "natural man" was little more than a mass of errors.

This mind, although secondary to the real self, puts all the vitality of a deeper mind into its falsities. The central idea here is identification. Man's false or negative identity is the self he takes himself to be when under bondage to opinion. Quimby's experiments with hypnotism had taught him that whatever the mind accepts as true is real *to that mind* as long as the acceptance continues. To accept an opinion as true is to take it to oneself, so identifying with it that one lives by it, permitting it to give tone to one's whole mentality. . . . The remarkable power of imagery over the human mind, coupled with its subconscious influence, was one of the chief of Quimby's discoveries.

The question is, granted dominion of a given group of negative images centering about a disease-pattern, how is it possible to detach the soul from this "false identity?" To answer this question is to follow Quimby in his next step after he changed from a mental to a spiritual point of view.

Plainly, if intuition under the guise of the spiritual senses, the power of directed receptivity, and the power of the spirit to project itself towards another spirit, is *latent in each one of us*, there is some common ground of spiritual powers in our primary self. In Quimby this primary self had become active so that he could view the mentality of a patient on all its levels, discerning repressions and patterns and also potentialities. There must be some way to arouse the latent primary self in the patient. This could not be accomplished by a word of command (as in hypnotism). The real self could not be aroused by mere suggestion. It must be appealed to by Truth, by what Quimby called Science, with its power to dispel opinion. The power of this spiritual appeal can be nothing less than Wisdom (God or Spirit). Wisdom is the common basis of our existence as spiritual beings.

In this Wisdom we live, move, have our being. Through Wisdom we are intimately related: spirit can touch spirit.

Quimby was led to this conviction because of the upliftments and insights of his inner experience when sitting by the sick, inwardly seeking to heal them and set them free. He found that the life or power with which his spirit came in contact on the higher activity level was not an energy he controlled or tried to control: it was Wisdom to which he became open when he discriminated the identity of the natural man from the identity of the spiritual man. In seeking Wisdom's guidance and cooperating with it he did not try to impress his own mentality on the patient's mind. That would have been no better than hypnotism. His objective was to rise from the level of natural mentality to the level of divine creation, so that the imagery and efficiency of perfect health should utterly dispel the disturbing patterns, repressed emotions and the other adverse mental factors.

The greatest step made by Quimby in developing his technique was in realizing that the primary self--created and reared in the image and likeness of Wisdom for health and freedom, spiritual living and spiritual progress--*is not sick*, does not sin, is not really the slave it appears to be. For granted the truth it is possible to arouse by inner realization *the true man*. The thinking, willing, acting self which the patient takes himself to be (when unenlightened) must be readjusted according to this true or real man. This process involves detaching the patient's "natural senses"--his attention, thought, volition, emotion; his striving for freedom and self-realization, long held in bondage--from external things and attaching his consciousness to the "true" which dispels the false.

> This accomplished as the essential change, the other stages of the therapeutic activity readily follow.
>
> It is imperative to take the clue from Wisdom in all these matters, for here is the basis of all that is immutable, while the world of opinions is always subject to change. The spirit is untouched by either error or suffering, sin or misery, because it *lives* in its integrity in the divine image. Moreover, Wisdom is present with us to guide the spirit intuitively as an agent of healing. Wisdom is the active principle in which the human spirit resides. We can grow in responsiveness to its guidance by utilizing our spiritual senses, by the realization that Wisdom is indwelling, is equal to every occasion as the source of eternal truth.[1]

At this point Dresser introduces some comparisons with later teachings, which are not strictly relevant here. Disease is "*an experience*, ... not an *entity* which seizes a person like an animal."[2] Disease is "always a relationship within personality[;] ... it is the *person* who is ill, notably in all nervous and emotional disorders."[3]

> Quimby was far from saying that "Matter is an unreal illusion." He carefully called attention to *what man takes matter to be in certain* connections only, because man is in such connections under bondage to opinion. That is to say, an illusion is due to misinterpretation, as in construing a pressure- sensation so that it seems to indicate

---

[1]*Ibid.*, pp. 16-21.

[2]*Ibid.*, p. 21.

[3]*Ibid.*

disease of the heart. But the object mistakenly named still remains a fact to be accounted for when we acquire the knowledge that truly applies. Man invents mental worlds without number. But these are not the realm of nature in space and time. Nor are they the heavens of the spiritual world. Nature is not *maya* (illusion), as Hindoo philosophers have declared, nor is it basically due to *avidya* (ignorance). Ignorance certainly plays havoc with us all. But it is not cosmical in power.[1]

Elsewhere Dresser says:

> The essential point to note... is that matter is plastic to thought; it is that in which, on the one hand, the thought of God takes shape, and, on the other, the embodiment of human belief. In any case we must look to the direction of consciousness anterior to it, as the source of its changing states and of its life.
> There is all the more reason for affirming and dwelling upon the reality of the good when we understand, not merely believe, that this constant realization of the true is just as constantly effacing all that is harmful in matter, and is receiving actual and substantial expression in the visible world. When we understand that "all that is seen by the natural man is mind reduced to a state called matter," we no longer confuse [1] matter, [2] spiritual matter or mind, and [3] soul or Spirit, while according due recognition and reality to each.
> It was thus characteristic of Dr. Quimby not to deny anything--except the reality of disease as something by itself--but to see it, if possible, in its

---

[1] *Ibid.*, p. 22.

true light and in considering matter he always regarded it from the idealist's point of view, and, while not ignoring it, never attributed to it that reality of life and power which belongs to God alone.[1]

Dresser observes, summarizing with regard to Quimby's technique, that applying it

for the benefit of others is to come into intuitive touch with the patient's mentality, to see what this mentality discloses, and what the negative identification is, as in mistaking a given pain for a disease one has heard about. The second step is to turn radically away from the patient's secondary self by rendering oneself receptive to Wisdom in two respects: with reference to the divine ideal of health, freedom, power, as the standard by which we were all created; and with regard to the patient's particular need, the special insight for that individual, placed as he is amidst contending forces. Quimby, with his remarkable powers of concentration, was uncommonly successful in thus changing the direction of his mind, by attaching his spiritual senses to what was to him fundamentally real and true. His realization of the Truth or Science was sufficiently powerful so that the patient's mind partook of it, the incentive coming from it, although the first results were subconscious. By "realization" one means the positive life or power *by feeling it*, making of the realization an *experience*. Prayer is not the word here. The realization is dynamic, it takes hold, strikes home, and home is where the spirit is.

---

[1] Horatio W. Dresser, "Dr. Quimby's Theory of Matter," *Unity*, LX (June, 1926), 538.

Yet even the silent treatment was a part only of the technique. For no one can be set wholly free from error until he *sees* it. Given evidence that the silent activity was effective, Quimby began his explanations in order to "take down the structure called disease" and show how it was reared. Since the first aches or pains were incidental, and could have been construed by avoiding falsities, it is well to recover the implied activity and redirect it. To see how we miscreated and misdirected is to realize the effectiveness of a power we did not know we possessed. Now at last we can "right about face" into the true direction.[1]

Dresser now takes note that the Calvinistic religious beliefs of Quimby's day were at the bottom of much illness, so Quimby had to help his patients escape

---

[1]Dresser, "Quimby's Technique," pp. 22-23. Some terminology not originated with specifically this matter in mind may be employed helpfully here. It has been said that when "Will agency," free initiative, "freely turns to God for renewed strength, in humble faith in God's forgiveness and good will, forces are let loose in the life of that personality which his own free will now can readily accept, and allow to work for the greater good one feels obligation to at the time. But this help, this grace, is not forthcoming apart from a self-committing act of will agency." Peter A. Bertocci, *Free Will, Responsibility, and Grace* (New York and Nashville: Abingdon Press, 1957), p. 106. The act of acceptance allows the influx of divine wisdom-life-love-power to be increasingly important with relation to will power, which is "the measure of control determined by its interplay with other factors [in addition to will agency] in the total choice situation." Bertocci, p. 37.

from theologians as well as physicians.

With regard to Quimby and depth psychology, Dresser says:

> Had Quimby been content to remain a merely mental therapist, he might have begun somewhat as Freud did by tracing emotional suppressions to infantilisms. For he had abundant evidences of the concealed "mechanisms" which have been identified as complexes. But the releasing of emotions associated with the illness was part only of the process, and incidental. The whole selfhood was involved, and analysis alone could not disclose that. The whole furniture of the mind was at stake. What the analysts have termed the "transference" was included in what Quimby learned concerning mental atmospheres. Had his technique stopped with analysis he would have been unable to make the complete *explanation* which was the *cure*.[1]

The explanation was not simply a theoretical matter that is applied alike in all cases. Dresser stresses:

> granted the presence of indwelling Wisdom, the significant principle is guidance or wisdom for the occasion, for the individual, and no two cases are the same. The attitude of receptivity to Wisdom as power and life, guidance and quickening love, is wholly unlike that of utilizing suggestion as the primary force. Quimby gave his spirit to Wisdom with a fullness of response such that his personality as a whole was actuated by the experience. Hence his remarkable power of concentration (formerly used in *controlling* the

---

[1] Dresser, "Quimby's Technique," pp. 24-25.

mind of Lucius) was secondary in comparison with the depth and scope of his spiritual realization. All his mental powers were instrumental; what was more central was his spirit actuated by Wisdom.

This contrast between the spiritual and the mental was also implied in Quimby's distinction between divine truth and man's opinion, the Christ in each of us and "the man Jesus" who exemplified the true Science of Life and Happiness, and between the spirit, the "real" or "scientific" man in each one and the "false identity" or conditioned self. Hence the psychological factors are to be understood by noting what was implied when Quimby shifted from the intuitive diagnosis in the first stage of the technique to the second stage or interior realization. The whole process at work in the "silent treatment" was indeed *silent* because Quimby found that he could work directly with the patient's subconsciousness, could address himself to the spirit within, in fact that he must do so before the patient could cooperate. The actual state of the patient was much deeper than is apparent to any one save the therapist realizes because it includes the emotional depths, the bondages, repressions and conflicts grouped by the analysts under the term "complex." Quimby . . . could discern the heart of those depths so as to give himself to the realization at the point and in the manner most needed by the patient.

Thus the rapport with the patient was an important part of the technique. No less important was Quimby's power of "absenting" himself, as he called it, from the negative identification and thus diagnosed which held the patient in bondage. Thus the shifting of attention from the diagnosis to the realization was a turning-point. Quimby made this transition with force because he could intensively concentrate. The truth concerning the patient's real self (the part that cannot be sick) was the central consideration: the truth was grounded in God's wisdom or design. The qualification that part of us is not and cannot be sick was not a weak but a strong one, in contrast with the qualifications which we usually make. Hence Quimby could give himself to his conviction with all the force of his long experience in discerning the inner life. The real man in all of us is of course ready to be set free. But we live in relative darkness. What is needed is the coming of spiritual light, "the light which lighteth every man born into the world," the light that can penetrate all darkness whatever the bondages. Quimby found that he could bring this light. Hence the various references in his writings to the "the dark places" in which he found his patients enveloped. His patients, by divine birthright, possessed the requisite power of "openness" or receptivity through which wisdom from above could come. Given this illumination, the old identification could give place to the new.

Although the principle of identification is secondary it is highly important, as we have noted in the foregoing, because the mind, being limited in scope, can function actively in but *one direction at a time*. Hence it is that a "direction of mind" can make all sorts of things (one by one) *as real as life itself*. The given "direction" carries identification with it, for it includes the process known as attention, which is central to the human mind. A direction, however, as the term is used here, is more than the shifting of interests of the moment as our minds ordinarily shift. This directivity not only implies a change of thought, an exchange of mental imagery, as one object gives place to another: the direction carries *activity* (as power) with it, so that the whole mind becomes absorbed by what is thus accepted. Unwittingly a man may take home to himself the very miseries he would cast out. If he knew that the process of identification is his own act his procedure would be radically different. To give assent because of ignorance is indeed to fall into a pit of confusions. By contrast the directivity toward light and freedom has the added power of the "realization of truth," the power of Wisdom sustaining our conviction. The realization profoundly and truly *becomes an experience*, a new experience of the divine presence. On this level there is peace, the peace which knows no disturbance or fear. On this level there is imbuing love, quickening guidance. The efficiency is not then in the finite thought, the human will, not even in the imagery or suggestion which helps to make the realization definite: the power rests with God as Wisdom. For there is no strength in anything human that is not in deepest truth a sharing of divine power.

It is difficult to see the force of this teaching unless we take up a position on a level from which we can look down on the play of life (on "Wisdom's amusements," Quimby says) where man is mistaking himself for a being of flesh and blood, generating woes by misusing his mentality. On the upper level man is intact, complete as a spirit, with all requisite powers so that if death were to occur he would be found adequately equipped for existence in the spiritual world. Quimby grew into this conviction through experiences with the sick in the more critical instances when a patient was actually rescued from imminent death, especially when the separation between soul and body had partly taken place. Man is indeed *a complete spirit* because he is independent of the body *so far as his enduring powers are concerned*. To gain this insight is to base one's whole view of life upon it, always regarding the spirit as centrally real.

What then is consciousness? It is this interchange of activity between spirit, mind, and body through which we become aware of the activities in which we are living. We think and move most directly with Wisdom when we think from the spirit, think *with* the spirit. Thus to think is to follow what comes, what is given: not interposing our own ideas, not trying to direct or control. The type of thought is that of the divine image and likeness, not that of man's inventions. I repeat: Quimby did not when directing his attention to a patient try to convey his *own* thoughts or imagery. Believing that the divine image-likeness (Love and Wisdom) is latent and can become active, his part was that of an awakener or light-bearer. He believed in direct relationship or contact because by experience he could discriminate between a transfer of thought on the mental level and the *experience* of cooperating with Wisdom on the spiritual level. Furthermore, his experience in helping the sick led him to see that the indwelling life, when curative, works through the organism to the point needed, for example, in dissolving and carrying away a tumor through the process he called a "chemical change."

What is it in our nature that is most responsive, most likely to be touched into central activity? The immediate or intuitive side, the love-nature rather than the intellectual side. Quimby did not develop a theory of the emotions at this point. He did not discriminate what has been technically called feeling or feeling-tone in contrast with the emotions. Noting the fact that a patient was suffering from emotional congestion, he turned directly to the center or heart. Fear was, he found, the worst of the besetting emotions, almost the basis of disease in its entirety. Granted this conclusion, Quimby gave himself to the realizational truth of "perfect love" as the dynamic which casts out fear. Error and truth, fear and love cannot rule in the same household. To establish the truths of the divine image and likeness is to drive the errors away.

Yet while the spiritual emphasis falls on the unifying curative realization, Quimby's conversations with his patients were often of an analytical type. For the patient needed to know the genesis of the particular fear or pattern in some detail in order to be convinced, notably in instances in which doctrines of the churches were involved.... It was plain that he made no claims in his own behalf. He sought rather to take himself out of the way that each patient might behold the vision for himself. Thus the whole procedure was spiritual in the best sense of the word. Had Quimby taken any credit to himself he might have claimed that he had received a "revelation." He himself would then have become an authority, and attempts might have been made by his followers to found a new religion. But such a scheme would have been utterly absurd. This would have meant a reversion to the bondages from which Quimby had set people free. It would have meant exalting the finite ego to the first rank. Self-assertion would then have been the prevailing direction of mind. But the true prevailing affection is love of Wisdom, whose instruments we may become by demonstrating the unchangeable in the changing. Hence Quimby claimed no more for himself than the functions of a light-bearer carrying the torch of Wisdom into the dark places and disclosing the realities hidden there.[1]

---

[1] *Ibid.*, pp. 28-33.

APPENDIX C

EVANS BIOGRAPHICAL MATERIAL

The chief source of information on Warren Felt Evans is an article that contains references to "private journals and other material"[1] furnished by the Evans family but no longer known of by the family nor thus far found anywhere [1962; later, some located in Dartmouth]. The article itself is scarce. It begins:

> Next to Phineas Parkhurst Quimby, the founder of the modern spiritual healing movement, the first disciple of his to become a mental therapeutist, the Reverend Warren Felt Evans, M.D., was the most intuitive and original investigator and teacher that the movement has produced.[2]

Evans was born on December 23, 1817, in Rockingham, Vermont, and died on September 4, 1889, in Salisbury, Massachusetts.[3]

> His boyhood was spent on his father's farm, and his early education was that furnished the youth of his day by the district school. No information is available respecting his mental habits at this time.

---

[1] William J. Leonard, "Warren Felt Evans, M.D.," *Practical Ideals*, X (Sept.-Oct., 1905), 4.

[2] *Ibid.*, and X (Nov., 1905), 22; *Dictionary of American Biography*, VI (1931), 213-14.

[3] *Ibid.*, X (Sept.-Oct., 1905), 4.

That he must have early developed a love of study is evident from the fact that he entered Chester Academy, in his native State, to fit for college when nearing his eighteenth year. This is all the more apparent when it is understood that his father was unable to assist him and that he had to depend upon his own efforts to meet the expenses of his education. This was true of him until the end of his college course. . . . He was admitted to Middlebury College in Vermont in the year 1837, where he remained until the following spring, when he entered Dartmouth College. He did not complete the course, but left in the middle of the Junior year. He makes no note of the reason for cutting short the usual college course. It may be conjectured that after five years of self-denying economy in procuring the means to carry him through his academic career, he was eager for the more independent position that the profession offered to which he had no doubt been looking forward since he began his studies. Two important incidents in his life at this period, which he recorded many years afterward in a brief chronological table, upon which I am drawing for some of these early data, point in this direction. One of these is found in the note concerning his first sermon, which he preached at Bellows Falls, Vermont, January 1, 1839, only a very short time before he left college, which was in the spring of the year 1839. This was no doubt a trial sermon, given for the purpose of securing from the church authorities the necessary official sanction to become a minister. The other important incident recorded is his marriage, on June 21, 1840, to Miss Charlotte Tinker of Chelsea, Vermont.[1]

---

[1] *Ibid.*, pp. 4-5.

Healing Hypotheses 307

On "July 1, 1840, he was appointed by the New Hampshire Conference minister of the Methodist Episcopal Church at Peacham, Vermont."[1]

>His experiences were not unlike those of other Methodist clergymen of his time in New England. ... The itinerant system of his church carried him to many towns, nearly all of which were in New Hampshire after his first settlement. These were Goffstown, Pembroke, Northfield, Rindge, Marlow, Newport (1850), Concord (1852), Lisbon (1854), Claremont (1856), and West Unity (1860). His two last pastorates were in Massachusetts, at Lawrence (1858), and Salisbury (1861). He was recognized by his contemporaries of the pulpit as one of the most scholarly and most thoughtful of preachers. His assignment to Concord, New Hampshire, was a proof of this, for here his denomination had need of its most gifted clergymen, as it was the seat of a divinity school [that became Boston University] whose professors and students constituted an important part of the minister's congregation. He was a young man of 34 when assigned to this parish, and he discharged the duties so well that he was honored with a second appointment. His learning was also availed of by the theological school, when occasion required his services as a substitute for absent professors. His special qualifications for teaching in such an institution were his acquaintance with church history and his familiarity with the Greek text of the New Testament. He was, it may be said, a life-long student of the New Testament in the original Greek, which he read, as he somewhere says, with the same facility as he did the English

---

[1]*Ibid.*, p. 6.

translation.[1]

Apart from his academic services, the ministerial career of Evans was not so usual as the information thus far given indicates. He departed from the ordinary in both his health and his religious experiences.

He records, "In June, 1835, I turned my attention to religious things and connected myself with the Congregational Church."[2] However,

> Before he reached his twenty-first year, he had embraced what was then known as the Oberlin view of sanctification[3] and left the Congregational Church to join the Methodist Episcopal body, where this view had a more hospitable reception than elsewhere. In his personal life and in his preaching, the phase of Christian experience fostered by this doctrinal belief was constantly emphasized. In his hands it developed into none of the extravagances and fanaticisms which have characterized many of its adherents. He never for a moment claimed to have attained perfection. What he was ever seeking was what he termed "a higher and deeper experience in religion," an experience that included a conscious communion with God, "a calm happiness of unbroken fellowship with Him," to give a favorite phrasing of his thought to be found quite often in his published works as well as in his or private

---

[1] *Ibid.*, p. 7.

[2] *Ibid.*, p. 11.

[3] Stressing perfection, perhaps pointing toward New Thought. See *Encyclopaedia of Religion and Ethics*, IX (1917), 736.

journal.[1]

Evans writes:

> At times my soul has had a clearer sense of the Allness of God than I ever before experienced. One night on my bed my soul lost itself to the All. It seemed to me that there was nothing but God; that he was the life, the support, the substance of everything which exists. I thank God for rest in the All-pervading Deity. This inward consciousness of God, this living and moving in the Divine element has made all times and places alike. . . . Sometimes I find formal prayer to be an impossibility. I enter my closet and hold my soul in the Divine presence. I can only sweetly rest in the will of God, while my heart from its inmost centre silently breathes out the prayer, the holiest in earth or heaven:
> "May thy will, not mine, be done,
> May thy will and mine be one."
> Prayer is becoming with me an inward life. The soul in a ceaseless current flows out after God. Its desires silently flow into my soul.[2]

Also:

> I have recently enjoyed a deeper consciousness of the love of God, his boundless and everlasting love, than I ever before reached. . . . I have found that my growth in the spiritual life has gone forward by new manifestations of God to my consciousness and every successive stage of that

---

[1] Leonard, *op. cit.*, p. 12.

[2] *Ibid.*, pp. 12-13, ellipses by Leonard.

growth has been based upon, and preceded by, some new and enlarged view of God. . . . Long have I found God so near to me that I could not move without moving in Him. I am floating in the depths of the ocean of the Infinite Life. But that Life seems to me to be Love.[1]

And:

I feel a great love for spiritual truth. I love truth as intensely as a miser loves gold. I am not conscious in myself of any prejudice that would prevent my embracing what was clearly true. I throw open my soul and turn it imploringly towards the eternal source of light and knowledge.[2]

Dates for these quotations are not provided by the biographer, but they are from a "spiritual journal" that was "not carried beyond 1865."[3] They are presented by the biographer as if recording events before those to be given next.

Writing probably in the early 1860's Evans says:

Several years ago while thirsting for a more satisfying knowledge of divine things than the current superficial literature of the church could supply, I was led to pray the Lord most sincerely to lead me to some book or books which could satisfy this inmost need. I had been previously led to study with interest and profit the mystic authors.

---

[1] *Ibid.*, pp. 13, ellipses by Leonard.

[2] *Ibid.*, pp. 13-14.

[3] *Ibid.*, p. 11.

From Madam Guyon, Fenelon, Kempis, Tauler and others I found something that was valuable. But all was vague and indefinite. While in a book store in the city of Portsmouth I saw on the shelf a work entitled "Athanasia, or, Foregleems of Immortality." [A footnote adds: "By Rev. E. H. Sears, a Unitarian writer of wide reputation."] It was deeply impressed on my consciousness that this was an answer to my earnest prayer. I consequently bought two copies, retaining one and presenting another to a brother in the ministry. The views of that excellent little volume came to my soul as rain upon a thirsty soil. In a foot note I observed a reference to the work of Swedenborg on "Divine Love and Wisdom." It was forcibly impressed upon my mind that the views of the book were those of Swedenborg and that what I had earnestly longed for would be found in him. I accordingly sent to Boston and procured his principal works. I may truly say that what my soul long yearned for I had found. I believed his teachings, for I could not do otherwise. I inwardly saw their truth.[1]

The biographer observes:

> The date of that momentous visit to Portsmouth is not given, nor is there anywhere an allusion to the exact time when he began the study of Swedenborg, though the year 1856 seems to be the date, as he notes in his journal on December 1, 1860, that for four years his theological opinions had been undergoing a revolution. Early in the year 1858 his recorded meditations show the

---

[1]*Ibid.*, p. 14.

influence of the new teacher.[1]

He evidently believed at first that he could consistently hold these new views of religion and remain in his place in the Methodist pulpit, for he proclaimed these views, as he says in a published letter, "in private conversation and in the pulpit." He says: "it appeared to me that I might be called by Providence to diffuse those higher views and religious teachings through the church of which I had long been a member and a sincere preacher. It was very natural to suppose that truths which had been so greatly blessed to my comfort would be eagerly embraced by all, as soon as they were made acquainted with them."

So eager was he to propagate these "glorious and all-satisfying truths," as he called them, and so fully persuaded was he that they needed only to be proclaimed to his Christian brethren to be welcomed by them, that he wrote a book embodying them in a most lucid and impressive form. He called it "The Celestial Dawn, or, Connection of Earth and Heaven."[2]

The manuscript of this book was finished on February 19, 1861,[3] and was published in the fall of

---

[1]*Ibid.*, p. 15.

[2]*Ibid.*, p. 8.

[3]*Ibid.*, part 2, X (November, 1905), 7; since all references to Leonard before this have been to the first part, no mention of parts has been made. The article is divided into sections, but no reference is made to them in the citations here.

Healing Hypotheses

1862.[1]

Although Evans avoided referring to Swedenborg by name in advancing Swedenborg's views, "soon after this book was put in circulation, evidences accumulated of the dissatisfaction created among his Methodist friends with the views advocated."[2] On April 4, 1864, Evans writes:

> This day has been an epoch in my spiritual history. I have sundered my connection with the Methodist Episcopal Church. It is not a step that has been hastily taken, but has long been considered. For five years past the providence of the Lord seems to have led me to this result. The failure of my health while preaching at Lawrence, my partial recovery and then, after another attempt to preach in the old church, the failure of my health again, seemed to me the voice of God that my labors as a Methodist preacher were by his will closed. My poverty and sufferings while my health would not admit of my laboring, not calling

---

[1] *Ibid.*, part 1, p. 8. This was not his first publication; Leonard notes:

His authorship dates from the year 1860, when he issued a booklet in advocacy of a higher Christian experience than it seemed to him to be the aim of the church to encourage. He entitled it "Divine Order in the Process of Full Salvation." It is not a polemic by any means, but a most kindly tender plea for a perfect consecration of the life to the will of God.... About the same time, perhaps a little earlier in the year, a larger book dealing with the same theme was issued and was named "Happy Island, or, Paradise Restored." No copy of this book has been accessible.... [part 3, X (December, 1905), 9.]

[2] *Ibid.*, part 1, p. 9.

forth any help from the church for which I had expended all my energies served to wean me from it. The suspicion of heresy and even of insanity that rested upon me for the views expressed in "The Celestial Dawn," and the cold shoulder that was turned toward me by my brethren, were a part of the permissive providence of the Lord leading in the same direction. I have been led to this decision by a higher power against which it has been vain to struggle. I have felt myself for years floating before a current of providences that was bearing me towards the New Church and out of the Old. I now feel a sense of freedom that is a great relief to my mind. I have been brought by the Divine mercy of the Lord from darkness into light. I wish here to record my grateful sense of the divine goodness to me in all His dealings with me. He has heard my sincere and oft-repeated prayer that He would lead me into all truth. I have learned to trust all to His management. I only pray to be of use to the souls of others. I long to impart the Divine treasures, in mercy given to me, to all receptive Souls.[1]

"A few days" later

he notes the baptism of himself and wife by Rev. Thomas Worcester, D. D., of the New Church, by which they became members at large of that religious body. He did not become a pastor in his new relations, but consented to serve as a missionary of the Massachusetts Association. He was still in feeble health and he says in his journal, "My consent was based on my confidence in the Lord and in his Word. One thing I know, that so far as a soul will hold itself in readiness to impart,

---

[1] *Ibid.*, part 1, p. 10.

the Lord will give. "With what measure ye mete, it shall be measured to you again." I long to engage in some higher use than I have apparently filled the last few years—years of preparation."

These words were written in August, 1864. Little did he know that the yearning of his heart to be of "some higher use" was to be gratified in the way it was. He had been satisfied to have been physically able to carry the message of the New Church to the few in New England who might be willing to hear it. But his "years of preparation" were for a "higher use." Instead of being the prophet of a small religious body and the evangel of a narrow province, he was to become the pioneer apostle[1] of a worldwide spiritual movement which many believe is destined to redeem the world from sin, sickness and death.[2]

For years Evans was burdened with sickness and also from time to time managed to overcome it through spiritual means.[3] His biographer describes him when nearly 47 as

> of medium stature, of slight build, and [carrying] an infirmity of many years standing, known in medicine by the name of fistula, which, together with a disordered nervous system, had caused him many a breakdown . . . and would have totally

---

[1] A term used in the title of his earlier article, later issued as a pamphlet by H. H. Carter of Boston, "The Pioneer Apostle of Mental Science," *Practical Ideals*, VI (July-August, 1903), 30-37, a brief account of Evans.

[2] Leonard, *op. cit.*, part 1, pp. 10-11.

[3] *Ibid.*, part 1, p. 7.

wrecked the life of a less stalwart soul.[1]

"Before he had finished his studies preparatory to entering the ministry"[2] he had a faith healing of "a most aggravated and obstinate dyspepsia."[3]

> He gives a glimpse of how he must have been handicapped ... even in his earlier pastorates when he makes such a minute as this: "I have carried into the pulpit a load of bodily infirmities enough to cause me to sink in any other work. Sometimes Christ has stood by me, and the rush of the divine energy into my soul has raised me above all my weakness." He continued to grow more feeble, so that all the later years of his ministry were marked by periodical suspensions of his work from this cause, and even when he was at his post there was devotion to duty under great suffering a large part of the time.[4]
> After one of the breakdowns spoken of, which occurred early in the year 1859, while pastor at Lawrence, Massachusetts, he makes this note in his journal on September 19, 1859: "My health so completely failed me last April that I could not preach. I have not preached for more than six months. There was a time when I could not so much as read. But during this complete prostration of my nervous system my soul has tranquilly reposed in God. Far down below my trembling

---

[1] *Ibid.*, part 2, p. 3.

[2] *Ibid.*, part 2, p. 4.

[3] *Ibid.*

[4] *Ibid.*, part 1, p. 7.

nerves there is a region of soul where all is still and silent." Here is the earliest evidence we have that the new teaching [of Swedenborg] was enabling him to look away from the body and its sensations and to rest in the calm spot at the inmost centre.[1]

From his past expressions, one might think him perfectly capable of making such an observation irrespective of his new views.

"Early" in 1860 Evans writes:

> I have thought much of the power of a living faith, by which I mean a faith that is connected with love, or which proceeds from love. Such a faith is power, and it seems to me that its power is but little understood. In the primitive church the power of faith was understood. In the church of the future it will be so again. Once faith had power over disease. Here, undoubtedly, was no violation of the laws of nature, but the unfolding of a higher law. A law is only the mode of the divine action. Faith once gave the mind power over the material world, to some extent. All causation, all force lies in the spiritual world or in some mind, uncreated or created. The phenomena of the outward world are effects, the causes of which are in the world of mind. [A reference to the faith that removes mountains is omitted by the biographer.] Our Saviour expresses in these words, I believe, the law of the soul's power over matter. In the future this law will be more fully developed.

---

[1] *Ibid.*, part 2, p. 3.

I pray the Lord to increase my faith.[1]

A month later,

under date of April 12, 1860, Dr. Evans is found dwelling upon his physical condition and utters the first word of his that I have met with as to the mental origin of disease. "My health," he writes, "is not yet adequate to the full work of the ministry. I long for strength to employ it in the work so dear to my heart. . . . I have hope of regaining my former power. The Lord is my strength. 'He is the health of my countenance and my God.' I will find in Christ all that I need. He can cure every form of mental disease, and thus restore the body, for disease originates generally, if not always, in the mind." There is little doubt that he was helped to this conclusion respecting the mental origin of disease by his study of Swedenborg's "Science of Correspondence," where he found such teachings as this: "There is not anything in the mind to which something in the body does not correspond, and this which corresponds may be called the embodying of that."

Three weeks later, under date of May 4, 1860, we find him taking a more positive attitude towards his infirmity and rallying his spiritual forces to overcome it. He writes: "My soul has great peace at the centre, through there is often much disturbance at the surface. My nervous system has been so prostrated that trembling seizes upon me in the performance of the simplest services. I know not the occasion of it nor the remedy for it. But relying on God, from whom is all life and all good, I am resolved to put it away as

---

[1] *Ibid.*, part 2, p. 4.

an evil that is a sin against God, because it unfits me for His work. I consecrate myself and all that I am and hope to be to the uses of Christ's kingdom. This evil that has almost crushed the life out of me must cease. I will be myself, that is, what God would have me to be.[1]

Less than a year later, after finishing *The Celestial Dawn*,

he had so far triumphed over conditions that he was able to accept an invitation to the pastorate of the Methodist Episcopal church of Salisbury, Massachusetts. In making a memorandum of his settlement there, he says: "Through the blessing of God and in answer to prayer, my health is improved. I lay hold upon Christ as my life and as the 'health of my countenance and my God.'" The day of his entire redemption was yet in the distance. Ill health was still to be his portion. But he was a student of his own case, and was gaining, all unaided, save by the Spirit, a deeper knowledge of the spiritual laws to be availed of in healing, of which in the coming years he was to become the first eminent expounder. His invalidism was being used by the Spirit to prepare him for the great service he was to render the world.[2]

On Sunday March 30. 1862, Evans writes:

It is now two months since I have preached otherwise than in private conversation. I have passed through a painful sickness, and am yet far

---

[1]*Ibid.*, part 2, p. 6, ellipsis by Leonard.

[2]*Ibid.*, part 2, p. 7.

from being fully restored. I have had some rich experiences of Divine things and some heavenly views. . . . God has given me an earnest spirit of supplication for some days past for restoration to health that I may be made the messenger of good to souls. My faith has grasped Christ as the Life, the eternal Life. My soul lives wholly from Him, and my body from my soul. Hence in saving the soul he saves the body. . . . That the body should be saved from an abnormal, disorderly condition by faith violates no law of nature, for it is the eternal order of God that faith saves the soul, and the body's life is derived wholly from the vital spirit it encloses. The omnipotence of God acts according to the eternal order He has established. This order is expressed by Christ when he said many times to those He healed in soul, and thus in body. "Thy faith hath saved thee." In absolute self despair, I have looked to Him who is the only Life. With stubbornness of faith—a faith He has imparted, hence the faith of God—I have said with humble boldness. "I know thou dost save.". . . Through faith I have conjunction with the one and only Life. "I shall yet praise Him who is the health of my countenance and my God." I hear His voice, a voice that sent life to thrill through the decaying body of Lazarus. "Go in peace, thy faith hath saved thee." I have no hope from physicians and drugs. They are as powerless as the staff of Elijah in the hands of Gehazi to raise the widow's son. May Christ eternally unite me to Himself by granting me this great favor.[1]

Later in 1862 Evans records:

---

[1] *Ibid.*, part 2, p. 8, ellipses by Leonard.

This has been a remarkable day in my experience, a new epoch in my spiritual history. My faith was put to the trial, and through Christ gloriously triumphed. I enjoyed an extraordinary season in prayer. Out of the deeps I cried unto the Lord and He heard me. While sinking, like Peter, I seized hold of Christ, and walked upon the abyss as if it had been marble. I touched Him who is the Life, and life thrilled through my whole being. More than twenty years ago, after a long season of desolation and self-imposed condemnation, Christ spake me whole, soul and body. There is a faith to which the Divine power always responds, "Go in peace, thy faith hath saved thee." With holy violence I laid hold upon Him who has become my salvation. I live because Christ lives. Here is the connection of cause and effect. I no longer live, but Christ liveth in me. I am dead and my life is hid with Christ in God. I feel myself saved—perfectly well, soul, spirit and body. The eleventh-day of August is laid up in everlasting remembrance. From this time forth I live a life of faith. There is a faith that puts the soul in vital connection with the one only Life. I am saved on this eleventh day of August. All is well. Christ is bringing me up to a higher plane of divine life. I now bid an eternal farewell to the experience described in the seventh chapter of Paul's epistle to the Romans. The day of freedom dawns at length.[1]

Eight months after this, Evans observes,

I see how it is that by believing I have the thing for which I am praying causes me to have it. It is

---

[1]*Ibid.*, part 2, pp. 9-10.

implied that the faith is divinely imparted. It proceeds from God. Faith is truth and truth from God is something real and substantial. If one prays for recovery to health and the Lord gives him to believe that he is recovering, that faith is only the truth that it is so, received from the Lord. To believe that I am being recovered to health, if that faith is self originated, accomplishes nothing. But if my belief of it is a truth received from God, or if my faith is the faith of God, it becomes a substantial reality. Faith in its essence is truth, and truth is substance. Hence the author of the epistle to the Hebrews says, "Faith is the substance of things hoped for." Now if the Lord imparts to me a Divine conviction that a certain blessing is mine, that faith being the substance of what I desire, puts me into an actual realization of what I am praying for.[1]

It may have been about this time that Evans first went to Quimby. Not much seems to be known about this, although Leonard said that "every effort has been made to fix the time of the interviews, as well as to ascertain precisely what help Dr. Evans obtained from Dr. Quimby."[2]

Leonard reports,

> I consulted George A. Quimby of Belfast, Maine, his father's secretary during the last years of his practice.... He writes, "I know nothing about Mr. Evans' connection with my father except that he came to Portland to see him. I was either away at the time or else his stay was so brief that it made

---

[1] *Ibid.*, part 2, p. 11.

[2] *Ibid.*, part 2, p. 1.

no impression on my mind." The distinguished practitioner, Dr. J. H. Dewey, who was intimately acquainted with Dr. Evans, ... was also requested to give such information as he might possess on the point in question. He says, "In our earlier conversations we often referred to Dr. Quimby and his healing work, in which Dr. Evans told me of his visit to him, which, I think, was while he was yet preaching in the Methodist church and before Mrs. Eddy was healed by Quimby. [Leonard here adds the footnote: This would make the time of the visit to be in 1862, as it was in October of that year when Mrs. Eddy went to be treated. Dr. Dewey, however, admits that he is not certain of the date.] It was his acquaintance with Dr. Quimby's method that led to the modification of his views on the law of mental, or spiritual, healing, which he afterward so fully set forth in his own books on the subject."[1]

It is to the father of Horatio W. Dresser that one must look for most of the information on this topic. Julius A. Dresser writes:

> That able writer upon Mental Science, Dr. W. F. Evans, pays the following tribute to Quimby, in his second volume, entitled "Mental Medicine." He says: "Disease being in its root a *wrong belief*, change that belief, and we cure the disease.... The late Dr. Quimby, of Portland, one of the most successful healers of this or any age, embraced this view of the nature of disease, and by a long succession of most remarkable cures ... proved the

---

[1]*Ibid.*, part 2, p. 15. It will be noted that Dewey refers to only one visit, although no point is made of it, and it could be a typographical error.

truth of the theory . . . . Had he lived in a remote age or country, the wonderful facts which occurred in his practice would have now been deemed either mythical or miraculous. He seemed to reproduce the wonders of the gospel history." Dr. Evans obtained this knowledge of Quimby mainly when he visited him as a patient, making two visits for that purpose, about the year 1863, an interesting account of which I received from him, at East Salisbury, in the year 1876. Dr. Evans had been a clergyman up to the year 1863, and was then located in Claremont, N.H. But so readily did he understand the explanations of Quimby, which his Swedenborgian faith enabled him to grasp the more quickly, that he thought he could himself cure the sick in this way. Quimby replied that he thought he could. His first attempts on returning home were so successful that the preacher became a practitioner from that time, and the result has been great growth in the truth and the accomplishment of a great and a good work during the nearly twenty-five years since then. Dr. Evans's six volumes upon the subject of Mental Healing have had a wide and well-deserved sale.[1]

---

[1] Julius A. Dresser, *op. cit.*, pp. 20-21, rev. ed., pp. 26-27, ellipses by him. The omissions, from p. 210 of the work cited, are "By faith we are made whole. There is a law here the world will some time understand and use in the cure of the diseases that afflict mankind." "effected by psychopathic remedies, at the same time" "and the efficacy of that mode of treatment." In an unindicated omission immediately after "wrong belief" is "in the sense explained above." *Gospel* is capitalized by Evans. Leonard quotes J. A. Dresser as above at part 2, pp. 1-2 and at greater length the Evans quotation on Quimby at part 2, pp. 12-13, and observes that this is the only

Being desirous of having all the light possible thrown upon the relations which existed between Dr. Quimby and Dr. Evans at the time under review, I communicated with the widely-known writer and author, Horatio W. Dresser, asking for such recollections as he might have of his father's views. Through his courtesy I have permission to quote him as follows: "The impression I got from my father was that Dr. Evans' Swedenborgian belief and philosophical knowledge admirably fitted him to understand Dr. Quimby's theories and methods. It was evidently a case where a word to the wise was sufficient. Hence Dr. Evans very soon concluded that he could heal in the same way. Evidently, too, the method of silent treatment--this was probably the chief novelty to Dr. Evans--was one that he was prepared to appreciate at once. Of course the help which Dr. Quimby gave him was the convincing evidence. Dr. Quimby saw Evans' ability and encouraged him to take up the mental healing practice. My father always esteemed Dr, Evans highly and, so far as I know, held that his exposition of the mental method and theory was in entire harmony with the Quimby teaching.[1]

Leonard adds in a footnote, "Dr. Evans' publisher, H. H. Carter, of 5 Somerset street, Boston once remarked to the writer that Mr. [J. A.] Dresser always commended the books of Dr. Evans to his patients, especially 'The Divine

---

reference to Quimby published in the books on healing by Evans.

[1] Leonard, *op. cit.*, part 2, pp. 14-15.

Law of Cure.'"[1]

Dresser says:

> In 1863, Mr. Quimby received as a patient one who was to accomplish a very important work in the promulgation of the new theory and practice of healing. This was Rev. Warren Felt Evans, of Claremont, New Hampshire. Mr. Evans had been in poor health for several years, having suffered from a nervous breakdown coupled with a chronic disorder that had failed to respond to the methods of treatment then in vogue. Having heard of Mr. Quimby's remarkable cures [Leonard says that "how Dr. Evans learned of Dr. Quimby's work in Maine there is no means of determining"[2]], he visited Portland on two occasions to receive treatment by the new method. His expectations were more than realized. Mr. Evans was not only healed of his maladies, but became so deeply impressed by the practice and teachings of the new method and later began to apply it, having first developed the implied philosophy in his own terms. The turning-point came one day while in conversation with Mr. Quimby. Mr. Evans remarked that he believed he could cure by the same method and Mr. Quimby encouraged him to think that he could. Accordingly, Mr. Evans made the venture as soon as opportunity offered, after his return home, and the first attempts were so successful that the way opened for him to devote the remainder of his life to authorship and the

---

[1] *Ibid.*, part 2, p. 15n.

[2] *Ibid.*, part 2, p. 12.

healing of the sick.[1]

Leonard is less sure about some of this:

> When Dr. Evans learned the secret of Dr. Quimby's method, we can easily believe that he was captivated by it since he had long before come to believe that the healing works of Jesus were wrought through an understanding of mental and spiritual laws, and that it was along these lines, indeed, that he himself had been endeavoring to secure relief from his physical ills. It must have been an interesting moment when those two original thinkers came together to compare notes on this great subject, the one having proved himself a master in the practical application of principles which the other had intuitively discerned as possibly capable of such an application on the part of anyone. He was there as a patient, Mr. Dresser tells us, but with what benefit to his health we are not told. That he drew out of Dr. Quimby all that he had in him to give respecting his theories and methods we cannot for a moment doubt. Neither can we doubt that he was an apt pupil and carried away, and made his own, all that the teacher had to offer. The conviction that he could make use of the same methods in healing soon possessed him, and he was confirmed in it by the encouraging word of the veteran practitioner.[2]

> While the date cannot be fixed with precision when Dr. Evans undertook to make a test

---

[1]Dresser, *A History of the New Thought Movement*, pp. 71-72.

[2]Leonard, *op. cit.*, part 2, pp. 13-14.

of healing others by spiritual methods, it is almost beyond question that it was not later than the year 1863. That even at this time he had any thought of giving his life to this work there is no reason to suppose, for we have already learned that in August, 1864, he was arranging to become a missionary of the New Church. More than a year after this date, he writes in his journal of his "great desire to preach the gospel again," and devotes several pages to setting forth what he conceives to be the preparation a minister needs to become an effective preacher. He probably had come to believes that a minister should fulfil the commission given by Jesus to the early disciples and add the ministry of healing to the preaching of the word, and intended to do so if he resumed the pastoral office. But the way to his return to that office, as we have noted, was still closed by reason of feeble health, though he preached more or less as a missionary of the New Church. Among his literary remains are the manuscripts of some of the sermons he prepared during that period. Like the true son of the spirit that he was, he waited only for Divine guidance. It came, and he consecrated himself to a healing ministry as wholly and unselfishly as he ever did to the work of the pulpit and the pastorate.[1]

If he did not begin [his healing practice] as early as the year 1863, he was evidently giving much attention to the practice in 1865, for there are indications in his journal of the study he was then making of disease and its treatment. In one place he says: "Last night, at 2 o'clock, I awoke from sleep and received an important suggestion relating to the removal of diseased conditions from

---

[1] *Ibid.*, part 2, p. 2.

the body. Where a disease tends to produce a particular and unhealthy mental condition, as melancholy or low spirits by dyspepsia or diseased liver, if the opposed mental state can be induced it will tend to cure the disease. This is a principle of great extent. Disease should be studied in relation to its effects upon the mind and then the states of mind that are antagonistic to the disease may be induced through the spiritual world." As this is the very first deliverance of Dr. Evans on record after he began his mental healing practice, it will have special interest for his many friends. It is valuable also as giving a glimpse of the original and intuitive method that was to characterize his career as the first public expounder of spiritual therapeutics.

He was living in Claremont, New Hampshire, at this time, where he bought a little home five or six years before, and to which he returned in April, 1862, after his breakdown in his pastorate in Salisbury, which proved to be the conclusion of his pastoral career. During his forced retirement here he was not content to act the part of an invalid. He was busy in 1862 in getting his book, "Celestial Dawn," through the press and with official duties connected with the schools of the place. In the summer of 1863, to aid his son who had lost his right arm in the Civil War, he bought a periodical business and conducted it until the wounded boy was able to take charge. In the midst of these activities, he was consulting with Dr. Quimby, and making his first experiments in mental healing. Here in Claremont was the scene of his first triumphs as a practitioner and here he gathered the material for his first book, "The Mental Cure," which ... was the earliest work to set forth the principles of metaphysical healing.[1]

The doctorate of Evans was in medicine. Leonard gives little information on it, but mentions that

> medical science interested him from early life, and he pursued the study of it, not to gain a degree, but simply to add to his store of knowledge. After he began his practice as a mental healer he received a diploma from a chartered board of physicians of the Eclectic School, certifying to his qualifications and giving him the [space in original] M.D., a title which he used in his circulars, but never in his books.[2]

It is not clear when this took place.

> From the first, patients were received in the home [of Evans]. When they removed from Claremont to Salisbury in 1869 this practice was followed during a part of every year. An office was probably opened in Boston about the year 1867, as certain data indicate, [at this point Leonard adds the footnote: It was in 1867 that Dr. Evans and his wife united with the New Church Society in Bowdoin street, Boston, having been members "at large" of the denomination. This indicates that they must have had an office in Boston at that date. This is the belief of the present senior pastor, Rev. James Reed, who was then an associate pastor.] when the custom of spending only the winter and spring months in the city was

---

[1] *Ibid.*, part 2, pp. 15-16.

[2] *Ibid.*, part 2, pp. 17n-18n.

inaugurated which was continued for nearly twenty years. In 1873 they removed from a leased house in Salisbury to one they had purchased there. The summers were not the least busy part of the year with them. They maintained the home in the country for the purpose of serving the sick to greater advantage than was possible for them to do in Boston. The house was enlarged to accommodate a goodly number, and yet was often too small to meet the demands made upon it by applicants from all parts of the land. Here, as in Boston, this noble pair lived to serve, without money and without price if need be, all who came to them for help... . His compensation consisted of freewill offerings.[1]

Mrs. Frances A. Pettengill, of Salisbury, remembers

seeing him and the impression the sight of him made on me with his long white beard and a sort of feeling of mystery. I am 85 yrs. old but was pretty young when I saw him about town.... I can't think of another person in town, my age, who would remember him.[2]

In an interview on May 28, 1962, she mentioned that he was individual in his characteristics, that she did not recall his treating sick people, nor his mingling with the townspeople, nor his attending the Methodist church that she had attended for 80 years, and that he served in 1861. Presumably, he did not attend it. She recalled that he used to go to some other place; presumably, it was Boston, although she associated him with Washington, D.C.

---

[1] *Ibid.*, part 2, pp. 19-20.

[2] Letter of October 9, 1962.

He seems not to have made any very lasting impression on Salisbury. The Washington connection may have been from a Post Office job there of his wounded son, Franklin, reported by Mrs. Charlotte Marshall, great granddaughter of Evans, interviewed on May 29, 1962; she added that Evans had a winter apartment on Beacon Hill and an office nearby. Nothing was known about his connection with Quimby. Mrs. Marshall indicated that many of his patients were nervously unsettled women who had reached menopause.

The Salisbury death records list his September 4, 1889, death as from disease of brain and his occupation as doctor.

After the publication of his last book in 1886, he started another, but did not finish it.

According to information received from Horace B. Blackmer, Recording Secretary of the General Convention of the New Jerusalem in the U.S.A., on April 9, 1962, Evans was not ordained in the New Church, but was a licentiate or lay leader for five years,

> authorized to teach and lecture about the doctrines of our church, and to conduct religious services upon request in the absence of an ordained clergyman. He entered into this work for the first year with considerable vigor, but his health gradually curtailed the extent of his efforts, and at the end of the time (1869) he "did not ask to have his license renewed." (His assistance in Sabbath services during most of this period were accorded our society in Contoocook, N.H.) From the point of view of our church, his books written after his acquaintance with Dr. Quimby, departed materially from Swedenborgian teachings.

Curiously enough, this town was rather near the birthplace of Mary Baker Eddy; there seems to be no indication that they ever met, but they were patients of Quimby probably within a year, apparently lived in adjoining communities when Evans moved back to Salisbury, and of course shared Boston. Whether there is a justification for the suggestion that she was influenced by him[1] is not within the scope of this study.

Presumably, the most important factor in the development of his thought was his own seeking attitude and mystical experiences that accompanied it. In addition to his religious experiences, he also had psychical ability. J. H. Dewey writes to Leonard:

> I was quite intimately acquainted with Dr. Evans from the time he first came to Boston to begin his healing work. He was both a seer and healer. I had the most unmistakable evidence of his ability at times to accurately diagnose the conditions of an absent patient and to so effectually treat him that the patient was fully conscious of the treatment at the time, though no previous arrangement had been made for it. My acquaintance with him was at a time when it was of the greatest help to me in my own independent studies along these lines, and my memories of him are of the most agreeable kind. He was a man of unusual insight and ability and an absolutely independent and discriminating thinker, as his published writings most fully demonstrate.[2]

Dewey in a book quotes at length from Evans on the brain, including the following, and includes in his introductory remarks the observation, "It may be well ... to remark that Dr. Evans writes from practical experience,

---

[1] An unsigned entry on Evans in *The National Cyclopaedia of American Biography*, XXIII (1932), 430.

[2] Leonard, *op. cit.*, part 4, *Practical Ideals*, XI (January, 1906), 16.

having demonstrated the general truth of the doctrines in his own person."[1]

> On the dividing line between sleeping and waking, the mysterious dream-land, the mental powers become greatly exalted and quickened, so that the experiences and perceptions of hours, and even weeks and months, are crowded into moments. The mind breaks loose from its material thraldom, the limitations of time, place, and sense, and asserts its innate freedom. It sees without the external eye, and to distances almost unlimited. It perceives distant objects, persons and things, something as we see the image of an absent friend in the mind, only with more objective clearness, and they do not appear to be in the mind, but external to it, like the scenery around us in our every-day life. There are those who can enter this state at will. It has become, in fact, their normal condition. We have experimented much with it, putting it to severe tests, a thousand miles away, and have found it as reliable as our ordinary vision. The power of thus suspending the action of the cerebrum, possessed by a scientific person, is of great value in the diagnosis of disease. It is a condition of the highest wakefulness, though physiologically it is a state of sleep, and has been denominated somnambulism. It may exist when the external senses are not oblivious to the objects surrounding us. It is a waking up from their usually dormant state of the undeveloped powers of our inner life.[2]

---

[1] John Hamlin Dewey, *The Way, the Truth and the Life* (New York: J. H. Dewey Publishing Company, 1988, 1st ed.?), p. 259.

[2] W. F. Evans, *The Mental-Cure*, pp. 105-08.

Especially since Leonard does not tell of such experimentation recorded in the Evans journal, it seems likely that it was something inspired by Quimby, quite possibly taken up as part of the silent method of healing.

APPENDIX D

DRESSER'S EARLY BIOGRAPHICAL DATA

In an undated note to his son, Dresser says:

> I came across a few biographical data the other day, while looking over some of my papers, and I thought you might like the paper; so I have copied it off. This tells something about myself previous to the time of biographical sketches in such works as "Who's Who." So here you are.
>
> Horatio Willis Dresser, born January 15, 1866, 7 A.M., Yarmouth, Maine. Moved to Webster, Mass., (from Westbook, Maine) in autumn of 1866. Father owned and published *The Webster Times*, a weekly newspaper, until 1874. Visited grandparents in Yarmouth nearly every summer. Father's health broke down, family moved to Dansville, N.Y., April, 1874: near the health home there. First attended school in Dansville, at age of 8. Visited Maine in June, 1876, where last saw grandfather. Returned to Dansville, and family went to Denver, Colo, in July; we camped at Manitou, in foothills of Pike's Peak, that summer. Father bought house on Welton St., Denver, where we spent the winter. House sold, moved to California, in March, 1877. Lived in Oakland and Napa. Attended grammar school in Oakland, while we lived at 1967 Grove St. First occupations for pay: selling lampshades and distributing physician's cards from door to door. Moved to Willows, Colusa Co., at terminus of Cal. Pacific R.R., where father was station agent. Began to

learn railroad and telegraph business from father and his assistant, the operator. Became telegraph operator for a small line running north from Willows to Germantown and Oakland, 1879. Also messenger for Western Union. All moved to Pinole, on main line of Central Pacific, 18 miles from Oakland, in 1881. Station agent and telegraph operator in father's name (father too ill to work and could not telegraph). Salary, 75,00 [sic] per month. Also agent for Wells Fargo and Co's Express, and telephone agent for a powder co. Visited Southern Cal. on vacation, Feb., 1882.

Left with family for Boston, May 11, 1882; arrived Boston, May 17, and Yarmouth same day, on visit to grandmother. Spent summer in Yarmouth and Auburn (worked at latter place in Chas. Cushman's shoeshop, keeping accounts in the stitching-room at $1,00 [sic] per day). Father in Boston that summer in water business. Resigned in Auburn and went to Boston, Oct. 1, 1882. Lived at 215 W. Springfield St. Attended Chauncey Hall School two days, took bookkeeping lessons, and studied arithmetic and elocution (to overcome defect in speech [apparently successfully overcome]). Seriously ill in November. Parents took up practice of mental healing at 14 West Chester Park (now part of Mass. Ave). Family moved to Hotel Boylston, cor. of Tremont and Boylston, for summer of 1883; then to Hotel Howland, 218 Columbus Ave., for year. Worked as clerk for a time in store of Health Food Co., 199 Tremont St., (Mr. W. H. Pratt, agent). Moved to Hotel Huntington (later the Nottingham), Huntington Ave. and Blagden Street, Aug., 1884. Parents practising and teaching mental healing. Gave service for a time to Geo. M. Whitaker, owner and editor of the New England Farmer (wrote shorthand and read proof). Became business manager and bookkeeper, 1886-1888. Resigned position, and took French lessons preparatory to going to Europe. Practised mental healing in co-operation with parents, beginning in 1884. Sailed for Europe with Hooker-Swain party, June 16, 1888. Had private tutor in English, fall and winter of 88-89. With family in Fort Edward, N.Y. summer of 1889. Lectured in co-operation with parents, fall of 1889, at new home, 19 Blagden St., opposite the rear of the Huntington. Europe with party, summer of 1889, as part assistant to Hooker-Swain. Fitted for Harvard under tutor, 1890-91. Entered as special, fall of 1891, after failing to pass entrance exams in June. Studied in Dublin, N.H. (where family spent summer, 1892). Passed exams. in fall and entered as regular student. Father d. May 10, 1893. Left college for time, but returned for final exams. Spent summer with mother and brothers, Intervale, N.H. Tried college for a while in the fall, but left on account of ill-health in December. Lost all credit for junior year. We lived at 481 Beacon Street on[e] year. Lectured with mother to small classes there, early months of 1894. Asked to print second lecture, "The Immanent God," first publication. Rewrote other lectures and published first book, "The Power of Silence," May 10, 1895. We moved next to 105 Irving St., Cambridge; wrote second book, "The Perfect Whole," there[.] Returned to Harvard for part-time work as special student. Received A. B. out of course, 1905; A.M., as earned in 1904. See Who's Who for list of books and other occupations.

APPENDIX E

DRESSER'S LETTER TO EL ON CHRISTIAN SCIENCE

Hartsdale, N.Y.
April 3, 1953

Dear El.

You may wonder how a person can go about discriminating between the truths implied in Christian Science and the half-truths which are seriously misleading, and I will tell you a little story. Once a young woman from the ordinary walks of life came to call on me, in Boston, to discuss just such matters as half-truths imply. She was not an educated woman. She had little knowledge of life or of systems of belief. But she had the directness of a mind true to itself and she wanted to see things for herself. In a library in Brooklyn she happened upon a book of mine, "The Power of Silence," in which the principles of healing which I acquired from Quimby's teaching were set forth, and she read and read with absorbing interest. Then her C. S. teacher and healer learned that she was reading my book and absolutely forbade her to read it, adding to this command the usual fallacies by which C. S. people had tried to keep the truth about Mrs. Eddy from becoming known; and all this with the show of authority by which a dictator puts himself over. Now, this simple-minded woman was not satisfied. She wanted to know whether what she had been told about my book and about me was true, or whether she had been lied to. So she traveled on to Boston, secured an appointment to talk with me, and presented her problem. Of course it was a simple matter to go back to the early history when father and mother were with Quimby and

Mrs. Patterson-Eddy was there, partly grasping Quimby's ideas but partly getting a chance to exercise her love of power. This woman knew I had the truth, for I could set her mind at rest on every p[o]int. Then she returned to Brooklyn and kept on reading my book. Her teacher-healer learned this fact and called the woman to account before a church committee. She was asked the direct question if she was reading my book, and said Yes. Furthermore, she explained, I have been on to Boston to see for myself, and have learned the truth about Mrs. Eddy. Then the committee put her out of the C. S. organization. Now that's the sort of thing that would settle the matter for anybody, and this is but one instance with regard to people who, as truth-lovers, have followed the matter through. But I have known others who, lacking that woman's directness and sincerity, hedged and compromised. For example, I once knew the right hand man who as Mrs. Eddy's associate had access to everything including Mrs. Eddy's diary. It was that little book, he told me, that gave him the convincing evidence that what I had set forth about Mrs. Eddy (including father's pamphlet) was true. But what did he do? "There's money in it," he said; "the C. S. people have got millions and you cannot buck up against them." So he withdrew from my acquaintance when as a right-hand man, he could have done more than any other person to set the C. S. people free. That was a sort of Judas temptation, was it not?

    Now of course I have had the advantage in clearing matters up for sometime C. S. people. For people soon saw I had no axe to grind and knew what I was talking about, for I had known all the people who were closest to Quimby, I had all the manuscripts and everything else, and could hand on Mrs. Eddy, so to speak, for people to gaze at. The discrimination turned on this: Quimby did two great things for people. He penetrated the "false identification" by which people's ills had been built up---as in case of the medicos who persuaded my mother she had spinal complaint when she had nothing of the sort; or, in case of my father, who seemed to be headed for "consumption" but needed to be set free from his Calvinism, which Quimby said was "killing" him---and dispelled that diagnosis to the wind; and, if people were willing, he showed them up to themselves, as he was ready to do in case of Mrs. E., but she wouldn't take it. This meant, in Quimby's own words, "she has no identity in truth," (reported to me by one of Quimby's patients). So she began her work with a lie and kept it up, ostensibly a well woman while under the care of medical doctor after medical doctor, taking remedies and trying treatments but never overcoming [t]he shaking palsy. That's what comes when a person is not true to self. Now if anybody thinks I have fabricated this account of a strange case, I am ready to accept the challenge, as in conferring with that very genuine woman from Brooklyn who would not take No for an answer.

So there you are.
As ever,
[signed on carbon copy] H.W.D.

APPENDIX F

DRESSER'S LETTER TO MRS. BROWNE ON EXTRASENSORY PERCEPTION

The book referred to below appears to be Eileen J. Garrett's *Telepathy* (New York: Creative Age Press, Inc., 1941).

South Hadley, Mass.
February 8, 1943

Dear Mrs. Browne:

The book on "Telepathy" raises a highly important question as to the validity of experiences purporting to originate, as causes are concerned, from the "other world." Such a doubt as the book itself suggests would naturally arise after a time, since alleged messages might be generated from within or alleged presences conjured up as if such presences were more than merely psychological.

I am perhaps in a position to resolve the doubt to a large extent. So you may be interested to know how I acquired the attitude that has borne the test of time.

Back in the 80's when there was marked interest in psychical research in Boston, with Mr. Richard Hodgson present as secretary, over from England for a while in connection with investigations, I was selected by a very influential person affiliated with the Society for Psychical Research to be given a college education at Harvard with a view to preparing me later as a so-called "scientific medium." Evidentially speaking I was supposed to have the requisite sensitivity for such a function. The question whether a man, so trained, could or would yield his organism for mediumistic activities was apparently not raised. I was not informed by my patroness concerning the reason for supplying the money for four years at Harvard. This of course was not an honest procedure. I was to be told in due time. I was prompted to accept the meager amount granted me--meager because my patroness, a queen without a kingdom outside of her estates in Boston, Lenox and Bar Harbor, went over to the university and ascertained the least possible amount on which a young man could squeeze through college, and then granted me just that sum--because I wanted a Harvard University education in order to develop my interests in philosophy. I continued on my way during a year of preparation with a tutor, and two years at Harvard before the concealed plan was exposed. Then my patroness invited me to visit in her luxurious home, Bar Harbor, I was taken out to ride one afternoon, and the plan was disclosed. A firm believer in individuality and its preservation, I declined to be shaped by such a pattern. I dropped that queen in due time and when I could do so secured money enough to complete my education, as the saying is, in accordance with my own convictions.

To go back a bit. We as a family, father, mother and I, declined all ouvertures [sic] for experimentation in psychical matters, howbeit at that time Hodgson hadn't even accepted telepathy as an established fact, and we were known as having proved it long before. The reason was this: there is a superior value in psychical experiences coming *unsought* amidst natural circumstances in contrast with prearranged conditions for purposes of proof. For prearrangements imply the possibility of projections or anticipations which might mar the whole proceding.

In line with this view of the matter, I adopted an attitude when I was about 18 which I have maintained ever since. The implications are these:

1. What appertains to me spiritually is likely to be bestowed or given. If it comes, it brings its own evidence. Not having sought it, never having tried to repeat it, I have good reason to believe it was real--real as a "gift."

Healing Hypotheses 347

    2.   With a few rare exceptions, it is better not even to experiment with telepathy, but rather to take it as a matter of course. So with clairvoyance or clairaudience. If it comes, well and good. If it does not come, why still well and good.
    3.   Mediumistic experiences were to be excluded from the word "go" because I was already too sensitive to "mental atmospheres" and needed to avoid increased psychical receptivity.
    4.   It is possible to retain the attitude of a mere observer, listening, thinking, noting what comes, without making the least effort even to hold onto any intimation given from outside or beyond, however full of grace from heaven it seemed to be.
    5.   It is desirable to attribute a high place in one's makeup to intuition, psychic impressions, and so on, as valid on their own level in terms of abilities on our part for participating in such experiences as an *uninvited* guidance, a clairvoyant awareness of a person's condition at a distance, or any clairaudient item, like a communicating word from a "voice" not reasoned away (as do psychologists) on the hypothesis of hallucination.

With the evidences of more than a half-century since I adopted the above outlined attitude, I can now look back over cherished experiences which I believe have disclosed most of the types of psychical experience. The telepathic experiences have been most numerous, and I believe the book is sound in its teachings in connecting telepathy with emotions. I have had comparitively *[sic]* few experiences of clairvoyance that are outstanding, but a sufficient number to discriminate the type in contrast with telepathy. I have heard words from a distance as if uttered in my ear when there was no clairvoyance and no telepathy otherwise than that of this limited experience. I was near enough to mediumship for two years, 20 to 22, to fear that I might succumb to it. I see no reason to doubt that a few experiences affiliated with people who have passed on were real, but I have my own factual basis for belief, namely, the brevity of any such communication--a brevity that was not marred by an effort on my part to enlarge upon a message by keeping it going. The fact that but few messages of any sort have come during the last quarter century leads to no doubt on my part concerning the validity of experiences occurring years ago. For my interpretation is that communications are vouchsafed when needed. So if years pass without any outstanding event, why, once more, well and good. If I need guidance, it will come. If I never reach out to a person who has passed on, I shall have more evidence when and if communicating experiences come. I have never closed the inner door save in a case of an officious correspondent whom I will call Mrs. Psychic who took it upon herself to travel to Brooklyn psychically to discover when I arrived and otherwise to follow me at a distance until I had to tell her I had shut her out and that was that. That same mortal is now trying to induce me to promise to come back to her from the beyond if I go first or to be ready for her presence if she departs first. Once more I have written 'Nothing doing.'

It seems to me that if I had yielded to mediumistic experiences, I would eventually come to doubt the validity of the communications, for I would know that I had acquired the habit and that habit often keeps us "going through the motions."

Mrs. Piper's organism obviously acquired the habit so that messages purporting to come from the beyond during the years of experimentation with this famous medium regularly began with the same words, so a friend who copied many of the messages on the typewriter told me.

The experiences which some people have had with automatic writing as the basis may have conveyed actual messages from the beyond at first. But the recipient's mind, accustomed to the experience after a time, may have picked up the thread and may have done a lot of elaborating.

"Telepathy" surely gives the right clue in rejecting

the view that the whole content of psychical experiences is supplied by the subconscious. I can readily identify the reference to the superconscious as something other than the subconscious. I believe it *normal* to be in touch with other modes of reality on the higher level. The subconscious does not generate those modes, although the subconscious might later follow some of the deliverances reproductively.

A symbol as described in this book might derive its initial reality from above, but might assimilate some of its content from below. I once had a symbolical experience so profoundly real for me that it has been to a considerable extent a basis of faith ever since. Yet by a reminder only it was partly affiliated with the subconscious. I could not dissolve the experience into a mere by-product of the subconscious because it was so plainly a deliverance or gift from above.

Why do I believe so heartily in my own experiences while to a large extent doubting those of other people? Because, for one thing, I have not gone out in quest of them but have let them come and have never practised or sought mediumship. Whereas personal experience is so often rejected because it *is* personal, I am convinced that the personal tone establishes the evidence, as in a telepathic communication from my mother years ago, identifiable by its personal quality in contrast with the remoteness that might enter in case of a mere experiment with a stranger. The scholars have been inclined to reject experiences between friends. But it is friends who *know*, notably in my relationship with my parents in the early years, my nearness to a young woman cousin, and, in later years, telepathy in case of a patient who was especially in affinity.

I believe we possess powers of communication, clairvoyance, and the rest, that are in abeyance, remaining potential in this life with most of us, as absorbed as we are in externalities. But with a few these powers are awake. We who know them by experience did not try to awaken in this respect. The awakening came naturally, in my case in connection with therapeutic interests in helping people from the time I was about 17.

There was a great advantage, you will notice, in beginning one's adventures in this realm with an other than personal or experimental motive in mind, namely a desire to help people out of their troubles through silent spiritual healing. As a matter of course one put faith in the Divine Presence as source of guiding wisdom. In the same way one had faith in intuition as a higher mode of knowing. The teaching that we are "members one of another" and that mental atmospheres tend to mingle came as readily. No less easily came the observation that telepathy alone could not explain silent healing. Some people insisted that it did. For some patients got the "thought" which seemed to them decisive. But those of us who carried on the practice knew that the words were subordinate to the realizational experience as a whole. So we refused to select out the telepathy and experiment with that to convince critics like Dr. Hodgson. I refused to succumb to the plans of my queen-patroness because I knew that mediumship would be a minor part of my psychical life. I deliberately trained my mind to the limit inphilosophy at Harvard to be as critical as the best of them, the doctor's degree being the sign that I had passed muster.

The experience is perhaps unusual: to have in one's own person the whole range of abilities from almost mediumship (when I was 22 or so, as above stated) to a critically analytical power sufficient to dissipate into thin air many psychical experiences which others have found convincing.

The author of "Telepathy" is the only person I have known about who could pass through mediumship and out into the clear light of doubts as to the validity of communications received through her. Ordinarily, some have the experiences, others the critical acumen with the requisite training.

I believe it is possible to have the experiences and

Healing Hypotheses 351

keep them intact while also giving oneself the training that would seemingly make possible the complete undermining of anything allegedly psychical. Much depends on being sufficiently grounded in inner experiences before taking the critical training.

One can, for example, retain intuitional abilities to the full as *if* "uneducated," while on the other hand receive the analytically critical training which enables psychologists to reason away intuition as non-existent.

In other connections I have given some of the reasons, in my book, "The Open Vision," for example.

In most people the inner "degree," as Swedenborg explained, is closed. Hence they are natural-minded and nothing more, while in this the natural world. In the few this degree is open. So they have what Swedenborg calls spiritual perception (I use the term intuition to cover this kind of perception). Hence these people discern by spiritual-mindedness. St. Paul also contrasts the two.

On the lower level, as I call it, of natural-mindedness one may well push doubt to the limit, explaining away right and left if one can.

Thus, when my queen-like patroness tried to get a psychical message when I was visiting her in Bar Harbor by putting her hand on mine while I held the pencil for automatic writing and she asked a question into the air, the pencil wrote plainly only so far as her mind and mine *agreed*, the rest being a blur. So the content of the writing was plainly attributable to her mind and mine, and nothing more.

When I sat one night with a table-tipping group the table-stuff ran into chaos because, the strongest mind present, was sceptical of any validity. That mind being mine, the experiment was ruined.

The only occasions when I have been present during a medium's trance the whole content of the experience was explicable by reference to what the medium delivered by aid of her clairvoyance plus what she derived from the subconscious mind of people present.

As an exhibit of clairvoyance in one instance the evidence in favor of clairvoyance was excellent, for I could give the requisite verification. But as alleged evidence of a spirit-presence the result was nil.

I state these matters without egotistic presumption because the abilities by which I judge were *given*: I did not acquire them or think them out.

You see, I put in first rank the upper-level experiences signalized as superconscious, together with the spiritual capacities which such experiences imply. This then is the real primacy of the inner life. Hence the insistence in all my writings on the discernment from within-outward which I believe to be the real clue to the original Christianity. Mentation is subordinate to spiritual perception. Body follows mind as an instrument. Natural-mindedness is and remains external. Only by internality can we see things in adequate light.

I cannot then see that doubts imported from externality apply to what we cognize as real by internality. By spiritual perception we already know what is real, for it was given from within or above. What is given is what generates conviction.

Share this letter with the author of "Telepathy," if you like (I forget her name, and the book is in Brooklyn), but ask her to send it back to me as it is a sort of first draft only.

Sincerely,
H. W. Dresser [signed]

Continued, February 23.

While in general I agree with the author of "Telepathy," there is one point on which I radically disagree. Naturally, as one who has had mediumistic experience, she puts much stress on the organism. So, as naturally, she bases telepathy on physical experiences with special reference to the *glands*.

Here she mistakes the organic accompaniment for the process taking place in connection with it, as one might uncritically assume that because a cerebral activity takes place in connection with thoughts, *therefore* it is the brain that thinks. This would involve a fallacy.

If telepathy were as dependent on the organism as this writer believes, in the other life we would be at a loss for means of communication. Swedenborg has made plain the fact that thought interchange is the usual mode of communication in the spiritual world, where all our thoughts are "open" for others to discern.

We have, then, *spiritual*, not organic, powers, such that in this life some of these powers are awake and are active in case of telepathy while others are quiescent. The primary ability is in the *spirit*. Thus we can on occasion think with the spirit, as Swedenborg puts it. Some people are so immersed in natural or external-mindedness that the only thinking they supposedly do is with the brain. But the brain is the organic basis for this life only. Telepathy at its best is *direct* communication from spirit to spirit, as if space did not exist. That is why, when I was in Switzerland in 1888, I communicated with mother, then in Vermont, as if I were actually present with her. She recognized me by my quality, as she had become accustomed to such discernment through her experiences in spiritual healing. Whatever the status of the brain or the glands, such matters were incidental. The bodily organism could be shuffled off and the interchange could take place just as well.

There might indeed be a sort of low-level interchange here in this life, chiefly dependent on the condition of mind-body. Witness the mixture of atmospheres occurring in case of infatuation, the two young people involved in it being mostly active on the biological plane. So telepathy would seem to be psychophysical and nothing more, the emotions with their bodily basis being predominant. But it is not the low-level experiences what disclose the principle in question. In higher-level experiences the psychophysical condition is a minor matter. These approximate the activity which, as Swedenborg describes it, is customary in the "other" life.

Swedenborg was sufficiently awake to these differences to give an adequate account of them. Mediumistic experiences occur on such a low level, amidst so much confusion, that Swedenborg warned people to have nothing to do with them at all. They would lack the requisite psychology. They could not discriminate a fallacy from a truth.

The advantage gained in keeping clear of mediumship is this: there is a probability that if one follows the successive deliverances of psychical experiences through the years the way will be disclosed for interpreting in and with the spirit by subordinating the psychophysical conditions as incidental.

The author in question has, to be sure, followed the lead of her own experiences, and so has advanced beyond the theoretical level of those who construe in terms of such experiments as those at Duke University. But a greater advance will be possible when she discerns the nature and limitation of psychophysical experience.

If either you or the author is inclined to make comments on this viewpoint, please return my letter with such comments.

[Initialed on original,   H.W.D.
but not on carbon copy].

APPENDIX G

PARALLEL QUOTATIONS FROM BOTH EDITIONS OF DRESSER'S
THE POWER OF SILENCE

(italics added)

First Edition

[p. 25] Either then,--note he alternative,--God put forth his own *being as* the world, immanent yet transcendent, and is with it, transforming it through phenomena, as much now, in this age, in these changing times, in this room, as in the irrevocable ages of the past, or there is no God at all. For whatever exists is a part of and within the one Reality. Nature's God, the immanent God, is the only possible God. Let me repeat. Either God is revealed through the cohesive force which holds matter together, and holds the planets in their positions in space, through the love which

Second Edition

[p. 30] Either, then--note the alternative--God put forth *H*is own *life in* the world, and is immanent yet transcendent, is present in it, transforming it in this age as truly as in the irrevocable ages of the past, or there is no God. Let me repeat. Either God is revealed through the cohesive force which holds matter together, and holds the planets in their positions in space, through the love which draws man to man, and the fortunes and misfortunes which characterise his progress, through the insensible gradations by which our politics are changing and draws man to man, and the fortunes and misfortunes which characterize his progress, through the insensible gradations by which our politics are changing and our [p. 26] conflicts are making us true men and women, or there is no divine Father at all; for science tells us of no other development but that of ever-gradual and never-ceasing evolution, due to resident forces.

Life, then, all life, yours and mine, all that holds it together and links it with the eternal forces of the universe, is a continuous, divine communication. There is no separation between our own souls and that Spirit in whom, in the most literal sense, we live and move and have our being, between the world in which we live and that eternal Reality of whose substance and of whose activity it is a part. The life which sleeps in the rock, dreams in the plant, and awakens to consciousness in man, is the same, the one great life, which is revealed our own conflicts are making us true men and woman, or there is no divine Father. For the true Father is the God of experience, the Supreme Reality which experience reveals, which makes experience possible. He is the God of action, the God of the concrete. It is our own concrete experience that makes God's presence known. God is not the same as our experience. He is not identical with the world. But the world is from moment to moment real by virtue of His immanent presence.

Life, then, ultimately speaking, is a continuous, divine communication. There is no real separa[p. 31]tion between our souls and the Father in whom, in the most literal sense, "we live and move and have our being." All nature reveals God--the sea, the sky, the mountains, the complex life of great cities, the simple life of the country, the admiration of the poet, the thought and feeling of all men, all nations, all

Healing Hypotheses

just as clearly in the fortuitous changes that spur us on to progress as in the exact movements of the planets. All nature reveals God. The sea, the sky, the mountains, the complex life of great cities, the simple life of the country, the admiration of the poet, the thought and feeling of all men, all nations, all books, all churches, all religions. All thinkers, all artists and lovers of the beautiful, are feeling after him. All state in their own terms, and according to their degree of intelligence, the conception of a divine Father, which I have tried to make clear as it [p. 27] appears to me; namely, that he *is* nature, yet more than nature, personal, yet more than person; on the one hand, the great unit, omnipresent force and substance whence all things and beings proceed, impersonal, infinite, unknown, transcendent, indefinable; on the other hand, relatively known, books, all churches, all religions. All thinkers, all artists and lovers of the beautiful, are "feeling after" Him.

God, then, is *revealed in* nature, yet He is more than nature can manifest. He is Person, yet in a sense is beyond personality, as we ordinarily conceive of it. On the one hand, He is omnipresent power which all forces exemplify, the source of the substance which all forms contain, the basis of life whereby all beings exist. Yet He is more than this, He is Spirit, Intelligence, apprehended rather by the supreme insight of the soul than through objective experience. He is Power, yet also Love; the Author of the total universe, yet near enough so that Jesus, most truly of all, named Him "Father" in a particularly personal sense. His complete nature is made known, if at all, in the total universe. Yet He is as genuinely knowable in human life. Hence God is at once a Spirit finite, immanent, personal; an intelligent power, large enough to be the author of all life, and near enough so that Jesus could name him Father, and so that we can perceive his activity in our daily lives; an omnipresent Reality, whose complete nature is revealed in the total universe, and so much as we can comprehend in our own lives; a Spirit which has no form, but which all forms reveal; a God who is unknown and unperceived in this larger and deeper sense, except by those who have thought and suffered deeply, he whom we refuse to recognize when we look afar into the heavens for a god of our own fancy; a God who is not only immanent, but *is that in which he dwells*,--a continuous, all-pervasive, all-pervaded Spirit; a Friend who is just as near to us in this present happy moment as in the countless aeons of eternity of which this fleeting moment is an integrant part.

without form, and the Essence which all forms reveal, the all-loving Father who is unknown and unperceived in this larger and deeper sense, except by those who have [p. 32] thought and suffered deeply, He whom we refuse to recognise when we look afar into the heavens for a god of our own fancy; who is not only immanent, but who *is also independent of that in which He dwells*; the Friend who is as near to us in the present moment as in the countless aeons of eternity, of which this fleeting moment is a part.

[p. 34] Were we not thus *intimately related to* the Father, there would be some place where He does not exist.

[p. 30] Were we not thus *a part* of the one omnipresent Reality, there would then be some place where the Reality does not exist; and it would not then be omnipresent.

APPENDIX H

SOME PERIODICALS RELATED TO NEW THOUGHT

In addition to periodicals referred to above in connection with New Thought or otherwise easily discoverable in writings relating to New Thought [chiefly *New Thought* of the International New Thought Alliance, *Unity* and *Daily Word* of Unity, *Science of Mind* of the United Church of Religious Science, and *Creative Thought* of Religious Science International] and to religious healing in general, there are some others that deserve mention because they at least overlap the New Thought field. Among them are:

Gate Way: Journal of the Spiritual Frontiers Fellowship, 1229 Hinman Avenue, Evanston, Illinois [now *Spiritual Frontiers*, Spiritual Frontiers Fellowship International, P.O. Box 7868, Philadelphia, PA 19101]. The journal identifies itself as a reporter of applied psychics and a forum of diverse opinion. It is published ten times a year by the nondenominational Spiritual Frontiers Fellowship, which formulates no doctrine and espouses no opinion. The Fellowship is a nonprofit corporation formed in March, 1956, to encourage study, within the Christian Movement, of psychic phenomena as related to prayer, spiritual healing, and personal survival (immortality). [Its academic affiliate, The Academy of Religion and Psychical Research, P.O. Box 614, Bloomfield, CT 06002, publishes *The Journal of Religion and Psychical Research* and the *Proceedings* of its annual conferences.]

He Is Able: A journal dedicated to aid the revival of the Ministry of Healing in the Methodist Church, published monthly by the Fellowship of the Healing Christ, 802 Cherry Street, Chattanooga, Tennessee. As stated in *He Is Able*, April, 1963, (no volume number, but the first issue was April, 1961), p. 3.

> *HE IS ABLE* is dedicated to the restoration of the Ministry of Healing in the Methodist Church. It is operated on a non-profit basis and its life depends upon contributions. All work done on the magazine is on a volunteer basis. Currently the monthly distribution is 2,500 copies, of which approximately 1,800 are paid subscriptions.

The Fellowship has a missioner who travels from church to church. Among the books listed by the Fellowship Book Store are some New Thought ones.

The Lund Re-View, published by Harold Woodhull Lund, 754 Clinton Avenue, Bridgeport 4, Connecticut. The first issue of this monthly periodical was that of August, 1962. The view presented is that of a Christian Scientist who has left the Christian Science church, but continues to use the term Christian Science, unlike those who late in the nineteenth century were inspired by Christian Science but acceded to Mrs. Eddy's desire to reserve the name for her own expression of such views. This publication is representative of a monistic interpretation of Christian Science that objects to what it considers the dualistic interpretation of official Christian Science. For information on such differences of interpretation see Braden, *Christian Science Today*, passim.

A Metaphysical and Symbolical Interpretation of the Bible by Mildred Mann. Published by the Society of Pragmatic Mysticism, 101 West 57th Street, New York 19, New York [now c/o Leonebel Connaway, RR # 1, Box 800, Pawlet, VT 05761]. Mrs. Mann [now deceased] is the leader of the Society, which is dedicated to the "Practice of the Presence of God in the Every Day World." The teachings are essentially those of New Thought. They are an excellent example of the conscious blending of mystical insights from various religious traditions.

[*Noetic Sciences Review*, Institute of Noetic Sciences, 475 Gate Five Road, Suite 300, P.O. Box 909, Sausalito, CA 94965. The Institute is "to broaden knowledge of the nature and potentials of mind and consciousness, and to apply that knowledge to the enhancement of the quality of life on the planet."]

APPENDIX I

LETTERS OF QUIMBY'S WIDOW, SUSANNAH B. (HARDEN) QUIMBY

(Perhaps first drafts or copies of letters to be sent; some capitalization and punctuation inserted without use of *sic*)

In Boston University's Quimby Collection in the Special Collections of the Mugar Memorial Library

1. To Mrs. Clarke (on Quimby's illness and death):

Mrs Clarke I received your letter of affectionate inquiry and must alas confirm the sad and painful reality of [originally "truth that"] of my hus[band's] death ["and" crossed out][.] He had for some time previous to giving up been much exhausted [originally "wearied"] and complain [*sic*] of weariness at any exertion and that night of the fire he was so much excited [wo]rked so hard that he never seemed to get rested [so tha?]t when his daily duties were ended he would lie [dow]n too weary and nervous to sleep. [H]e dismissed his patients about the middle of Nov[. 1865] and gave up for rest, thinking freedom from professional duties would restore him, but a fever ensued, and he died but two months. [H]is decline [originally "illness" or "sickness"] was rather gradual [originally there followed "but never from the first did he"], untill [*sic*] the few last days he sank rapidly.

O [?] Mrs Clarke such a loss as his precious life is to me, to the sick and suffering and to the whole community[.] I cannot feel reconciled, and cannot understand dark and mysterious providence, that one so useful and beloved should be taken [originally followed by "but alas it is so (?) hard and sad"][;] and every object about our happy home speaks of the sad and bereavement.

I am very glad to hear Mr. Clarke is so much improved[.] I have often thought of you both and of your loving devotion to him [originally followed by "in his"][.] [M]ay his health be restored and your life be long and happy.
We have had a very strange [?] mild and open winter very little snow, and consequently business very dull, as our country trade depends wholy [sic] on snow for traveling[.] [W]ith kind regards to your husband and love to yourself[,] [V]ery truly yours Fanny [?, presumably a nickname for Susannah]

2. To Julius Dresser (on the future Mary Baker Eddy and possible succesors of Quimby):

Mr Dresser my dear friend,
You were very kind and thoughtful to write me, and send Mrs. P[atterson's] production and I highly appreciate the favor. I like to hear of her occasionally. Her lines are truly lofty and appropriate. Did I not know her, they would be beyond my comprehension, and therefore uninteligable [sic], but I understand her, and know her mode of praise. I think she might have sent me a copy, but she does not like me, so would not gratify me enough, or notice me by sending them. I agree with your views of her exactly. She is ever aiming at her own popularity and endeavoring to build herself up at some others expense. She evidently thought when she so strongly endorsed the Dr theory at her first visit to him that he would put her forward to explain *for him his doctrine*, and she never fully abandoned the idea while he lived. She last summer visited B[elfast] (bringing a rich friend with her to bear expenses) and hung around and talked, at last, proposed (through her friend) giving a lecture, but the Dr did not encourage it, and did not invite her to [other side of the sheet:] *preach* for him at all, so she did not stay long. I have thought she would eventually go into spiritualism, heart and hand. She said she did join them sometimes and

would get quite excited and carried away while talking about them. Her case as she describes it is sad, and had I never seen her or heard her talk I might have more sympathy or believe she was in the frightful condition she represents, but she is so extravagant in her expressions and does not *always adhere closely to truth* that I have less confidence perhaps than I ought. I do not doubt but what you might effect a cure on her or others if you felt inclined to give your attention that way. My *hus* often spoke of your devotion to his theory, and how happily you received his ideas. And if his mantle would fall on you, I should be very glad, and my heartfelt sympathy would go with you. Did Geo tell you his father released him from any obligation to follow his practice? He did so and I am very glad, for it was never congenial to his feelings and had his father left him without releasing him he would have felt his father's wish ought to be regarded, and his own would so conflict that he would not [have] been fit for any business at all. He now feels free, and the experience he had and the many truths he has received will I trust abide and keep him from many snares he might otherwise fall into. He has now gone to N.Y. at the invitation of a cousin there in business. He will assist him to find employment if he likes to remain there. Accept my congratulations in your new relations as parent. May your [breaks off at this point]

3. Probably to Julius Dresser (on Annetta and Horatio Dresser and a Quimby article):

I am glad to hear your wife is so well. Give her my love and kindest regards and that dear boy a good hearty kiss. Your papers I have on hand [?] for which I am much obliged. I sent you our Bel[fast] papers which are not much to brag of. I enclose an article on rest [?] that my hus sent me while he was in P[ort]l[and]. Thought it very sensible and worth preserving. Perhaps you may think it worth copying. The first part has some *big words* such as [?] are apt to use to impress people with their *mightyness* [sic]. I shall always be glad to hear from you. Wishing your success and prosperity, I remain your friend Mrs Q. Since I commenced this letter we have had a very severe storm and the mails are delayed so this letter will be old before you get it.

[The above is written on top of, or perhaps underneath--one cannot tell by use of the naked eye--the following on the same sheet of paper.]

4. To Miss Deering (on disposition of Quimby's watch chain):

Miss Dearing
I want to say to you that the watch chain you gave my husband, I have given my brother. I wanted some one that I loved and one that would prize it for his sake should have it, and also one that my husband would like should have it. Neither of the sons needed it and my Brother had done kind offices that I could not pay, and I felt that one of his treasures would be very dear to him so I gave him the chain. Ans June 20

3. Probably to Julius Dresser, of a later date than the above writing to him, judging by George Quimby's having a job, whereas he was looking for one above (on her feelings and Quimby's desire to publish):

I cannot speak of any special experience or manifestations more than a sudden feeling of nearness ["and sense of joy from it" (?) crossed out]. Perhaps when some touching occurs [sic] or some joyful inteligence [sic] has come a feeling will ["sometime" crossed out] flash over me that I might have were he nearby [?] like what one feels at suddenly meeting a friend and the sensation remains although the stern reality will force itself on me that I cannot see him. Your position now as Ed[itor] I often think of and wish my hus might have lived to see it. He always longed for a paper and would I think [have] had one had he lived. He ["always" crossed out] found it so hard to get anything printed and he so longed to lay some of his experiences before the public. Perhaps tis better as it is, but I cannot fathom it. I wrote Geo and sent your Brother [?] address as I thought he would like to call on him. He is a good deal confined as he is book keeping and does not have much leisure. He boards in Brooklyn. He is at Thayer & Sargent, 26 South Street. I have just res a letter from Emma [Ware?]. She is in Wash visiting her brother.

APPENDIX J

THE HEALING IDEALISM OF P. P. QUIMBY, W. F.EVANS, AND THE NEW THOUGHT MOVEMENT

C. Alan Anderson
Professor of Philosophy and Religion, Curry College

Probably the most consciously philosophical popular movement in the life of the American nation throughout the past century is what William James called the American people's "only decidedly original contribution to the systematic philosophy of life."[1] James referred to this academically much neglected group of approaches to applying idealism in daily life as the "Mind-cure movement," and included in it both Christian Science and various non-Christian Science forms of "health mysticism." However, James emphasized the New Thought[2] side of Mind-cure. He characterized the

---

[1]William James, *The Varieties of Religious Experience* (New York: New American Library, A Mentor Book, 1958, originally 1902), pp. 88-89.

[2]The most complete survey of New Thought is Charles S. Braden, *Spirits in Rebellion: The Rise and Development of New Thought* (Dallas: Southern Methodist University Press, 1963). See also J. Stillson Judah, *The History and Philosophy of the Metaphysical Movements in America* (Philadelphia: The Westminster Press, 1967), and the books of Horatio W. Dresser, especially (Dresser ed.) *The Spirit of the New Thought* (New York: G. P. Putnam's Sons, 1917), and *A History of the New Thought Movement* (New York:

movement as "a deliberately optimistic scheme of life, with both a speculative and a practical side,"[1] and the basic purpose of "the systematic cultivation of healthy-mindedness."[2] Particularly on its practical side it has been considered appropriately as a religion, but it is a religion rooted more in philosophical attitude and exploration than in revelation (at least if one omits Christian Science, and it largely will be omitted here, both because of its claims of revelation and because of space limitations). Sydney E. Ahlstrom deals with New Thought, Christian Science, and related outlooks, such as the positive thinking of Norman Vincent Peale, as "harmonial religion," "those forms of piety and belief in which spiritual composure, physical health, and even economic well-being are understood to flow from a person's rapport with the cosmos."[3] Ahlstrom sees harmonial religion as

> a vast and highly diffuse religious impulse that cuts across all normal lines of religious division. It often shapes the inner meaning of the church life to which people formally commit themselves. . . . Some of its motifs probably inform the religious life of most Americans. During the 1960's, moreover, one could note a steady growth in the

---

Thomas Y. Crowell Co., 1918). For a more recent New Thought anthology see Ernest Holmes and Maud Allison Lathem (eds.), *Mind Remakes Your World* (New York: Dodd, Mead & Co., 1941).

[1] James, *op. cit.*, p. 87.

[2] *Ibid.*, p. 85.

[3] Sydney E. Ahlstrom, *A Religious History of the American People* (New Haven and London: Yale University Press, 1972), p. 1019.

strength of this general impulse, while closely related but more esoteric forms of religion [of occult and Eastern types having much in common with some forms of New Thought] . . . seemed to thrive even more vigorously.[1]

New Thought, which acquired its name about 1895 after being called Mental Science and other names, may well be the quintessential blend of American spirituality and practicality. As expressed in the Declaration of Principles which appears in each issue of the quarterly *New Thought*, the movement affirms

> [1] the inseparable oneness of God and man, the realization of which comes through spiritual intuition, the implications of which are that man can reproduce the Divine perfection in his body, emotions, and in all his external affairs. [2] the freedom of each person in matters of belief. [3] the Good to be supreme, universal, and eternal. [4] that the Kingdom of Heaven is within us, that we are one with the Father, that we should love one another, and return good for evil. [5] that we should heal the sick through prayer, and that we should endeavor to manifest perfection "even as our Father in Heaven is perfect." [6] our belief in God as the Universal Wisdom, Love, Life, Truth, Power, Peace, Beauty, and Joy, "in whom we live, and have our being." [7] that man's mental states are carried forward into manifestation and become his experience through the Creative Law of Cause and Effect. [8] that the divine Nature expressing Itself through man manifests Itself as health, supply, wisdom, love, life, truth, power, peace, beauty, and joy. [9, this omitted from the paper,

---

[1]*Ibid.*, p. 1020.

since it was omitted inadvertently from International New Thought Alliance publications for years] that man is an invisible spiritual dweller within a human body, continuing and unfolding as a spiritual being beyond the change called physical death. [10] that the universe is the body of God, spiritual in essence, governed by God through laws which are spiritual in reality even when material in appearance.

James saw as sources (1) the four Gospels, (2) Emersonianism, (3) Berkeleyan idealism, (4) "Spiritism, with its message of 'law' and 'progress' and 'development,'" (5) "optimistic popular science evolutionism," (6) Hinduism, and especially (7) the intuitive belief of the movement's leaders in "the all-saving power of healthy-minded attitudes."[1] Other writers have added Neoplatonism[2] and Spinozism[3] to the list. Except perhaps for James's last source, all this misses the most impressive immediate origin, the work of a self-educated Yankee genius, Phineas Parkhurst Quimby (1802-1866), and his followers.

Quimby, who lived almost all of his life in Maine, was a clockmaker, daguerreotypist, and inventor who

---

[1]James, *op. cit.*, pp. 87-88.

[2]Woodbridge Riley, *American Thought: From Puritanism to Pragmatism* (New York: Henry Holt and Co., 1915), p. 49, and John Wright Buckham, *Mysticism and Modern Life* (New York and Cincinnati: The Abingdon Press, 1915), p. 62.

[3]Gaius Glenn Atkins, *Modern Religious Cults* and Movements (New York, Chicago, London, and Edinburgh: Fleming H. Revell Company, 1923), pp. 215-17, drawing on Josiah Royce's *The Spirit of Modern Philosophy*.

obtained patents on a lock, chain saw, and steering gear for ships.[1] But his most important contributions followed his investigation of mesmerism and the interpretations of it given by several of its practitioners, who might be called America's pre-Socratic philosophers. With apparently little knowledge of philosophy, they boldly ventured into new worlds of experience and speculation, attempting to explain reality as seen in the light of their hypnotic feats. Largely following an old esoteric tradition, they taught the existence of an invisible, magnetic, electric fluid connecting the mesmeric operator with his receptive subject. As a result of his experimentation with mesmerism in the late 1830's and 1840's, Quimby concluded that there was no mesmeric fluid, but that one mind acts directly on another. In an unpublished manuscript of this period, Quimby observed, "The fluid which really exists, is in the mind of the operator, being like Berkley's [sic] composition of matter,

---

[1]Some of Quimby's autobiographical words have not been published, but are contained in C. Alan Anderson, "Horatio W. Dresser and the Philosophy of New Thought" (unpublished Ph.D. dissertation, Boston University Department of Philosophy, 1963), Appendix A, pp. 200-52, quoting Quimby's early writing extensively. See George A. Quimby, "Phineas Parkhurst Quimby," *The New England Magazine*, VI (March, 1888), 267-76, largely reprinted, with minor changes, in Horatio W. Dresser, *Health and the Inner Life* (New York and London: G. P. Putnam's Sons, 1906), which also contains other valuable material on and by Quimby. See also Horatio W. Dresser (ed.), *The Quimby Manuscripts* (New York: Thomas Y. Crowell Co., two editions, both 1921), especially chs. 1-6, and Georgine Milmine, *The Life of Mary Baker G. Eddy and the History of Christian Science* (New York: Doubleday, Page & Company, 1909), especially ch. 3.

made up of ideas, impressions &c."[1] One might suppose that Quimby, who wrote that in the mesmeric state "the bodily senses cease to act--impressions are now conveyed directly to the mind--all space + time, in this state, is annihilated,"[2] discovered a kindred soul in Berkeley. However, this was not the case. Quimby briefly referred to Berkeley at this time, as he did to others, including Epicurus, Lucretius, Plato, and Hume, but Quimby did not attempt to work out a thoroughgoing conventional idealism, perhaps because he was drawing on common sense realism as discovered in reading Thomas C. Upham of relatively nearby Bowdoin College.[3] The extent to which Quimby wrote of philosophers, especially Upham, has been unknown or ignored by previous writers on Quimby. Nevertheless, although one can point to these and such other conceivable influences as Swedenborg,[4]

---

[1] Anderson, *op. cit.*, p. 219.

[2] *Ibid.*, p. 214.

[3] *Ibid.*, especially pp. 204, 205, 208, 209, 220, and 247-49. See also Riley, *op. cit.*, ch. 5 and Herbert W. Schneider, *A History of American Philosophy* (2nd ed., New York and London: Columbia University Press, 1963), pp. 210-11, on common sense realism.

[4] Judah, *op. cit.*, pp. 149-50; H. W. Dresser, *Handbook of the New Thought*, pp. 193-94; H. W. Dresser, *A History of the New Thought Movement*, p. 318; John Whitehead, *The Illusions of Christian Science* (Boston: The Garden Press, 1907), p. 224. See also Robert Peel, *Mary Baker Eddy: The Years of Discovery* (New York, Chicago, San Francisco: Holt, Rinehart and Winston, 1966), pp. 162-63.

Healing Hypotheses

mesmerist John Bovee Dods,[1] and "the Poughkeepsie seer," Andrew Jackson Davis,[2] consideration of Quimby's own experiences and reflections on them essentially justifies the claim that Quimby "was not in any sense a borrower, after he took up the theory of mesmerism and found how meagre was the supposed science, and branched out into the field of his own investigations."[3] Neither Quimby nor his early followers until the 1880's appeared to take note of Emerson.[4]

In exploring mesmerism Quimby discovered most remarkable phenomena, including the extrasensory perception of his mesmerized assistant. As Quimby's experimentation with mental powers progressed, he discovered that without the aid of mesmerism his mind could operate beyond conventionally accepted boundaries and that he could help others to make contact with divine Wisdom, which would correct the human errors which he held to be the sources of illness. He maintained that the explanation or the Truth is the cure. No longer was he concerned simple with the influence of one human mind on another; he had discovered the central importance of allowing the divine mind to express itself in one's life. There is a deeper level of selfhood, one's true self, which can rise above bodily appearances and enable healing to

---

[1] Peel, *op. cit.*, pp. 153-54. Cf. Dresser, *Health and the Inner Life*, pp. 21-22. See also Anderson, *op. cit.*, pp. 25-33 and additional references given there; see p. 223 for early critical comments of Quimby on Dods.

[2] Peel, *op. cit.*, pp. 160-63, and Judah, *op. cit.*, pp. 52-56 and 151-54.

[3] Dresser (ed.), *The Quimby Manuscripts*, 1st ed., p. 12, 2nd ed. p. 18.

[4] Anderson, *op. cit.*, pp. 153-55 and sources cited there.

take place. In his ultimate Science of Health and Happiness, as he called his outlook, Quimby considered matter, in the words of his leading expositor, "plastic to thought; it is that in which, on the one hand, the thought of God takes shape, and, on the other, the embodiment of human belief,"[1] which often impresses sickness on the body. Quimby used more confusing, less clearly philosophical, terminology in his at least implied idealism of healing than he did in his early lecture notes. Quimby died without publishing his manuscripts, and many of them remain unpublished, but some of his Portland patients carried on his work in divergent ways.

If the pioneering, persistently questioning, often condemned Quimby was the Socrates of the New Thought movement,[2] Warren Felt Evans (1817-1889) was its Plato. By the time that Evans finished publishing, from 1869 to 1886, his six books (one of which appeared in five languages) on mind and healing, New Thought scarcely could help being "a series of footnotes"[3] to Evans. Evans studied at Middlebury and Dartmouth, became a Methodist minister and later a Swedenborgian lay leader, was healed with the aid of Quimby, became a healer in Boston and Salisbury, Massachusetts, and received a medical degree from an eclectic medical school the identity of which has

---

[1]H. W. Dresser manuscript, "Quimby's Technique," quoted *Ibid.*, p. 266. Cf. Alfred North Whitehead, *Adventures of Ideas* (New York: The Macmillan Company, 1933), p. 99, on nature as plastic.

[2]Milmine, *op. cit.*, p. 45, refers to Quimby as "a mild-mannered New England Socrates."

[3]Alfred North Whitehead, *Process and Reality: An Essay in Cosmology* (New York: The Macmillan Company, 1929), p. 63, in the famous reference to "the European philosophical tradition" as "a series of footnotes to Plato."

not been discovered.[1]

After first taking a more Swedenborgian approach, Evans came to see his work as "an attempt to construct a theoretical and practical system of phrenopathy, or mental-cure, on the basis of the idealistic philosophy of Berkeley, Fichte, Schelling, and Hegel."[2] Evans called one of his chapters "The Creative Power of Thought, or Hegel's Philosophy as a Medicine."[3] Evans referred to his philosophy as a Christian Pantheism "which does not destroy the individuality of man, nor separate God from the universe which he continually creates out of Himself, nor sunder Him from the activities of the human soul by the intervention of second causes."[4] This pantheism or panentheism, as he might have called if the term had been available to him, foreshadowed current process philosophy in various ways, including emphasis on God interpreted in accordance with his loving relationship with us, the primacy of feelings, and divine-human partnership in the ongoing process of creativity. Some of Evans' observations relevant to process thought, as well as to New Thought, are:

> Creation is not now an accomplished event. It is not a thing done, but one that is in the process of being done. The divine idea is not yet fully

---

[1] The basic biographical writing on Evans is William J. Leonard, "Warren Felt Evans, M. D.," *Practical Ideals* X (Sept.-Oct., 1905), 1-16, X (Nov., 1905), 1-23, X (Dec., 1905), 9-26, and XI (Jan., 1906), 10-26, quoted at length in Anderson, *op. cit.*, Appendix C, pp. 273-96.

[2] W. F. Evans, *The Divine Law of Cure* (Boston: H. H. Carter & Co., Publishers, 1881), p. 9.

[3] *Ibid.*, Ch. 16.

[4] *Ibid.*, p. 42.

realized or actualized. The world is an unfinished picture. As the Platonists would say, it is in a state of *becoming*. The divine idea, the universal divine life, a mysterious power of order and arrangement, is at the very centre and heart of things, struggling to work itself out into a complete material expression. Universal nature is moved from within by the Universal Mind, of which our minds are a part.[1]

If life is love, then all the physiological processes must be modified by our affectional states. ... The life of God is love. His love is an infinite desire to impart his own good to others.[2]

By the power of silent thought, which in its nature is a *tacit speech*, we can deposit in the fruitful soil of the *unconscious mind* of an invalid the living germ of a better condition. ... The Spiritual nature of man acting through the will and imagination, and determined to a definite aim by love and faith, is the most *real force* in the universe, for thoughts are not "trifles light as air," but are substance and divinely living things.[3]

Desire alone is powerless; and thought alone is lifeless and inefficient. They must be combined in a harmonious unity.[4]

[If] the inmost soul of man is the outcome or

---

[1] W. F. Evans, *The Primitive Mind-Cure* (Boston: H. H. Carter & Co., Publishers, 1885), p. 124. Italics in original, as in all these quotations.

[2] W. F. Evans, *The Mental-Cure* (Boston: H. H. & T. W. Carter, 1869), p. 216.

[3] Evans, *The Primitive Mind-Cure*, p. 85.

[4] *Ibid.*, p. 135.

offspring, or offshoot, of the Universal Soul, and is a manifestation under finite limitations of the first creative Principle ... then the inner nature of man must of necessity share in a degree the attributes of the world-creating Power. It is made in the image of God, and so far *is* God. ... Just so far as we know God, we become God, and so far *is* God. ... Just so far as we know God, we become God, and can to the same extent do divine works. . . . As all matter exists only in mind, it follows that all modifications of the mind effect changes in *that appearance* which we call matter. ... The body is but a part of the external world, and both are to us what we think and believe them to be.[1]

Evans's reference to matter as an appearance, and he even calls it "an illusion or deceptive appearance that is perceptually changing with our ever-varying mental states,"[2] points up the chief philosophical contrast between New Thought and the Christian Science established by another former Quimby patient, Mary Baker Eddy (1821-1910). In New Thought matter is recognized as an appearance of spirit, or one way in which God makes himself known, even if sometimes so unclearly as to invite the term illusion; yet it is never altogether unreal. In Christian Science matter is considered utterly unreal, the erroneous product of mortal mind, which itself is unreal. Thus New Thought has a form of idealism, while Christian Science, although asserting the allness of God, is left with an almost Zoroastrian dualism of God and the powerful nonentity that is mortal mind.

As Borden Parker Bowne observed with regard to

---

[1] *Ibid.*, pp. 94-95.

[2] *Ibid.*

Christian Science,[1] it is experimentation, rather than metaphysical speculation, that will determine the truth of claims of fact. However, metaphysics can be helpful in encouraging or discouraging the needed experimentation. To conceive of the possibility of an occurrence is a step toward bringing it about. That the direct application of thought and feeling to change material conditions beyond customarily controlled voluntary bodily motions seems strange is partly a tribute to long-prevalent metaphysical convictions as to the limits of mental power. Perhaps only now are we entering a sufficiently open-minded period to begin to assess New Thought adequately. This is thanks in part to scientific progress in psychosomatic medicine and parapsychology, to new philosophical interest in such fields as medicine, genetics, and psychology, to ecologically-stimulated concern over the status of nature, and to the popularity of various Oriental and occult theories and meditative practices, most of the essentials of which have been found in New Thought for many years. With widespread awareness of exotic sources of teachings like those of New Thought, it is all the more appropriate that we recognize the American contributions. Moreover, New Thought is especially deserving of attention and emulation because of its, especially Evans's, attempt to put its concerns into the fullest metaphysical perspective.

From: *Philosophy in the Life of a Nation: Papers Contributed to the Bicentennial Symposium of Philosophy*, New York: Bicentennial Symposium of Philosophy, City University of New York Graduate Center, 1976, pp. 279-283; reprinted in *The Journal of the Academy of Religion*

---

[1]Borden P. Bowne, pamphlet *Philosophy of Christian Science* (New York: Eaton & Mains; Cincinnati: Jennings & Graham, n.d.), p.9.

and Psychical Research, II, January, 1979, 25-30. This may well have been the only academic recognition of New Thought in connection with the Bicentennial of the United States.

APPENDIX K

THE MARCH OF METAPHYSICS

Metaphysics is the branch of philosophy that seeks to understand the most basic nature of all reality, to discover what anything must be like in order to be at all. Religion is a way in which people combine their beliefs, attitudes, and actions in relation to whatever they consider to be most important (generally including a belief about the existence and nature of a God or gods).

VARIOUS OUTLOOKS

1. The mythological prelude: the attempt to come to terms with the universe through the use of imaginative, storytelling insight.

2. The Milesian curtain raiser: rational thought, rather than poetic storytelling, produces the conclusion that everything comes from one thing, generally conceived to be a physical something, such as water or air.

3. The Heraclitean essential insight: process and Logos: balanced becoming.

4. The Eleatic denial of change: static being.

5. The atomistic compromise of changeless material atoms with change through rearrangement: materialism, mechanism.

6. The Socratic recognition of oneself as immortal soul.

7. The Platonic embrace of Eleatic changelessness for full reality, but mind as self-moving, soul of the world, non-material Forms.

8. Aristotelian side track with a God of isolated aloofness.

9. Epicurean application of atomism in a pain-

avoiding search for sheltered contentment.
        10.   Stoic practical psychology of mind control for virtue, (alignment with Nature, Reason, God), combined with freedom-denying pantheism.
        11   Jesus' apotheosis of love and practical, direct application of awareness of presence of God to remedy human problems, especially of health.
        12.   Neoplatonic blend of mysticism and emanation, an uneasy balance of monism and dualism.
        13.   The Medieval muddle of flip-flopping between Plato and Aristotle.
        14.   Protestant Reformation provided no clear resolution of problems.

MATERIALISM or **NATURALISM** (Only matter or lifeless energy is real) and **MECHANISM** (Everything acts in a machine-like way, non-teleological [non-purposive]):
        15.   Hobbes (1588-1679) and La Mettrie (1709-51) advanced materialism.
        16.   Newton (1642-1727) united scientific discoveries into the "Newtonian world machine."

DUALISM (Mind and matter are equally real.):
        17.   Descartes (1596-1650) and Locke (1632-1704) presented a dualism of mind and matter.

IDEALISM (Everything is mental or spiritual.):
Theoretical:
        18.   Leibniz (1644-1716) converted atoms from matter to mind, but considered them "windowless" and called them *monads* (units) in a *panpsychism*, an idealism of many minds.
        19.   Berkeley (1685-1753) discarded material substance, and Hume (1711-1776) dropped spiritual substance, leaving only phenomena. Kant (1724-1804, responding to skepticism Hume, saw mind as orderer of experience, but denied possibility of knowing things in themselves. Fichte (1762-1814), Schelling (1775-1854), and

Hegel (1770-1831) (followed by such thinkers as Bradley [1846-1924] and Royce [1855-1916]) sought the thing itself and produced an idealism of one mind (absolute idealism).

20. Einstein (1879-1955), Planck (1858-1947), and other scientists demolished earlier materialistic science (but its assumptions continue to prevail in commonsensical view of reality), and replaced substance with essentially lifeless process (activity, change) as basic.

21. Bowne (1847-1910) (followed by Brightman [1884-1953] and Bertocci [1910-1989]) formulated Personalism (personal idealism), emphasizing the indispensability of personhood for a sound metaphysics.

22. Whitehead (1861-1947) (combining Plato, Leibniz, and 20th century physics) formulated his "philosophy of organism" or process philosophy, recognizing the quanta (momentarily-existing bursts of energy) of physics as living, interrelated units that he called *occasions of experience*, the building blocks, the "concrete" actualities in terms of which everything must be explained (the *ontological principle*). Avoiding the *fallacy of misplaced concreteness*, material things are recognized as collections or aggregates (abstractions or constructions) of occasions. God selects from possibilities (*eternal objects*, like Plato's Forms or Ideas) and provides them to occasions of experience as they start to develop; the occasions blend these potentialities with the influences of the past in order to produce new creations, which immediately are converted from subjectivity to objectivity, and (in *objective immortality*) forever influence all later-developing occasions of experience. Persons are successions of highly complex occasions that preside over the successions of vast collections of less complex occasions constituting their bodies. Hartshorne (born 1897) independently developed his similar views and advanced a *panentheism* that recognizes all as in God and the universe as God's body.

Applied (directly by mind, as well as indirectly in mental control of muscles to do work):

23. Traditional (Substance) New Thought drew on the insights and practices of Quimby (1802-66), Evans, Hopkins, C. Fillmore, Cramer, Troward, E. Holmes, and others, and accepted substance idealism.

24. Process New Thought builds on the same foundations, but goes beyond them to substitute a process idealistic view of reality, including a growing, fully personal God, serial selfhood, evolving natural laws (recognized as abstract formulations of habitual interactions), and personal immortality, as well as objective immortality. God is morally unchanging as perfect good, acting in such ways as to promote the maximum satisfaction of every bit of existence. God is perfect love-intelligence, understood as involving a recycling process of (1) offering to each occasion of experience the best, individually tailor-made possibilities, (2) allowing freedom of choice in co-creation with God, (3) appreciatively, perfectly preserving all effort-accomplishment as the completed occasion, and (4) presenting it to upcoming occasions as part of the past, in relation to which newly-offered perfect possibilities are to be blended by the new occasion.

APPENDIX L

HIGHLIGHTS OF THE IMMEDIATE BACKGROUND AND NATURE OF PROCESS NEW THOUGHT

OLD WESTERN RELIGIOUS THOUGHT

God is separate from the world.
Healing is either miraculous or medical intervention with the natural course of events.

(CONVENTIONAL, SUBSTANCE) NEW THOUGHT

God is all. Healing is receiving of God's general offering of good that requires acceptance by individual initiative (in varying degree accepting divine guidance) in using impersonal law. Reality is enduring substance.

FROM OLD TO NEW SCIENCE See Alfred North Whitehead, *Modes of Thought* (New York: Macmillan, 1938), Lecture Seven.

Matter in the basic form of changeless atoms has been replaced by equivalence of matter (as splittable atoms with subatomic particles) and energy. Energy is recognized as coming in momentarily-existing bursts or packets (quanta). Energy is essentially lifeless, and life a curious accident in the midst of the gigantic accident that is the universe. Earlier belief in the discreteness of things is replaced by recognition of things as interrelated in fields of force.

PROCESS NEW THOUGHT: God is all, but is more clearly recognized as the mind or personality of the universe, recognizing the universe as God's body. Healing is receiving of God's specifically-designed good, offered uniquely to each one. There is no acting, impersonal law, but the regularity, reliability, constancy of God's love may be considered at least its equivalent. Reality is not enduring substance, but is a vast collection of momentarily-developing units of experience.

Process New Thought is a combination of (a) the broad idealistic outlines and techniques of conventional (substance-oriented) New Thought, (b) the essential insights of the process-relational, panentheistic views of such thinkers as Whitehead and Hartshorne, and (c) an emphasis on the metaphysical centrality of personhood, characteristic of Bowne and his successors in (Boston) Personalism. In somewhat greater detail, Process New Thought is characterized by the following:

1. It accepts science's discovery of a process-relational outlook, but with a Whiteheadian recognition of the creative, living nature of the bursts of energy (called *occasions of experience* by Whitehead), with energy recognized as what we experience as feeling. There is nothing actual (concrete) except these units of experience. There is *freedom* in some degree at all levels of concrete existence since all experience has at least a little freedom. Process Philosophy is a *panexperientialism*; all concrete (actual) existence is experience, not passive stuff, whether considered matter or mind. Occasions of experience are the basic building blocks of reality.

2. *Life* is that in which there is (a) *aim* (relatively free choice of possibilities), (b) *creative activity* (transforming potentiality into actuality), and (c) *enjoyment* of the process (of creating a new unity out of the combined many coming to an occasion from the past-- which is composed of a multitude of earlier choices). Lifeless things are abstractions from (collections of) momentarily subjectively-aware, creative, living units (occasions of experience).

3. The creative process is the taking of the

many of the past and blending their influence with divinely-given possibilities, thus producing unique new creations, which are new unities of all that has been. The job of all existence is the creation of new unities. "The many become one, and are increased by one." See quotations below.

4. As the new many are created, they are added to God's awareness, resulting in God's endless growth.

5. Process New Thought takes care not to commit the *fallacy of misplaced concreteness* (mistaking the abstract for the concrete). The concrete, actual is found in occasions of experience, rather than the aggregates (collections) of them (abstractions from them) that constitute physical things and ourselves as existing more than a moment. We have serial selfhood. Instead of being things that *have* experiences, we *are* the experiences that, considered together make up the things. We (the moments-old or decades-old abstractions) are successions of occasions of experience; we have serial selfhood.

6. Living in the moment is required by serial selfhood. Since concretely one has only a moment to live, one should make the most of it. Understanding that we are new creations moment by moment can provide a powerful psychological impetus to drop old limitations and to accept divinely-given opportunities for fullest living.

7. After a moment of subjective (self-aware, not necessarily conscious) existence a subject (occasion of experience) becomes an everlasting object, which influences everything that comes later. Preservation of all effort in *objective immortality*, the state of perfect preservation of each subject-become object. Although doubted by some prominent process thinkers, there is personal *subjective immortality*, in which there is the perpetuation beyond bodily death of lines of development of personal occasions of experience (and probably less complex animal occasions) that preside over occasions

making up physical bodies.

8. Ultimate power is the lure of God's persuasive (rather than coercive) love-beauty.

9. The wisdom-love-beauty of God is the initial aim that begins each occasion's reaction to the influence of the past constituting the situation in which it comes into existence. God's love-wisdom is offered not as general possibilities available to everyone, but as specific, tailor-made plans for the particular occasion of experience, taking into account the character of the occasions in the line of development with which the occasion in question is especially identified. The presence of God as initial aim (*indwelling Christ*, in New Thought terminology) justifies the New Thought claim that what is sought already has been attained; the ultimate that any occasion can accomplish is to accept completely its initial aim.

10. The personality of God is the mind of the universe.

11. The hierarchy of existence is explained in terms of increasing clarity of awareness of inclusiveness; the higher the level in the hierarchy, the clearer the awareness, the more obvious the intelligence, the more fully personal; God has the utmost in clarity-intelligence-personality. There is nothing beyond the personal God.

12. Mystical experience is awareness of the larger context of existence, especially with regard to awareness of the divine love process, of providing initial aims, which is the giving activity of divine love, and the receiving of completed occasions, permanently keeping them, and making them available to all upcoming occasions--the receiving activity of divine love. The mystic leaps ahead of the usual human level of awareness in the continuum and realizes that order and love are one. Occasions have forward-looking poles, called mind, and backward-looking poles, called matter. The mystic is most consistently forward-looking, and universal- looking.

13. The universe is the body of God, body

understood as collection of immediate servants of presiding mind. One's own body is the servant both of God directly and of the portion of God that is one's "own" mind. Neither God nor the universe in some form (and perhaps many co-existing versions) had a beginning. God never was without a body (universe) of some type.

14. Mind within mind is the universal pattern. Each mind (occasion of experience) contains all earlier minds. (Occasions are unaware of other occasions developing at exactly the same moment, but this is no more practically important than the fraction of a second that it takes a message to travel from toe to brain or the roughly eight minutes that it takes light from the sun to reach us. On no reasonable theory can we know anything exactly as it happens.) All is present to everything; extrasensory perception is the basic type of awareness; sensory perception is just a narrowing of attention.

15. Time is real and is defined as the transition from one occasion of experience to the next. Experience is inconceivable apart from before-and-afterness. Freedom and creativity require a settled past and an open future. An "eternal now" of past, present, and future coexisting in their fullness is a denial of the reality of creative process; an "eternal now" may be an emotionally satisfying symbol of the comprehensiveness of God, but in reality there endless development. If process is basic to any part of reality, it must be basic to all of reality. Retrocognition is sharpened awareness of part of what is within an occasion. (It makes no difference whether one says that all the past is within God, or akashic records or oneself, for each contains all; separation is only relative.) Precognition is awareness of what is likely to occur, sharing in God's knowledge of probabilities; but the future holds surprises even for God, since freedom prevails.

16. Natural laws are abstractions that cannot act; they are changing (generally over vast periods of time) habits of interaction of occasions of experience, but unchanging pattern by which creation takes place by

blending of the past and the divinely-presented possible.

17. Treatment (for health, happiness, or whatever) is understood as enrichment (by awareness of divine reality of the healee by healer, or by more conventional methods) of most relevant part of the past of whoever or whatever is the object of concern (one cannot directly influence a developing occasion, so one influences the past out of which it comes, regardless of whether the healer understands that this is what is being done), in order to minimize contrast with the perfect possibility for new creation as offered by God in initial aim. Reduction of contrast makes it easier for the upcoming occasions to accept their initial aims. (The healer changes his or her own awareness by realizing the divine perfection of the one to be helped [or the physician administers a drug] and this changes part of the background out of which the upcoming occasions will arise, making it easier for the one being helped to select the divinely-offered aim.)

18. Relative separation of "God the One" from "God the many" in creation is in terms of stages of development of occasions. The start is pure God in the context of confrontation with the past (a vast collection of completed occasions of experience), but it is convenient to refer to distinctive later stages of aim and the resulting completed occasion as other than God, although in a comprehensive sense there is nothing but God.

19. A mind (occasion of experience) is not aware of anything beyond itself that is strictly contemporaneous, but this is no more inconvenient than the passage of a fraction of a second for a message to go from one's toe to his or her brain, or the roughly eight minutes for sunlight to reach us.

In short, Process New Thought is a practical, applied, clarified idealism, in which God is recognized as utterly personal, completely impartial, totally reliable, all-inclusive, unimaginably intelligent, completely loving (sharing--uniquely adapted for each occasion of experience--perfect possibilities for realization and completely accepting and preserving whatever anyone or anything makes of the divinely-provided potentialities). God is fully available and all-availing. Process New Thought is New Thought minus any instances of the fallacy of misplaced concreteness such as notions of changeless (non-growing) impersonal God, enduring substance, changeless and/or active law, and with the addition of insights such as the following from Alfred North Whitehead's *Modes of Thought* and *Process and Reality* and Charles Hartshorne's "The New Pantheism" in *The Christian Register*, May 20 and 27, 1936, (various omissions and combinations not noted) and *The Philosophy of Charles Hartshorne*:

[MT 135] [A] dead nature can give no reasons. All ultimate reasons are in terms of aim at value. A dead nature aims at nothing. It is the essence of life that it exists for its own sake, as the intrinsic reaping of value.

[MT 155-55] None of [the] laws of nature gives the slightest evidence of necessity. They are the modes of procedure which within the scale of our observations do in fact prevail... They exist as average, regulative conditions because the majority of actualities are swaying each other to modes of interconnection exemplifying those laws.... [T]o judge by all analogy, after a sufficient span of existence our present laws will fade into unimportance. New interests will dominate. In our present sense of the term, our spatio-temporal epoch will pass into the background of the past, which conditions all things dimly and without evident effect on the decision of prominent relations.

[MT 163] [I]n one sense the world is in the soul. ... [But] the soul itself [is] one of the components within the world. ... [My] present experience is what I now am. . . . The soul is nothing else than the succession of my occasions of experience, extending from birth to the present moment. Now at this instant, I am the complete person embodying all these occasions. They are mine. On the other hand it is equally true that my immediate occasion of experience, at the present moment, is only one among the stream of occasions which constitutes my soul.

[MT 164] [E]ach happening is a factor in the nature of every other happening.

[PR 32] The ultimate metaphysical principle is the advance from disjunction to conjunction, creating a novel entity other than the entities given in disjunction. The novel entity is at once the togetherness of the 'many' which it finds, and also it is one among the disjunctive 'many' which it leaves; it is a novel entity, disjunctively among the entities which it synthesizes. The many become one, and are increased by one.

[PR 254] Apart from the experiences of subjects there is nothing, nothing, nothing, bare nothingness.

[PR 254] On one side, the one becomes many; and on the other side, the many become one.

[PR 340] Each task of creation is a social effort, employing the whole universe. Each novel actuality is a new partner adding a new condition.

[PR 520] [Various] strains of thought . . . fashion God in the image[s] of [1] an imperial ruler, . . . [2] a personification of moral energy, . . . [3] an ultimate philosophical principle[, and 93) the Whiteheadian process-relational-organic view, which] does not emphasize the ruling Caesar, or the ruthless moralist, or the unmoved mover. It dwells upon the tender elements in the world, which slowly and in quietness operate by love; and it finds purpose in the present immediacy of a kingdom not of this world. Love neither rules, nor is it unmoved; also it is [p. 520] a little oblivious as to morals. It does not look to the future; for it finds its own reward in the immediate present.

[PR 521] God is not to be treated as an exception to all metaphysical principles, invoked to save their collapse. He is their chief exemplification.

[PR 522] [God] is the lure for feeling, the eternal urge of desire. His particular relevance to each creative act as it arises from its own conditioned standpoint in the world, constitutes him the initial 'object of desire' establishing the initial phase of each subjective aim.

[PR 526]   [God] is the poet of the world, with tender patience leading it by his vision of truth, beauty, and goodness.

[PR 532]   What is done in the world is transformed into a reality in heaven, and the reality in heaven passes back into the world. By reason of this reciprocal relation, the love in the world passes into the love in heaven, and floods back again into the world. In this sense, God is the great companion--the fellow-sufferer who understands.

[Hartshorne, NP]   A man has some awareness of the actions of his bodily cells; but what these cells do individually the man as a whole does not do, but only what these cells do in concert or together. We are cells in the body of God; for the most general bearing of our collective acts God is responsible, but not for our individual choices as such. . . . Omnipotence in the legitimate sense means all possible power over all things, but it does not mean "all the power in the universe as the power of one thing."
[T]he problem of evil is met in part by admitting a real division of power between God and finite creatures.

To say that we are parts of God is . . . only shorthand for saying that God feels our feelings (the same applies to our relation to our cells, except that our intuition of cellular feelings is vague and imperfect). Sympathy is the very meaning of unification in a truly spiritual philosophy.

Panpsychism [psychicalism]. . . abolishes the apparent implication of pantheism that God has a body composed of mere or dead matter. His material body is simply the minds inferior to him (as a man's cells to the man) collectively dominated by him, but also exercising influence upon him. *A body is the organization of one's immediate servants*. All things are the immediate servants of God, hence all nature is literally his body. But servanthood is limited by the principle of the division of power, and the action of the master is subject to reaction upon the master. This removes another paradox in the older theologies of a God upon whose action no counteraction can be exerted.

As the world acquires new content with the happening of new events, the things with which God sympathizes, the total contents of his sympathetic awareness, are added to and in this sense changed. Thus ethically God is forever the same unstinted love, but esthetically he is the ever-changing symphony of the world-process.

[God is] creative in the only sense in which creation is given any meaning by our experience. To create is to mold the course of events into correspondence with an idea. Men thus literally create each other when they mold each other's character by education and friendship. Thus the paradoxes of timeless purpose, together with those of non-sensitive ("impassive") love, and of action without reaction, are done away with once for all.

Personality is the only principle of wholeness, of integration, on a complex level such as the universe must involve, of which we have any experience. . . .[T]he scientist believes in a kind of unity or integrity of nature which he does not analyze. What could this unity be? If nature as a whole is a person of a supreme kind, then of course she will have certain ways of acting, for in such ways does personality express itself. . . .

[The attributes, characteristics, of God] were posited because they were required for an intelligible universe. . . . Atheism . . . declares that the world as a whole must forever be completely unintelligible to us [and] that there is no ultimate standard by which life can be ordered.

[PCH 691]   Of the dualities connected with psychicalism, the key one for me is, *singular and composite*.

Groups of sentient entities are not necessarily also sentient (fallacy of composition), nor are members of a group that as a whole does not feel necessarily insentient (fallacy of division). From whom did I first learn about this? It was not Whitehead but Leibniz, who saw it with the clarity of genius nearly three hundred years ago.

[PCH 692] Not only did I reason to psychicalism from my theism, but the converse reasoning also was important for me. If, without psychicalism, theism is incoherent, so, without theism, is psychicalism. How can many psyches, each of whom (Plato) is to some extent self-moved as well as moved by other self-movers, constitute an orderly cosmos [if there were no God]?

[PCH 700] My ultimate intuitive clue in philosophy is that "God is love" and that the idea of God is definable as that of the being worthy to be loved with all one's heart, mind, soul, and entire being. This definition I owe to Paul Tillich. I conclude that therefore love in its most generalized sense is the principle of principles. It is creativity, stressing one of its aspects. Whitehead says that "Love, imperfect in us is perfect in God." It is with his help that I have been able to generalize this to apply to nondivine actualities generally, Peirce hints strongly in the same direction and so does Bergson.

[PCH 700] Two important differences between my psychicalism and Whitehead's are that I conceive God as analogous to a "personally ordered society" rather than to a single actuality, and distinguish between God's Consequent Nature (CN), capturable in a concept, and the contingent states or instantiations of that nature--states knowable only intuitively and (to put it mildly) knowable adequately only by God. The CN in itself is part of the formal not the material side.... It is not contingent.

[PCH 700-701] Because Whitehead does not distinguish between consequent [upon what happens throughout the universe] *nature* and consequent *states* of God, or between divine concrete*ness* and instances of this abstraction, he obscures the truth that . . . The creative process has had no beginning.

APPENDIX M

ANCIENT AND MEDIEVAL ANTECEDENTS OF NEW THOUGHT

Most dates are approximate. Only the most uncertain have question marks.

EAST:
604-531	Lao Tzu: Taoism
600?	Zarathustra (Zoroaster): Zoroastrianism
551-479	Kung Fu-tzu (Confucius): Confucianism
550-480	Siddhartha Gautama, the Buddha (Enlightened One): (Buddhism)

WEST:
800?	Homer
750?	Hesiod
6th cent.	Theagenes of Rhegium: allegorical interpretation of myths
6th cent.	Pherecydes of Syros: reincarnation, diluted myth
624-546	Thales: abandoned myth, started philosophy, water *arche*
610-546	Anaximander: boundless
585-528	Anaximenes: air
580-497	Pythagoras: numbers, religious brotherhood
570-475	Xenophanes: critique of concepts of gods
544-483	Heraclitus: change (becoming, process) & Logos (order)
540-470	Parmenides: changelessness (being) Eleatic)
508	democracy begins in Athens
499-430	Zeno of Elea: changelessness (Eleatic)
499-428	Anaxagoras: "seeds" moved by mental particles

495-435	Empedocles: four "roots" moved by love and strife
470-399	Socrates (concept answer to ethical relativism, virtue as insightful knowledge, full soul immortality)
460-370	Democritus (& Leucippus, 5th Century): atoms
450-400	Age of Pericles (high Athenian culture)
445-365	Antisthenes: Cynic (unconventional virtuous living)
435-355	Aristippus: founded Cyrenaicism (raw hedonism)
431-404	Peloponnesian War (Sparta defeated Athens)
427-347	Plato (self-moving mind; real a world of Forms)
384-322	Aristotle (self-realization; isolated God; logic)
365-275	Pyrrho: Skeptic (knowledge impossible)
341-271	Epicurus: founded Epicureanism (refined hedonism; materialistic atomistic metaphysics)
336-264	Zeno of Citium: founded Stoicism (virtue the only good, brotherhood of all, peace of mind through conformity to Nature, or God, or Matter, or Fate, or Providence, which are synonymous in this deterministic pantheism)
215-130	Carneades: Skeptic
c. 150	Aristobulus: united Greek and Jewish thought; allegorical interpetation of Bible
96-55	Lucretius: Epicurean
? BCE-30 CE	Jesus, the Christ (the Messiah=Anointed One)
?-c. 64	Paul: invented Christianity?
30 BCE-50 CE	Philo: allegorical interpretation; negative theology; Logos between God and world
1st-3d. cents.	Gnosticism (hidden knowledge, dualism)
60-138	Epictetus: Stoic

121-180	Marcus Aurelius: Stoic
c. 150-215	Clement
c. 185-254	Origen
100 BCE-150	Neo-Pythagoreanism: One
204-269	Plotinus: One; emanation; mysticism
268	Goths invade Greece
313	Constantine's Edict of Toleration ends persecution of Christians, but he revokes it in 325 and makes Christianity the imperial religion and thereafter dissenters from the church are persecuted
325	Council of Nicaea opts for a view of Christ as divine and replaces classical approach to God through nature with trinitarian, faith-emphasizing Christian approach to nature through God who transcends human reason
330	Constantine moves his capital from Rome to Constantinople (earlier Byzantium, now Istanbul), capital of Eastern or Byzantine Empire for more than a millennium
354-430	Augustine
370	Asian Huns invade Europe
406	Vandals invade Gaul; Romans leave Britain
410	Goths sack Rome
425	Angles, Saxons, and Jutes invade Britain
433	Attila the Hun begins reign
476	Goths depose last Western Roman Emperor, Romulus Augustus; Middle Ages begin
529	Justinian closes Academy at Athens, formally ending Greek philosophy, and starts codifying laws
570-632	Muhammad
634	Muslims begin conquest of Near East and Africa
711	Moors invade Spain
732	Charles Martel defeats Moors at Battle of Tours, stopping Muslim advance into

	Europe
800	Charlemagne crowned Emperor of the West, political end of Dark Ages phase of Middle Ages
810-877	John Scotus Erigena
814	Arabic numerals established
900	Spain starts to drive out Moors; Mayas emigrate to Yucatan Peninsula
932	Printed books from woodblocks developed in China
1000	Vikings begin to explore North America
1033-1109	Anselm of Canterbury
1050-1121	Roscellinus
1054	Byzantine Empire breaks with Roman Church, with Eastern Church thereafter independent of Western Church
1059-1109	Al-Ghazali
1066	Normans conquer Britain (Battle of Hastings)
1079-1142	Bernard of Clairvaux,
1091-1153	Peter Abelard
1096	First Crusade to oust Muslims from Holy Land
1100	Polynesian Islands colonized
1126-1198	Averroes
1135-1204	Maimonides
1190	Genghis Kahn begins to conquer Asia
1193-1280	Albertus Magnus
1204	Crusaders capture and sack Constantinople
1210	Mongols invade China
1214-1294	Roger Bacon (not to be confused with Francis Bacon, 1561-1626)
1215	Magna Carta
1225-1274	Thomas Aquinas
1228	Sixth Crusade captures Jerusalem
1240	Mongols capture Moscow, destroy Kiev
1260	Kublai Kahn founds Yuan dynasty in China
1260-1327	Meister Eckhart

Healing Hypotheses 405

1265-1308	John Duns Scotus
1271	Marco Polo leaves for China to visit Kublai Kahn
1280-1347	William of Occam
1291	Crusades end as Muslims rout Christians in Palestine
1325	Aztecs found Tenochtitlan
1337	Hundred Years' War between England and France begins
1347	Bubonic plague spreads from China to Cyprus
1348	Black Death (plague) spreads to England
1351	Plague reaches Russia; European toll more than 25 million
1363	Tamerlane begins conquest of Asia
1368	Mongol dynasty ends in China; Ming dynasty begins
1390	Turks conquer Asia Minor
1401-1464	Nicolas of Cusa
1402	Tamerlane conquers Ottoman Empire
1431	Jeanne d'Arc burned as a witch at Rouen
1453	Hundred Years' War ends; fall of Constantinople to Ottoman Turks; traditional date for end of the Middle Ages and beginning of the Renaissance

APPENDIX N

MODERN WORLD AND NEW THOUGHT

Items most closely related to the "Metaphysical Movement" are indented once, wars twice; New Thought-related people are bolded; many important people, events, and books are omitted; dates of periods are highly debatable.

THE RENAISSANCE (1453 [fall of Constantinople]-1690 [Locke's *Essay Concerning Human Understanding*])

1463-1536	Erasmus: humanistic church reformer
1473-1543	Copernicus: heliocentric astronomy
1483-1546	Luther: Started Protestant Reformation
1509-1564	Calvin: absolute God, predestination
1519-1522	Conquest of Mexico
1548-1600	Bruno: infinite living universe, monads
1562-1598	Wars of Religion
1564-1642	Galileo
1618-1648	Thirty Years' War
1642-1649	English Civil War
1642-1727	Newton (1687 *Principia*)

THE ENLIGHTENMENT (1690-1781 [Kant's *Critique of Pure Reason*])

CONTINENTAL RATIONALISM
1596-1650	Descartes: metaphysical dualism: thought (mind) and extension (matter)
1632-1677	Spinoza: rationalistic pantheist
1644-1716	Leibniz: panpsychistic idealist

BRITISH EMPIRICISM
1561-1626	Francis Bacon: empiricist; knowledge is

	power
1588-1679	Hobbes: materialist
1632-1704	Locke: empiricist, mataphysical dualist
1685-1753	Berkeley: idealist; to be is to perceive or to be perceived
1711-1776	Hume: phenomenalist (Locke - material substance = Berkeley; Berkeley - spiritual substance = Hume)

OTHER

1651	Hobbes, *Leviathan*
1688-1772	Swedenborg
1689-1755	Montesquieu
1694-1778	Voltaire
1703-1758	Edwards
1706-1790	Franklin
1712-1778	Rousseau
1724-1804	Kant
1733-1815	Mesmer
1741	Handel, *Messiah*
1747	LaMettrie, *Man a Machine*
1748-1832	Bentham
1762-1814	Fichte
1768-1834	Schleiermacher
1771	Swedenborg, *True Christian Religion*
1770-1831	Hegel
1772-1833	Ram Mohan Roy
1775-1783	American Revolution
1775-1854	Schelling
1788-1860	Schopenhauer
1789-1802	French Revolution
1792-1867	Victor Cousin
1795-1872	John Bovee Dods
1798-1857	Comte
1799-1888	A. Bronson Alcott
1802-1866	**Quimby**
1803	Dalton's atomic theory
1803-1882	Emerson

1804-1872	Feuerbach
1805-1844	Joseph Smith
1806-1873	J. S. Mill
1807	Hegel, *Phenomenology of Mind*
1808	Goethe, Faust I
1809-1882	Charles Darwin
1810-1860	Theodore Parker
1812-1815	War of 1812
1813-1855	Kierkegaard
1815-1903	Renouvier
1817-1862	Thoreau
1817-1881	Lotze
1817-1889	**W. F. Evans**
1817-1892	Baha' Ullah
1819	Schopenhauer, *The World as Will and Idea*
1818-1883	Karl Marx
1820-1903	Spencer
1820-1895	Engels
1821-1910	M. B. Eddy
1824	Beethoven, *9th Symphony*; Byron, *Don Juan*
1826-1910	A. J. Davis
1830-33	Lyell, *The Principles of Geology*
1831-1891	Blavatsky
1832	Charles Babbage conceived the computer
1833	Wm. Whewell coined term "scientist"
1836-1886	Ramakrishna
1836	Emerson, *Nature*, started Transcendentalism
1838-1900	Sidgwick
1838-1893	**J. A. Dresser**
1842	Comte's materialistic positivism
1843-1935	**A. G. S. Dresser**
1846-1848	Mexican War
1835-1909	W. T. Harris
c. 1838	**Quimby** came upon Mesmerism
1839-1914	C. S. Peirce
1840's	**Quimby** wrote "lecture notes"
1842-1910	William James

1844-1900	Nietzsche
1844-1906	**M. Cramer** Divine Science
1848-1906	**A. B. Small** " "
1854-1914	**F. B. James** " "
1861-1945	**N. Brooks** " "
1845-1931	**M. Fillmore** Unity
1854-1948	**C. Fillmore** "
1846-1888	Anna Kingsford
1847-1910	B. P. Bowne
1847-1916	**T. Troward**
1851	Melville, *Moby-Dick*
1852	Stowe, *Uncle Tom's Cabin*
1852-1933	Vaihinger
1853-1925	**E. C. Hopkins**
1854	Thoreau, *Walden*
1855-1916	J. Royce
1858-1947	Max Planck
1859	Darwin, *The Origin of Species*
1859-1938	S. Alexander
1859-1938	Husserl
1859-65	**Quimby** wrote articles
1859-1941	Bergson
1859-1952	John Dewey
1861-1865	U. S. Civil War
1861-1925	R. Steiner
1861-1947	Whitehead
1862-1902	Vivekananda
1862-1933	**W. W. Atkinson**
1864-1936	Unamuno
1866-1954	**H. W. Dresser**
1869	**Evans**, *The Mental-Cure* (1st proto-New Thought book)
1869-1948	Gandhi
1871-1960	Flewelling
1872-1950	Aurobindo
1872-1970	Russell
1873	James Clerk Maxwell, *Treatise on Electricity and Magnetism* (leading to

	relativity & quantum theory)
1874-1948	Berdyaev
1875	Eddy, *Science and Health*; Theosophical Society founded
1875-1965	Schweitzer
1878-1965	Buber
1879-1955	Einstein
1880-1936	Spengler
1882	(British) Society for Psychical Research started
1883-1973	Jaspers
1884-1953	Brightman
1884-1975	Wieman
1884-1976	Bultmann
1885	American Society for Psychical Research started
1886-1965	Tillich
1886-1968	Barth
1887	**J. Dresser**, *The True History of Mental Science*
1887-1960	**E. Holmes** Religious Science
1888-1975	Radhakrishnan
1889-1966	Brunner
1889-1951	Wittgenstein
1889-1975	Toynbee
1889-1976	Heidegger
1892	International Divine Science Association founded by **Cramer**
1892-1971	Niebuhr
1893	The World's Parliament of Religions (popularized Eastern Religions in U. S.)
1893-1985	**Taniguchi** Seicho-No-Ie
1893	Hudson, *The Law of Psychic Phenomena*
1897	Hartshorne born
1898	Spanish-American War
1899	First "New Thought Convention," Hartford
1899	International Metaphysical League

	started, Boston
1900	Planck began quantum theory
1900	Freud, *The Interpretation of Dreams*
1901	Bucke, *Cosmic Consciousness*
1902	James *The Varieties of Religious Experience*
1905, 1907, & 1916	Einstein's theories of relativity
1905-1980	Sartre
1907	James, *Pragmatism*; Bergson, *Creative Evolution*
1908	Bowne, *Personalism*
1910-1989	Bertocci
1914	Earlier associations became International New Thought Alliance
1914-1918	World War I
1917-1922	Russian Revolution and Civil War
1921	**Dresser**, *The Quimby Manuscripts*
1929	Whitehead, *Process and Reality*
1929	Hubble proved universe expanding
1935-1936	Italo-Ethiopian War
1936-1939	Spanish Civil War
1937-1945	Second Sino-Japanese War
1939-1945	World War II
1948-1949, 1956, 1967, 1973	Arab-Israel Wars
1950-1953	Korean War
1960-1975	Vietnam War
1987	First paper on New Thought presented at an American Academy of Religion meeting, Boston, with start of discussions leading to founding of Society for the Study of Metaphysical Religion.
1988	**Seale**, *P. P. Quimby: The Complete Writings*
1991	Persian Gulf War
1991	First public session of SSMR held, Tampa.

APPENDIX O

PRACTICAL PROCESS PHILOSOPHY

from

A GUIDE TO THE SELECTION AND CARE OF YOUR PERSONAL GOD
by C. Alan Anderson
(Canton, MA: Squantum Press, 1991), pp. 46-49.

(1) You, the universe, and God are new every moment.

(2) You can make a significant new departures at any time. You can be burdened by the past much less than you probably believe.

(3) There is no reason for you to regret "your" past. You were not there. You did not exist a second ago, and you will not exist a second from now. Someone very much like you did and will, but he or she should be recognized as an ancestor or a descendant, someone to be appreciated in some way, but not identified with.

(4) No effort ever is wasted. All occasions of experience, including you, become objectively immortal when they complete their split-second subjective careers, and they influence everything forever, in some degree.

(5) Cooperation is essential. Unless something that you are committed to doing takes no more than a small fraction of a second, you are only a fleeting part of a relatively long cooperative program of many generations of [the abstraction that is considered] you. Needless to say, in many projects cooperation with other lines of development (other people and things) also is necessary.

The entire universe is involved in any act.

(6) You can't take it with you beyond your fraction of a second of awareness as a subject. However, nothing that you have ever is lost. It will be forever in God and in your successors, who in some degree will identify with you (however wisely or foolishly), most likely both before and after death. Make the most of the moment.

(7) You can afford to risk everything, to go for broke, in providing your greatest momentary satisfaction and the best background out of which your successors will arise. It is foolish to settle for less than the best: what God offers.

(8) Love is ultimate, as the universal recycling process. God as love gives the perfect initial aim to each occasion of experience. God allows the occasion to choose freely and enjoy fully, and then he accepts appreciatively the product of the occasion's choosing, which is the completed occasion itself. He arranges it in the universal pattern, and passes it along to coming generations.

(9) Recognizing God as love (which is wise, giving, sharing, participating in the experience of others) provides a full understanding of God's operations. The invariable reliability of God may tempt us to think of God as law, but the notion of law is only an approximation of what goes on as divine personal action. Law is a name for perfect love at work, for the consistency, uniformity, and dependability of God's personality. God is not a cosmic vending machine, and even if he were, process thought holds that the person who inserts the coin actually would not be the same person who receives the product. To consider God as law undermines God's place as initiator and your place as responder. Your originality lies in the character of your response to God.

(10) God is fully personal. It is because God is

perfectly personal that he is perfectly impartial, which probably is what most people mean when they say that God is impersonal. An impersonal God is a contradiction in terms, a monstrous impossibility, which, if it could be, would be the most ugly incongruity of existence. The personal ultimate, God, is indescribably loving, intelligent, and aware, so he provides an initial aim that is perfectly consistent with the occasion's background. This background includes the prayers, conscious or unconscious, of the occasion's "own" predecessors [in its own line of development] and of others. Moreover, by providing (and being present as) the initial aim, God lovingly gives tailor-made guidance, as no impersonal ultimate could do.

(11) Unity with God, as well as our seeming separation from him, can be understood in terms of phases of development of an occasion. At the beginning, as initial aim, clearly it is God; as it progresses in its choosing of its unique balance of the past and the possible (giving God a unique perspective on the whole) it is convenient to speak of it as if it were other than God, although it continues to be an individualization of God [one of God-the-many]. The fully developed mystic is one who is as consciously God at the completion of momentary creation as he or she was God at the beginning of creation a moment earlier.

(12) Understanding God, we appreciate the power of gentleness and of the futility of force. God acts as loving persuasiveness by presenting possibilities of perfection to lure us into acceptance of what he offers.

(13) Accepting what God offers may require our persistence and commonsensical action as parts of a process extending over generations of occasions.

(14) We can understand all kinds of treatment, ranging from taking an aspirin or undergoing surgery to affirmation or visualization, as ways of enriching the

immediate pasts of occasions (usually people) being helped. Treatment does this by reducing the discrepancies between their negative pasts and the possibilities presented by God as initial aims, enabling the occasions (people) to opt for the initial aims more easily.

(15) *Evil* is the acceptance of lesser possibilities [influences of the past] than God's initial aims offer. Any creation is good to the extent that it converts potentiality to actuality. But backward-looking, lesser-than-perfect blends are of less value than are more positive selections, both to the occasion in question and to God in his forming of the most beautiful whole. From the standpoint of any one developing occasion there is little point to speak of evil at all. That occasion was not in the past and it will not know the future, so its sole concern should be making the best of the present, which in itself never can be evil. Evil always is about might-have-beens, about the way that we wish that things were.

(16) All concrete, actual, reality is growing, evolving, in flux. The panentheistic personal God is never changing in loving, divine character, but is always expanding in experience. This is an awesome vision of an open future in which even natural laws (understood as habits of interaction) are subject to development and eventual practical dissolution (MT 155). Yet always there will be the changeless pattern by which occasions of experience arise by loving divine instigation, create and enjoy themselves by relatively free choice, and exist everlastingly as objects influencing all later occasions.

(17) To be is to be utterly dependent on God for existence and potentialities, free to find complete fulfillment in God, yet to hold an effective veto power over God through rejection of the possibilities that he presents to you.

(18) Your everlasting place in the all-encompassing reality is as a contributor to God. What you contribute is your unique perspective. Your perspective is most valuable when it is "directed to the end of stretching individual interest beyond its self-defeating particularity" (PR 23). This self-defeating particularity is what you attempt to overcome in linking yourself with the way of God, which ever more fully is to become your own way (the way of you and your descendants known by your name and approximately your appearance over the next minutes and decades). Our petty, if horribly prominent, desires can be satisfied only by subordinating them to the desire for God himself.

Your understanding and power to accomplish in all this is enhanced greatly by acceptance of (a) mysticism's experience of unity with God, (b) personalism's awareness of the centrality of personality for all levels of existence, (c) process thought's comprehension of the nature of the creative advance, and (d) New Thought's use of constructive techniques for achieving wholeness in all aspects of daily living. The outcome--a powerful tool for living effectively and beautifully--is a mystically-inspired, personalistic Process New Thought.

APPENDIX P: SOME PATHS TO BOTH FORMS OF NEW THOUGHT

Nonliteral interpretations:
Theagenes Stoics Aristobulus Sophists Gnostics Philo Clement Origen Augustine Swedenborg Quimby Kingsford

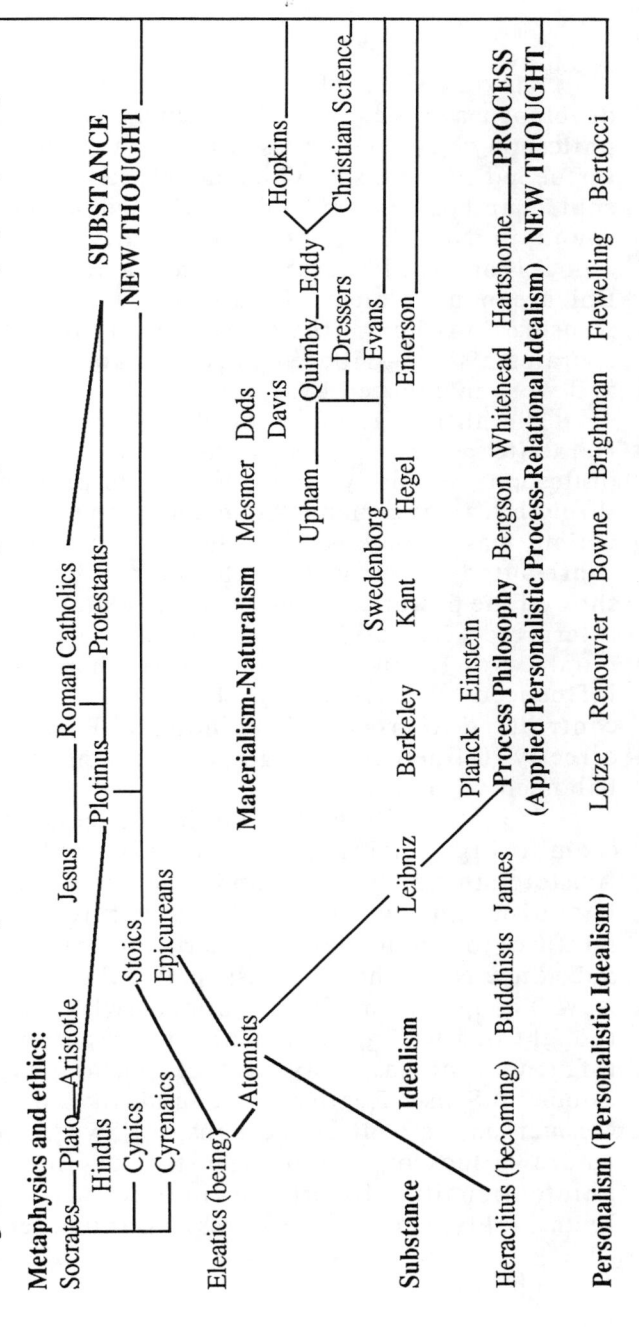

Metaphysics and ethics:

Socrates — Plato — Aristotle ⎯⎯⎯⎯⎯ Jesus ⎯⎯⎯⎯⎯ Roman Catholics
          Hindus   Plotinus
        Cynics   Stoics   Protestants   **SUBSTANCE**
        Cyrenaics Epicureans   **NEW THOUGHT**

Eleatics (being)
          Atomists   **Materialism-Naturalism**   Mesmer   Dods
                                                           Davis   Hopkins
                                                                 Upham ⎯ Quimby ⎯ Eddy
                                                                                   Dressers   Christian Science
                                                                       Swedenborg   Evans
                                                                                  Kant   Hegel   Emerson
                                     Berkeley
                                          Planck Einstein
Substance   **Idealism**   **Process Philosophy** Bergson Whitehead Hartshorne ⎯ **PROCESS**
                             Leibniz   (Applied Personalistic Process-Relational Idealism) **NEW THOUGHT**

Heraclitus (becoming) Buddhists James

Personalism (Personalistic Idealism)   Lotze Renouvier Bowne Brightman Flewelling Bertocci

Varying sides of Socrates inspired (1) Plato, who developed a largely idealistic, comprehensive system of philosophy; (2) the Cynics, whose rough championing of virtue led to Stoicism, which developed elements of mind control and pantheism, both of which much later would be found in New Thought, and (3) the Cyrenaics, whose espousal of the pleasures of the moment preceded refined Epicurean avoidance of pain and enjoyment of quiet pleasures. Although the Megarians are not shown above, Socrates also contributed to them; they were much like, and were influenced by, the Eleatics.

The antipodal views of Eleatic changelessness and Heraclitean change came together in the atomistic philosophy of many changeless units producing change through rearrangement. Atomism led to later materialism, which was expressed in Mesmer and in Dods, who contributed to New Thought to the extent that they showed the power of mind, however materialistically they interpreted it. Atomism, in revised forms emphasizing mind (with Leibniz) and energy (with recent scientists) influenced Whitehead and others whose thought contributed to Process New Thought. Process thinking is directly in line with the Heraclitean emphasis on change balanced with order.

The idealistic and healing influences of Christianity (combining insights of Jesus with Platonism, Aristotelianism, Judaism, and other views) blended with Hinduism and various mystical, esoteric, and occult mixtures to provide largely the theoretical background of Substance New Thought. Especially the practical side of New Thought came from Quimby (who worked out his thought in a background of his own experimentation and influences of [a] conventional philosophy, especially Common Sense Realism as found in Upham, and [b] Mesmerism, as well as, perhaps, [c] Swedenborg and [d] Andrew Jackson Davis), mostly as intentionally or unintentionally, directly or indirectly, interpreted by Evans, Eddy, Hopkins, the Dressers, and others. Berkeley,

Hegel, Emerson, and other idealists were drawn on as New Thought evolved.

Process New Thought developed directly out of Substance New Thought, with theoretical reinterpretations derived from Process Philosophy (which has some kinship with Buddhism) and Personalism.

From a process perspective, Quimby's Wisdom is individualized and active as initial aim; spiritual matter is creative, choosing activity of an occasion of experience; and the inadequate opinions of people (and the illnesses that they instigate) are the past, which the later development of aim in an occasion of experience generally tends to adopt more than to accept Wisdom fully.

APPENDIX Q: THEMES AND THINKERS CONTRIBUTING TO NEW THOUGHT

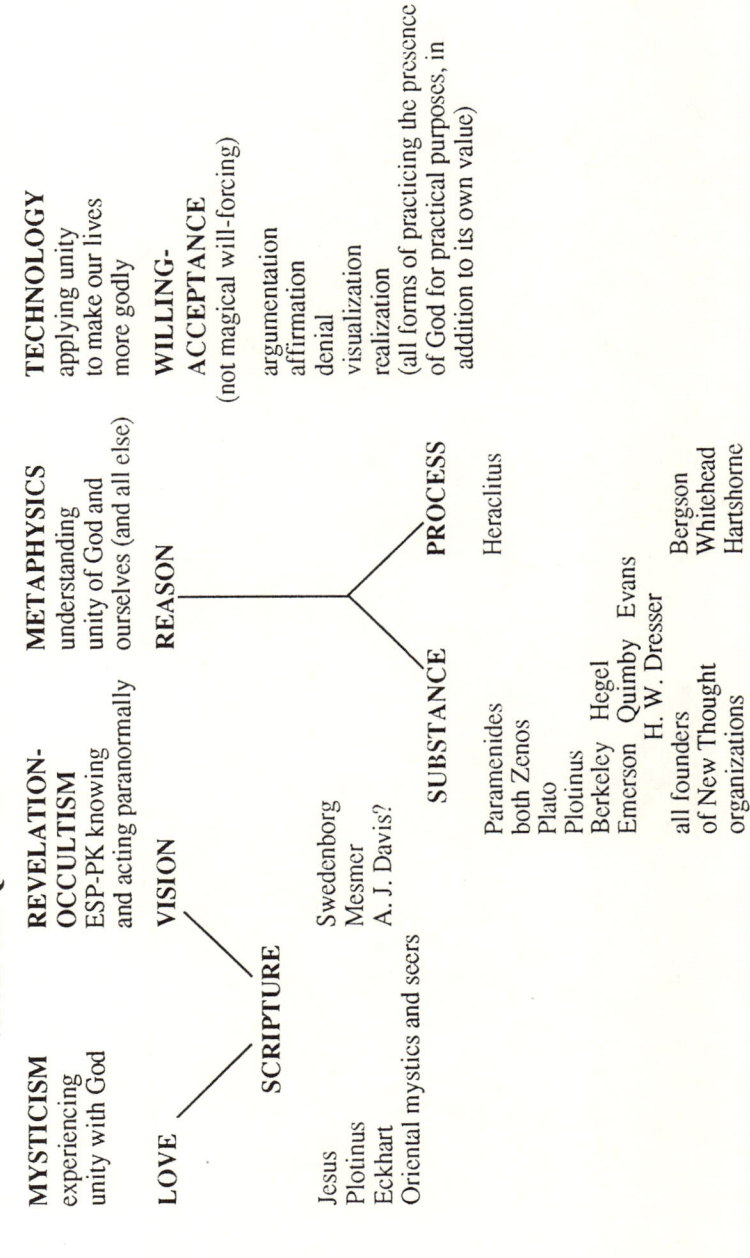

MYSTICISM	REVELATION-OCCULTISM	METAPHYSICS	TECHNOLOGY
experiencing unity with God	ESP-PK knowing and acting paranormally	understanding unity of God and ourselves (and all else)	applying unity to make our lives more godly

LOVE   VISION   REASON   WILLING-ACCEPTANCE
                                                                              (not magical will-forcing)

SCRIPTURE

                                                                              argumentation
                                                                              affirmation
                                                                              denial
                                                                              visualization
                                                                              realization
                                          SUBSTANCE   PROCESS
                                                                              (all forms of practicing the presence of God for practical purposes, in addition to its own value)

Jesus   Swedenborg
Plotinus   Mesmer
Eckhart   A. J. Davis?
Oriental mystics and seers

                                                       Parmenides   Heraclitus
                                                       both Zenos
                                                       Plato
                                                       Plotinus
                                                       Berkeley   Hegel
                                                       Emerson   Quimby   Evans
                                                                   H. W. Dresser   Bergson
                                                       all founders   Whitehead
                                                       of New Thought   Hartshorne
                                                       organizations

APPENDIX R

SOME CONTRASTS OF OLD AND NEW OUTLOOKS

OLD CHRISTIAN THOUGHT	SUBSTANCE NEW THOUGHT	PROCESS NEW THOUGHT
Reality is enduring substance.	Reality is enduring substance.	Reality is creative process.
Being is basic.	Being is basic.	Becoming is basic.
You **have** experience.	You **have** experience.	You **are** experience.
Soul is mortal substance.	Soul is immortal substance	Soul is a succession of momentarily-existing selves (serial selfhood).
Resurrection.	Subjective immortality.	Objective and subjective immortality.
God is largely transcendent (classical theism).	God is essentially immanent (pantheism).	God is immanent and transcendent (panentheism).
God creates out of nothing.	God emanates from divine fullness.	God creates by participating in blending of past and possible.

Universe is not part of God; it is matter and mind created by God.	Universe is part (in some interpretations, all) of God's being, is God's body.	Universe is part of God's becoming, is God's body.
Matter is lifeless stuff.	Matter is appearance of one mind (God).	Matter is collection of many relatively lowly minds.
God is changeless in theory, if not in practice.	God is changeless, except as responsive.	God is growing experientially, yet constant morally.
God is essentially love, yet is forcing.	God is essentially Love-Law.	God is essentially alluring, persuasive Love.
God is personal and in some degree capricious.	God is largely impersonal, and acts as law.	God is personal, impartial, and acts by giving initial aims.
God gives orders.	God gives general possibilities.	God gives tailor-made possibilities (initial aims).
God creates and sustains, yet seems inactive in one's life.	The burden of initiation largely is on us. God guides and responds.	God initiates. We must respond to God's guiding initiation of each moment.

Prayer sometimes changes God, who may give what is requested.	Prayer changes ourselves, who receive according to our beliefs, working through divine law shaping unformed substance.	Prayer helps create momentary self, giving immediate enjoyment and enriching the next self's past by becoming part of it, thereby making it easier for next self to accept God's initial aim.
Christ is identified with Jesus.	Christ is the presence of God permanently in each of us equally.	Christ is the presence of God, understood as initial aim of each momentary self (occasion of experience).
Law is divine command.	Law is active, divine, impersonal, automatic, intelligent, unconscious part of God.	Law is an abstraction, habits of interaction of occasions of experience.

APPENDIX S

QUIMBY, "THE DIFFICULTY OF INTRODUCING MY IDEAS"

It is appropriate to let the last words of this book be from Quimby. Without Quimby, Julius Dresser and Annetta Seabury might have died young, perhaps without meeting, and there would have been no Horatio W. Dresser. Evans probably would have promoted Swedenborgianism without seeing its implications for healing, for as long as his health allowed; and that might have been a short period. Mary Baker Eddy probably would have had no system of spiritual healing. Most likely, we should know nothing of Emma Curtis Hopkins or any of those who were touched by her life and teaching. Myrtle Fillmore might have succumbed to her illness, and Charles Fillmore might have continued as a businessman. William James probably would have produced *The Varieties of Religious Experience* without its lectures on "The Religion of Healthy-Mindedness." Possibly the degree and forms of acceptance of Eastern views popularized at The World's Parliament of Religions would have been different, with more (or less) direct acceptance, or with less acceptance apart from the avenues provided by New Thought groups. Ernest Holmes might have become a popular inspirational speaker, but probably without direct practical applications. Norman Vincent Peale might have labored in the ministry without ever attaining fame. Maybe somebody would have seen that Emerson's insights could be applied practically, but who? Perhaps Malinda Cramer would have come up with something out of Quaker and theosophical roots, but one scarcely can be sure that it would have been very much like what New Thought has become.

Possibly views such as those of Dods would have

produced a materialistic healing movement. Psychiatry and psychosomatic medicine presumably would have developed irrespective of Quimby's work. Perhaps the power of mind was enough "in the air" so that somebody else would have done something like the job that Quimby did in producing a blend of philosophy, science, religion, and healing. But the fact remains that it *was* Quimby who laid the foundation for the core of what has followed in New Thought, and in related areas.

Quimby's words (in Seale, ed., *The Complete Writings*, II, 303) quoted below reflect frustration, but I think that they imply hope, and that there is a broad--and possible--task of healing the world's outlook. They end with a question, which can be taken to suggest the need for continuing to explore, to reformulate, to remain, as Ernest Holmes put it, "open at the top." Quimby speaks for all who toil and soar in the project of providing the explanation--the healing hypothesis--that most effectively can cure the world.

> Introducing these ideas to the world is not an easy task, for the world like the sick cannot understand. For if they could, then there would not be any call for some other mode of reasoning. But the world, like a sick man, is in trouble and does not know how to free itself from the fetters that bind it. It is easy to take one individual case and apply the theory, but to take the world and give the causes and symptoms is not so easy a task. The world, like the sick, have no idea that what is said and believed has anything to do with their sickness, when all our troubles or nearly so are from our belief, directly or indirectly. Therefore, I have to take the world as a patient and show that the causes of man's trouble arise from his beliefs and these make him sick. Now the sickness is not the belief, but the belief is the cause directly or indirectly. So to cure, I have to destroy the belief

and then the sickness will cease. Then the question will be asked what is a belief?

BIBLIOGRAPHY

Part One: Writings Not Included in Dresser Bibliography
Part Two: Dresser Bibliography

H. W. Dresser writings wherever possible are listed chronologically. Generally where pages are not indicated, the information is from a Dresser typewritten list of some of his articles and the articles in question have not been seen in the publications listed. To the extent allowed by available information, the arrangement of periodicals and other categories is according to similarity of type of publication and approximate time of writing.

I. Writings not published by Swedenborgian groups

   A. Original appearance of his published books
   B. Apparently completed book manuscripts
   C. Pamphlets
   D. Other Writings
      1. Published
         a. Dresser-signed articles in his own periodicals: *The Journal of Practical Metaphysics* and *The Higher Law*
         b. Dresser articles in other periodicals
      2. Typewritten material

II. Writings published by Swedenborgian groups

PART ONE

Items Not Included in Dresser Bibliography

Allen, Abel Leighton. "New Thought," *Encyclopedia of Religion and Ethics.*

Anderson, John Benjamin. *New Thought its Lights and Shadows: An Appreciation and a Criticism.* Boston: Sherman, French & Company, 1911.

Anderson, Paul Russell and Max Harold Fisch. *Philosophy in America from the Puritans to James.* New York: Appleton-Century-Crofts, 1939.

Atkins, Gaius Glenn. *Modern Religious Cults and Movements.* New York: Fleming H. Revell Company, 1923.

Bach, Marcus. *The Unity Way of Life.* Englewood Cliffs, N.J.: Prentice-Hall, Inc., 1962.

Barrows, Charles M. *Bread-Pills: A Study of Mind-Cure.* Boston: Deland and Barta, Priners; Mutual News Company, Agents, 1885.

_____. *Facts and Fictions of Mental Healing.* Boston: H. H. Carter & Karrick, 1887.

Barrows, John Henry (ed.). *The World's Parliament of Religions.* Vol. 1. Chicago: The Parliament Publishing Company, 1893.

Bates, Ernest Sutherland and John V. Dittemore. *Mary Baker Eddy the Truth and the Tradition.* New York: Alfred A. Knopf, 1932.

Bertocci, Peter A. *Free Will, Responsibility, and Grace.* New

York and Nashville: Abingdon Press, 1957.

Braden, Charles Samuel. *Christian Science Today: Power, Policy, Practice.* Dallas: Southern Methodist University Press, 1958.
_____. *These Also Believe: A Study of Modern American Cults and Minority Religious Movements.* New York: The Macmillan Company, 1949.

Bromberg, Walter. *The Mind of Man: A History of Psychotherapy and Psychoanalysis.* New York: Harper & Brothers, 1959.

Cady, H. Emilie. *Lessons in Truth: A Course of Twelve Lessons in Practical Christianity.* Lee's Summit, Mo.: Unity School of Christianity, 1958, originally 1894.

The Christian Metaphysician. January-February, 1891.

Christy, Arthur. *The Orient in American Transcendentalism.* New York: Columbia University Press, 1932.

Clark, Elmer T. *The Small Sects in America.* rev. ed. Nashville: Abingdon Press, 1949.

Collyer, Robert H. *Mysteries of the Vital Element in Connexion with Dreams, Somnambulism, Trance, Vital Photography, Faith and Will, Anaesthesia, Nervous Congestion and Creative Function. Modern Spiritualism Explained.* 2nd ed. London: Henry Renshaw, 1871, originally Bruges, 1868.

Cousin, Victor (trans. O. W. Wight). *Course of the History of Modern Philosophy.* 2 vols. New York: D. Appleton & Company, 1852.

Curti, Merle. *The Growth of American Thought.* 2nd ed. New York: Harper & Brothers, 1951.

Dakin, Edwin Franden. *Mrs. Eddy: The Biography of a Virginal Mind*. New York: Charles Scribner's Sons, 1930.

Dawson, George Gordon. *Healing: Pagan and Christian*. London: Society for Promoting Christian Knowledge, 1935.

Dewey, John Hamlin. *The Way, the Truth and the Life*. 6th ed. New York: J. H. Dewey Publishing Company, 1888, perhaps the date of first publication.

Dictionary of American Biography.

Dods, John Bovee. *The Philosophy of Electrical Psychology*. New York: Samuel R. Wells, 1870, originally 1850.

_____. *Six Lectures on the Philosophy of Mesmerism*. New York: Fowlers and Wells, 1847.

Dresser, H. W., memorial. *Journal of the General Convention of the New Jerusalem in the United States of America for 1954*, p. 57.

Dwyer, Walter W. (ed. Florence M. Hehmeyer). *The Churches' Handbook for Spiritual Healing*. 4th ed. New York: Ascension Press, 1960.

Eddy, Mary Baker. *Science and Health with Key to the Scriptures*. Boston: Truestees under the Will of Mary Baker G. Eddy, 1934.

Evans, W. F. *The Celestial Dawn; or Connection of Earth and Heaven*. Boston: T. H. Carter & Company, 1864, originally 1862.

_____. *The Divine Law of Cure*. Boston: H. H. Carter & Company, 1881.

_____. *Esoteric Christianity and Mental Therapeutics*.

Boston: H. H. Carter & Karrick, 1886.

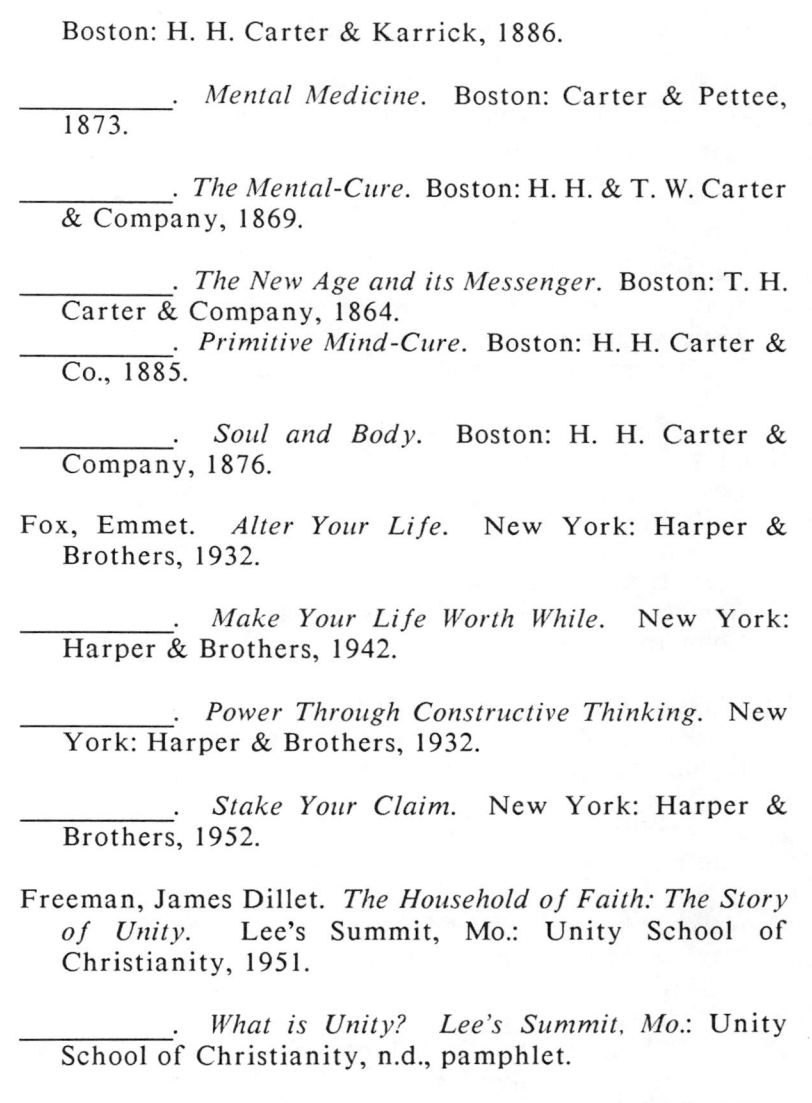

_____. *Mental Medicine.* Boston: Carter & Pettee, 1873.

_____. *The Mental-Cure.* Boston: H. H. & T. W. Carter & Company, 1869.

_____. *The New Age and its Messenger.* Boston: T. H. Carter & Company, 1864.

_____. *Primitive Mind-Cure.* Boston: H. H. Carter & Co., 1885.

_____. *Soul and Body.* Boston: H. H. Carter & Company, 1876.

Fox, Emmet. *Alter Your Life.* New York: Harper & Brothers, 1932.

_____. *Make Your Life Worth While.* New York: Harper & Brothers, 1942.

_____. *Power Through Constructive Thinking.* New York: Harper & Brothers, 1932.

_____. *Stake Your Claim.* New York: Harper & Brothers, 1952.

Freeman, James Dillet. *The Household of Faith: The Story of Unity.* Lee's Summit, Mo.: Unity School of Christianity, 1951.

_____. *What is Unity?* Lee's Summit, Mo.: Unity School of Christianity, n.d., pamphlet.

Frothingham, Octavius Brooks. *Transcendentalism in New England.* New York: Harper & Brothers, 1959, originally 1876.

Garrett, Eileen. *Telepathy.* New York: Creative Age Press, Inc., 1941.

Gaze, Harry. *Emmet Fox the Man and his Work.* New York: Harper & Brothers, 1952.

_____. *My Personal Recollections of Thomas Troward.* 3 booklets without publishing information, except 1958.

Goddard, Harold Clarke. *Studies in New England Transcendentalism.* New York: Hillary House Publishers, Ltd., originally Columbia University Press, 1908.

Holmes, Ernest. *New Thought Terms and Their Meanings.* Los Angeles: Institute of Religious Science and Philosophy, 1953.

Holmes, Ernest and Maud Allison Lathem (eds.). *Mind Remakes Your World.* New York: Dodd, Mead & Company, 1941.

James, William. *The Varieties of Religious Experience.* New York: The Modern Library, n.d., originally Longmans, Green and Company, 1902.

John, DeWitt. *The Christian Science Way of Life.* Englewood Cliffs, N.J.: Prentice-Hall, Inc., 1962.

Kingsford, Anna Bonus and Edward Maitland. *The Perfect Way; or the Finding of Christ.* 5th ed. London: John M. Watkins, 1923.

Leonard, William J. "The Pioneer Apostle of Mental Science," *Practical Ideals,* VI (July-August, 1903), 30-37.

_____. "Warren Felt Evans, M.D.," *Practical Ideals,*

X (Sept.-Oct., 1905), 1-16.
X (November, 1905), 1-23.
X (December, 1905), 9-26.
XI (January, 1906), 10-26.

Luckhurst, Kenneth W. *The Story of Exhibitions.* London and New York: The Studio Publications, 1951.

Mack, Gwynne Dresser. *Talking with God: The Healing Power of Prayer.* Pound Ridge, New York: New-Church Prayer Fellowship, 1960.

"The Magnetic Family," collection of articles, *Saturday Review*, XLV (February 3, 1962), 39-47.

Main Currents in Modern Thought, XIX (Sept.-Oct., 1962), 3-28, issue devoted to electrodynamic and psychodynamic fields.

Mann, Charles H. *Healing Through the Soul[:] Formerly Called Psychiasis: Healing Through the Soul.* Boston: Massachusetts New Church Union, 1900 copyright data.

Mathison, Richard. *Faiths, Cults, and Sects of America from Atheism to Zen.* Indianapolis: The Bobbs-Merrill Company, Inc., 1960.

Mayer, F. E. *The Religious Bodies of America.* 3d ed. St. Louis, Mo.: Concordia Publishing House, 1958.

Milmine, Georgine. *The Life of Mary Baker G. Eddy and the History of Christian Science.* New York: Doubleday, Page & Company, 1909.

Muelder, Walter G. and Laurence Sears. *The Development of American Philosophy.* Cambridge, Mass.: Houghton Mifflin Company, 1940.

Mulford, Prentice. *Prentice Mulford's Story.* New York: F. J. Needham, 1889.

National Cyclopaedia of American Biography.

New Thought [Quarterly]. Any recent back cover [then giving the Declaration of Principles of the International New Thought Alliance, now presented inside the publication, and restored to its completeness after some years of inadvertently omitting one of its sections].

Nordhoff, Charles. *The Communistic Societies of the United States.* New York: Hillary House Publishers, 1961, originally 1875.

Parrington, Vernon L. *Main Currents in American Thought.* Vol. 2. New York: Harcourt, Brace and Company, 1954.

Persons, Stow. *American Minds: A History of Ideas.* New York: Henry Holt and Company, 1958.

Poyen, Charles. Introduction to *Report on the Magnetical Experiments* made by the Commission of the Royal Academy of Medicine, of Paris, Read in the Meetings of June 21 and 28, 1831. Translated by Poyen. Boston: D. K. Hitchcock, 1836.

_____. *Progress of Animal Magnetism in New England.* Boston: Weeks, Jordan & Co., 1837.

Quimby, George A. "Phineas Parkhurst Quimby," *The New England Magazine*, VI (March, 1888), 267-76. [Now available in Ervin Seale, ed., *Phineas Parkhurst Quimby: The Complete Writings.* Marina Del Rey, CA: DeVorss & Co., 1988, I, 19-27.]

Quimby, Phineas P. See Dresser, ed., *The Quimby*

Manuscripts [and Seale, ed., *Phineas Parkhurst Quimby[:] The Complete Writings*].

_____. (ed. Erroll S. Collie). *The Science of Health and Happiness.* 2d ed. Processed, privately distributed, originally 1940.

Riley, Woodbridge. *American Thought from Puritanism to Pragmatism.* New York: Henry Holt and Company, 1915.

The Ruby (yearbook of Ursinus College), 1912 and 1913.

Schneider, Herbert W. *A History of American Philosophy.* New York: Columbia University Press, 1946.

Schneider, Herbert W. and Ruth Redfield. "John Bovee Dods," in *Dictionary of American Biography*, V, 353-54.

Sheldon, Henry C. *Theosophy and New Thought.* New York and Cincinnati: The Abingdon Press, 1916.

Snowden, James H. *The Truth About Christian Science.* Philadelphia: The Westminister Press, 1920.

Springer, Fleta Campbell. *According to the Flesh[:] A Biography of Mary Baker Eddy.* New York: Coward-McCann, Inc., 1930.

Studdert Kennedy, Hugh A. *Mrs. Eddy[:] Her Life, Her Work and Her Place in History.* San Francisco: The Farallon Press, 1947.

Tillich, Paul. "The Relation of Religion and Health: Historical Considerations and Theoretical Questions," *The Review of Religion*, X (May, 1946), 348-84.

Troward, Thomas. *The Law and the Word.* New York: Dodd, Mead & Company, 1950, originally 1917.

The Twentieth Century Biographical Dictionary of Notable Americans.

Tyner, Paul. "The Metaphysical Movement," *The American Monthly Review of Reviews*, XXV (March, 1902), 312-20.

Van Baalen, Jan Karel. *The Chaos of Cults: A Study of Present-Day Isms.* 5th ed. Grand Rapids, Michigan: Wm. B. Eerdmans Publishing Co., 1946.

Weatherhead, Leslie D. *Psychology, Religion and Healing.* rev. ed. New York: Abingdon Press, 1952.

Werkmeister, W. H. *A History of Philosophical Ideas in America.* New York: The Ronald Press Company, 1949.

White, Andrew D. *A History of the Warfare of Science with Theology in Christendom.* Vol. 2. New York: D. Appleton and Company, 1896.

Whitehead, John. *The Illusions of Christian Science.* Boston: The Garden Press, 1907.

Wilbur, Sibyl. *The Life of Mary Baker Eddy.* Boston: The Christian Science Publishing Society, 1923, originally 1907.

The World's Congress of Religions. Boston: Arena Publishing Company, 1893.

PART TWO

Dresser Bibliography

I. Writings Not Published by Swedenborgian Groups

A. Original appearance of his published books, chronologically listed according to dates of prefaces, which years are the same as publication years, except as noted.

1895, March 25. *The Power of Silence.* Boston: Geo. H. Ellis; 2nd ed., revised and enlarged. New York: G. P. Putnam's Sons, 1904, preface dated June, 1904.

1895, May 1. Annetta Gertrude Dresser the only author listed in book, but listed by Dresser in a typed note as among his books with himself as "joint author" and "incorporated in part in Health and the Inner Life," *The Philosophy of P. P. Quimby.* Boston: Geo. H. Ellis.

1896, September. *The Perfect Whole.* Boston: Geo. H. Ellis.

1897, January 1. *The Heart of It: A Series of Extracts from The Power of Silence and The Perfect Whole.* ed. Helen Campbell and Katherine Westendorf. Boston: Geo. H. Ellis.

1897, September 15. *In Search of a Soul.* Boston: Geo. H. Ellis.

1898, July. *Voices of Hope.* Boston: Geo. H. Ellis.

1899, February. *Methods and Problems of Spiritual Healing.* Boston: Geo. H. Ellis.

1899, August. *Voices of Freedom.* New York: G. P.

Putnam's Sons.

1899, no preface date. Julius A. Dresser. *The True History of Mental Science.* Revised with notes and additions by Horatio W. Dresser. New York: The Alliance Publishing Co. and Boston: The Temple Publishing Co., 1899, 1st ed. Boston: Alfred Mudge & Son, Printers, 1887. See Appendix E, "Letter to El," for a reference apparently to this work, possibly indicating more than later revisions by H. W. D.

1900, July. *Education and the Philosophical Ideal.* New York: G. P. Putnam's Sons.

1900, no preface date. *Living by the Spirit.* New York: G. P. Putnam's Sons.

1901, no preface date. *The Christ Ideal.* New York: G. P. Putnam's Sons.

1902, no preface date. *A Book of Secrets.* New York: G. P. Putnam's Sons.

1903, July. *Man and the Divine Order.* New York: G. P. Putnam's Sons.

1906, no preface date. *Health and the Inner Life.* New York: G. P. Putnam's Sons.

1907, no preface date. *The Greatest Truth.* New York: Progressive Literature Co.

1908, January. *The Philosophy of the Spirit.* New York: G. P. Putnam's Sons.

1908, July. *A Message to the Soul.* New York: G. P. Putnam's Sons, 1910.

Healing Hypotheses 445

1911, July. *Human Efficiency.* New York: G. P. Putnam's Sons, 1912.

1914, March. *The Religion of the Spirit in Modern Life.* New York: G. P. Putnam's Sons.

1917, January 1. Dresser (ed.). *The Spirit of the New Thought.* New York: Thomas Y. Crowell Company.

1917, no preface date. *Handbook of the New Thought.* New York: G. P. Putnam's Sons.

1917, no preface date. *The Victorious Faith.* New York: Harper & Brothers.

1918, no preface date. Dresser (ed.). *The World War*, Vol. XV of *The World's Story.* Boston: Houghton Mifflin Company.

1919, no preface date. *A History of the New Thought Movement.* New York: Thomas Y. Crowell Company.

1919, no preface date. *On the Threshold of the Spiritual World.* New York: George Sully and Company.

1920, no preface date. *The Open Vision.* New York: Thomas Y. Crowell Company.

1921, no preface date. Dresser (ed.). *The Quimby Manuscripts* (both editions the same year). New York: Thomas Y. Crowell Company.

1922, no preface date. *Spiritual Health and Healing.* New York: Thomas Y. Crowell Company.

1924, January. *Psychology in Theory and Application.* New York: Thomas Y. Crowell Company.

1925, April 1. *Ethics in Theory and Application.* New York: Thomas Y. Crowell Company.

1926, April. *A History of Ancient and Medieval Philosophy.* New York: Thomas Y. Crowell Company.

1928, January 3. *A History of Modern Philosophy.* New York: Thomas Y. Crowell Company.

1929, January. *Outlines of the Psychology of Religion.* New York: Thomas Y. Crowell Company.

1932, November. *Knowing and Helping People.* Boston: The Beacon Press, Inc., 1933.

B. Apparently Completed Dresser Book Manuscripts

Studies in Self-Knowledge and Inner Control. (Probably written at least partly during the last year of his life; under his name on a title page he refers to himself as "Author of 'Outlines of the Psychology of Religion,' etc. Formerly Consultant in Psychology, The Associated Clinic of Brooklyn, New York." He retired from this position in 1953.

The Secret of Perpetual Youth and Leaves from my Treasure Chest. (At least partly written in 1935 from a present reference to it on p. 6).

Dresser also wrote chapters for a work or works with the titles *Successful Techniques in Psychology* and *Successful Methods in Psychotherapy.*

C. Dresser Pamphlets

"The Inner Life Series," of pamphlets; listed as for sale by the author at South Hadley, Mass., and Harriet M. Van Der Vaart, 5616 Kimbark Avenue, Chicago; n.d.

An Outline for the Study of Jesus' Teachings.
Christ Today.
The Original Christian Science.

"The Way of Life Series," of numbered pamphlets, published by the Church of the Saviour, Unitarian, Brooklyn, New York, beginning in 1933 (not all dated):

The Conquest of Fear, 1933.
Inner Control, 1933.
Nervousness, 1933.
Sleeplessness, 1934.
Overcoming Worry.
Emotional Conflicts.
Habit, 1942.
Adjustments and Maladjustments.
Fatigue.
Subconsciousness, (a Dresser family source suggests 1945).

The True Christian Science, 1908 pamphlet not seen nor known whether part of a series.

D. Other writings

1. Published

a. Dresser-signed articles in his own periodicals

The Journal of Practical Metaphysics
Vol. I:

"A Forerunner of the Mental Cure" (May, 1897), 226-29.
"Spiritual Poise" (June, 1897), 253-60.
"Raja Yoga Philosophy" (July, 1897), 294-98.
"The Limitations of Psychology" (August, 1897), 323-29.
"Individuality" (September, 1897), 349-58.

Vol. II:
"The Problem of Evil" (December, 1897), 71-74.
"The Failure of the New Thought Movement" (January, 1898), 97-102.
"The Omnipresent Spirit" (April, 1898), 197-211.
"Character Building" (May, 1898, 237-45; continued in (June, 1898), 270-77.
"The Problem of Life" (July, 1898), 293-302; continued in (August, 1898), 329-39.
"Concentration" (September, 1898), 373-75.

The Higher Law
Vol. I:
"Beauty" (December, 1899), 1-5.
"The Spirit" (January, 1900), 33-39.
"Immortality I" (February, 1900), 65-74.
"Immortality II" (March, 1900), 101-107.
"Immortality III" (April, 1900), 133-140.

Vol. II:
"The Mystery of Pain and Evil" (July, 1900), 33-37.
"The Problem of Matter" (August, 1900), 65-75.
"An Ideal Metaphysical Club" (September, 1900), 105-109.
"The Social Problem" (October, 1900), 129-33.
"Real Life" (November, 1900), 166-71.

Vol. III:
"The Spiritual Ideal I" (January, 1901), 33-40.
"The Spiritual Ideal II" (March, 1901), 75-79.
"The Spiritual Ideal III" (May, 1901), 105-11.

Vol. IV:

"A Fundamental Question" (December, 1901), 153-56. By Henry Wood and H. W. Dresser.

Vol. V:
"The Need of Perspective" (May, 1902), 111-18.
"Expression" (June, 1902), 147-55.
"A Neglected Law" (July, 1902), 167-74.
"Glad Tidings" (August-September, 1902), 190-95.
"The Elements of Religion" (August-September, 1902), 204-11.

b. Dresser Articles in Other Periodicals

The Arena
"The Mental Cure in its Relation to Modern Thought," XVI (June, 1896), 131-37.
"Universal Freedom," XX (November-December, 1898), 568-84.
"What is the New Thought?" XXI (January, 1899), 29-50.
"Has Life a Meaning?" XXI (February, 1899), 162-82.
"Anglo-saxon in the East," XXI (March, 1899), 296-310.
"Possibilities of the Moral Law," XXI (April, 1899), 477-500.
"The Facts in the Case," first half of "Christian Science and its Prophetess," XXI (May, 1899), 537-50. The second half, "The Book and the Woman," by Josephine Curtis Woodbury, follows, pp. 550-70.
"The Harmony of Life," XXI (May, 1899), 612-28.
"The Genesis of Action," XXI (June, 1899), 777-90.
"The Inner Life," XXII (August, 1899), 246-57.
"An Interpretation of the Vedanta," XXII (October, 1899), 489-508.

Practical Ideals (Volumes III-XXIV examined)
Vol. VI:
"Doctor Quimby's Method" (November-December,

1903), 25-26,
A letter from *Boston Transcript*, no date given.

Vol. XI:
"The Quimby Discoveries" (March, 1906), 12-15.
"As to the Origin of Christian Science" (May, 1906), 22-24.

Vol. XVII:
"Mr. Quimby and the Emmanuel Movement" (January, 1909), 1-4.
"Limitations of the Emmanuel Movement" (January, 1909), 4-10.
"Spiritual Point of View in Mental Therapeutics [Healing, in table of contents]," I (February, 1909, 5-12.
"Spiritual Point of View in Mental Therapeutics [Healing, in table of contents]," II (March, 1909, 1-7.
"Spiritual Point of View in Mental Therapeutics," III (April, 1909), 9-14.
"About Christian Science" (April, 1909), 15-17.
"Notes on Mental Healing," I (May, 1909), 13-19.
"Notes on Mental Healing," II (May, 1909), 14-18.
"Notes on Mental Healing," III (August, 1909), 15-20.
"Notes on Mental Healing," IV (September, 1909), 3-8.
"The Law of Spiritual Healing," I (October, 1909), 9-16.
"The Law of Spiritual Healing," II (November, 1909), 9-12.
"The Law of Spiritual Healing," III (December, 1909), 19-23.

Vol. XIX
"The Victorious Attitude," I (January, 1910), 17-23. (Condensed from *A Message to the Well*.)
"The Victorious Attitude," II (February, 1910), 6-11.
"The Victorious Attitude," III (March, 1910), 17-23.

Vol. XX:
    "The Future Life," I (August, 1910), 1-9.
    "The Future Life," II (September, 1910), 7-12.

Vol. XXI:
    "Success Through Failure" (April-May, 1911), 18.

Vol. XXII:
    "Swedenborg," I (October, 1911), 1-6.
    "Swedenborg," II (November, 1911), 6-10.
    "Swedenborg," III (December, 1911), 1-6.

Vol. XXIII:
    "Swedenborg," IV (January, 1912), 7-10.
    (The volume number in this issue is printed incorrectly as XXII.)
    "Swedenborg," V (February, 1912), 11-16.
    "The New Thought" (April, 1912), 9-11.
    "What is Truth?" (I (September, 1912), 1-6.
    "What Is Truth?" II (October, 1912), 1-6.

Unity
    ["The Influence of Temperament on Health" XXVII (September, 1907), 129-33.]
    "The Affirmative Attitude" (April, 1920).
    "The Quickening Word" (July, 1920).
    "Instantaneous Healing" (May, 1923).
    "He That Overcometh" (January, 1925).
    "The Living Faith," LXII (May, 1925), 409-13.
    "The Laborer and His Hire," LXIII (August, 1925), 111-18.
    "Anxiety and Worry" (January, 1926).
    "Dr. Quimby's Theory of Matter," LXIV (June, 1926), 536-38.
    "True Prayer," LXV (September, 1926), 214-22.
    "Fresh Beginnings" (November, 1926).
    "Divine Guidance," LXVI (February, 1927), 118-24.
    "Contentment," LXVI (April, 1927), 319-26.
    "Justice," LXVI (June, 1927), 517-24.

"Faith," (January, 1928).
"Power," LXIX (August, 1928), 125-31.
"The Way Out," LXXVIII (April, 1933), 8-15.
"Spiritual Truths," LXXVIII (June, 1933), 18-26.
"Silence" (February, 1934).
"A Message to the Lonely" (April, 1934).
"Nonresistance" (November, 1934).
"The Believing Attitude" (January, 1936).
"The Abundant Life" (May, 1936).
"Spiritual States," LXXXVI (February, 1937), 18-27.
"Spiritual Gifts," LXXXVII (December, 1937), 16-25.
"Spiritual Security," LXXXVIII (February, 1938), 2-31.
"Spiritual Guidance" (October, 1940).
"Sufficient Unto the Day" (November, 1942), 24-30.
"Interpreting Our Past," CIII (July, 1945), 23-29.
"Weakness and Strength," CV (August, 1946), 22-29.

The following articles are listed, without dates, in a Dresser list of articles, but not in a list of his Unity-published articles supplied by Unity School of Christianity:

Unity
"Health Through Wisdom" [513-18]
"All Things Made New" [24-31]
"Overcoming Fear" [203-?]
"Spiritual Laws and Ideals"
["Prayer" 214-?]

Weekly Unity
"Spiritual Strength" XIII (March 18, 1922), 1-2.]

Christian Business
"Mental Atmospheres"

Christian Victory (?)
"Quimby's Technique."

Current Literature
"Put the Soul in Command" [excerpted from *Education and the Philosophical Ideal*], XXX (January, 1901), 109.

Current Opinion
"War as a Process of Moral Purification" [excerpted from *The Victorious Faith*], LXIV (February, 1918), 117.

Good Housekeeping
"Insure Your Health and Happiness," L (April, 1910), 470-72.
"An Invitation," L (April, 1910), 472-73.
"Action and Reaction," LI (July, 1910), 73-75.
"Domestic Harmony," LI (September, 1910), 283-85.
"A Talk to Our Policyholders[:] How to Acquire the Power to Think, to Will and to Live in Company with God," LI (October, 1910), 431-35.
["Letter to a Charity Worker" (perhaps from *Good Housekeeping*)]

Home Progress
"True Punishment," III (February, 1914), 288-90.

The following appear in the "Home History Circle," conducted by Dresser in *Home Progress* from April, 1915, through August, 1917, at which time the magazine ceased publication:

IV (April, 1915):
"Germany at War," 945-46.
"Epochs in German History," 946-52.

IV (May, 1915):
"Belgium, the Cock-Pit of Europe," 993-94.
"The Struggles of Belgium and Holland for Peace," 494-97.

"Types of Character in the Netherlands," 997-99.

IV (June, 1915):
"The Growth of Republicanism in Switzerland," 1041-43.
"The Position of Switzerland in History," 1043-47.
"Swiss Literature," 1050-51.
"The Influence of the Alps on Swiss Character," 1051-54.

IV (July, 1915):
"Russia Today," 1089-91.
"The Development of Russia," 1091-96.

IV (August, 1915):
"Austria and Germany and their Relations," 1135-40.
"Austria and the Balkans," 1147-50.

V (September, 1915):
"The Struggle of the Balkan States for Independence," 6-10.
"Constantinople and Turkey in Europe," 10-12.

V (October, 1915):
"Austria and Italy," 53-55.
"The Great Cities of Italy and their Part in European History," 55-58.
"Art as an Expression of Italian Genius," 58-61.
"Italy and the Modern Nations," 61-64.

V. (November, 1915):
"France and Germany," 101-03.
"The Wars of Napoleon and their Consequences," 103-07.
"The Common People Since the Revolution," 107-10.

V (December, 1915):
"Characteristics of the Spaniard," 149-51.

Healing Hypotheses 455

"Spain at the Height of Power," 151-57.
"The Expulsion of the Moors," 157-60.

V (January, 1916):
"The Voyages of Portuguese Discoverers," 197-99.
"Portugal in India and Africa," 199-203.
"Portugal and England," 203-209.

V (February, 1916):
"The Scandinavian Countires and the War," 245-47.
"Norwegian Scenery," 247-50.
"Scandinavian Mythology," 250-57.

V (March, 1916):
"The Position of Denmark in European History," 93-95.
"The Literature of Iceland," 295-96.
"The Discovery of the Poles," 298-305.

V (April, 1916):
"England Past and Present," 341-43.
"The Study of English History," 343-46.
"The Roman Period," 346-53.

V (May, 1916):
"How Britain Became England," 389-94.
"The Beginning of Literature in England," 394-98.

V (June, 1916):
"England Under Foreign Rule," 437-39.
"Results of the Norman Conquest," 439-44.
"Meaning of the Great Charter," 445-48.

V (July, 1916):
"Beginnings of the Reformation," 485-86.
"The Age of John Wiclif," 487-91.
"England during the Middle Ages," 491-96.

V (August, 1916):
"England on the Seas," 531-35.

"England's Golden Age," 535-39.
"The Age of Shakespeare," 539-44.

VI (September, 1916):
"Education in England," 5-7.
"The Growth of Education," 7-12.
"Francis Bacon and his Influence," 13-16.

VI (October, 1916):
"The Age of John Locke," 53-55 (not signed nor initialed, but probably by Dresser).
"Locke's Philosophy," 55-59.
"The Puritan Period," 59-64.

VI (November, 1916):
"The Victorian Age," 101-03.
"The Great Men of Science," 103-06.
"Literature and Life in the Victorian Age," 106-11.

VI (December, 1916):
"The Beginnings of History in Scotland," 149-51.
"The Influence of Scotland in English History," 151-57.
"Types of Scottish Literature," 157-60.

VI (January, 1917):
"The Union of England and Scotland," 197-99.
"The Orkney and Shetland Islands," 199-204.
"Characteristics of Scottish Philosophy," 204-08.

VI (February, 1917):
"The Struggle for Home Rule," 245-46.
"The Beginnings of History in Ireland," 246-51.
"The Development of Learning in Ireland," 251-55.

VI (March, 1917):
"The Welch People and their Place in History," 293-95.
"The Beginnings of Welsh National Life," 295-300.
"The Isle of Wight and the Channel Islands," 300-02.

VI (April, 1917):
   "The Study of American History," 341-43.
   "The Period of Discovery, 343-45.
   "China and the Portuguese Explorers," 345-46.

VI (May, 1917):
   "The Coming of the Colonists," 389-91.
   "Life in Colonial Times," 391-93.
   "Rural Life in the Colonies," 399-401.

VI (June, 1917):
   "The Discovery of Manhattan," 437-38.
   "New Amsterdam," 438-45.
   "William Penn and Quakers," 445-48.

VI (July, 1917):
   "Intellectual Life in the Colonies," 485-87.
   "The Beginnings of American Education," 487-92.
   "In the Days of King Philip," 492-96.

VI (August, 1917):
   "Beginnings of the Revolution," 533-35.
   "In Revolutionary Times," 538-41.
   "The Leaders of the Nation," 541-45.

Other Dresser articles from magazines and papers, as listed by him:

The Business Philosopher
   "Introducing a Contributor," by Martin L. Zook, about Dresser.
   "Laws of the Spiritual Life," (December, 1922).
   "Contentment" (1923).
   "Paul's Problem" (June, 1922).
   "The Subconscious" (July, 1922).
   "The Deeper Self" (August, 1922).
   "The Value of the Intellect" (September, 1922).
   "Interior Thought" (October, 1922).
   "The Power of Thought" (October, 1922).

"The Sphere of Thought"

The Golden Rule Magazine
"Horatio W. Dresser, Philosopher" ("An Appreciation by the Editor")
"What Moulds and Makes Men"

Boston Transcript
"The Emmanuel Movement"

Uncertain source
"Letter to a Charity Worker"

Twentieth Century Magazine
"Greenacre"

Meadville Theological Journal
"The Art of Health"

Friends Intelligencer (April 13, 1912)
"The Spirit in Daily Life"
"Seeking Guidance" (June 15, 1912)
"The Power of Jesus' Personality"

Nautilus, Holyoke, Mass.
"Bergson's Philosophy, Life and Intuition," Ch. I.
"Rational Optimism"
"The Basis of Spiritual Healing"
"First Impressions: Following Your Hunches"
"Inner Guidance"
"The Art of Resting"

The Gleaner (Dr. W. John Murray's magazine, New York)
[as the publication later was named]
"Intuition" (July, 1925)
"Coue and Quimby"
"The Inner Point of View"
"In the Secret Presence"

"Spiritual Efficiency"
"Living in the Present"
"Unmasking Our Minds," review (June, 1925).
"Miracles"
"Psychical Experiences in the Bible"
"Judging Others," used later as a sermon (October 23, 1942)".
"The Value of Effort," sermon.
"The Original Christian Science"
"Spiritual Influx and Health" (March, 1926). Published also as a New Church tract entitled "Spiritual Healing."
"Spiritual Correspondences" (April, 1926).
"Mind and Body in Health and Disease" (August, 1926).

2. Typewritten Material

H. W. Dresser "typed articles for patients or studies in the sort of work I have been doing in Brooklyn since the Fall of 1931," as referred to in February 23, 1944, letter to his daughter. These articles are listed in the order bound by Mrs. Herbert W. Browne.

"Suggestions for Daily Living" (2 pages).
"Silence--Repose--Meditation " (6 pages).
"Human Types" (10 pages).
"Aids in Determining One's Mental Type" (4 pages).
"Mental Types (7 pages).
"Our Mental Worlds" (13 pages).
"Subconsciousness" (14 pages).
"Imagination" (15 pages).
"Balance--Compensation--Adaptation" (11 pages).
"Self-Help" (12 pages).
"Modes of Self-Help" (5 pages).
"Confusions" (7 pages).
"Susceptibility to Environment and to People" (15 pages).
"The Nature and Use of Suggestion" (14 pages).

"Suggestion II" (3 pages).
"Reticence and Emotional Immaturity" (9 pages).
"Christ Today" (8 pages).
"Christian Therapy" (8 pages).
"New Light on Disease" (10 pages).
"Meditation" (9 pages).
"Practising for Security" (7 pages).
"The Nature and Wise Use of the Will" (19 pages).
"Impressions, Premonitions, Guidance" (23 pages, of which 19 are missing).
"Spiritual Gifts" (8 pages).

Among the many pieces of writing left by Dresser, not all of which it is feasible to list here, are the following, most of which seem to be in the same category as those next above: "Silence--Repose--Mediation " (2 pages).
"Inner Health" (9 pages).
"Memory" (8 pages).
"Notes on Habit-Formation" (6 pages).
"Notes on Human Personality" (16 pages).
"Detachment" (11 pages).
"The House of Peace. The Home of Security" (3 pages).
"What to Believe" (11 pages).
"Courage" (7 pages).
"G. B. Shaw's Philosophy of Life or Design for Living" (9 pages).
"Suggestions for Daily Practice" (9 pages).
"Christianity as a Way of Life" (15 pages).
"Steps in Self-knowledge" (13 pages).
"Living in the Present" (8 pages).
"Intuition" (11 pages).
"Guidance" (3 pages).
"Outline of the Human Self with reference to Experience in the Inner Life" (2 pages).
"Notes on Hunches, Impressions, Premonitions, Leadings, Intuition, etc." (18 pages).
"Outline of the Teachings and Methods of P. P. Quimby" (19 pages).

II. Writings Published by Swedenborgian Groups

The Helper
"Every Man a Church," LVI (November 10, 1915), 3-13.
"True Faith," LVIII (June 28, 1916), 3-14.
"Worshipping in Spirit," LVIII (November 29, 1916), 3-13.
"The New Idea of Man," LIX (January 24, 1917), 3-12.
"The Miracle of Every Day," LXVI (December 29, 1920), 3-9.
"The Divine Guidance," LXVII (February 23, 1921), 3-10.
"Spiritual Healing from a New Church Viewpoint," LXXI (February 7, 1923), 3-21. Also published as a pamphlet with the same title, in Philadelphia, n.d. See also his pamphlet *Spiritual Healing* (Patterson, N.J.: The Swedenborg Press, 1943).
"The New Thought and the New Church," LXXI (February 21, 1923), 3-17. Published in slightly condensed form as a pamphlet of the same title, Philadelphia, n.d.
"Brotherhood," LXXI (May 16, 1923), 3-15.
"The Lord is With Us," LXXII (December 26, 1923), 4-14.
"The Lord's Human Consciousness," LXXIII (January, 23, 1924), 9-25.
"The Upper Room," LXXVI (June 24, 1925), 9-20.
"The Value of Effort," CXIV (May 24, 1944), 1-7.

The New Christianity
"Pastoral Psychology," II (Summer, 1936), 57-60.
Review of *Tricks Our Minds Play on Us* by K. S. Stolz, and *The Art of Counseling* by Rollo May, V (Summer, 1939), 74.
"Concerning the Unconscious," VI (Spring, 1940), 47-49.
Review of *Man's Search for Himself* by Edwin B. Aubrey, VI (Autumn, 1940), 105-06.
"A Clinic for Damaged Lives," VI (Winter, 1940), 13-15.

"The Meaning of Inner States," VII (Autumn, 1941), 83-86. It is noted at p. 83 that this article was intended as a chapter of a contemplated, but apparently not completed, book, *The Psychology of Emanuel Swedenborg.*
"Religious Experience," VII (Winter, 1941), 17.
"The Sphere of Philosophy," VIII (Summer, 1942), 56-57.
Review of *Modern Marriage*, ed. by Moses Jung, VIII (Christmas, 1942), 95.
"The Value of the Doctrines," IX (Easter, 1943), 40-41.
Review of *Our Age of Unreason*, by Franz Alexander, IX (Summer, 1943). 69-70.
Review of *Religion and Health* by Seward Hiltner, IX (Summer, 1943), 69.

The New-Church Review
"An Estimate of the New Thought," I Exposition, XVIII (April, 1911), 161-79; II Criticism, XVIII (July, 1911). 354-70.
Review of *The New Testament Period and its Leaders*, by Frank T. Lee, XXI (April, 1914), 316-17.
"The Larger Charity" XXI (October, 1914), 535-47.
"True Humanism" XXIV (April,1917), 222-30.
Review of *The Psychology of Religion*, by George Albert Coe, XXIV (October, 1917), 636-38.
Review of *The Origin and Evolution of Life*, by H. F. Osborn, XXV (January, 1918), 158-60.
Review of *The Fellowship of Silence*, ed. by Cyril Hepher, *The Fruits of Silence*, by Cyril Hepher, and *The Empire of Silence*, by Charles Courtenay, XXV (April, 1918), 317-19.
"The Worship and Love of God," XXV (July,1918), 426-36.
Review of *Religion Rationalized*, by Hiram Vrooman, XXVI (October, 1919), 622-23.
"The New Thought and Spiritual Healing," XXX (April, 1923), 145-64.
Review of *Psychology for Bible Teachers*, by Edward

Annett, XXXII (July, 1925), 373-74.
Review of *A Short Psychology of Religion*, by G. J. Jordan, XXXV (April, 1928), 253-55.
Review of *Understanding Human Nature*, by Alfred Adler, XXXVI (January, 1929), 126-27.

The New-Church Herald
"Spiritual Healing from a New-Church Viewpoint," [republished from *The Helper*], IV (March 24, 1923), 177-81.
"The New Thought and the New Church," [republished from *The Helper*], IV (April 21, 1923), 244-47.
"Progress in the Church," [republished from *The New-Church Messenger*], V (February 2, 1924), 68-69.

The following six articles are excerpts from the projected book, *The Psychology of Swedenborg*:

"Love I," IX (March 17, 1928), 167-69.
"Love II," IX (March 24, 1928), 180-81.
"Remains," IX (September 22, 1928), 565-68.
"Memory I," X (January 19, 1929), 34-36.
"Memory II," X (January 26, 1929), 49-51.
"Disease-Health-Healing," X (April 27, 1929), 261-65.

"Spheres and Spiritual States," X (September 21, 1929), 562-65.
"Social Psychology," XI (February 1, 1930), 68-70.

The following twelve articles from *The New-Church Herald* are from *The Psychology of Swedenborg*. Their general title is "Swedenborg's Psychology." Their subtitles are given below:

"Mysticism I, " XI (August 23, 1930), 502-05.
"Mysticism II, " XI (September 6, 1930), 530-32.
"Psychical Research," XII (January 10, 1931), 18-21.
"Perception I," XIII (September 10, 1932), 546-48.

"Perception II, " XIII (September 17, 1932), 561-63.
"The Brain and Senses," XIII (October 15, 1932), 628-30.
"Sensation," XIII (October 22, 1932), 642-44.
"The Body," XIII (November 12, 1932), 689-92.
"Soul and Body," XIII (December 31, 1932), 800-803.
"Mental Activity," XIV (June 3, 1933), 336-40.
"Mental Origins I," XIV (October 7, 1933), 593-96.
"Mental Origins II," XIV (October 14, 1933), 615-16.

"Atmosphere," XVI (May 25, 1935), 249-50.

The New-Church Messenger
Vol. CXVI:
"The Pathway of Life" (March 19, 1919), 221.
Letter, "War Even to Annihilation," [reply to a report of his remarks to Massachusetts Woman's Alliance on "The Spiritual Results of the War," in March 19, 1919, issue, p. 234] (April 2, 1919), 268.
"Reaching People Where they Are," in a symposium, "Avenues of Approach," (April 23, 1919), 326.
Joint author with Adolph Roeder of "The Supernatural in Recent Literature (May 28, 1919), 424.
"The Renewing Life," (June 25, 1919), 503-05.

Vol. CXVII:
"To Lose Life or Find it" (October 15, 1919), 269.
"The Feeling Toward the Germans"(Octobor 15, 1919), 283-84.
"The Inward Light" (October 15, 1919), 375-77.

Vol. CXXIV:
"The Light of Truth" (January 3J 1923), 5-8.
"Swedenborg and the Universities" (January 10, 1923), 25-26.
"The Coming of the New Age" (January 31, 1923), 68-71.
"A Man of God" (March 7, 1923), 150-54.
"The Doctrine of Uses" (May 16, 1923), 312-15.

Healing Hypotheses

Vol. CXXV:
"The Vine and the Branches" (July 25, 1923), 53-55.
"The Divine Protection" (August 15, 1923), 96-99.
"Human Limitations" (October 24, 1923), 255-58.

Vol. CXXVI:
A letter (January 30, 1924) J 73-75.
"How the Bible was Written" (February 6, 1924), 87-91.
"Spirit of Truth" (March 12, 1924), 165-68.
"The Nature of Man" (March 19, 1924), 188-92.
"Recognizing the Lord" (April 30, 1924), 285-88.
"The Real Issue" (May 14, 1924), 319-23.

Vol. CXXVII:
"The Lord With Us" (October 29, 1924), 322-25.
"Of the Abundance of the Heart" (December 17, 1924 433-36.

Vol. CXXVIII:
"Seeking Guidance" (January 21, 1925), 37-40.
"Interpretation" (April 29, 1925), 288-90.
"The Sphere of Imagination" (May 20, 1925), 344-46.
"Verification" (June 3, 1925), 376-78.

Vol. CXXIX:
"Spiritual Healing," (September 9, 1925), 637-39.

Vol. CXXXII:
"Responsibility," (February 9, 1927), 92-95.

Vol. CXXXIII
"The Psychology of Hell," (October 12, 1927), 272-74.

Vol. CXXXIV:
"Feeling and Pleasure" (January 11, 1928), 24-27.
"Swedenborg and Evolution" (March 7, 1928), 164.
"Swedenborg's Sanity" (March 28, 1929), 204-07.

Vol. CXXXVI:
"Complexes" (April 17, 1929), 254-56.
"Self-Love" (May 22, 1929), 336-38. Published under the incorrect title, "Complexes."
"Swedenborg's Science" (June 5, 1929), 365-67.

Vol. CL:
"Spiritual Influx," (March 11, 1936), 169-70.

Vol. CLXVI:
"Spiritual Therapy in Action[:] Is Religion in Practice," (May 25, 1946), 167-68.

Vol. CLXVIII:
"Swedenborg's Psychology," (May 8, 1948), 154-56

Vol. CLXIX:
"On Classifying Swedenborg,"(January 29, 1949), 39-40.
"Intermediate Experiences," (August 27, 1949), 278-80.

Vol. CLXXI:
"On Interpreting the Scriptures," (March 10, 1951), 87-88 and 90-91.
"Reasons for Mystical Experiences[:] Often Due to Immaturity," (June 30, 1951), 218-20.

Vol. CLXXII:
"On Psychology and Religion," (February 9, 1952), 55-56.
"Vagaries of Superstition," (May 17, 1952), 175.

Vol. CLXXIII:
"The Psychology of the Bible; Sermon on Mount is Especially Concerned," Part I, (February 21, 1953), 67-68 and 70. Part II, (March 7, 1953), 87-88.
"The Apostle Paul[:] Study of His Limitations," (May 30, 1953), 181-82.
"The Problem of Will; Our Natures Resist Efforts to Regenerate It," (October 3, 1953), 323-25.

Vol. CLXXIV:
 Dresser column, "With the Practicing Psychologist," began in CLXXIV : (January 9, 1954), 27, and continued in:
 (January 23, 1954), 45.
 (March 6, 1954), 92.
 (April 3, 1954), 122.
 (May 1, 1954), 157-58.

SUPPLEMENTARY BIBLIOGRAPHICAL NOTES

1992

The bibliography of Dresser writings is incomplete, although very slightly amplified over the original version. Many years ago I complied a supplement to the bibliography; unfortunately all copies of it have disappeared. It dealt largely, if not entirely, with Dresser writings in Swedenborgian periodicals.

For those who want entry points to the writings of the great process thinkers, Whitehead and Hartshorne, I suggest:

Alfred North Whitehead, *Modes of Thought* (New York: Macmillan, 1938).

Charles Hartshorne, *Omnipotence and Other Theological Mistakes* (Albany: State University of New York Press, 1984).

A notable introduction to the field of process thinking:

John B. Cobb, Jr. and David Ray Griffin, *Process Theology: An Introductory Exposition* (Philadelphia: The Westminster Press, 1976).

An excellent anthology of writings from ancient to recent, organized in a process perspective:

Charles Hartshorne and William L. Reese (eds.), *Philosophers Speak of God* (Chicago: The University of Chicago Press, 1953).

For much on the philosophical underpinnings of Process

New Thought, see two notable volumes in The Library of Living Philosophers, now published by Open Court Publishing Company, La Salle, Illinois: Paul Arthur Schilpp (ed.), *The Philosophy of Alfred North Whitehead*, 1941 and 1951, and Lewis Edwin Hahn (ed.), *The Philosophy of Charles Hartshorne*, 1991.

David Ray Griffin and Huston Smith, *Primordial Truth and Post-modern Theology* (State University of New York Press, 1989) is a helpful exchange of views on the issue of an impersonal ultimate vs. a personal God.

Charles S. Braden, *Spirits in Rebellion: The Rise and Development of New Thought* (Southern Methodist Press, 1963) remains the best and most complete and reliable history of New Thought. While I was a graduate student, Charles S. Braden called on me, and I shared information on Evans with him. Shortly after I completed work on my dissertation, this book appeared.

Martin A. Larson, *New Thought Religion: A Philosophy for Health, Happiness, and Prosperity* (Philosophical Library 1986, revision of 1985 original edition titled *New Thought, or, A Modern Religious Approach*) emphasizes possible Swedenborgian influences.

J. Stillson Judah, *The History and Philosophy of the Metaphysical Movements in America* (The Westminster Press, 1967) covers a wider field.

Sydney E. Ahlstrom, *A Religious History of the American People* (New Haven and London: Yale University Press, 1972) covers a much wider field. Ahlstrom uses the term *harmonial religion* for the metaphysical movement. See Appendix J.

Gail Thain Parker, *Mind Cure in New England: From the Civil War to World War I* (Hanover, New Hampshire:

University Press of New England, 1973) covers a narrower field, as do:

C. Alan Anderson, *Contrasting Strains of Metaphysical Idealism Contributing to New Thought*; Monograph #1 (Santa Barbara, Calif.: Society for the Study of Metaphysical Religion, 1991).

Ervin Seale (ed.) *Phineas Parkhurst Quimby[:] The Complete Writings*, 3 vols. (Marina del Rey, Calif: DeVorss & Company, Publishers, 1988).

Ervin Seale, *Mingling Minds: Some Commentary on the Philosophy and Practice of Phineas Parkhurst Quimby* (Linden, New Jersey: Tide Press, 1986).

Mason A. Clark (ed.), *The Healing Wisdom of Dr. P. P. Quimby* (Los Altos, Calif.: Published by the author, distributed by DeVorss, 1982).

Erroll Stafford Collie, *Quimby's Science of Happiness: A Non-medical Scientific Explanation of the Cause and Cure of Disease* (Marina del Rey, Calif: DeVorss, 1980).

Of related interest are:

Catherine L. Albanese, *Nature Religion in America: From the Algonkian Indians to the New Age* (Chicago and London: The University of Chicago Press, 1990), which includes valuable "Suggestions for Further Reading."

Richard M. Huber, *The American Idea of Success* (New York: McGraw-Hill Book Company, 1971), with consideration of character, mind power, and personality ethics, in part continued in

Stephen R. Covey, *The Seven Habits of Highly Effective People: Restoring the Character Ethic* (New York: Simon and Schuster, 1989).

Ann Braude, *Radical Spirits: Spiritualism and Women's Rights in Nineteenth-Century America* (Boston: Beacon Press, 1989).

Stephen Gottschalk, *The Emergence of Christian Science in American Religious Life* (Berkeley, Los Angeles, London: University of California Press, 1973).

It would be fruitless to attempt to go into greater detail here about the growing amount of research and writing--much of it unpublished--related to New Thought. Suffice it to say that whereas when I began my research I was almost alone in the field, now there is a growing group of scholars doing much to remedy the academic neglect of New Thought. There even is the Society for the Study of Metaphysical Religion.

ABSTRACT

This is a prolegomenon to the study of (1) the early philosophy of Horatio Willis Dresser (1866-1954) as it relates to New Thought and (2) the philosophical foundations of New Thought as they relate to Dresser.

New Thought is a philosophical-religious movement which originated in the United States in the nineteenth century. While it seeks to provide a complete approach to life, its primary field of emphasis has been healing by nonphysical means.

New Thought's background is provided by the ancient tradition of religious healing, American philosophy largely of the nineteenth century, and speculation inspired by phenomena produced by mesmerism, also known as animal magnetism.

Mesmerists reported not only hypnotic effects that now commonly are accepted, but also "higher phenomena," including telepathy and clairvoyance, which served both to stimulate speculation and to retard acceptance of mesmerism.

The most commonly accepted explanation of all mesmeric phenomena in the first half of the nineteenth century was a holdover from earlier speculation on magnetism and astrology. This view assumes that one person can influence another through an invisible but material entity referred to as fluid. This came to be identified with electricity, which also was considered a fluid.

The "electrical psychology" of John Bovee Dods (1795-1872) distinguished differing densities of matter under the names of mind, matter, and the electricity that connects mind and matter.

A similar description is given by Phineas Parkhurst Quimby (1802-1866), who engaged in healing and maintained that "the explanation is the cure." Quimby holds that there is "spiritual matter" between mind and matter. But, unlike the case of Dods, the Quimby view is an idealism, especially as interpreted by Dresser.

The example and views of Quimby helped to inspire Warren Felt Evans (1817-1889) to develop a healing practice and an idealistic philosophy. He was the first to publish books on the "new" healing, Quimby having written but not published.

Evans starts with a conventional theism expressed in Swedenborgian terms, and moves to a view that he calls "Christian Pantheism." His is not so much a fully thought-out philosophical system as it is a collection of idealistic conclusions of various philosophers. Early in his philosophizing in regard to healing, Evans places considerable emphasis on the nonintellectual aspects of life, treating healing as the willing acceptance of divine assistance. Later he stresses the role of thought, maintaining that it and existence are one; hence, thought is adequate for attaining desired ends.

In the 1890's the later views of Evans and those who agreed with him came to be known as New Thought.

Dresser begins with an acceptance of pantheism. However, he prefers not to call it that; he holds that although God is expressed as man and Nature, the reserving of some of God unmanifested removes his view from pantheism. Dresser soon comes to reject pantheism, as now will be seen.

As Dresser's interest in epistemology heightens, he places increasing emphasis on analysis of experience. In this he begins with an indiscriminate whole of experience, and maintains that one gradually becomes aware of himself in relation to an other. For Dresser there is no meaning in the uninterpreted immediate. Hence, he rejects any claim of knowledge from unreflective mysticism. Thus he discards pantheistic mystical pronouncements, and relies on a commonsense separation of God from man and nature.

Dresser's philosophy is developed in contrast with New Thought, which asserts that God is all and perfectly good, and that one need only realize this state of affairs adequately in order to have a perfect life. Dresser challenges New Thought to prove its claims. In the absence of proof to the contrary, Dresser assumes that God and the world and man are separate, and that thinking will not result in such remarkable effects as New Thought claims.

However, Dresser does accept experiences of healing as being of divine origin. On the strength of his own examined extrasensory perception he maintains that there is a qualitative difference between spiritual experiences and merely psychical ones. He holds that it is to the higher, spiritual, level of activity that one should turn to find God and whatever healing may be given by God's grace. This higher level is marked more by love than by thought. Hence he considers inadequate the New Thought practice of mental affirmation of God's presence in order to accomplish healing.

Being in sympathy with the New Thought aims of healing and general human betterment, and, before delving deeply into philosophy, even accepting pantheism, Dresser's writings were popular in New Thought circles in the late 1890's and early 1900's. However, as he found New Thought generally unreceptive to scholarly examination, he turned increasingly to psychology and to the Swedenborgian New Church as fields of his activity.

New Thought and Dresser went their own ways. There is no reason for concluding that Dresser managed to bring New Thought in any significant degree toward his essentially orthodox views. However, he was recognized as a New Thought writer, accepted offices in New Thought organizations, and--judged by the popularity of his books--probably aided New Thought considerably around the turn of the century in its general aim of helping people to realize the availability of God.

In recent decades, probably with little or no Dresser influence, New Thought has shown some indications of moving in directions favored by Dresser. It has become somewhat more scholarly; some of its groups now offer various courses having philosophical, theological, and psychological content. Also there has come to be considerable recognition that thought unaided by a higher realization of divinity is unable to accomplish fully its healing aims. However, unlike Dresser, New Thought remains firmly pantheistic.